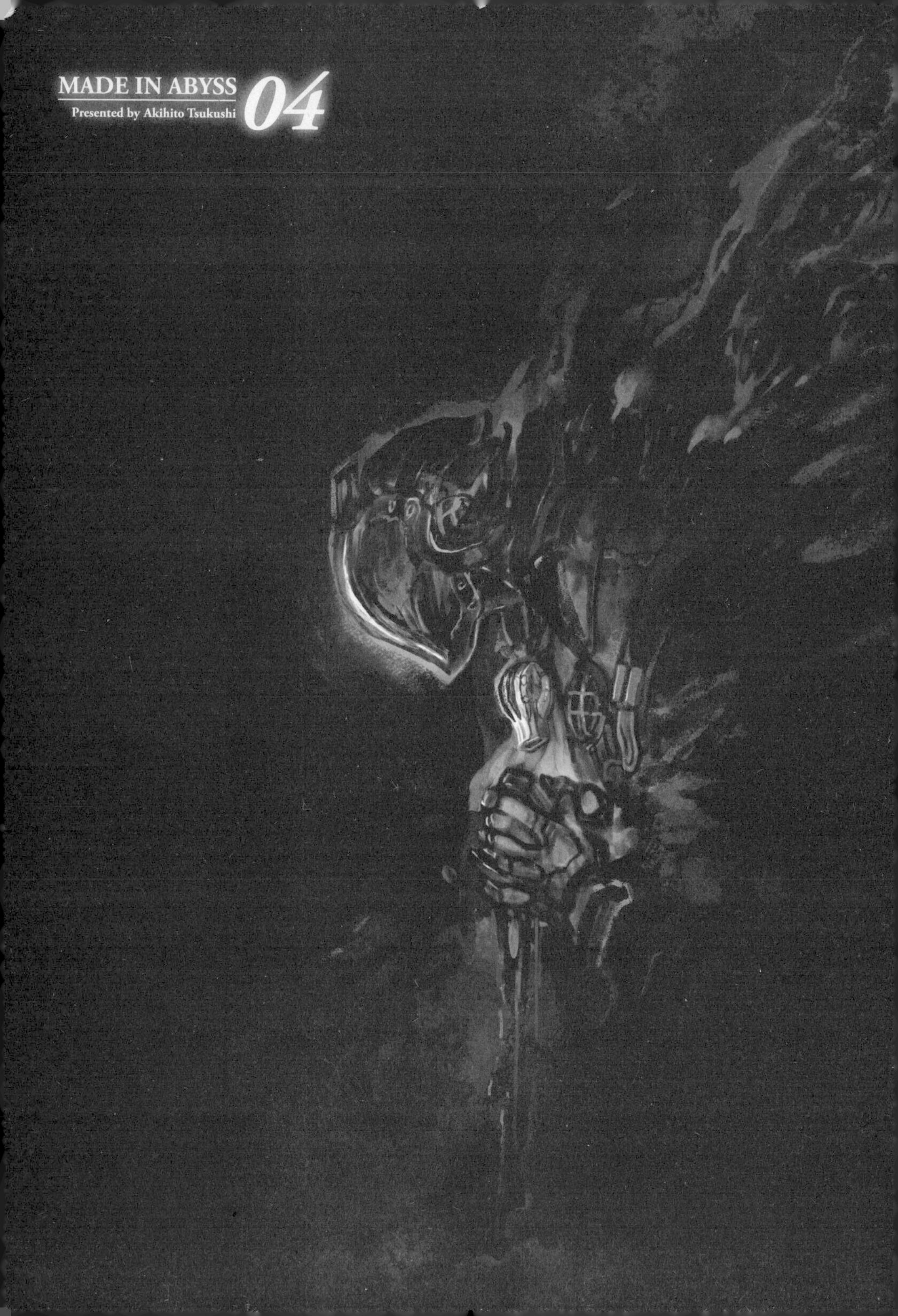
MADE IN ABYSS 04
Presented by Akihito Tsukushi

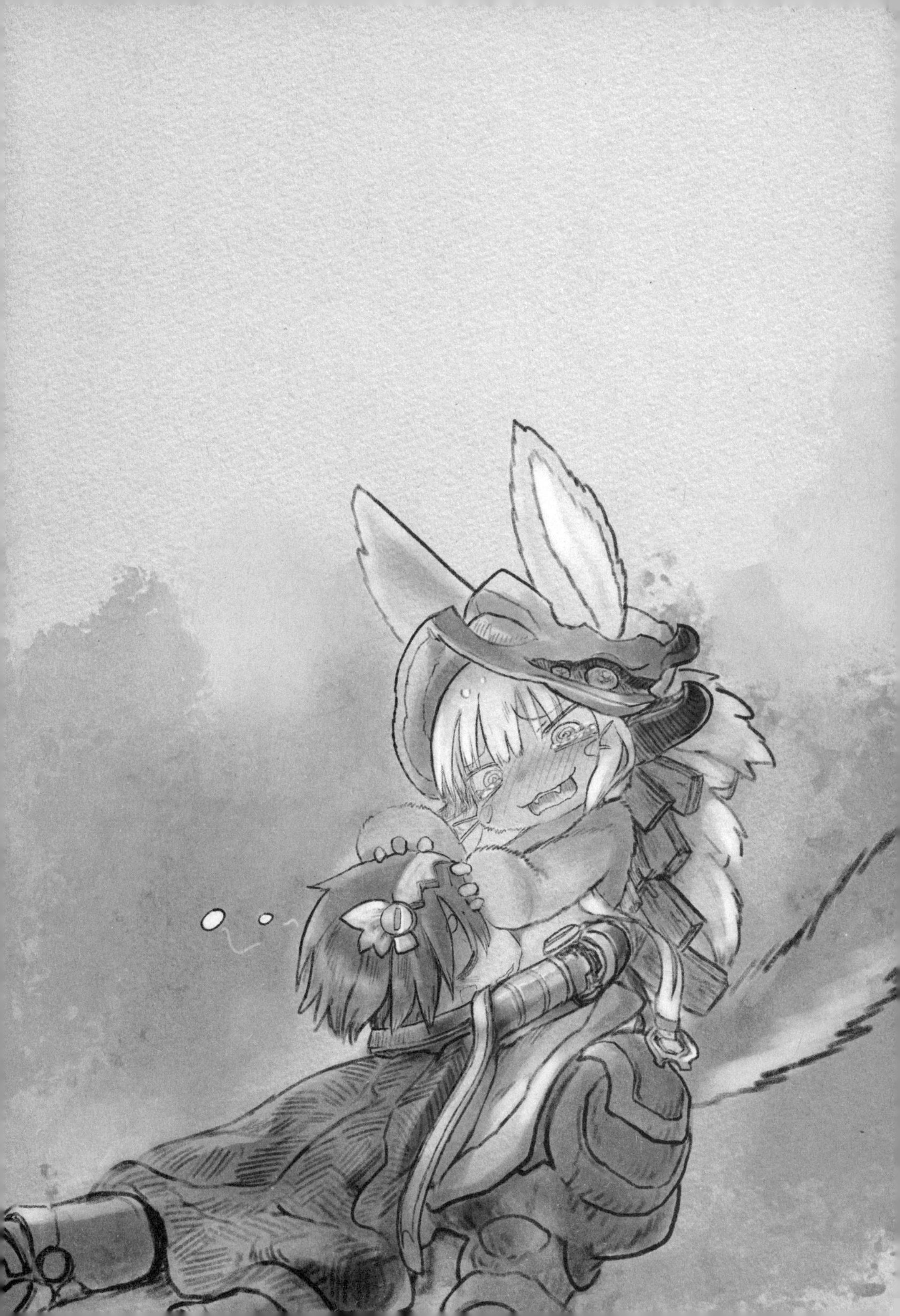

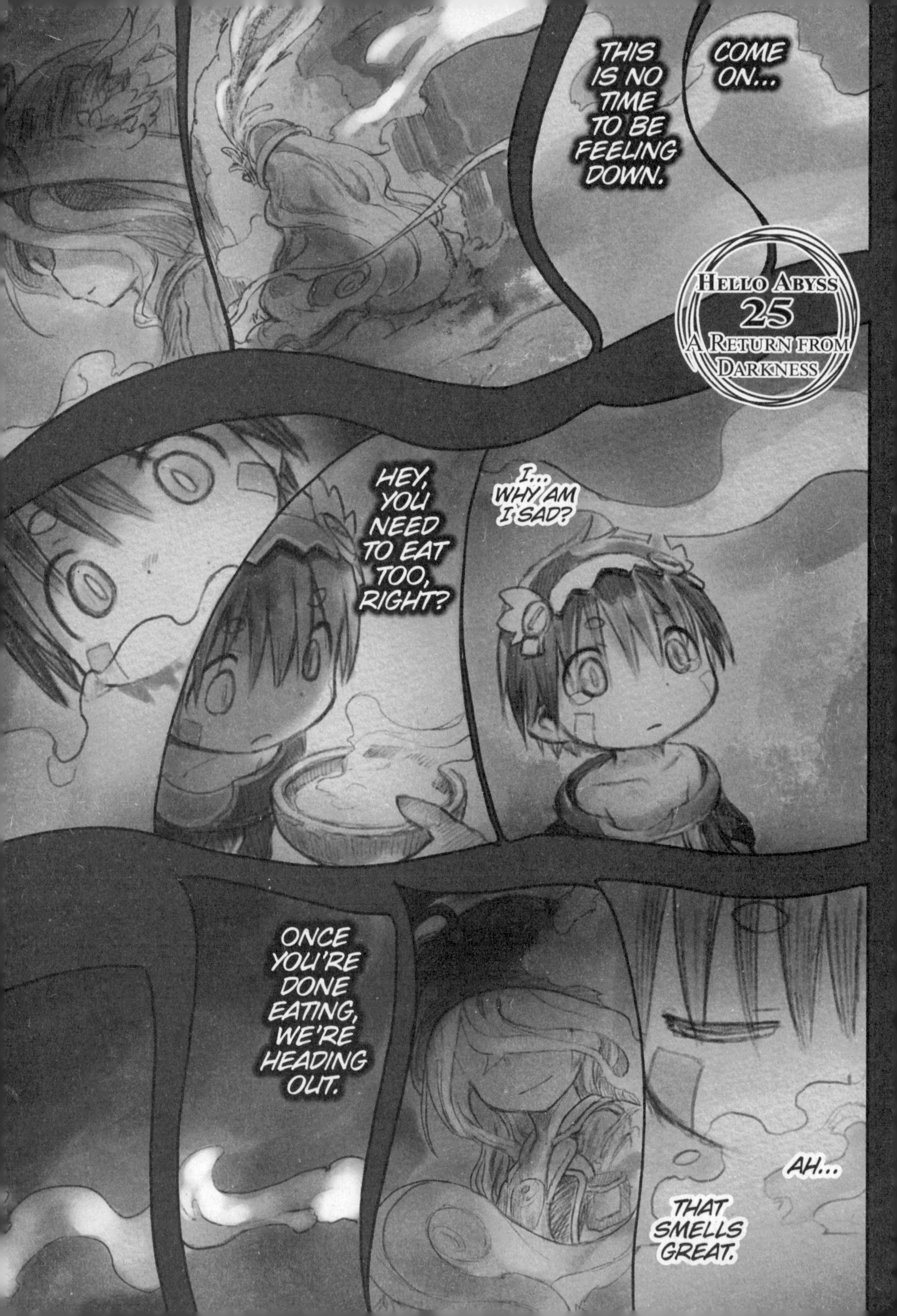
COME ON...
THIS IS NO TIME TO BE FEELING DOWN.
HELLO ABYSS 25 A RETURN FROM DARKNESS
I... WHY AM I SAD?
HEY, YOU NEED TO EAT TOO, RIGHT?
AH...
THAT SMELLS GREAT.
ONCE YOU'RE DONE EATING, WE'RE HEADING OUT.

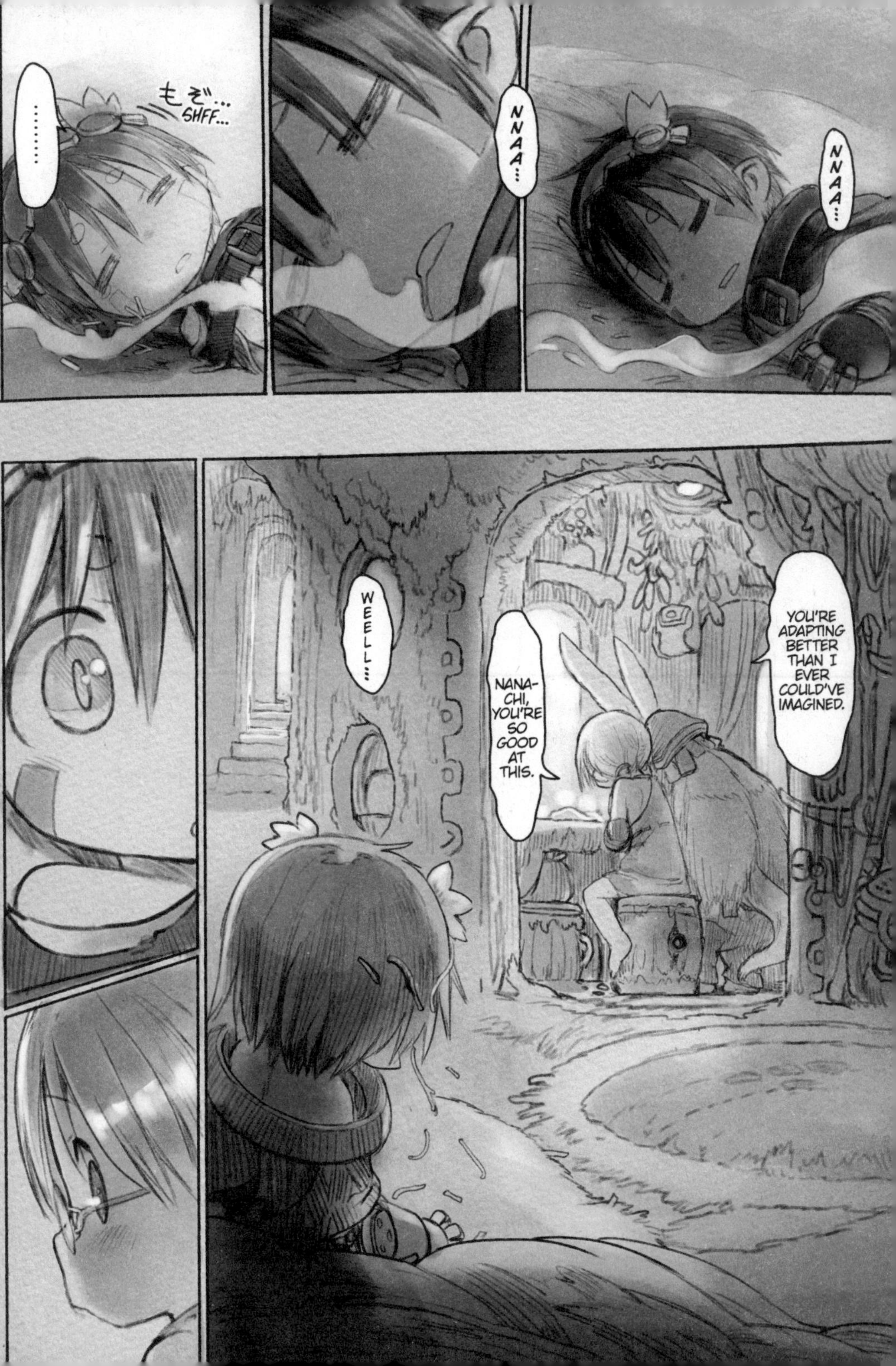
NNAA...
NNAA...
もぞ... SHFF...
....
YOU'RE ADAPTING BETTER THAN I EVER COULD'VE IMAGINED.
NANA-CHI, YOU'RE SO GOOD AT THIS.
WEELL...

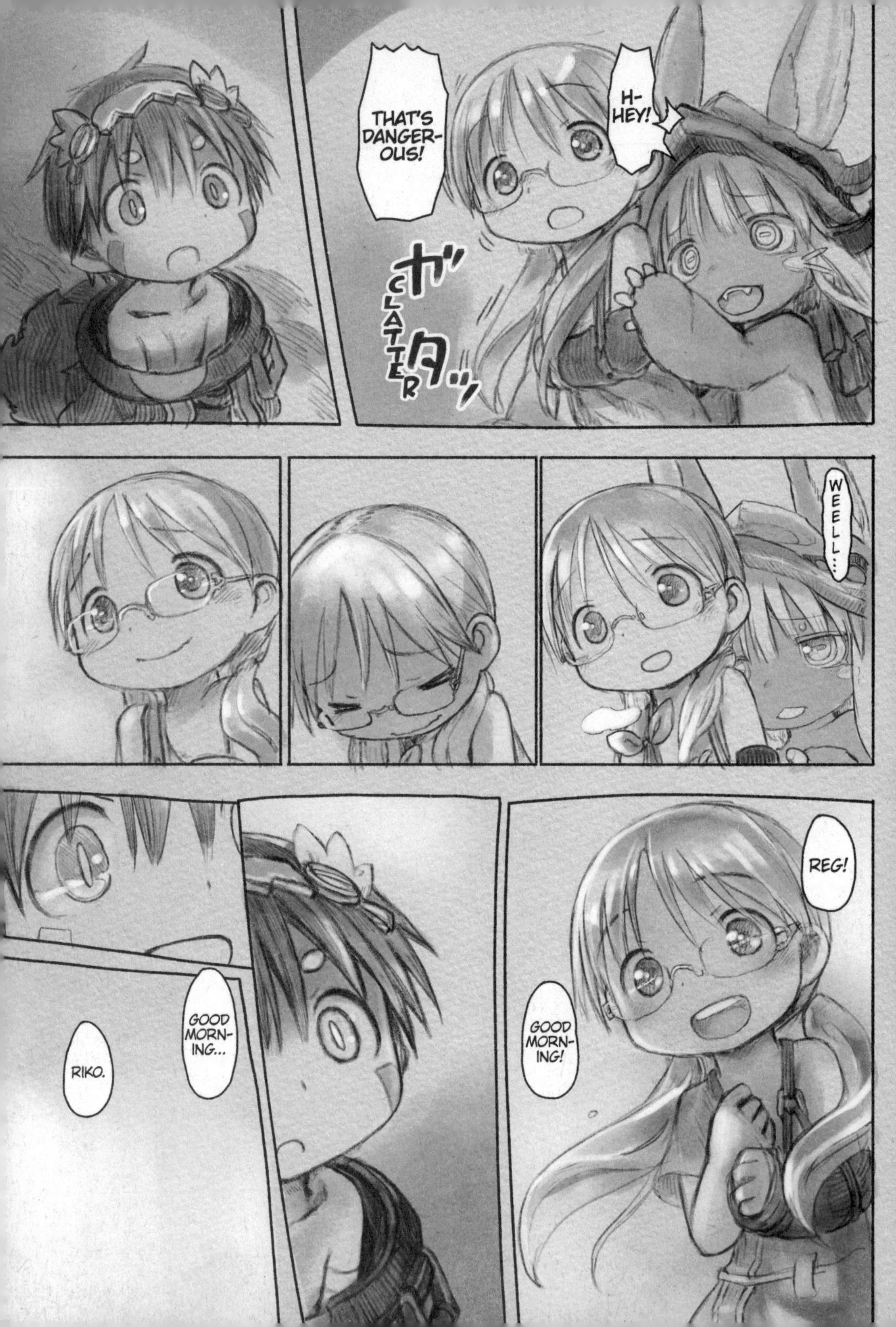
H-HEY!
THAT'S DANGER-OUS!
ガタッ
CLATTER
WEELL...
REG!
GOOD MORN-ING!
GOOD MORN-ING...
RIKO.

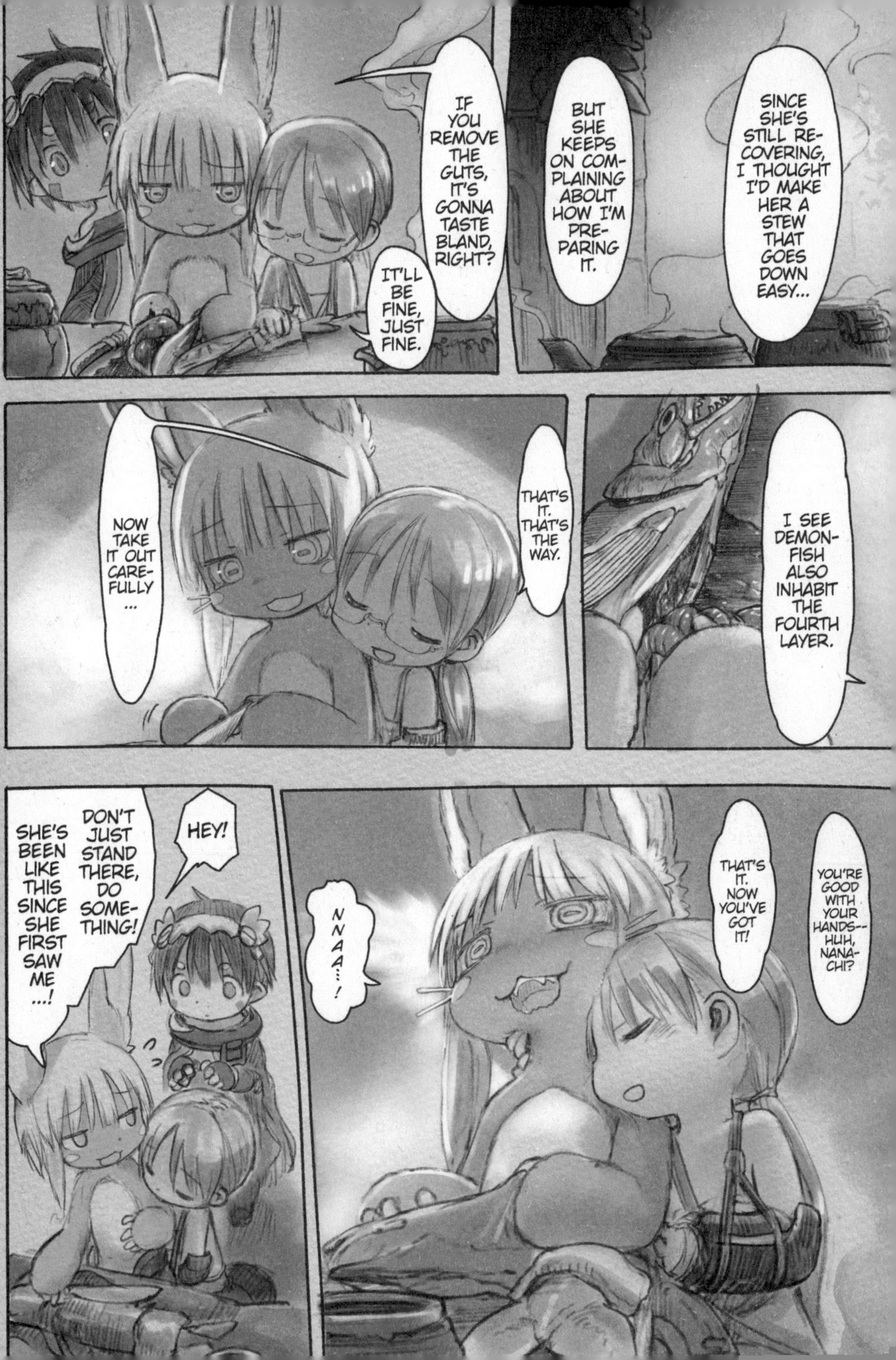
SINCE SHE'S STILL RE-COVERING, I THOUGHT I'D MAKE HER A STEW THAT GOES DOWN EASY...
BUT SHE KEEPS ON COM-PLAINING ABOUT HOW I'M PRE-PARING IT.
IF YOU REMOVE THE GUTS, IT'S GONNA TASTE BLAND, RIGHT?
IT'LL BE FINE, JUST FINE.
I SEE DEMON-FISH ALSO INHABIT THE FOURTH LAYER.
THAT'S IT. THAT'S THE WAY.
NOW TAKE IT OUT CARE-FULLY...
YOU'RE GOOD WITH YOUR HANDS-- HUH, NANA-CHI?
THAT'S IT. NOW YOU'VE GOT IT!
NNAAA...!
HEY!
DON'T JUST STAND THERE, DO SOME-THING!
SHE'S BEEN LIKE THIS SINCE SHE FIRST SAW ME...!

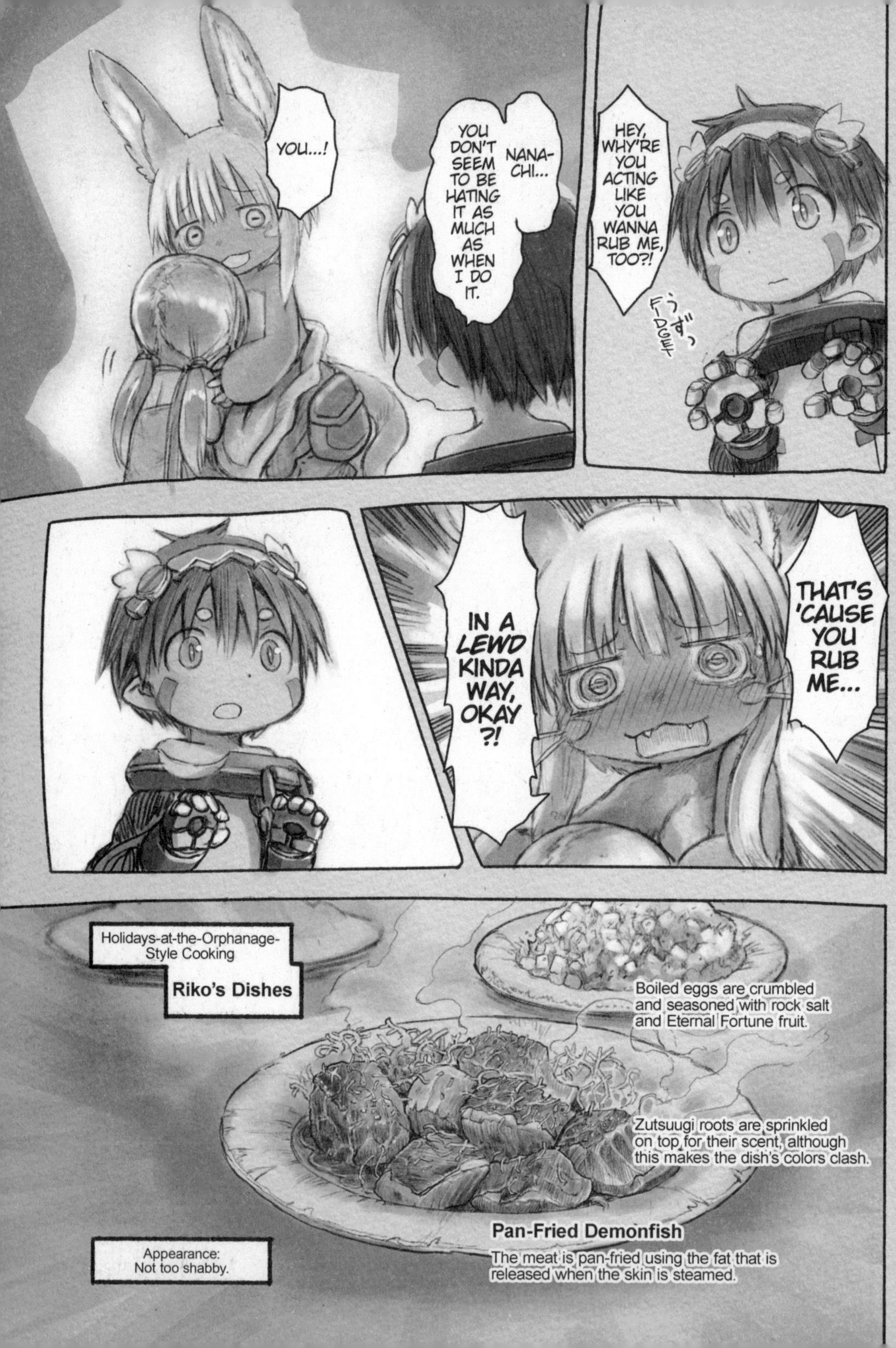
HEY, WHY'RE YOU ACTING LIKE YOU WANNA RUB ME, TOO?!
うずっ
FIDGET
NANA-CHI...
YOU DON'T SEEM TO BE HATING IT AS MUCH AS WHEN I DO IT.
YOU...!
THAT'S 'CAUSE YOU RUB ME...
IN A LEWD KINDA WAY, OKAY?!
Holidays-at-the-Orphanage-Style Cooking
Riko's Dishes
Boiled eggs are crumbled and seasoned with rock salt and Eternal Fortune fruit.
Zutsuugi roots are sprinkled on top for their scent, although this makes the dish's colors clash.
Pan-Fried Demonfish
The meat is pan-fried using the fat that is released when the skin is steamed.
Appearance: Not too shabby.

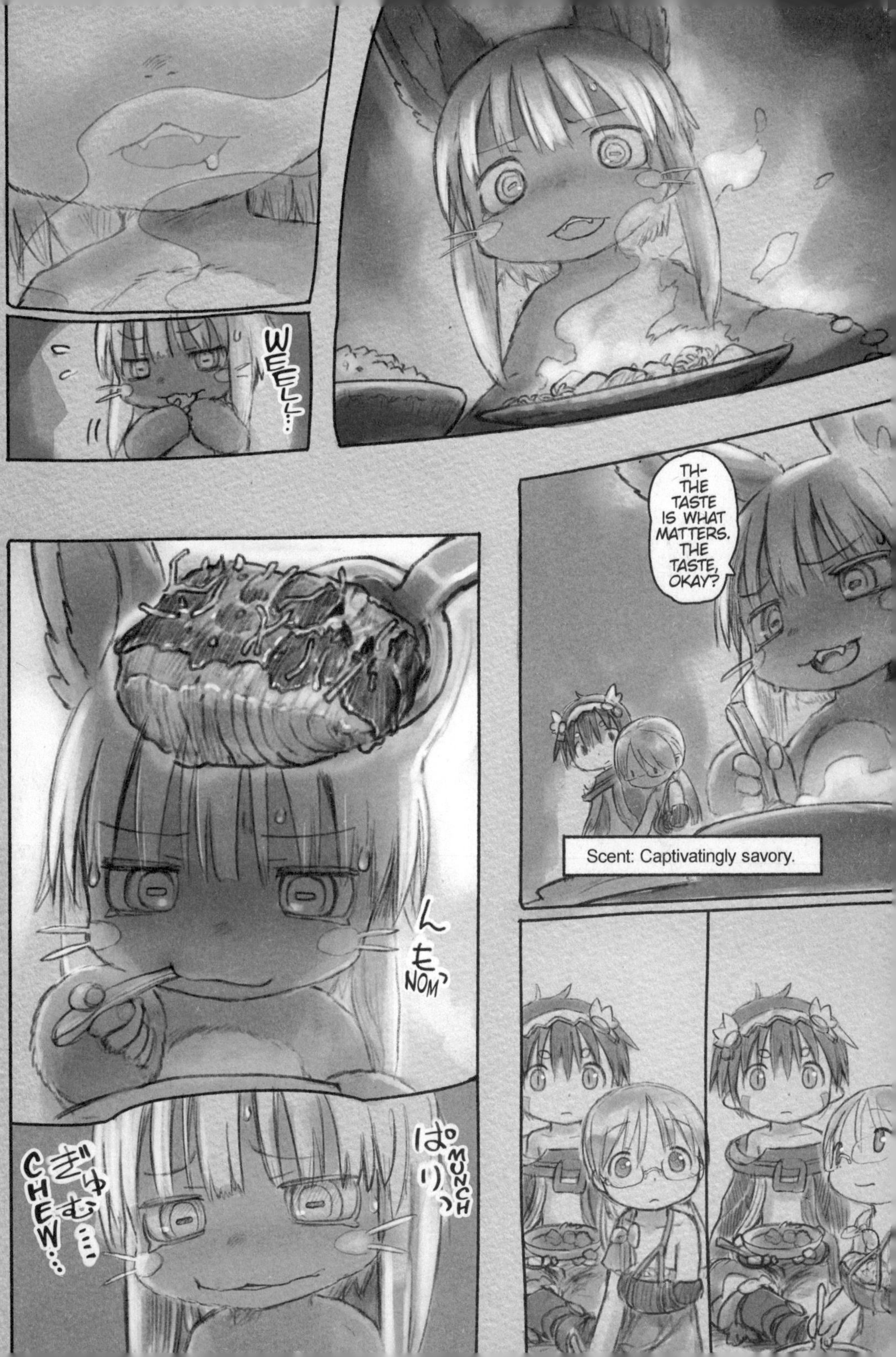
WEEELL...
TH-THE TASTE IS WHAT MATTERS. THE TASTE, OKAY?
Scent: Captivatingly savory.
んむ
NOM
ぱりっ
MUNCH
ぎゅむ…
CHEW...

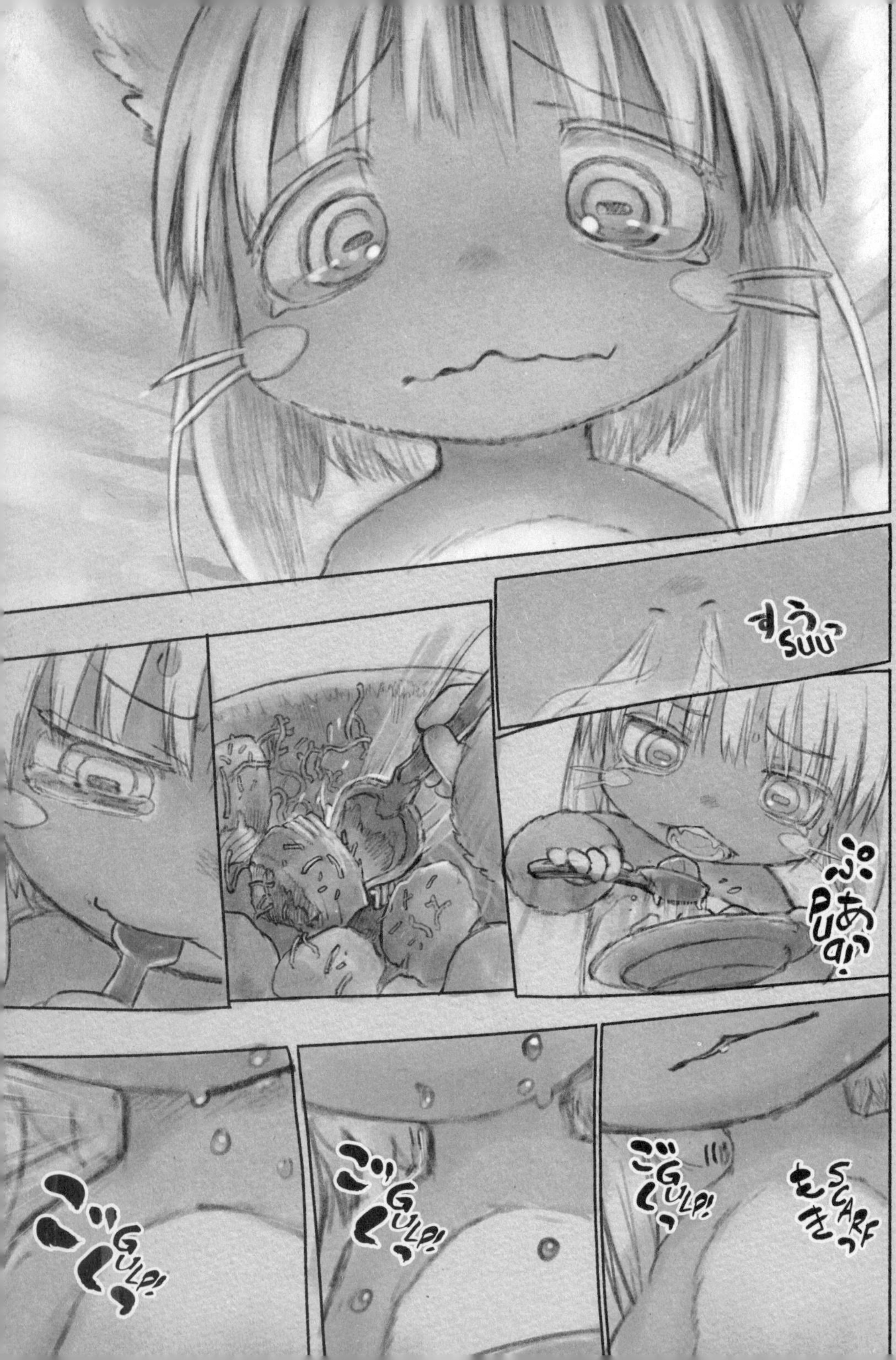
すうっ
SUU
ぷあっ
PUA!
もきっ
SCARF
ごくっ
GULP!
ごくっ
GULP!
ごくっ
GULP!

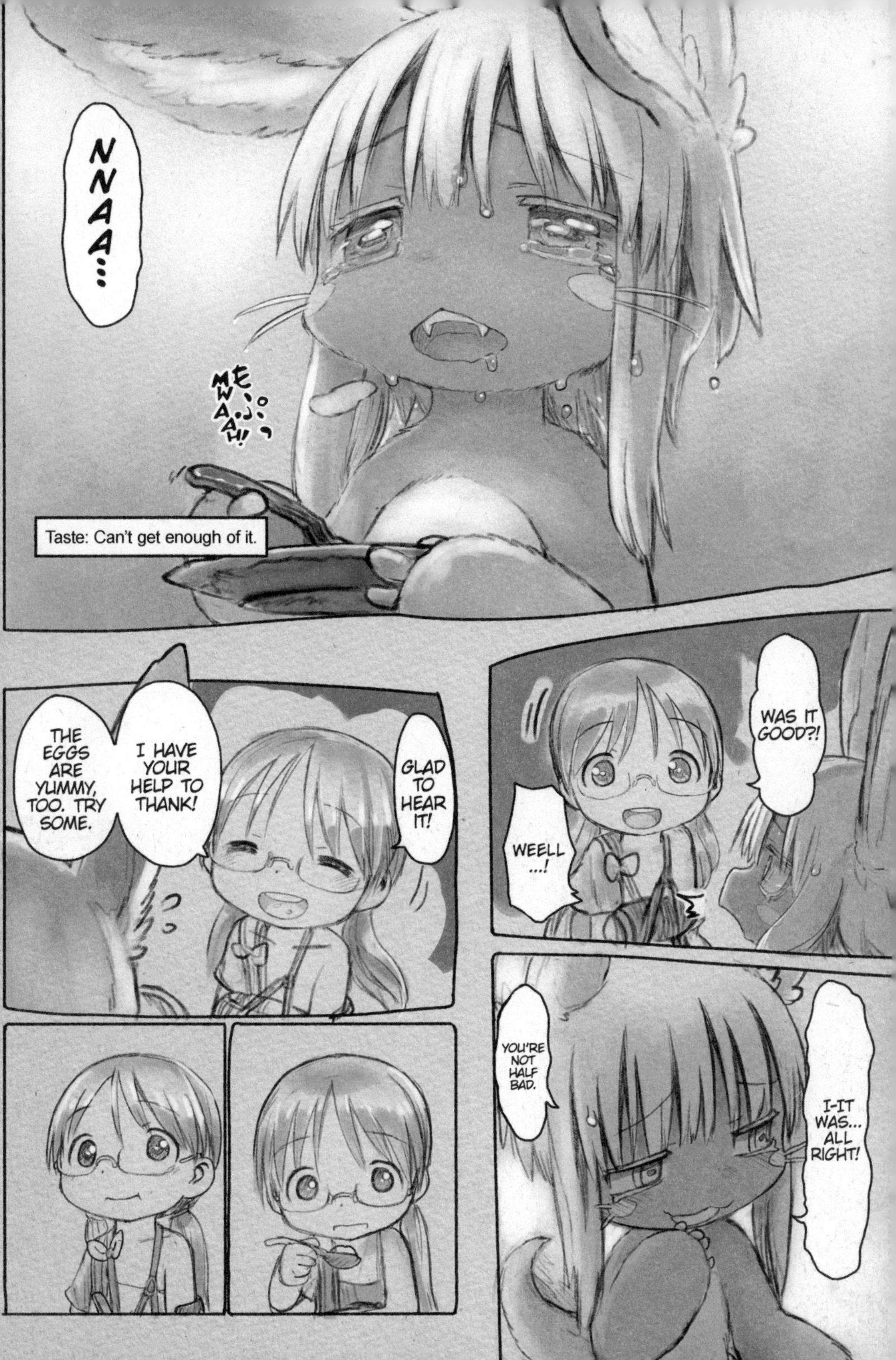
NNAA...
MEWAAH!!
Taste: Can't get enough of it.
WAS IT GOOD?!
WEELL ...!
GLAD TO HEAR IT!
I HAVE YOUR HELP TO THANK!
THE EGGS ARE YUMMY, TOO. TRY SOME.
I-IT WAS... ALL RIGHT!
YOU'RE NOT HALF BAD.

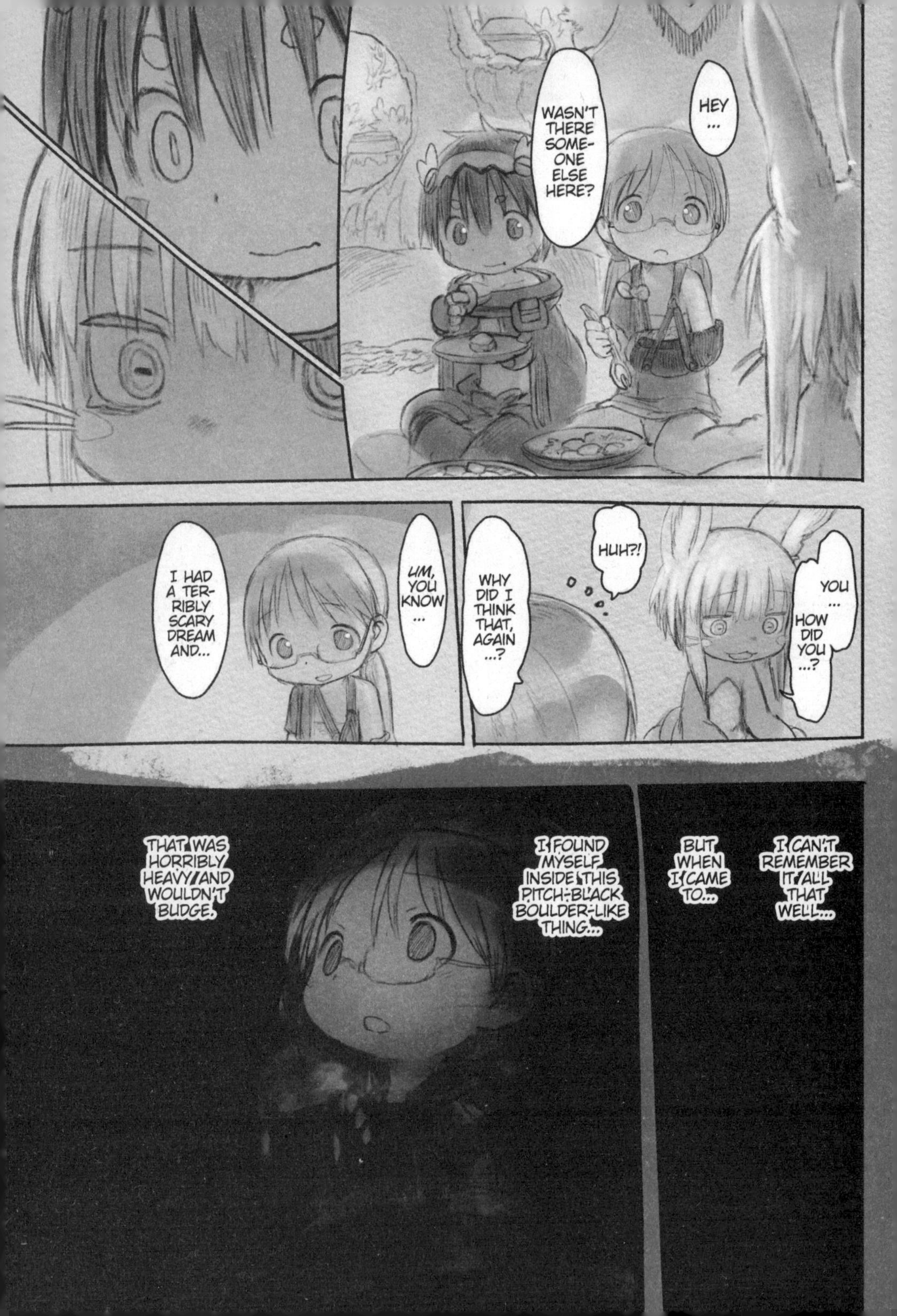
HEY ...
WASN'T THERE SOMEONE-ONE ELSE HERE?
YOU ... HOW DID YOU ...?
HUH?!
WHY DID I THINK THAT, AGAIN ...?
UM, YOU KNOW ...
I HAD A TER-RIBLY SCARY DREAM AND...
I CAN'T REMEMBER IT ALL THAT WELL...
BUT WHEN I CAME TO...
I FOUND MYSELF INSIDE THIS PITCH-BLACK BOULDER-LIKE THING...
THAT WAS HORRIBLY HEAVY AND WOULDN'T BUDGE.

AT FIRST, THERE WAS THIS CAVITY INSIDE IT THAT WAS ABOUT THE SAME SIZE AS ME...
BUT IT KEPT GETTING SMALLER AND SMALLER.
IT WAS SO PAINFUL, SO AGONIZING.
SQUISH...
IT GOT SO I DIDN'T EVEN UNDER-STAND WHAT I WAS ANYMORE.
I EVEN FORGOT HOW TO SPEAK.
I WAS SCARED-- SO SCARED-- AND I JUST KEPT CRYING...
THEN I HEARD CRYING...
BUT IT WASN'T COMING FROM ME...

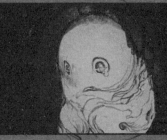

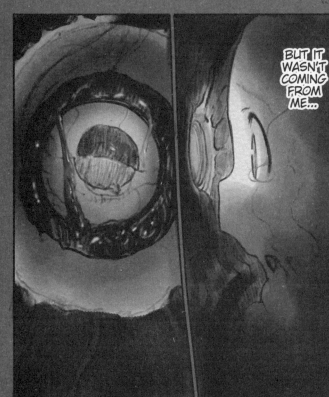

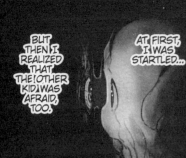

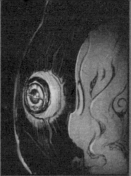

?!
AT FIRST, I WAS STARTLED...
BUT THEN I REALIZED THAT THE OTHER KID WAS AFRAID, TOO.
THAT HELPED EASE MY MIND, IF JUST A LITTLE.
THEN, YOU SEE, I STAYED LIKE THAT FOR QUITE A WHILE...
EVEN WHEN I GOT SCARED, THERE WAS THIS GIRL RIGHT IN FRONT OF ME WHO WAS EVEN MORE FRIGHTENED.
I COULDN'T TALK...
BUT WITH MY EYES ALONE...
I KEPT ON TELLING HER...
"IT'LL BE OKAY, IT'LL BE OKAY..."
THEN I SMELLED SOMETHING LIKE SMOKE...
AND THE CRYING...
STOPPED...

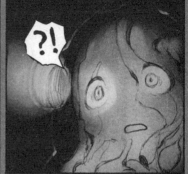

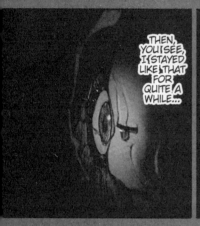

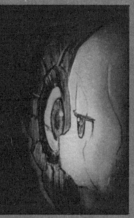

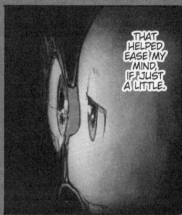

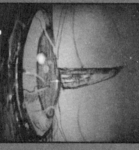

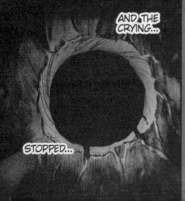

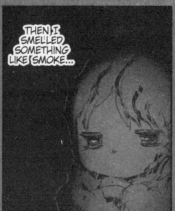

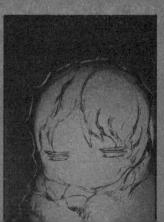

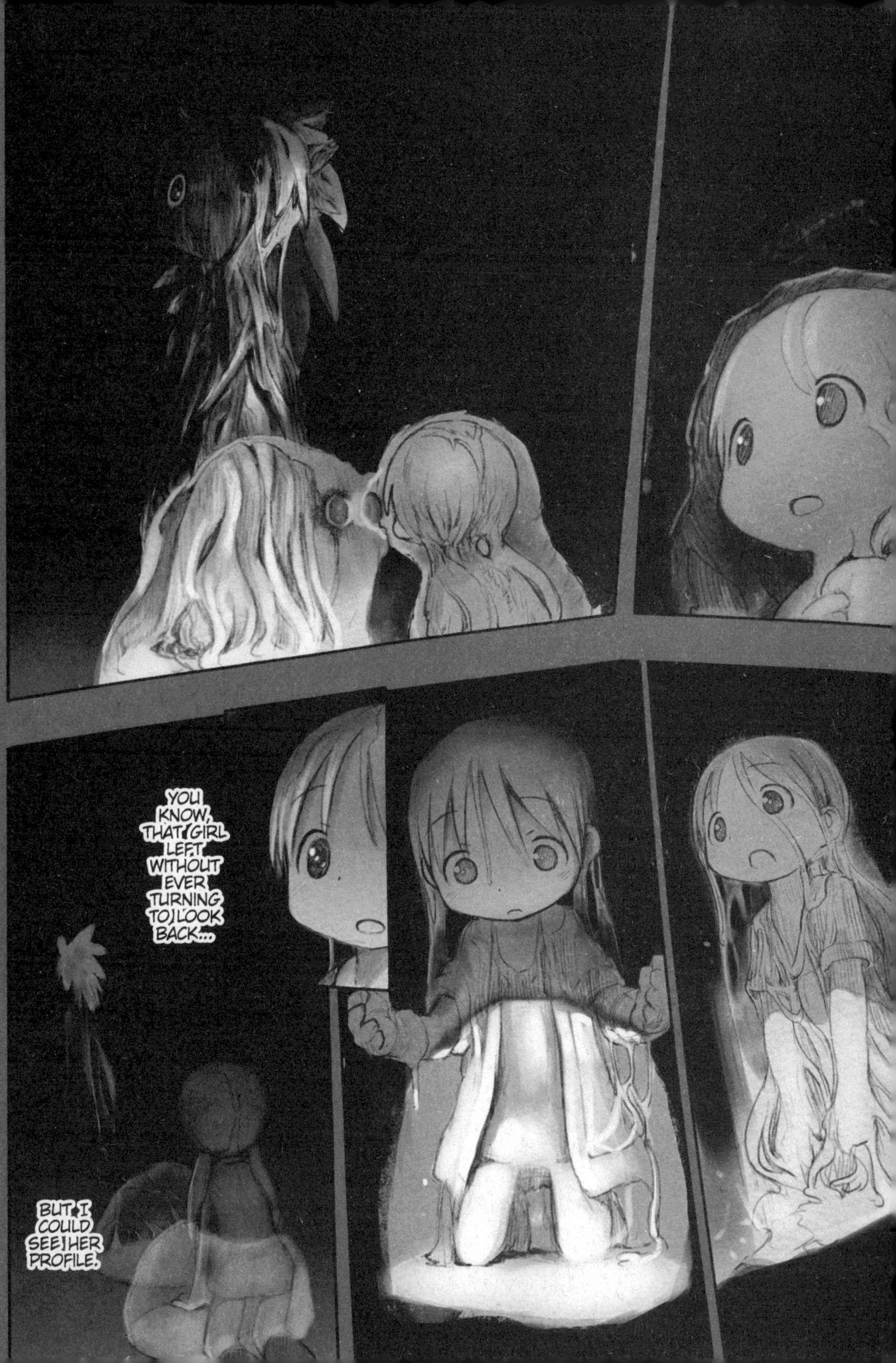
YOU KNOW, THAT GIRL LEFT WITHOUT EVER TURNING TO LOOK BACK...
BUT I COULD SEE HER PROFILE.

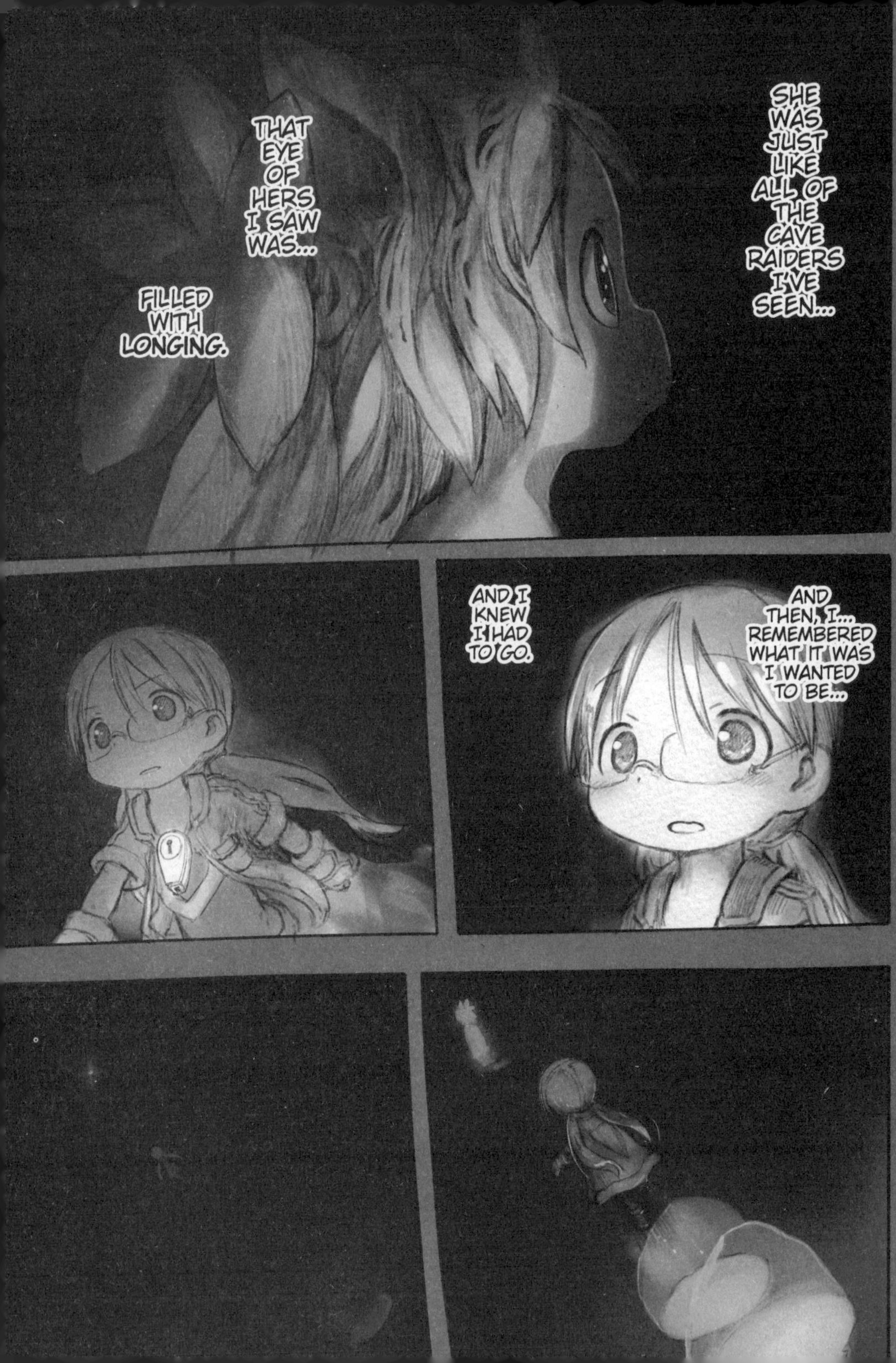
SHE WAS JUST LIKE ALL OF THE CAVE RAIDERS I'VE SEEN...
THAT EYE OF HERS I SAW WAS...
FILLED WITH LONGING.
AND THEN, I... REMEMBERED WHAT IT WAS I WANTED TO BE...
AND I KNEW I HAD TO GO.

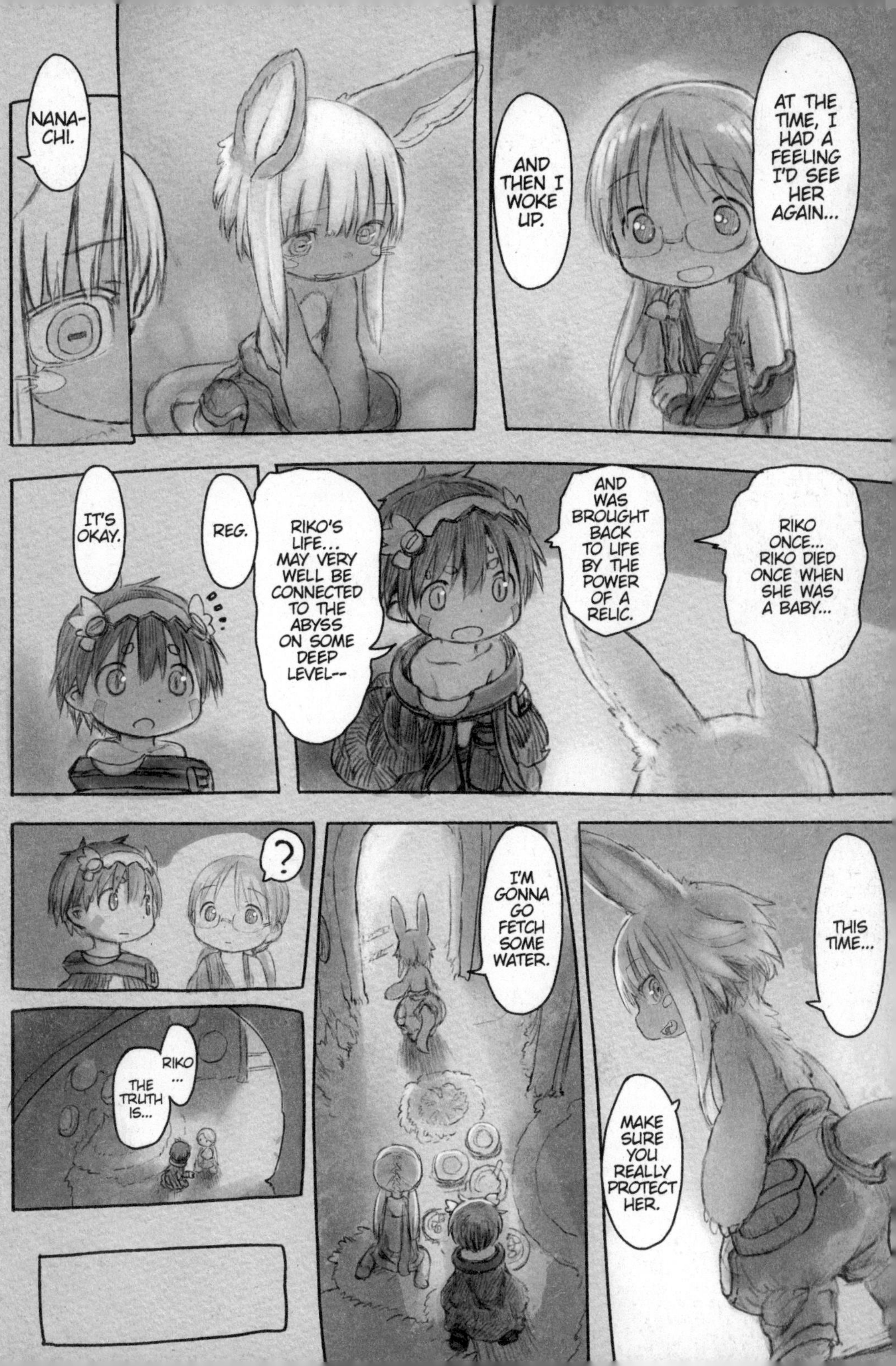
AT THE TIME, I HAD A FEELING I'D SEE HER AGAIN...
AND THEN I WOKE UP.
NANA-CHI.
RIKO ONCE... RIKO DIED ONCE WHEN SHE WAS A BABY...
AND WAS BROUGHT BACK TO LIFE BY THE POWER OF A RELIC.
RIKO'S LIFE... MAY VERY WELL BE CONNECTED TO THE ABYSS ON SOME DEEP LEVEL--
REG.
IT'S OKAY.
THIS TIME...
MAKE SURE YOU REALLY PROTECT HER.
I'M GONNA GO FETCH SOME WATER.
?
RIKO...
THE TRUTH IS...

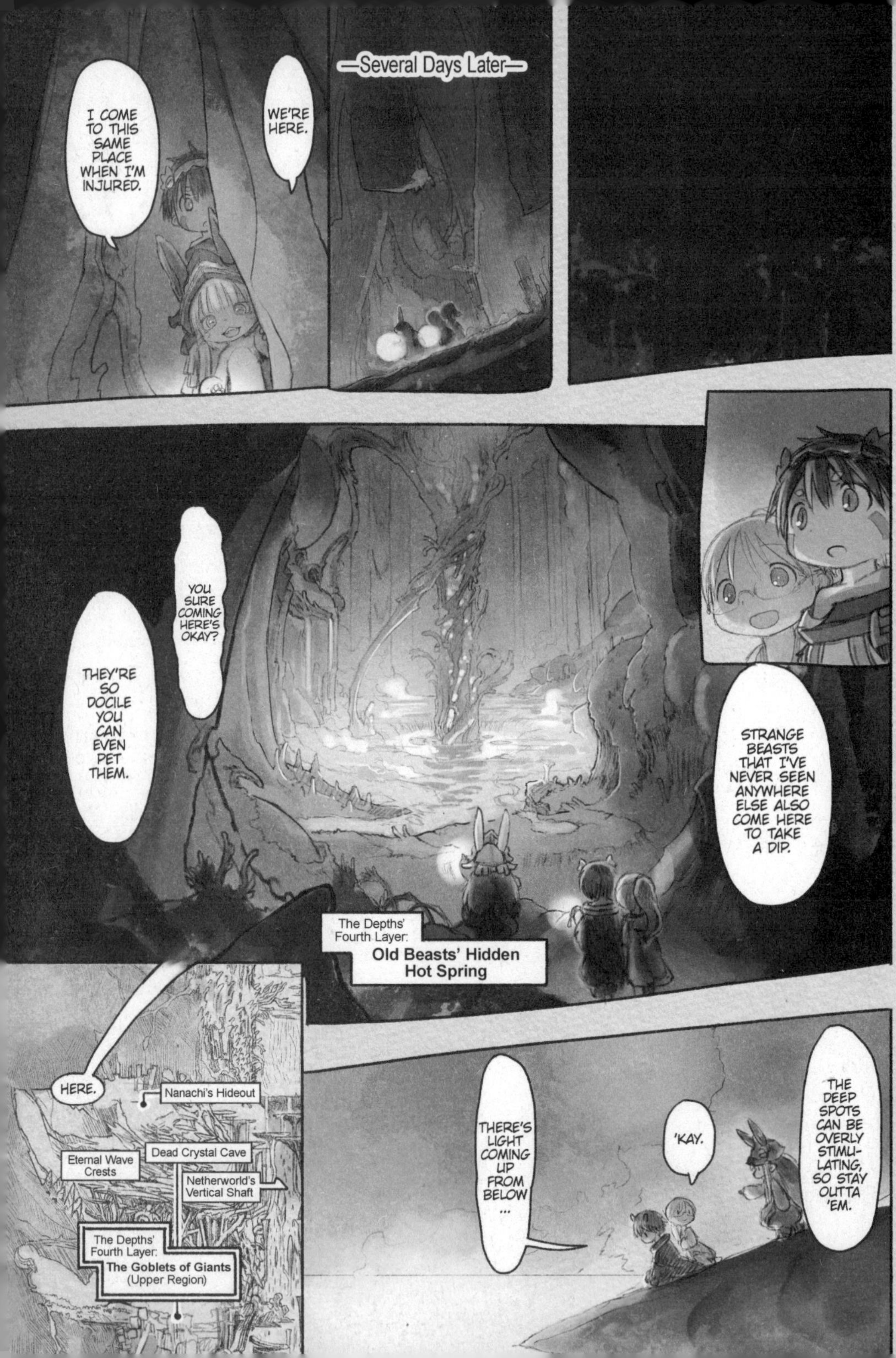
—Several Days Later—
WE'RE HERE.
I COME TO THIS SAME PLACE WHEN I'M INJURED.
STRANGE BEASTS THAT I'VE NEVER SEEN ANYWHERE ELSE ALSO COME HERE TO TAKE A DIP.
YOU SURE COMING HERE'S OKAY?
THEY'RE SO DOCILE YOU CAN EVEN PET THEM.
The Depths' Fourth Layer:
Old Beasts' Hidden Hot Spring
THE DEEP SPOTS CAN BE OVERLY STIMULATING, SO STAY OUTTA 'EM.
'KAY.
THERE'S LIGHT COMING UP FROM BELOW...
HERE.
Nanachi's Hideout
Dead Crystal Cave
Eternal Wave Crests
Netherworld's Vertical Shaft
The Depths' Fourth Layer:
The Goblets of Giants
(Upper Region)

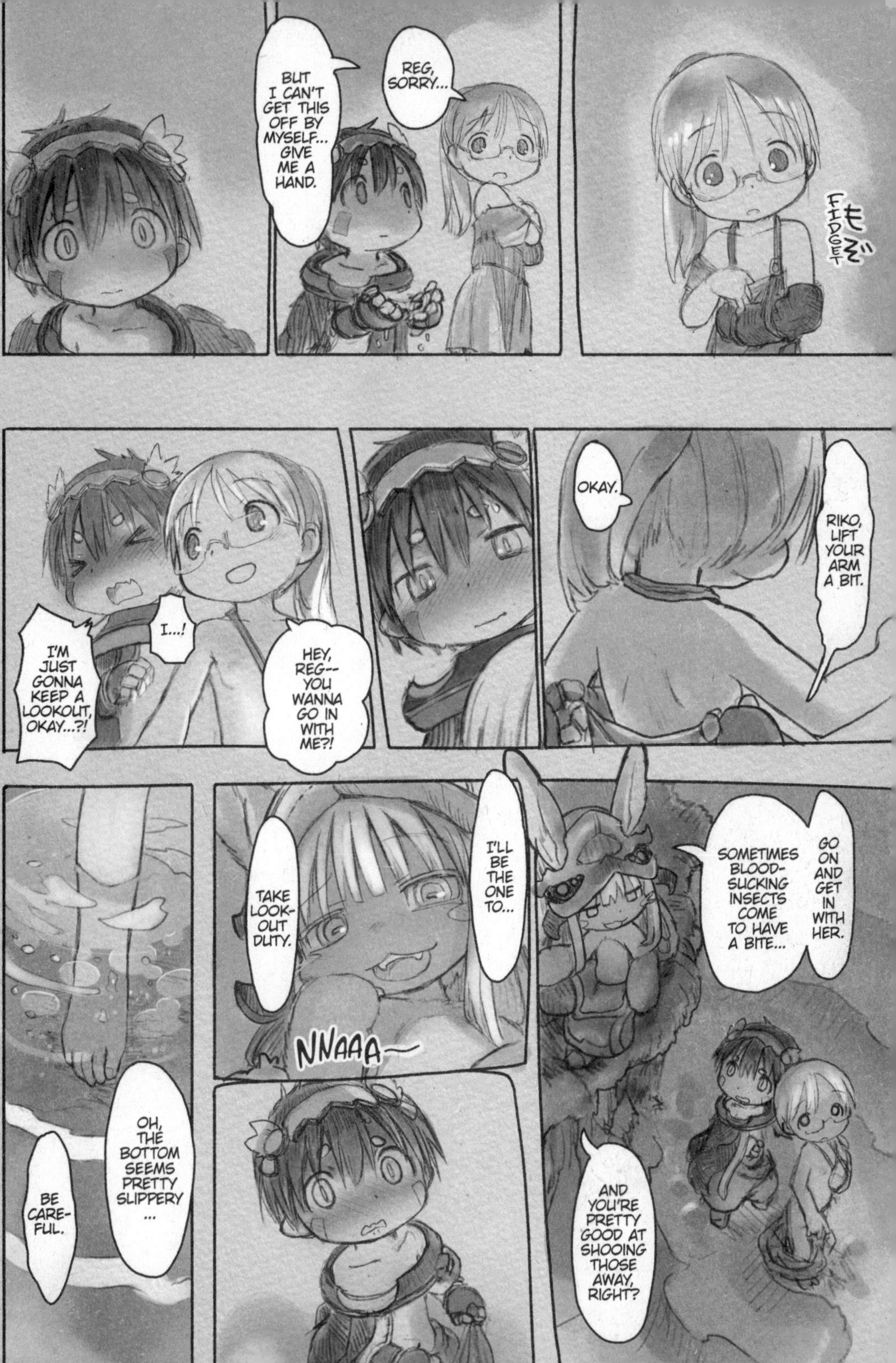
FIDGET
REG, SORRY...
BUT I CAN'T GET THIS OFF BY MYSELF... GIVE ME A HAND.
RIKO, LIFT YOUR ARM A BIT.
OKAY.
HEY, REG-- YOU WANNA GO IN WITH ME?!
I...!
I'M JUST GONNA KEEP A LOOKOUT, OKAY...?!
GO ON AND GET IN WITH HER.
SOMETIMES BLOOD-SUCKING INSECTS COME TO HAVE A BITE...
AND YOU'RE PRETTY GOOD AT SHOOING THOSE AWAY, RIGHT?
I'LL BE THE ONE TO...
TAKE LOOK-OUT DUTY.
NNAAA~
OH, THE BOTTOM SEEMS PRETTY SLIPPERY...
BE CARE-FUL.

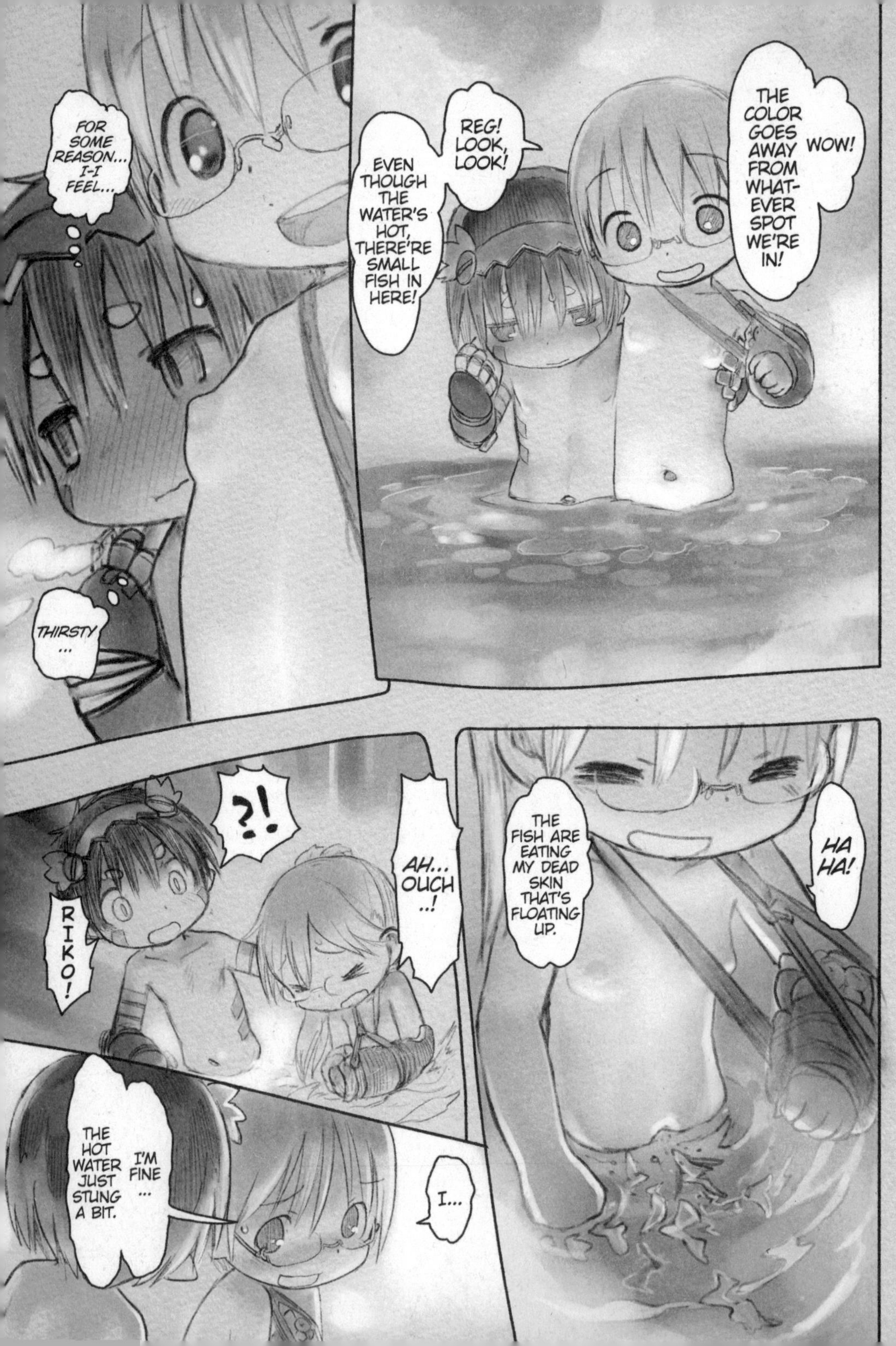
WOW!
THE COLOR GOES AWAY FROM WHAT-EVER SPOT WE'RE IN!
REG! LOOK, LOOK!
EVEN THOUGH THE WATER'S HOT, THERE'RE SMALL FISH IN HERE!
FOR SOME REASON... I-I FEEL...
THIRSTY...
HA HA!
THE FISH ARE EATING MY DEAD SKIN THAT'S FLOATING UP.
AH... OUCH..!
?!
RIKO!
I...
I'M FINE...
THE HOT WATER JUST STUNG A BIT.

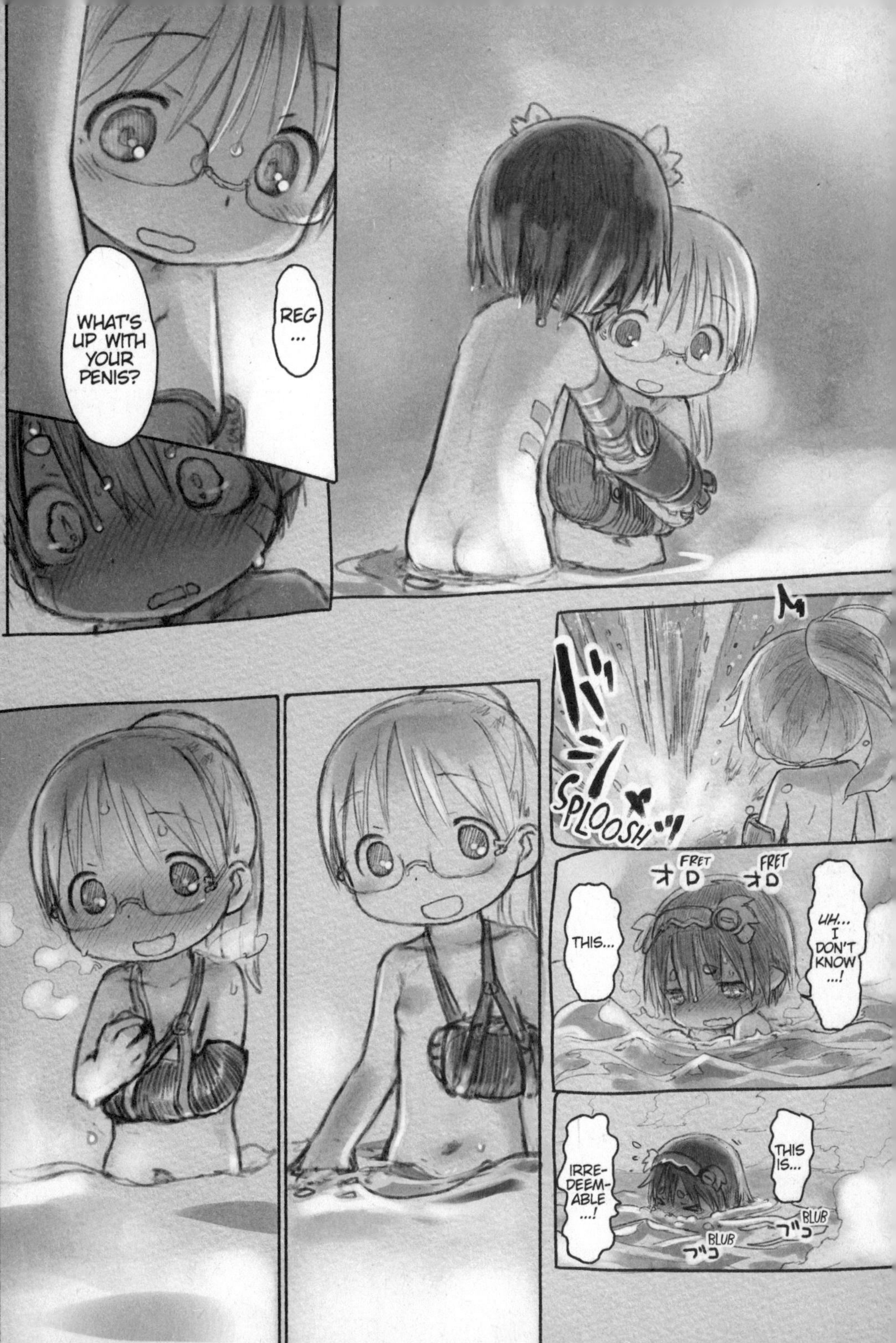
REG ...
WHAT'S UP WITH YOUR PENIS?
SPLOOSH
FRET FRET
UH... I DON'T KNOW ...!
THIS...
THIS IS...
IRRE-DEEMABLE ...!
BLUB
BLUB

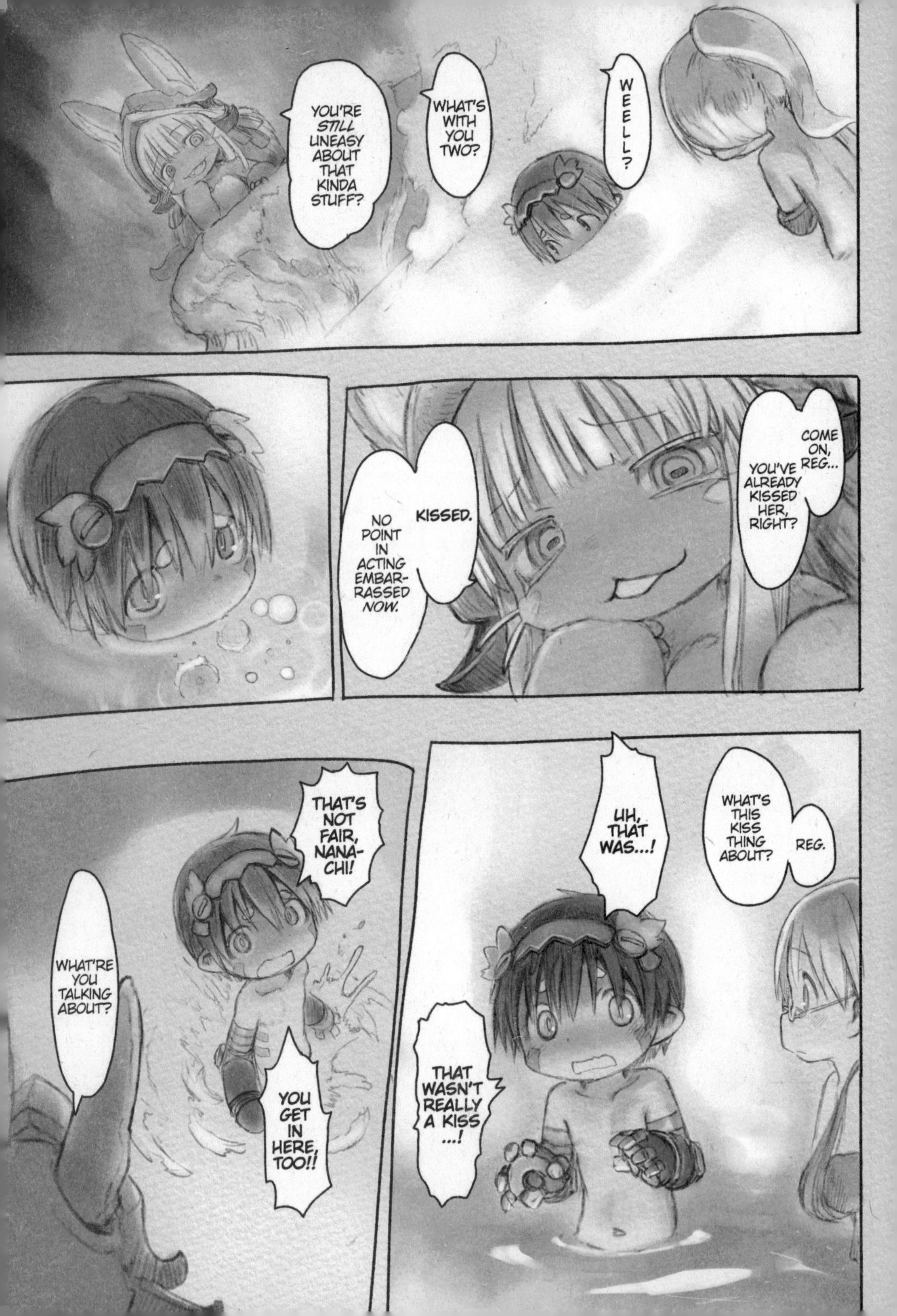
WEELL?
WHAT'S WITH YOU TWO?
YOU'RE *STILL* UNEASY ABOUT THAT KINDA STUFF?
COME ON, REG... YOU'VE ALREADY KISSED HER, RIGHT?
KISSED.
NO POINT IN ACTING EMBARRASSED *NOW.*
WHAT'S THIS KISS THING ABOUT?
REG.
UH, THAT WAS...!
THAT WASN'T REALLY A KISS ...!
THAT'S NOT FAIR, NANACHI!
WHAT'RE YOU TALKING ABOUT?
YOU GET IN HERE, TOO!!

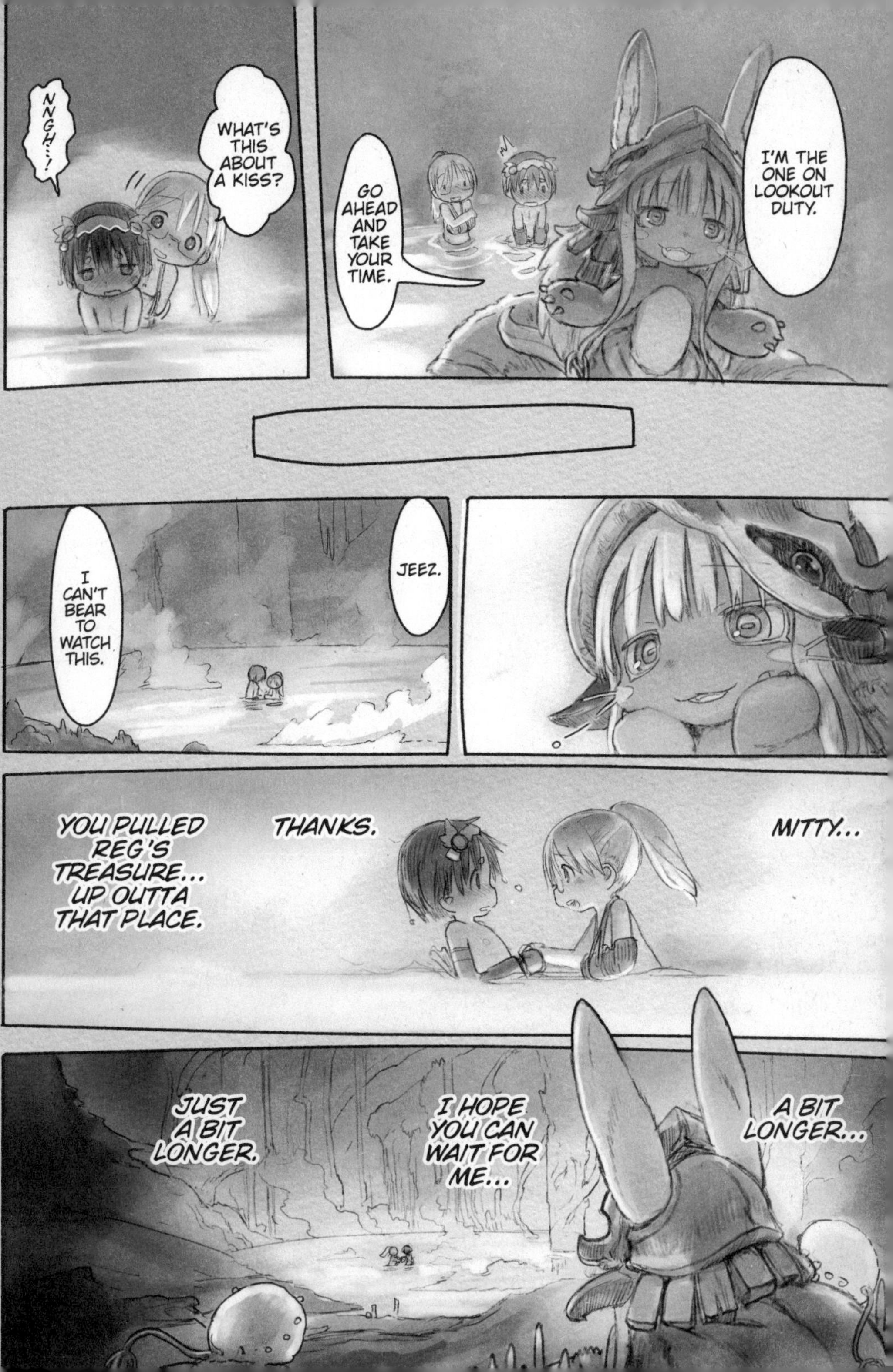
I'M THE ONE ON LOOKOUT DUTY.
GO AHEAD AND TAKE YOUR TIME.
WHAT'S THIS ABOUT A KISS?
NNGH...!
JEEZ.
I CAN'T BEAR TO WATCH THIS.
MITTY...
THANKS.
YOU PULLED REG'S TREASURE... UP OUTTA THAT PLACE.
A BIT LONGER...
I HOPE YOU CAN WAIT FOR ME...
JUST A BIT LONGER.

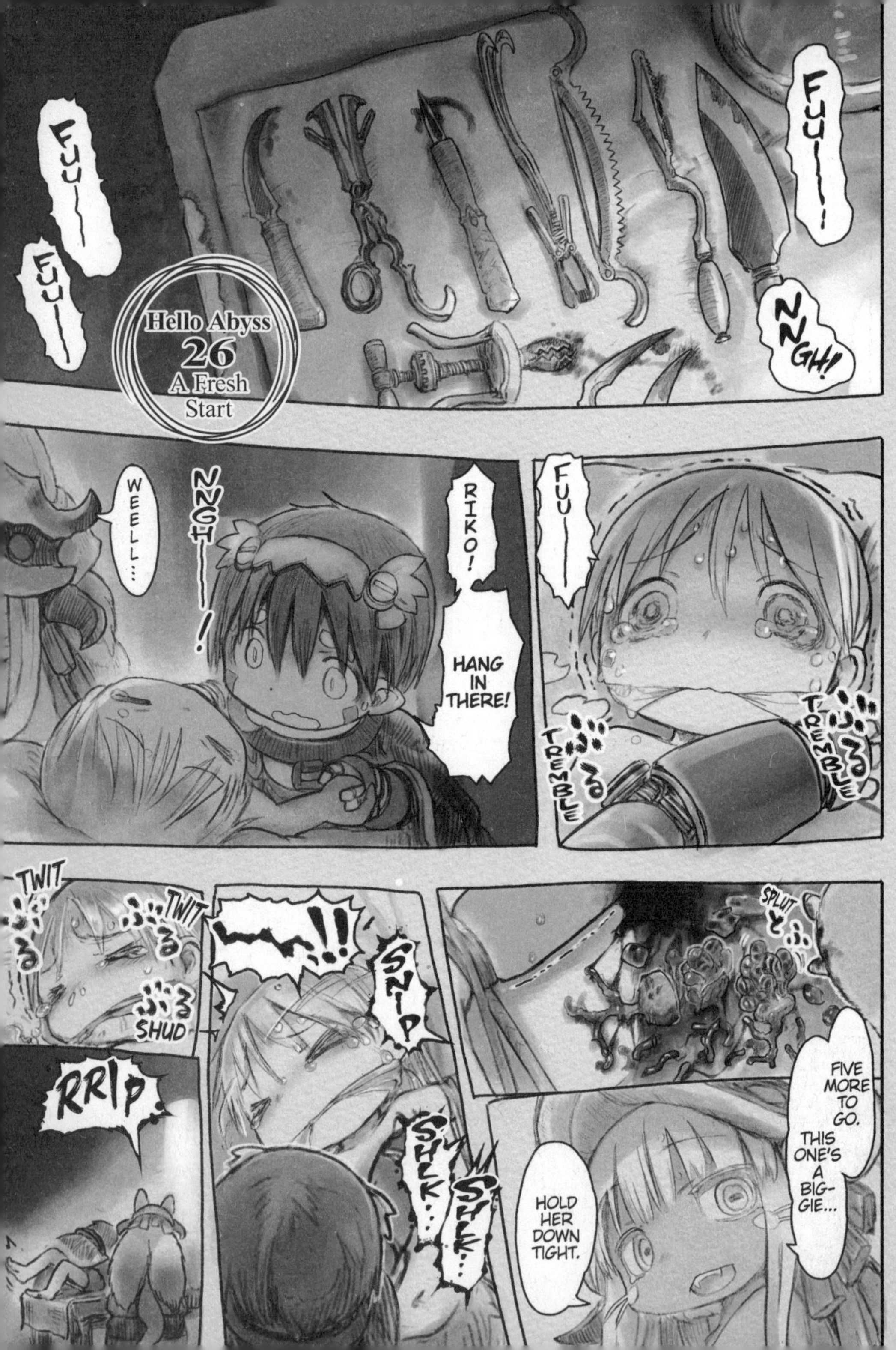
FUU—!
NNGH!
FUU—
FUU—
Hello Abyss 26 A Fresh Start
FUU—
TREMBLE
TREMBLE
RIKO!
HANG IN THERE!
NNGH—!
WEELL...
SPLUT
FIVE MORE TO GO. THIS ONE'S A BIG-GIE...
HOLD HER DOWN TIGHT.
—!!
SNIP
SHLK...
SHLK...
TWIT
TWIT
SHUD
RRIP!

ば
た
FLAIL

ば
た
FLAIL

ば
た
FLAIL

じ
PSSSHHH...
わ
あ
ぁ..

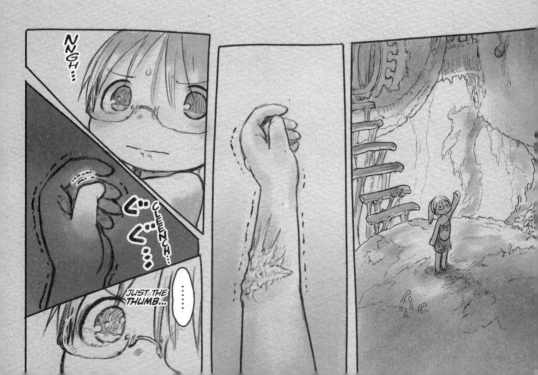

NNGH...

ぐ..
ぐ..
CLEENCH!

JUST THE
THUMB...

.....

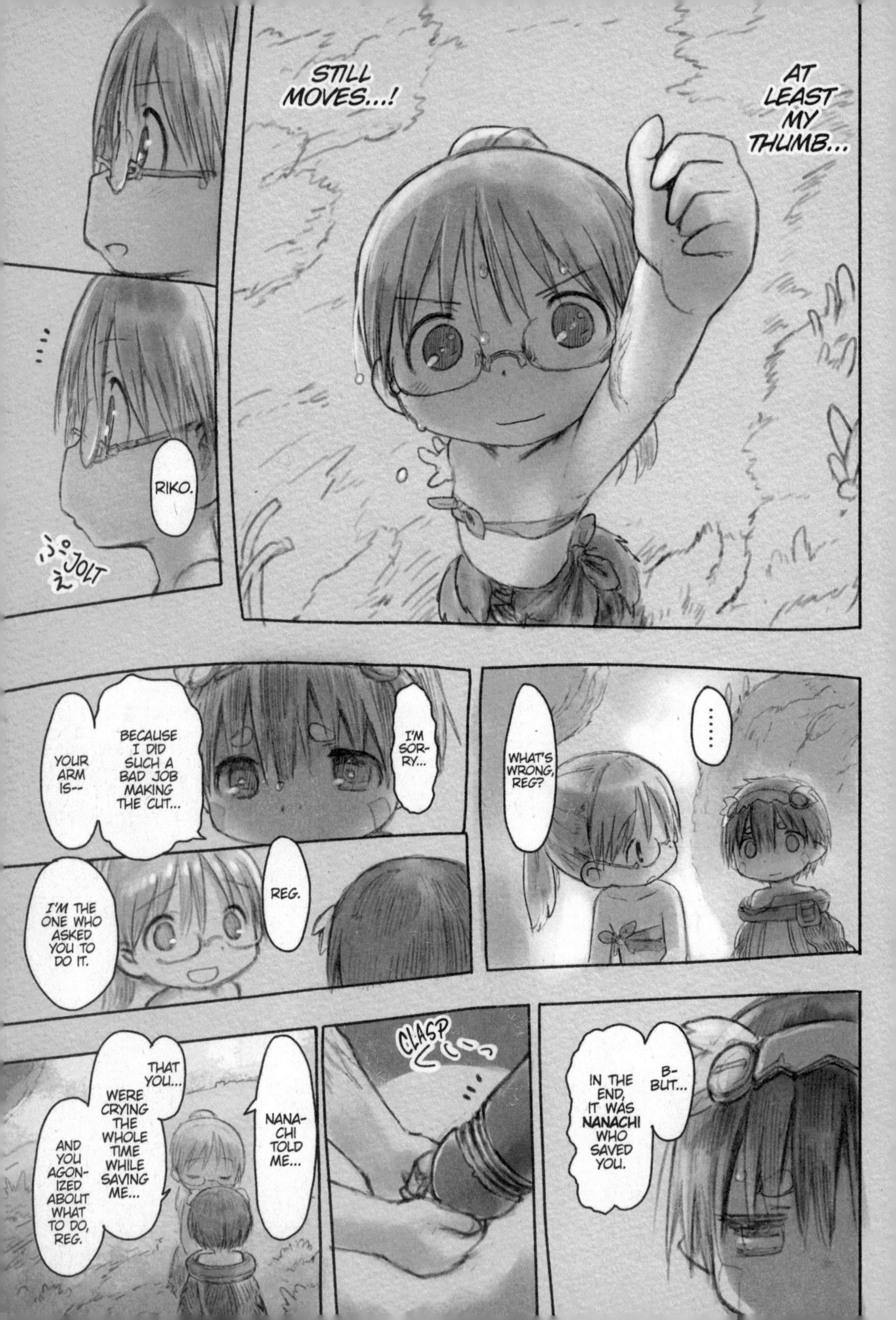
AT LEAST MY THUMB...
STILL MOVES...!
...
RIKO.
JOLT
......
WHAT'S WRONG, REG?
I'M SORRY...
BECAUSE I DID SUCH A BAD JOB MAKING THE CUT...
YOUR ARM IS--
REG.
I'M THE ONE WHO ASKED YOU TO DO IT.
B-BUT...
IN THE END, IT WAS NANACHI WHO SAVED YOU.
CLASP
..
NANA-CHI TOLD ME...
THAT YOU... WERE CRYING THE WHOLE TIME WHILE SAVING ME...
AND YOU AGONIZED ABOUT WHAT TO DO, REG.

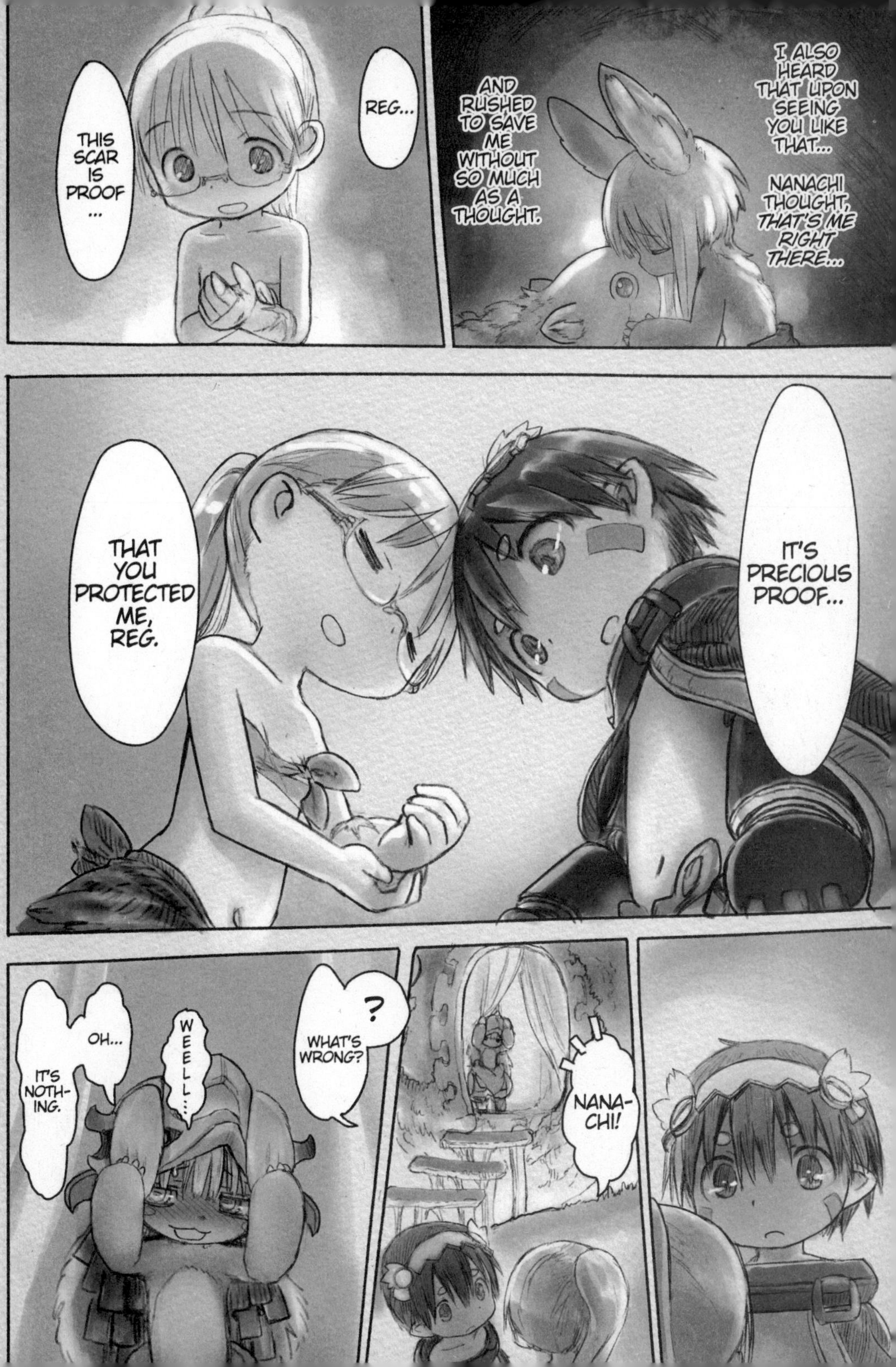
I ALSO HEARD THAT UPON SEEING YOU LIKE THAT...
NANACHI THOUGHT, THAT'S ME RIGHT THERE...
AND RUSHED TO SAVE ME WITHOUT SO MUCH AS A THOUGHT.
REG...
THIS SCAR IS PROOF...
IT'S PRECIOUS PROOF...
THAT YOU PROTECTED ME, REG.
NANA-CHI!
?
WHAT'S WRONG?
WEELL...
OH...
IT'S NOTH-ING.

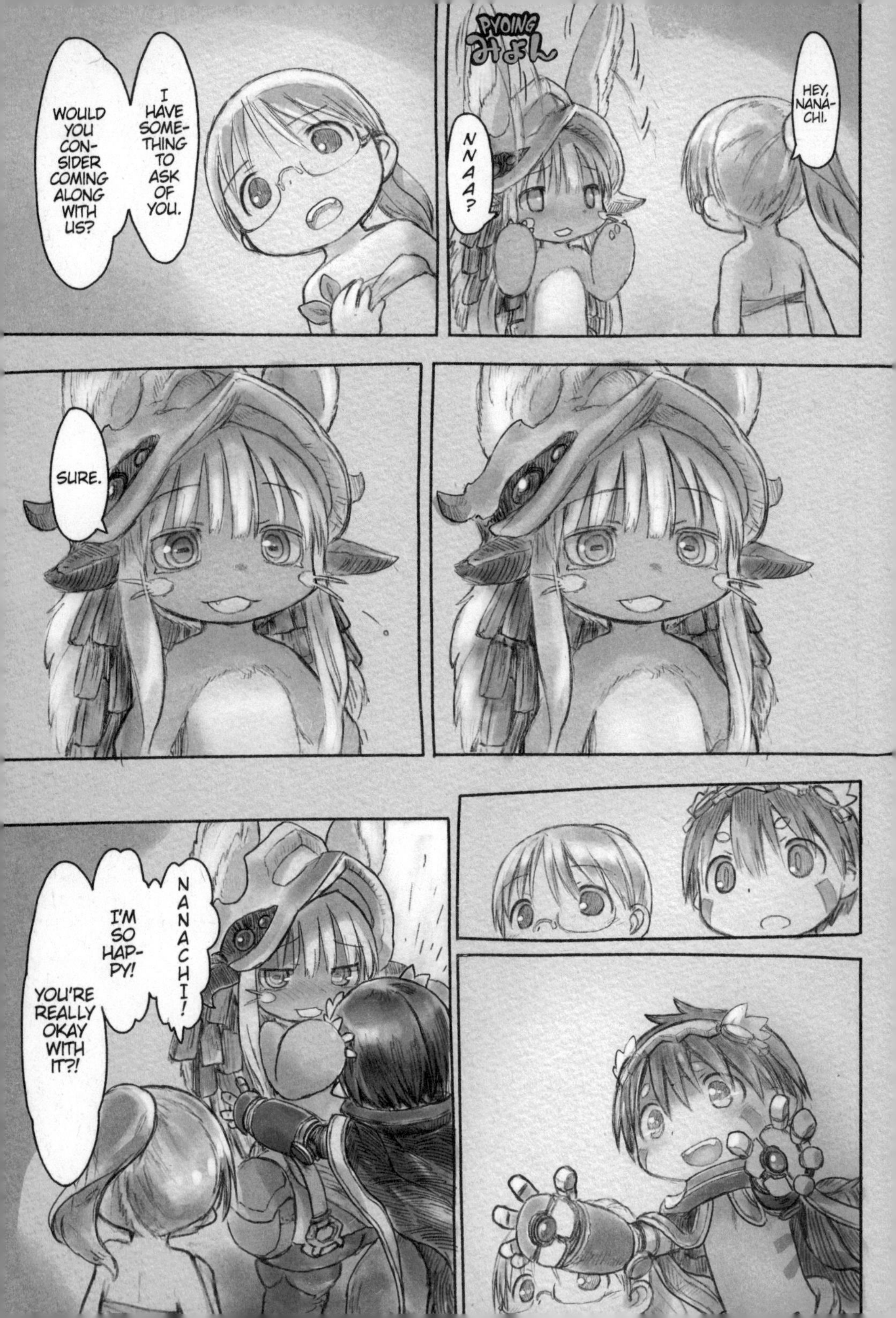
HEY, NANACHI.
PYOING
みょん
NNAA?
I HAVE SOMETHING TO ASK OF YOU.
WOULD YOU CONSIDER COMING ALONG WITH US?
SURE.
NANACHI!
I'M SO HAPPY!
YOU'RE REALLY OKAY WITH IT?!

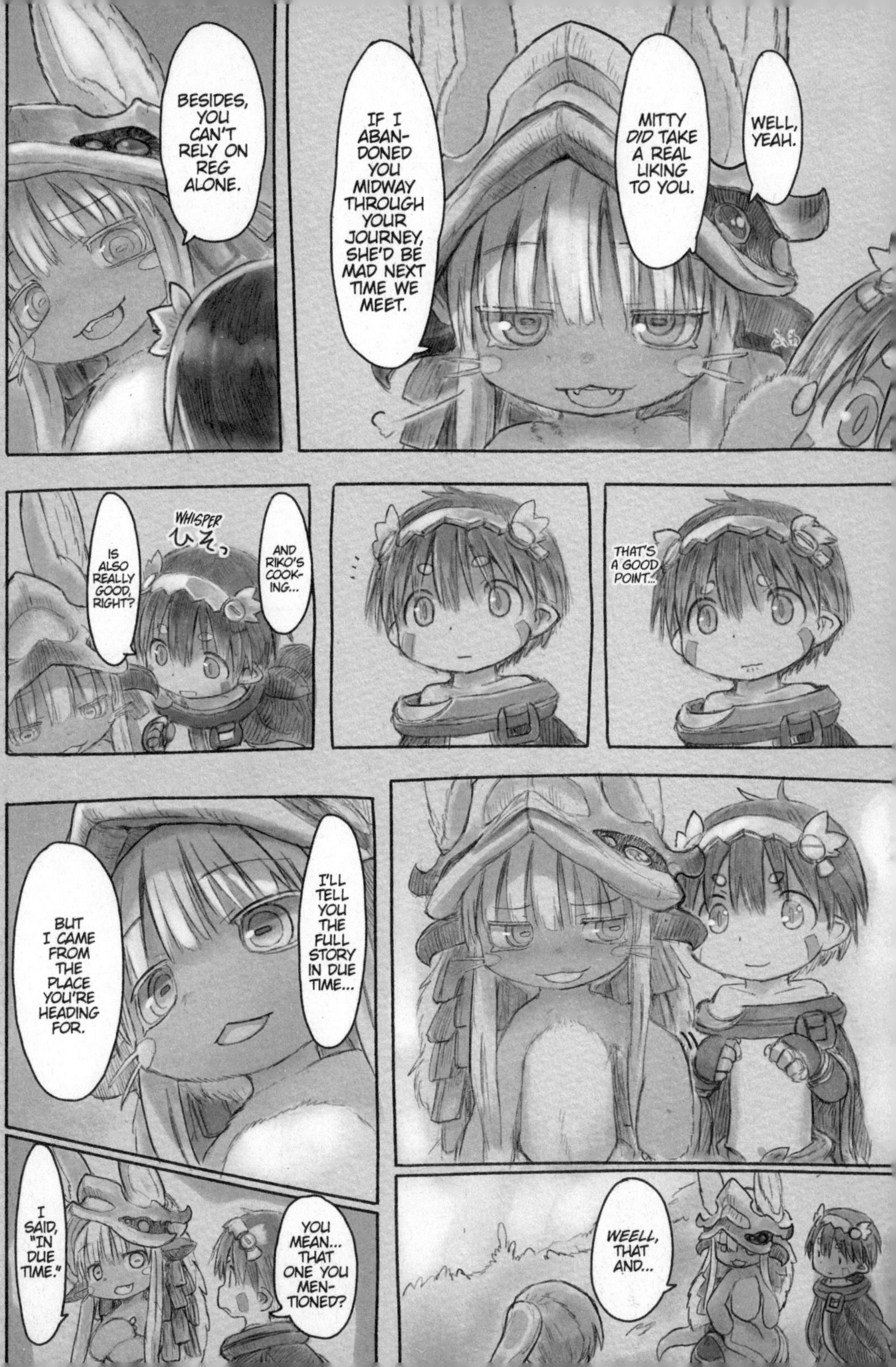
WELL, YEAH.
MITTY DID TAKE A REAL LIKING TO YOU.
IF I ABANDONED YOU MIDWAY THROUGH YOUR JOURNEY, SHE'D BE MAD NEXT TIME WE MEET.
BESIDES, YOU CAN'T RELY ON REG ALONE.
THAT'S A GOOD POINT...
AND RIKO'S COOKING...
WHISPER
IS ALSO REALLY GOOD, RIGHT?
I'LL TELL YOU THE FULL STORY IN DUE TIME...
BUT I CAME FROM THE PLACE YOU'RE HEADING FOR.
WEELL, THAT AND...
YOU MEAN... THAT ONE YOU MENTIONED?
I SAID, "IN DUE TIME."

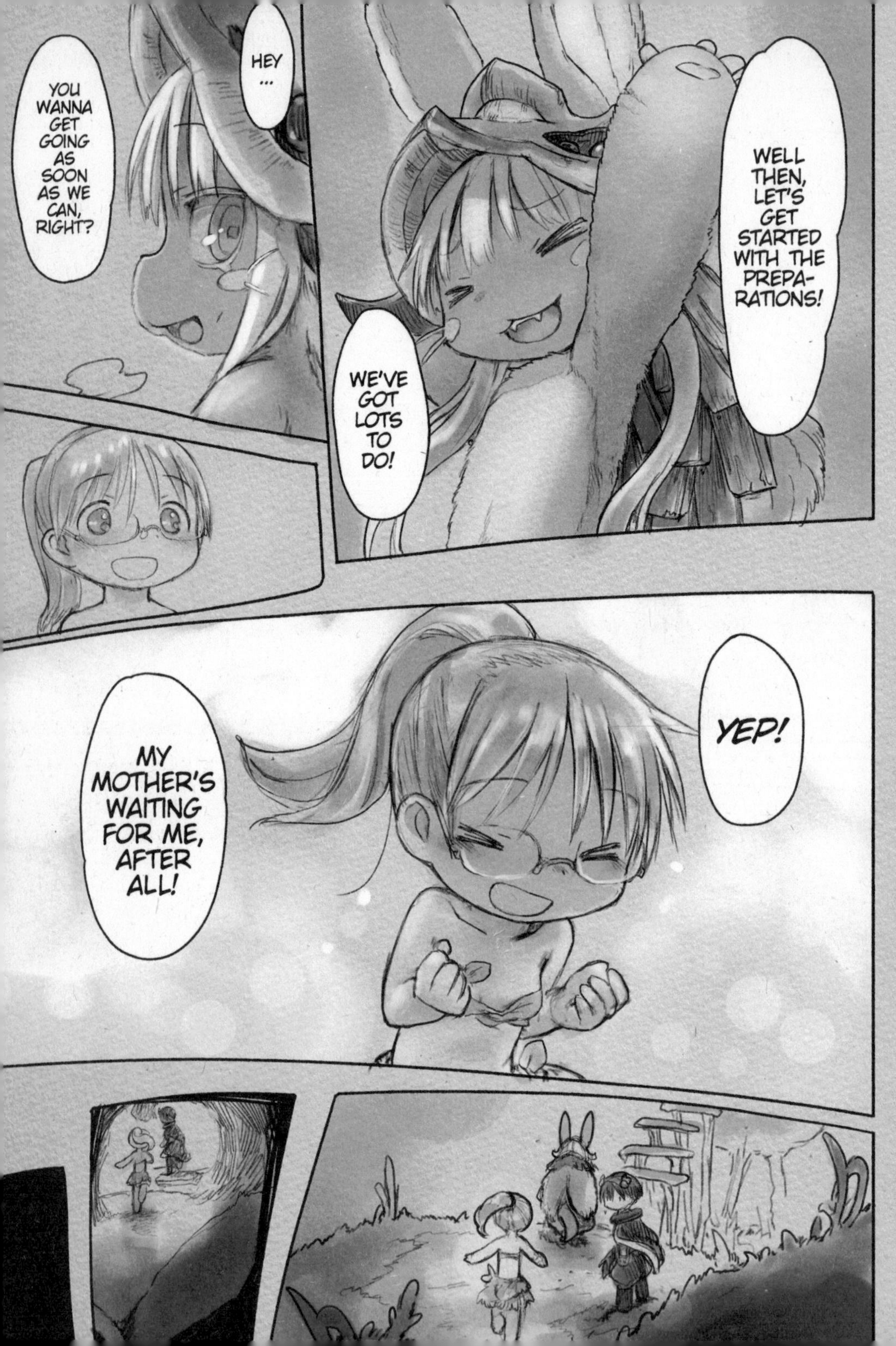
WELL THEN, LET'S GET STARTED WITH THE PREPA-RATIONS!
WE'VE GOT LOTS TO DO!
HEY ...
YOU WANNA GET GOING AS SOON AS WE CAN, RIGHT?
YEP!
MY MOTHER'S WAITING FOR ME, AFTER ALL!

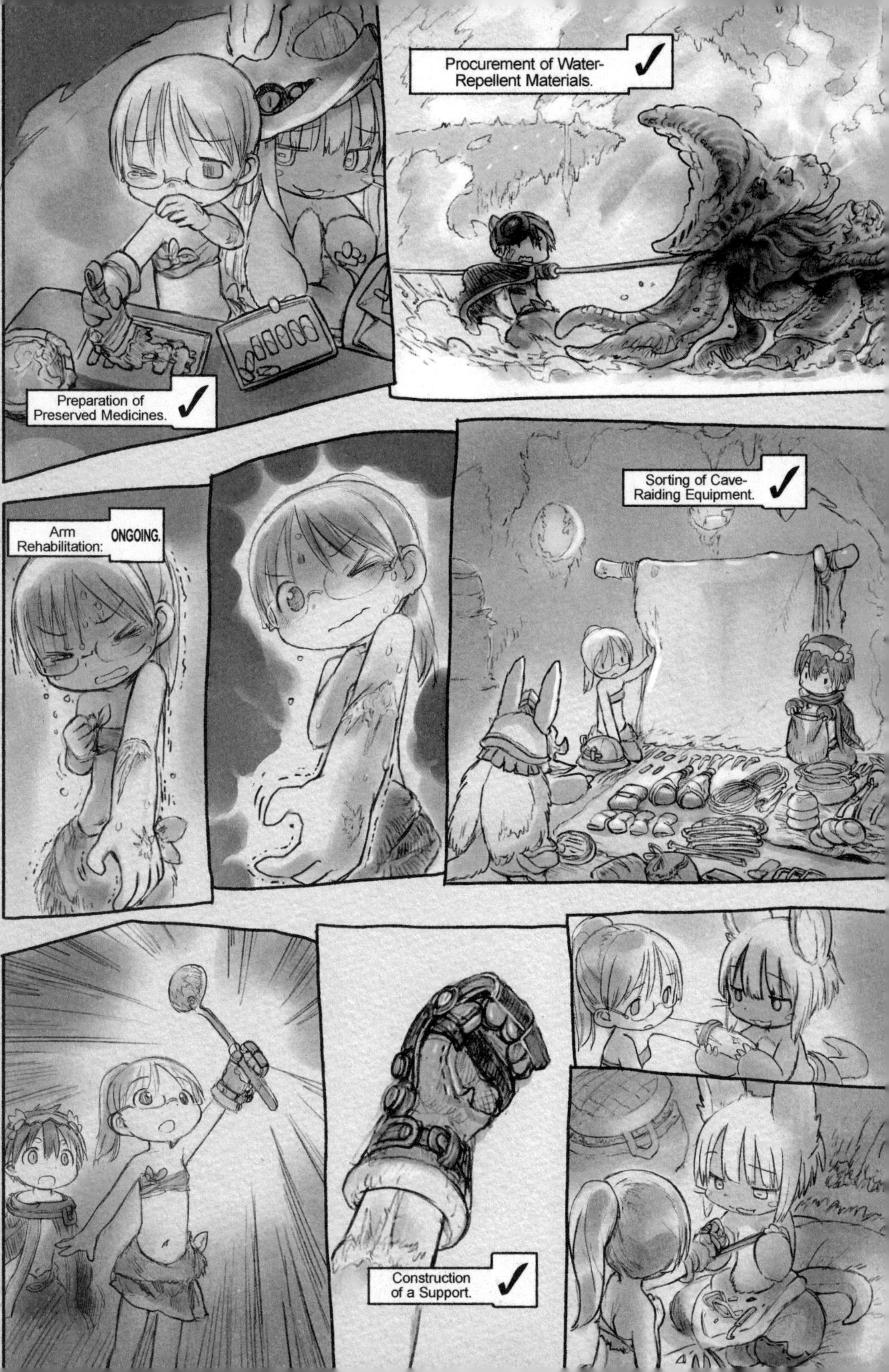
Procurement of Water-Repellent Materials. ✓
Preparation of Preserved Medicines. ✓
Sorting of Cave-Raiding Equipment. ✓
Arm Rehabilitation: ONGOING.
Construction of a Support. ✓

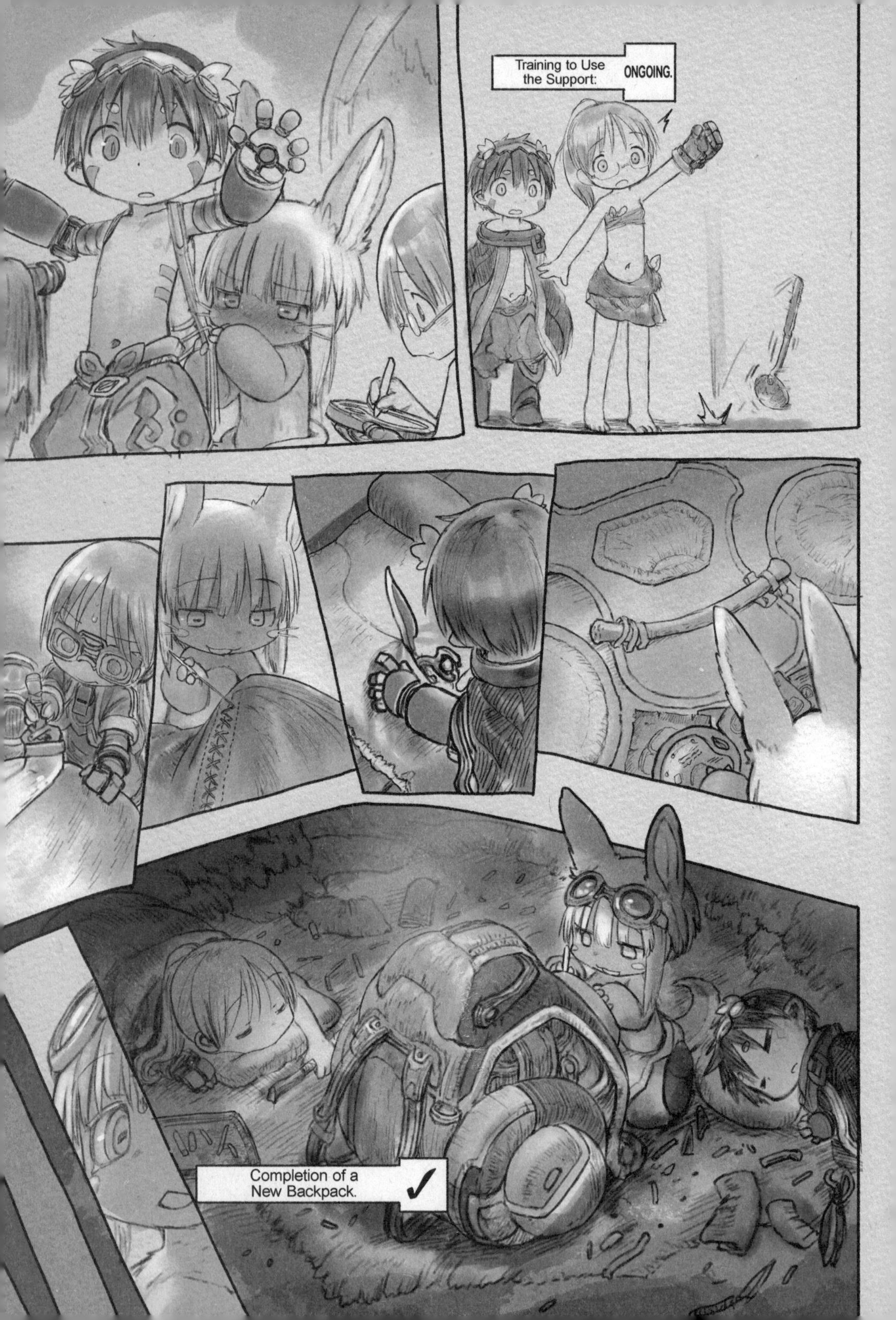
Training to Use the Support: ONGOING.
Completion of a New Backpack. ✓

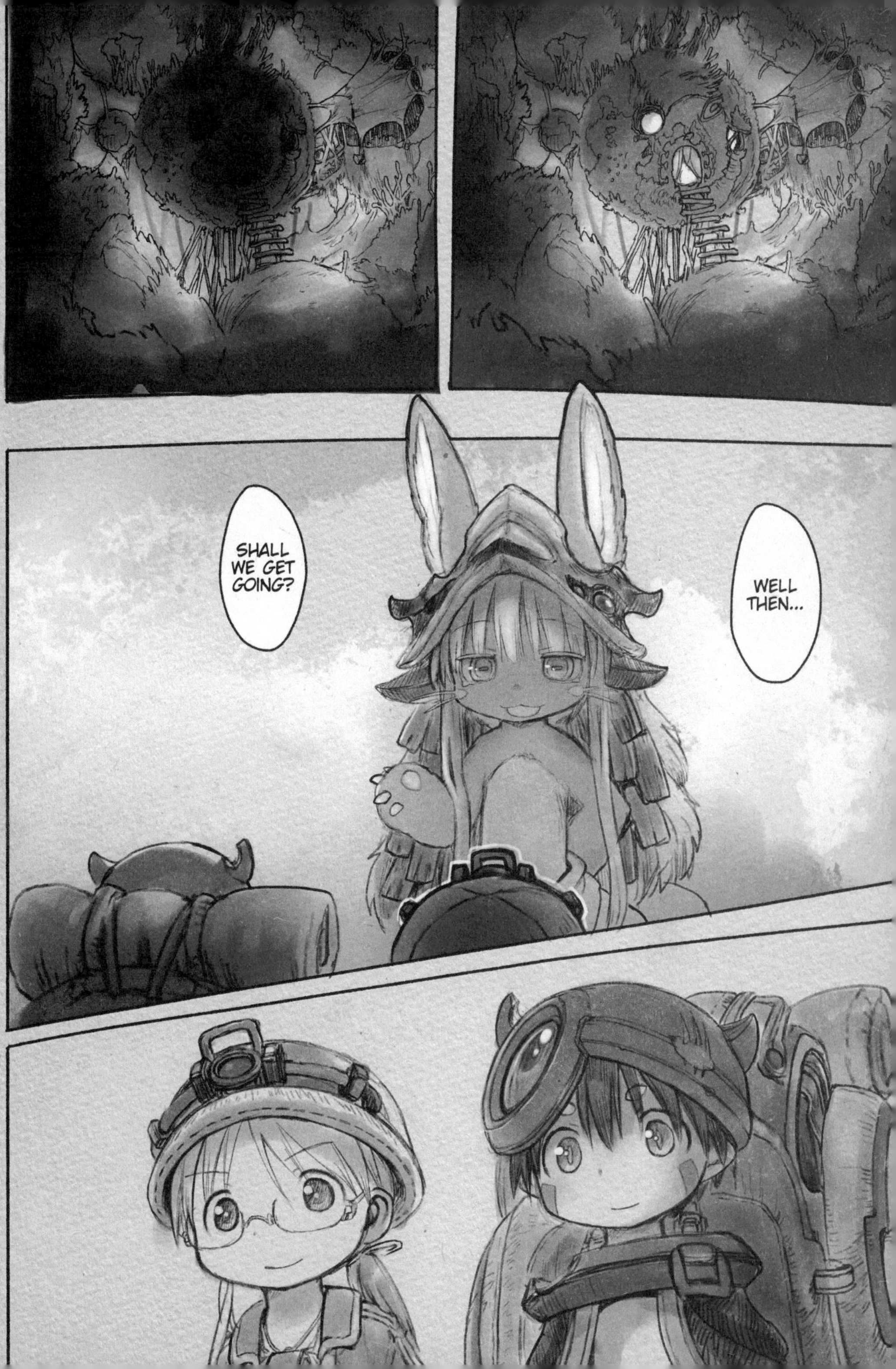
WELL THEN...
SHALL WE GET GOING?

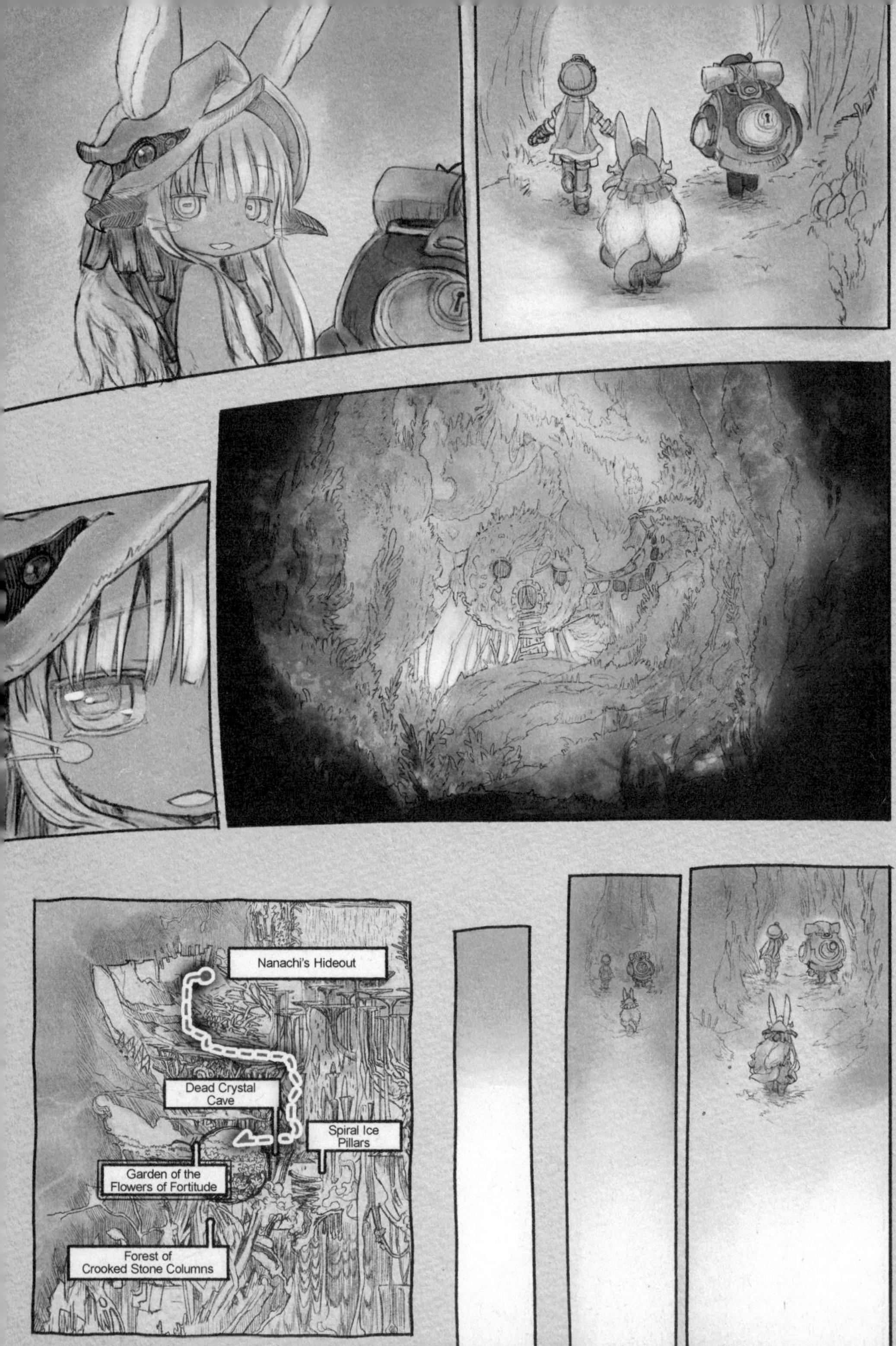
Nanachi's Hideout
Spiral Ice Pillars
Dead Crystal Cave
Garden of the Flowers of Fortitude
Forest of Crooked Stone Columns

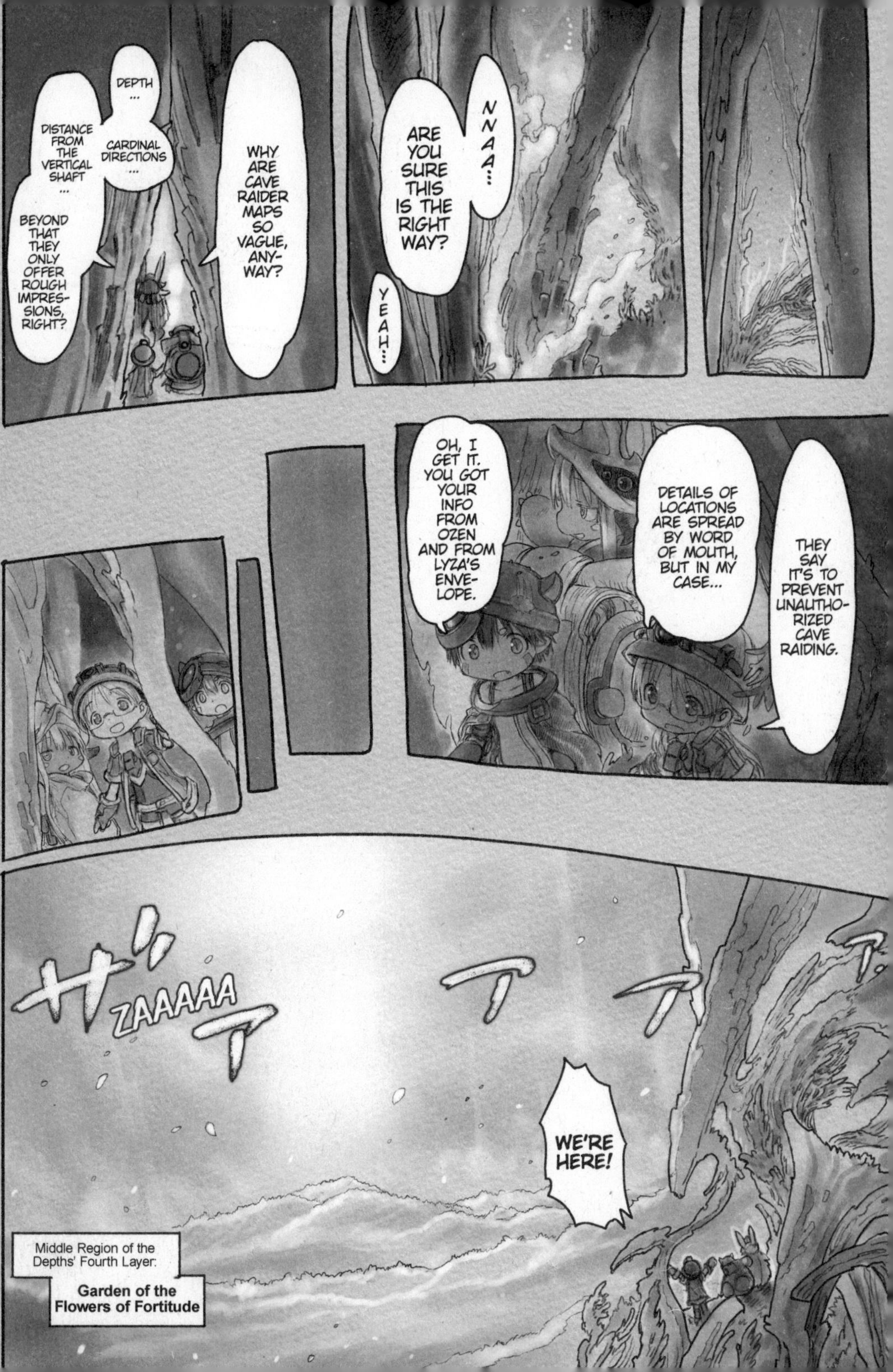
NNAAA...
ARE YOU SURE THIS IS THE RIGHT WAY?
YEAH...
WHY ARE CAVE RAIDER MAPS SO VAGUE, ANYWAY?
DEPTH...
CARDINAL DIRECTIONS...
DISTANCE FROM THE VERTICAL SHAFT...
BEYOND THAT THEY ONLY OFFER ROUGH IMPRESSIONS, RIGHT?
THEY SAY IT'S TO PREVENT UNAUTHORIZED CAVE RAIDING.
DETAILS OF LOCATIONS ARE SPREAD BY WORD OF MOUTH, BUT IN MY CASE...
OH, I GET IT. YOU GOT YOUR INFO FROM OZEN AND FROM LYZA'S ENVELOPE.
ZAAAAA
WE'RE HERE!
Middle Region of the Depths' Fourth Layer:
Garden of the Flowers of Fortitude

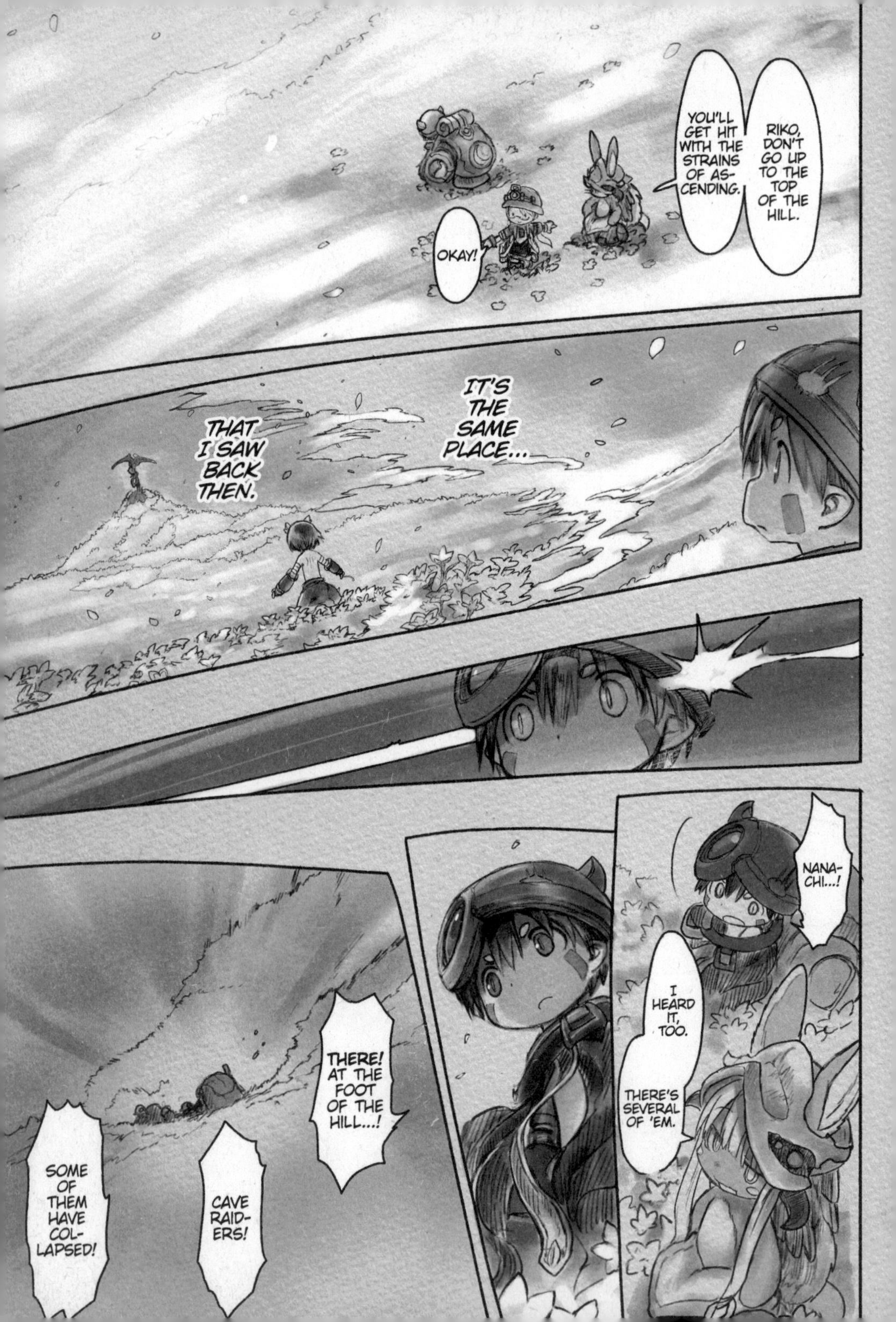
RIKO, DON'T GO UP TO THE TOP OF THE HILL.
YOU'LL GET HIT WITH THE STRAINS OF ASCENDING.
OKAY!
IT'S THE SAME PLACE...
THAT I SAW BACK THEN.
NANACHI...!
I HEARD IT, TOO.
THERE'S SEVERAL OF 'EM.
THERE! AT THE FOOT OF THE HILL...!
CAVE RAIDERS!
SOME OF THEM HAVE COLLAPSED!

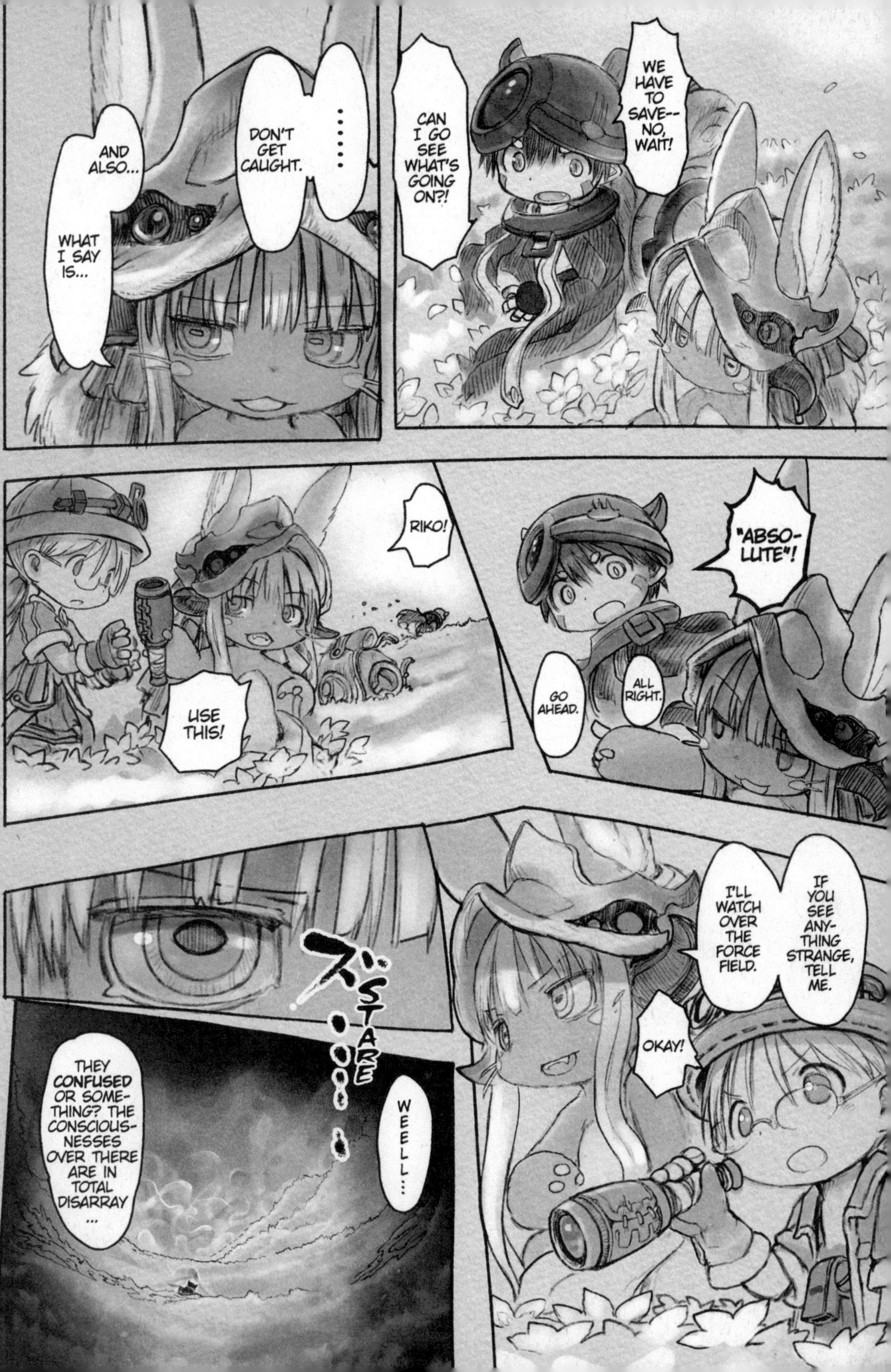
WE HAVE TO SAVE--NO, WAIT!
CAN I GO SEE WHAT'S GOING ON?!
......
DON'T GET CAUGHT.
AND ALSO...
WHAT I SAY IS...
"ABSOLUTE"!
ALL RIGHT.
GO AHEAD.
RIKO!
USE THIS!
IF YOU SEE ANYTHING STRANGE, TELL ME.
I'LL WATCH OVER THE FORCE FIELD.
OKAY!
STARE
WEELL...
THEY CONFUSED OR SOMETHING? THE CONSCIOUSNESSES OVER THERE ARE IN TOTAL DISARRAY...

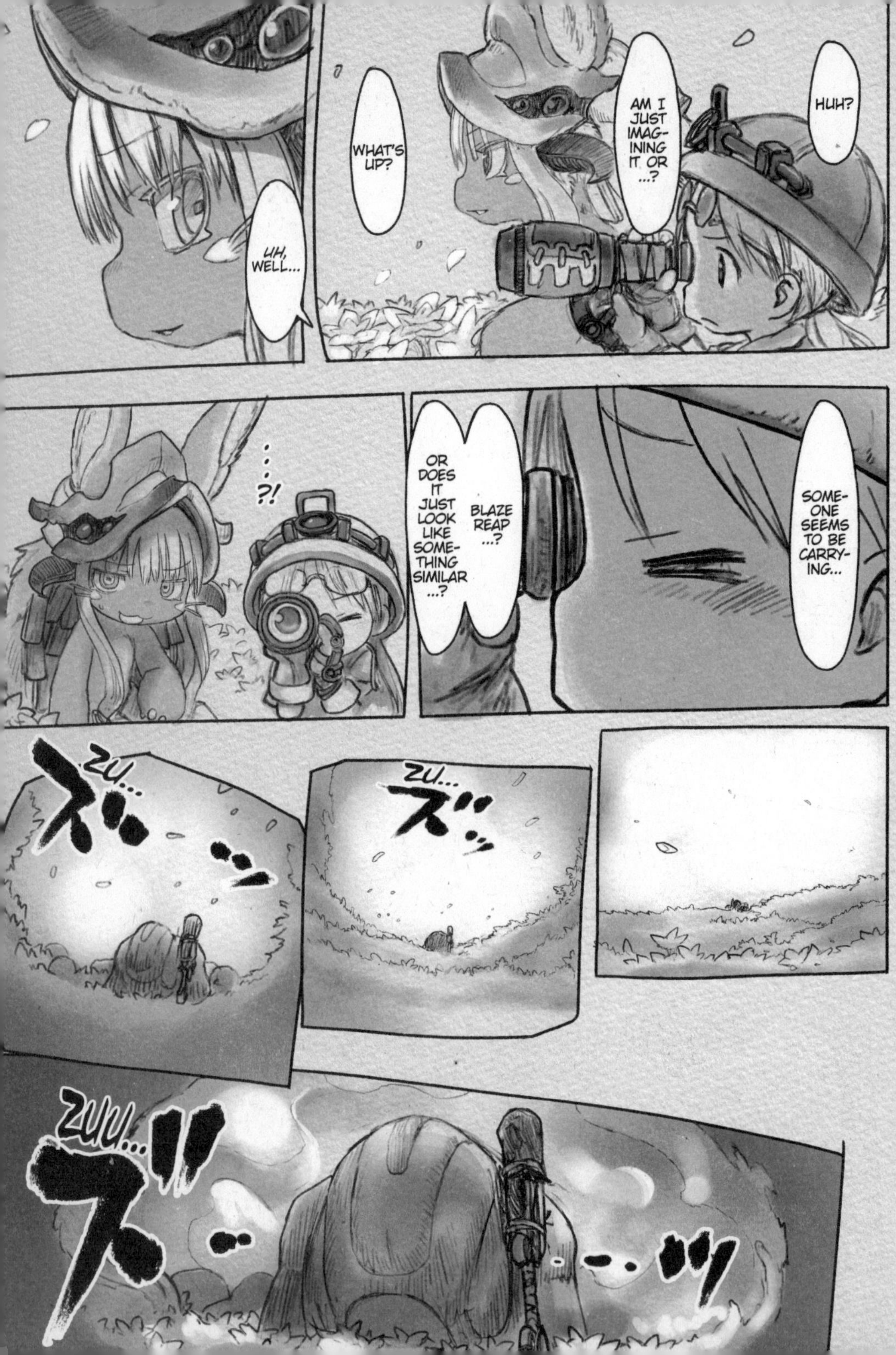
HUH?
AM I JUST IMAGINING IT OR ...?
WHAT'S UP?
UH, WELL...
SOMEONE SEEMS TO BE CARRYING...
BLAZE REAP ...?
OR DOES IT JUST LOOK LIKE SOMETHING SIMILAR ...?
...?!
ZU...
ZU...
ZUU...!!

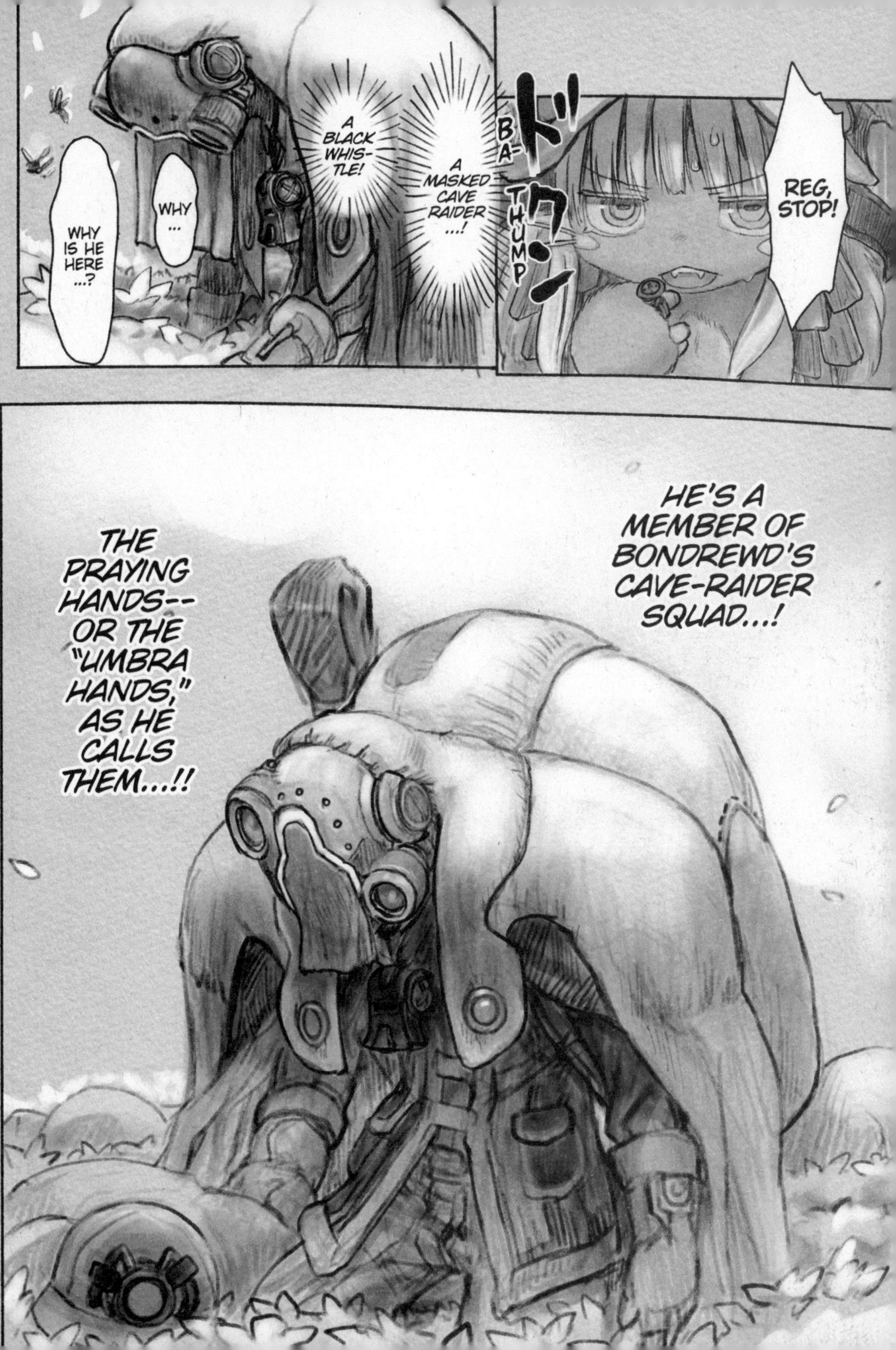
REG, STOP!
BA-THUMP
A MASKED CAVE RAIDER ...!
A BLACK WHISTLE!
WHY ...
WHY IS HE HERE ...?
HE'S A MEMBER OF BONDREWD'S CAVE-RAIDER SQUAD...!
THE PRAYING HANDS-- OR THE "UMBRA HANDS," AS HE CALLS THEM...!!

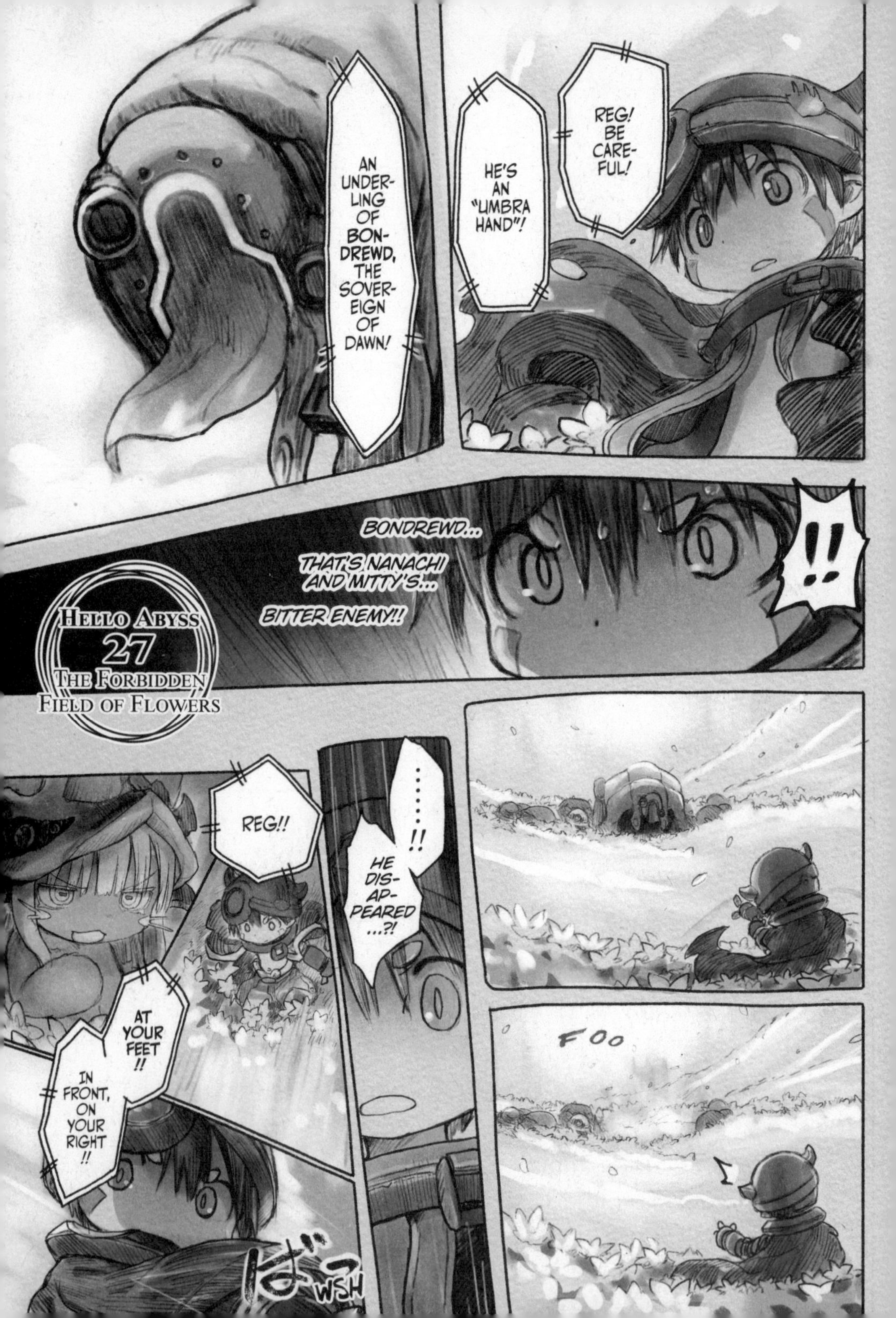
REG! BE CARE-FUL!
HE'S AN "UMBRA HAND"!
AN UNDERLING OF BONDREWD, THE SOVEREIGN OF DAWN!
!!
BONDREWD...
THAT'S NANACHI AND MITTY'S...
BITTER ENEMY!!
HELLO ABYSS 27 THE FORBIDDEN FIELD OF FLOWERS
FOO
......!!
HE DIS-AP-PEARED...?!
REG!!
AT YOUR FEET!!
IN FRONT, ON YOUR RIGHT!!
WSH

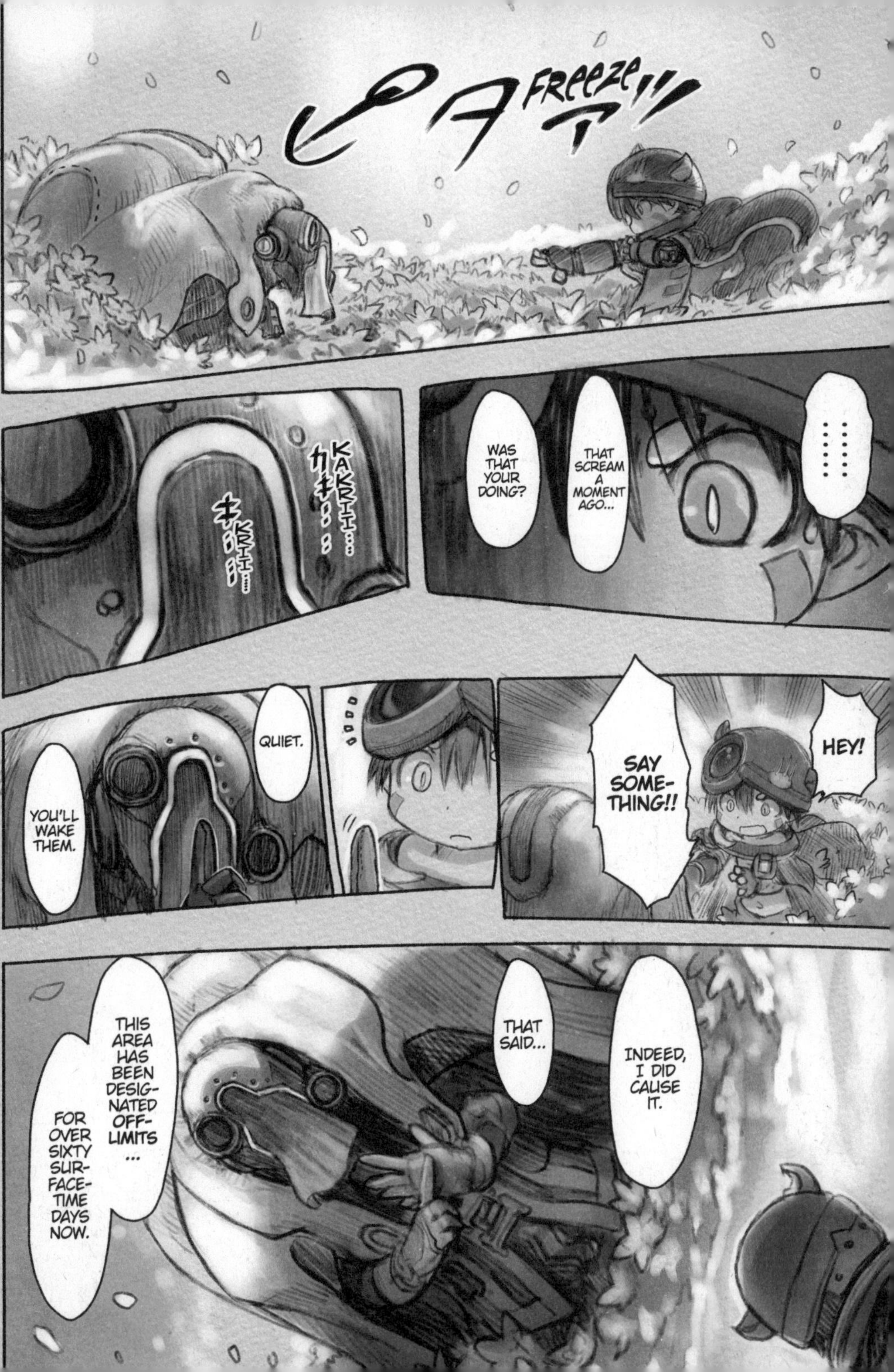
FREEZE!!
......
THAT SCREAM A MOMENT AGO...
WAS THAT YOUR DOING?
KAKRII... KRII...
HEY!
SAY SOME-THING!!
QUIET.
YOU'LL WAKE THEM.
INDEED, I DID CAUSE IT.
THAT SAID...
THIS AREA HAS BEEN DESIG-NATED OFF-LIMITS...
FOR OVER SIXTY SUR-FACE-TIME DAYS NOW.

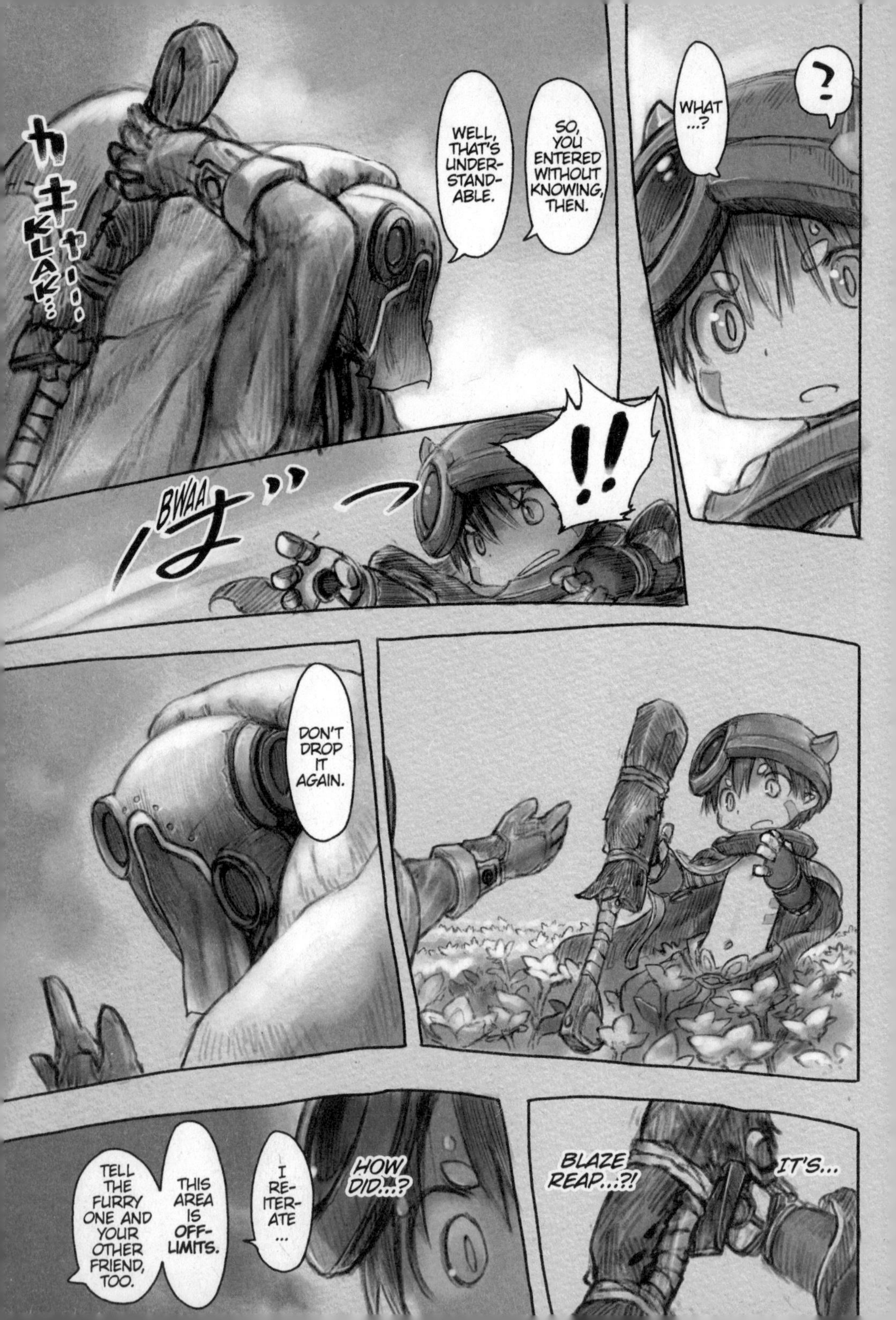
?
WHAT ...?
SO, YOU ENTERED WITHOUT KNOWING, THEN.
WELL, THAT'S UNDER-STAND-ABLE.
カキャ…
KLAK...
!!
ばっ
BWAA
DON'T DROP IT AGAIN.
IT'S...
BLAZE REAP...?!
HOW DID...?
I RE-ITER-ATE ...
THIS AREA IS OFF-LIMITS.
TELL THE FURRY ONE AND YOUR OTHER FRIEND, TOO.

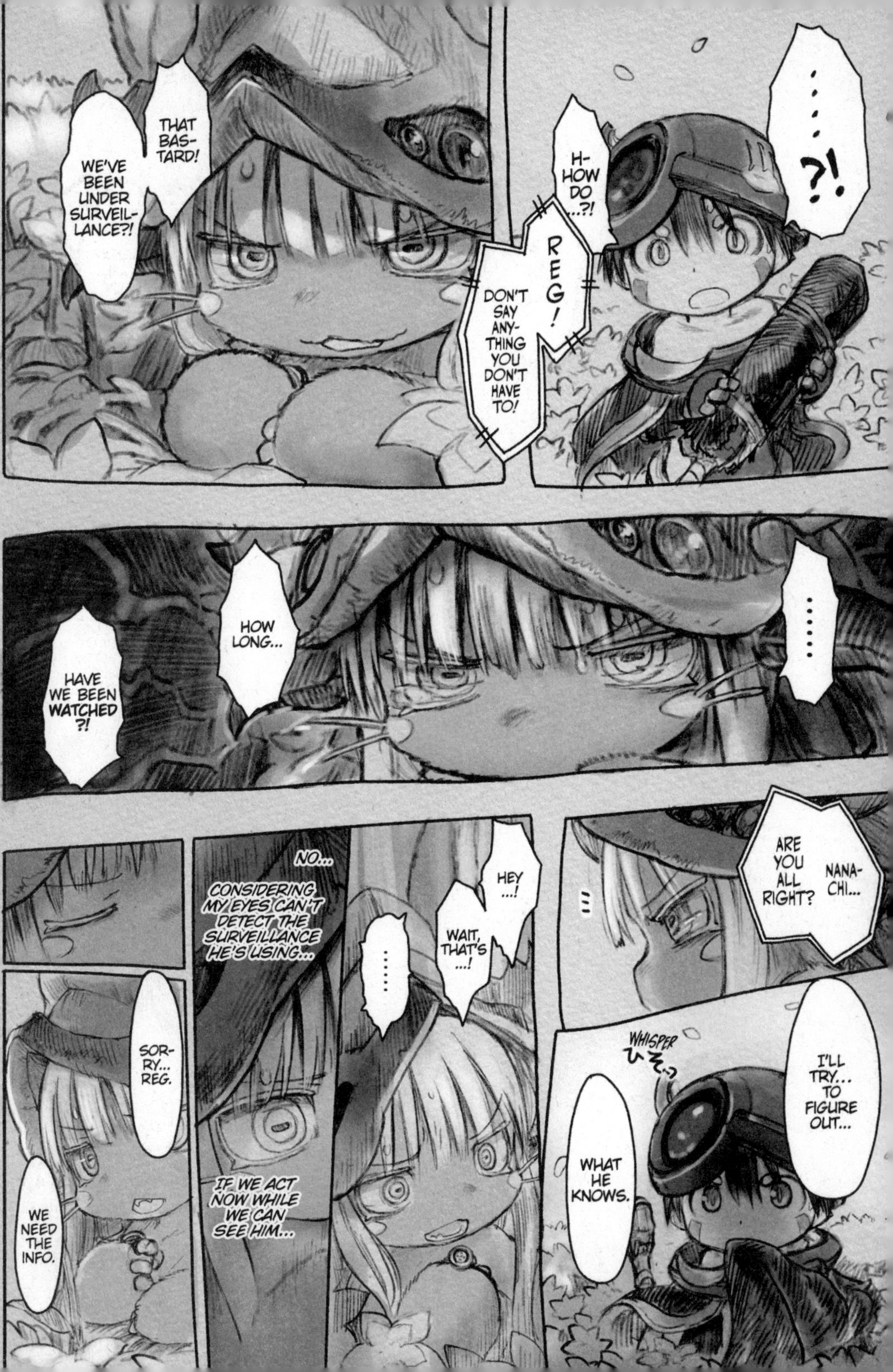

...?!
H-HOW DO...?!
REG!
DON'T SAY ANYTHING YOU DON'T HAVE TO!
THAT BASTARD!
WE'VE BEEN UNDER SURVEILLANCE?!
......
HOW LONG...
HAVE WE BEEN WATCHED?!
NANA-CHI...
ARE YOU ALL RIGHT?
...
I'LL TRY... TO FIGURE OUT...
WHISPER
WHAT HE KNOWS.
HEY...!
WAIT, THAT'S...!
......
NO...
CONSIDERING MY EYES CAN'T DETECT THE SURVEILLANCE HE'S USING...
IF WE ACT NOW WHILE WE CAN SEE HIM...
SORRY... REG.
WE NEED THE INFO.

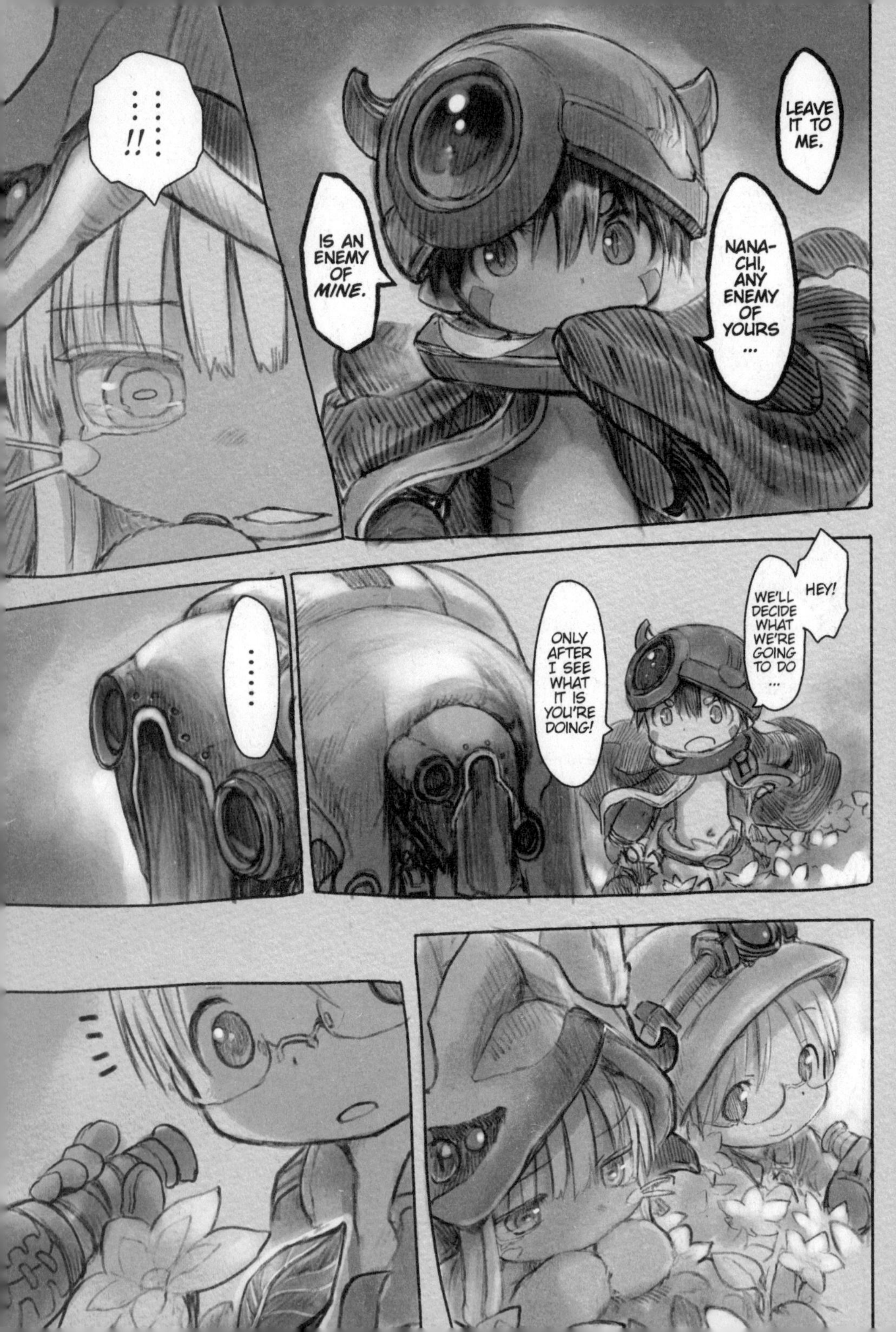
LEAVE IT TO ME.
NANA-CHI, ANY ENEMY OF YOURS ...
IS AN ENEMY OF MINE.
......!!
HEY!
WE'LL DECIDE WHAT WE'RE GOING TO DO ...
ONLY AFTER I SEE WHAT IT IS YOU'RE DOING!
......

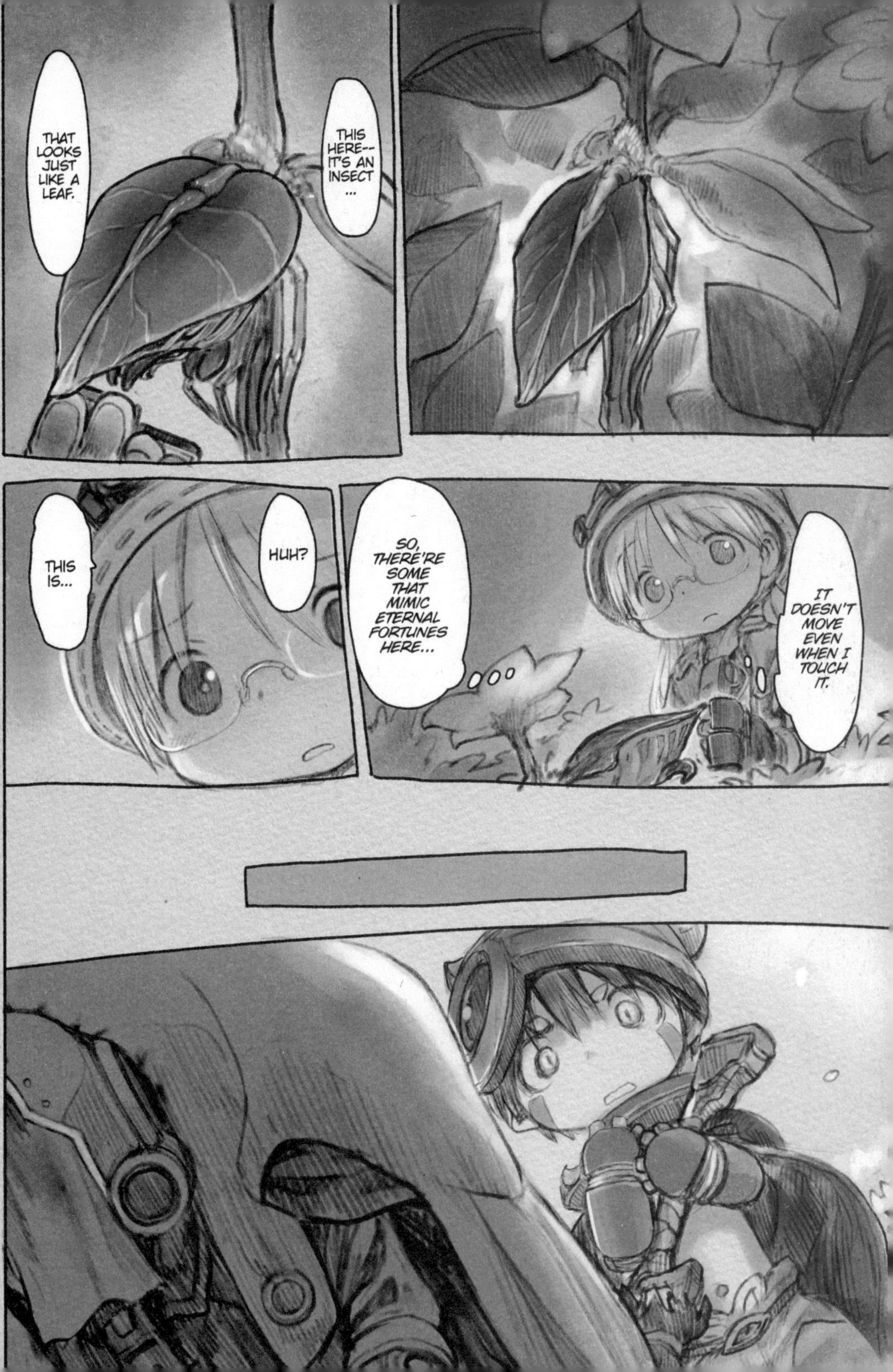
THIS HERE-- IT'S AN INSECT ...
THAT LOOKS JUST LIKE A LEAF.
IT DOESN'T MOVE EVEN WHEN I TOUCH IT.
SO, THERE'RE SOME THAT MIMIC ETERNAL FORTUNES HERE...
HUH?
THIS IS...

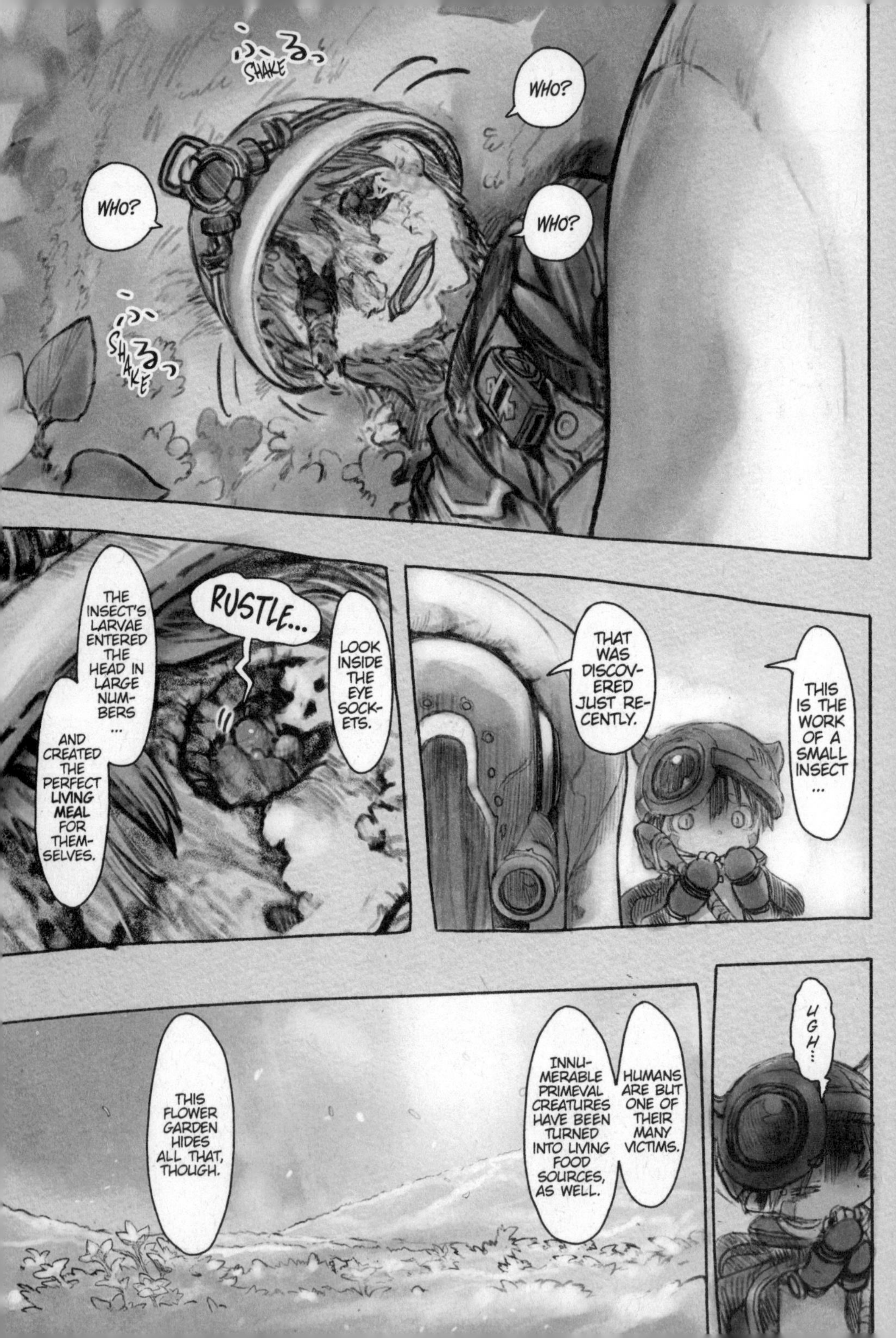
SHAKE
WHO?
WHO?
WHO?
SHAKE
THIS IS THE WORK OF A SMALL INSECT...
THAT WAS DISCOVERED JUST RECENTLY.
LOOK INSIDE THE EYE SOCKETS.
RUSTLE...
THE INSECT'S LARVAE ENTERED THE HEAD IN LARGE NUMBERS...
AND CREATED THE PERFECT LIVING MEAL FOR THEMSELVES.
UGH...
HUMANS ARE BUT ONE OF THEIR MANY VICTIMS.
INNUMERABLE PRIMEVAL CREATURES HAVE BEEN TURNED INTO LIVING FOOD SOURCES, AS WELL.
THIS FLOWER GARDEN HIDES ALL THAT, THOUGH.

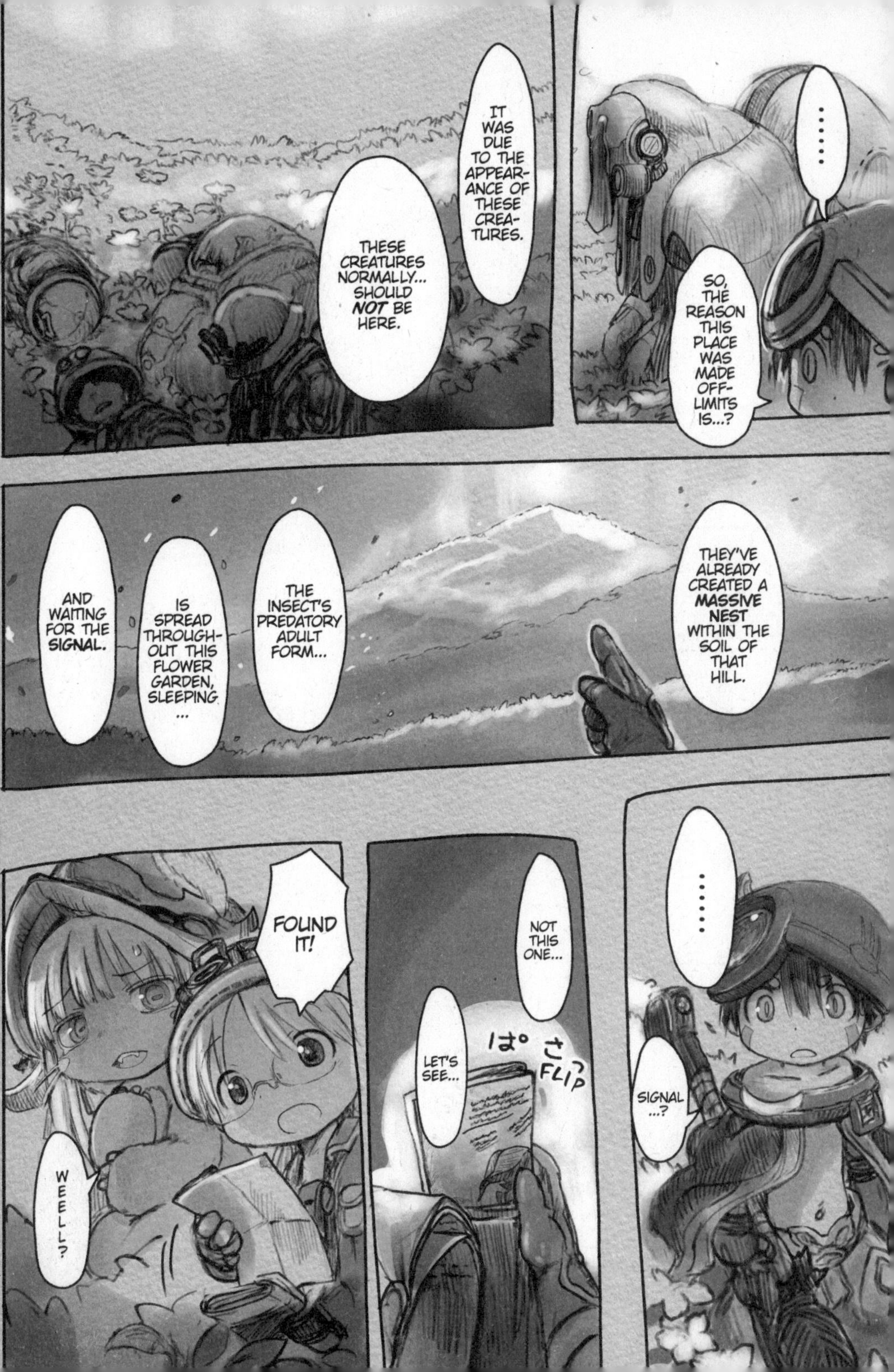
......
SO, THE REASON THIS PLACE WAS MADE OFF-LIMITS IS...?
IT WAS DUE TO THE APPEARANCE OF THESE CREATURES.
THESE CREATURES NORMALLY... SHOULD NOT BE HERE.
THEY'VE ALREADY CREATED A MASSIVE NEST WITHIN THE SOIL OF THAT HILL.
THE INSECT'S PREDATORY ADULT FORM...
IS SPREAD THROUGHOUT THIS FLOWER GARDEN, SLEEPING...
AND WAITING FOR THE SIGNAL.
......
SIGNAL...?
NOT THIS ONE...
ぱさ
FLIP
LET'S SEE...
FOUND IT!
WEELL?

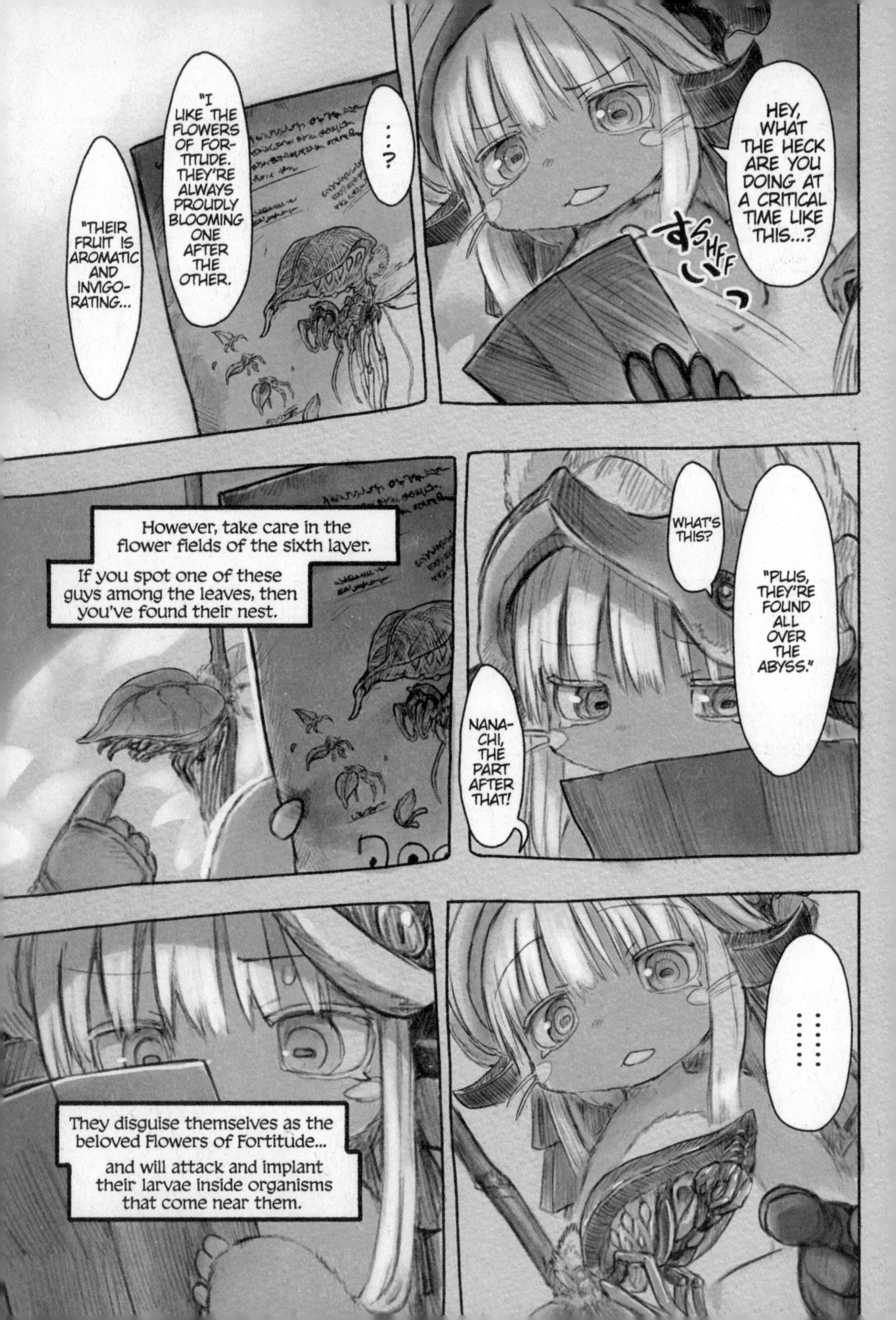
HEY, WHAT THE HECK ARE YOU DOING AT A CRITICAL TIME LIKE THIS...?
SHFF
...?
"I LIKE THE FLOWERS OF FORTITUDE. THEY'RE ALWAYS PROUDLY BLOOMING ONE AFTER THE OTHER.
"THEIR FRUIT IS AROMATIC AND INVIGORATING...
"PLUS, THEY'RE FOUND ALL OVER THE ABYSS."
WHAT'S THIS?
NANACHI, THE PART AFTER THAT!
However, take care in the flower fields of the sixth layer.
If you spot one of these guys among the leaves, then you've found their nest.
......
They disguise themselves as the beloved Flowers of Fortitude...
and will attack and implant their larvae inside organisms that come near them.

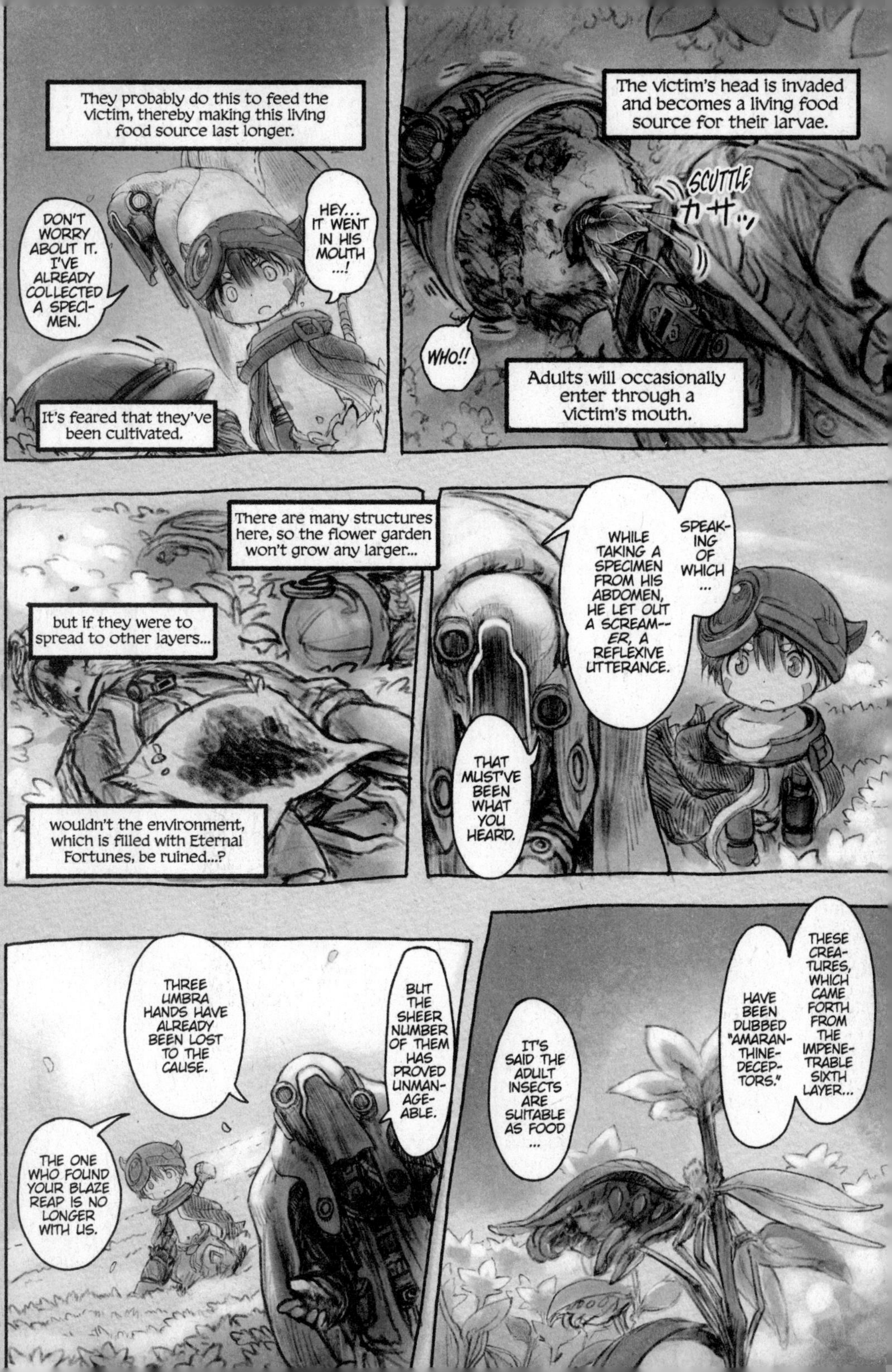
The victim's head is invaded and becomes a living food source for their larvae.
SCUTTLE
カサッ
WHO!!
Adults will occasionally enter through a victim's mouth.
They probably do this to feed the victim, thereby making this living food source last longer.
HEY... IT WENT IN HIS MOUTH ...!
DON'T WORRY ABOUT IT. I'VE ALREADY COLLECTED A SPECI-MEN.
It's feared that they've been cultivated.
SPEAK-ING OF WHICH ...
WHILE TAKING A SPECIMEN FROM HIS ABDOMEN, HE LET OUT A SCREAM-- ER, A REFLEXIVE UTTERANCE.
THAT MUST'VE BEEN WHAT YOU HEARD.
There are many structures here, so the flower garden won't grow any larger...
but if they were to spread to other layers...
wouldn't the environment, which is filled with Eternal Fortunes, be ruined...?
THESE CREA-TURES, WHICH CAME FORTH FROM THE IMPENE-TRABLE SIXTH LAYER...
HAVE BEEN DUBBED "AMARAN-THINE-DECEP-TORS."
IT'S SAID THE ADULT INSECTS ARE SUITABLE AS FOOD ...
BUT THE SHEER NUMBER OF THEM HAS PROVED UNMANA-GEABLE.
THREE UMBRA HANDS HAVE ALREADY BEEN LOST TO THE CAUSE.
THE ONE WHO FOUND YOUR BLAZE REAP IS NO LONGER WITH US.

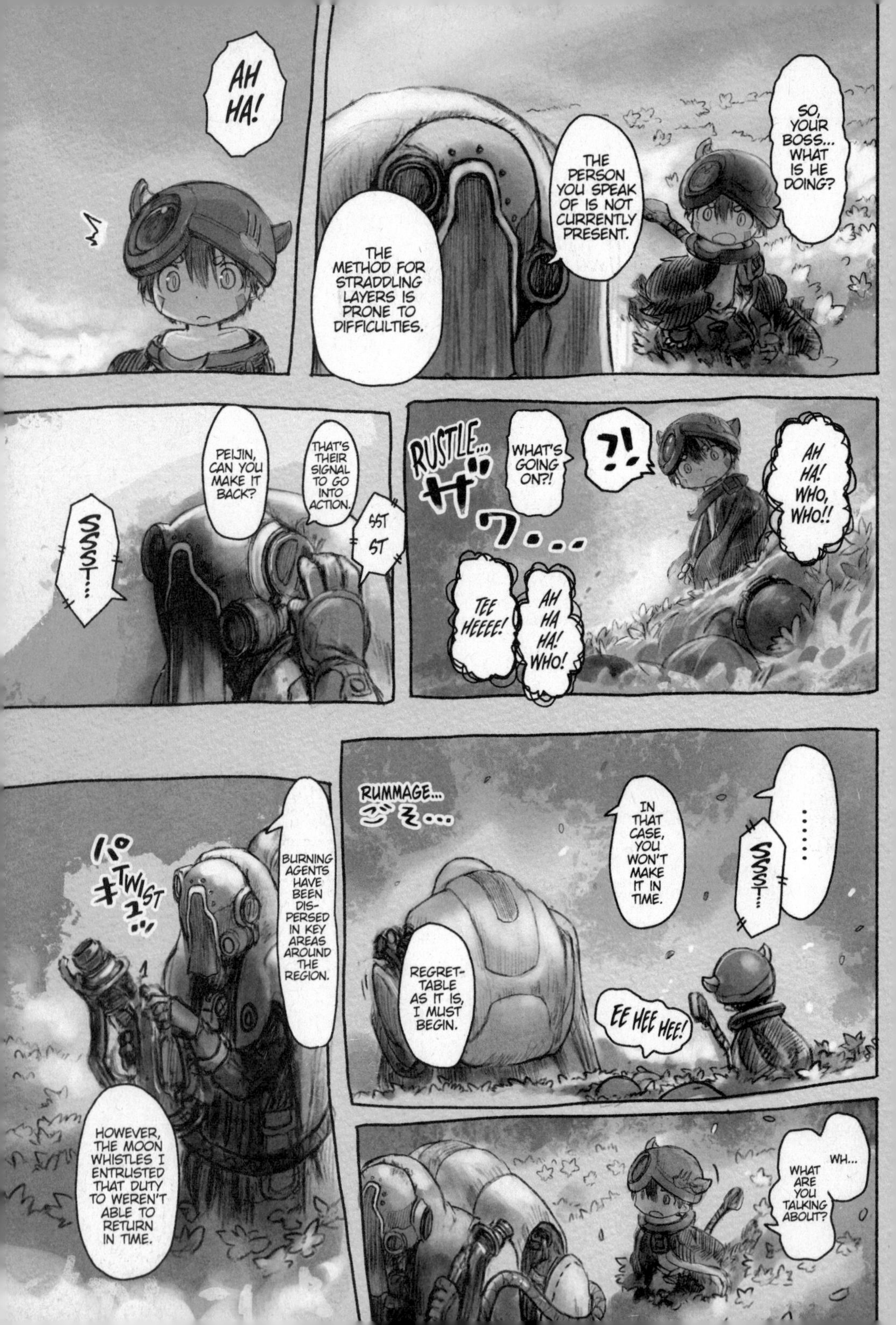
SO, YOUR BOSS... WHAT IS HE DOING?
THE PERSON YOU SPEAK OF IS NOT CURRENTLY PRESENT.
THE METHOD FOR STRADDLING LAYERS IS PRONE TO DIFFICULTIES.
AH HA!
AH HA! WHO, WHO!!
?!
WHAT'S GOING ON?!
RUSTLE...
ザワ...
AH HA HA! WHO!
TEE HEEEE!
THAT'S THEIR SIGNAL TO GO INTO ACTION.
PEIJIN, CAN YOU MAKE IT BACK?
SST ST
SSST...
......
SSSST...
IN THAT CASE, YOU WON'T MAKE IT IN TIME.
RUMMAGE...
ごそ...
REGRET-TABLE AS IT IS, I MUST BEGIN.
EE HEE HEE!
WH... WHAT ARE YOU TALKING ABOUT?
BURNING AGENTS HAVE BEEN DIS-PERSED IN KEY AREAS AROUND THE REGION.
パキュッ
TWIST
HOWEVER, THE MOON WHISTLES I ENTRUSTED THAT DUTY TO WEREN'T ABLE TO RETURN IN TIME.

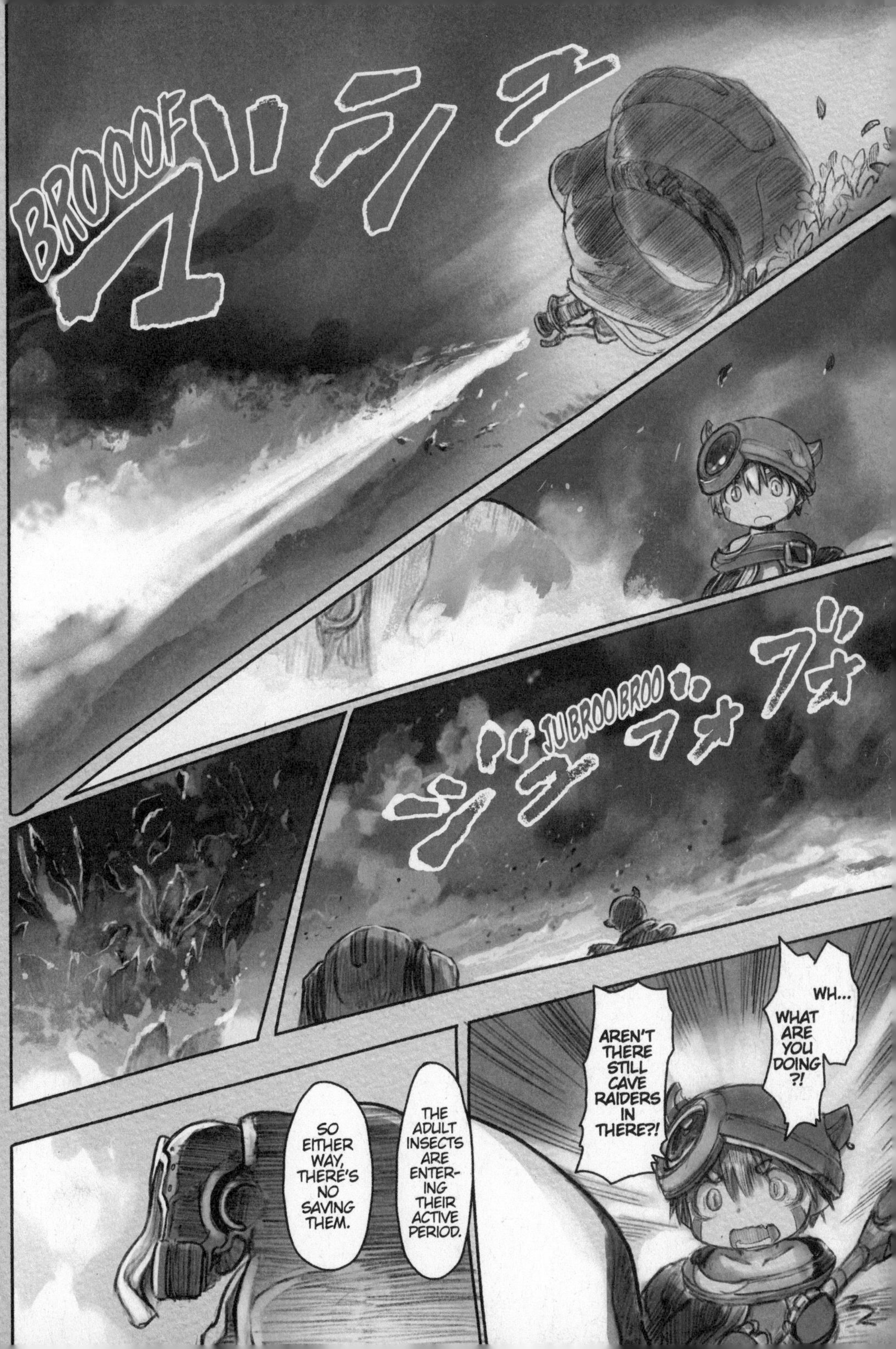
BROOOF
JU BROO BROO
WH... WHAT ARE YOU DOING?!
AREN'T THERE STILL CAVE RAIDERS IN THERE?!
THE ADULT INSECTS ARE ENTERING THEIR ACTIVE PERIOD.
SO EITHER WAY, THERE'S NO SAVING THEM.

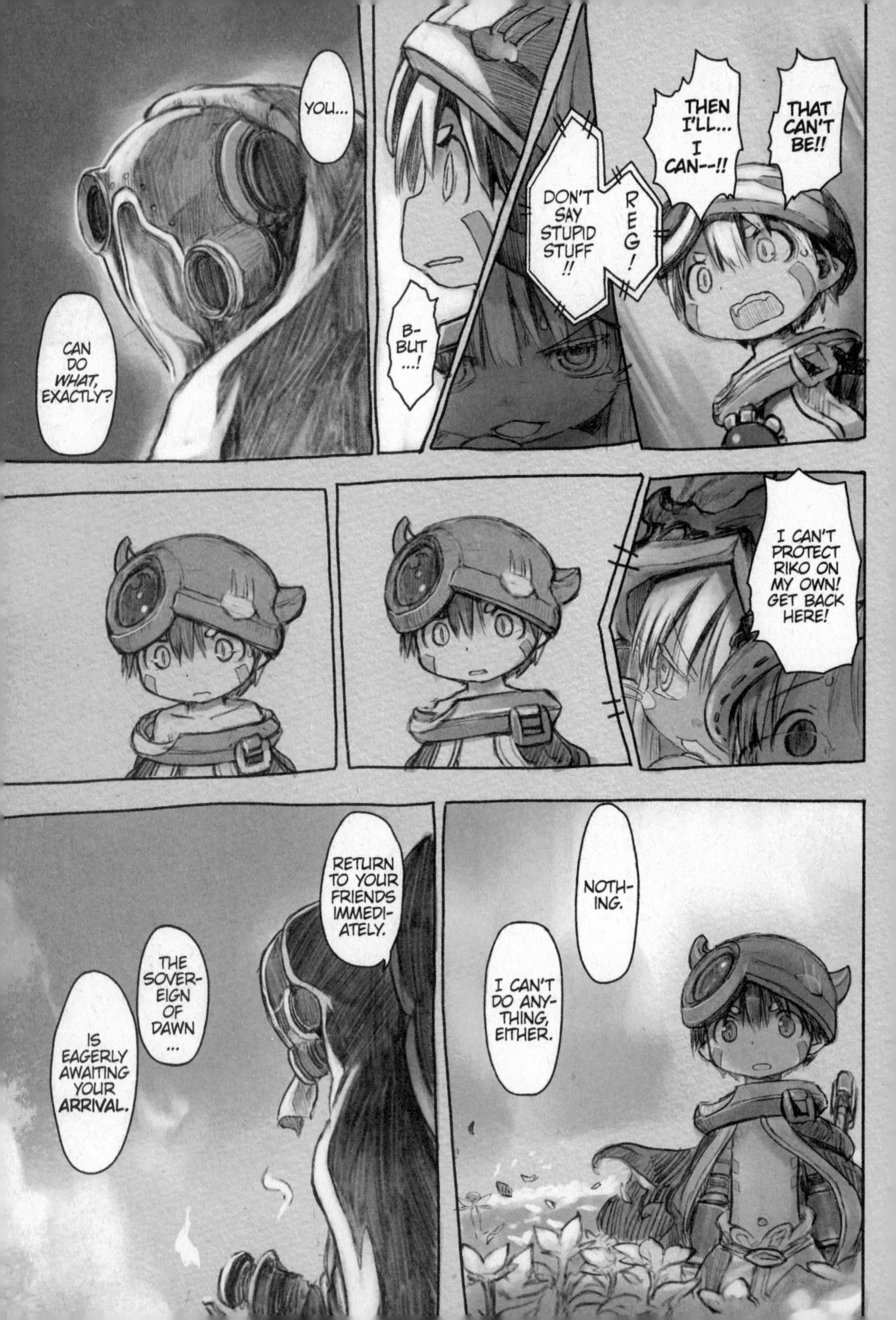
THAT CAN'T BE!!
THEN I'LL... I CAN--!!
REG!
DON'T SAY STUPID STUFF!!
YOU...
B-BUT...!
CAN DO WHAT, EXACTLY?
I CAN'T PROTECT RIKO ON MY OWN! GET BACK HERE!
NOTH-ING.
I CAN'T DO ANY-THING, EITHER.
RETURN TO YOUR FRIENDS IMMEDI-ATELY.
THE SOVER-EIGN OF DAWN...
IS EAGERLY AWAITING YOUR ARRIVAL.

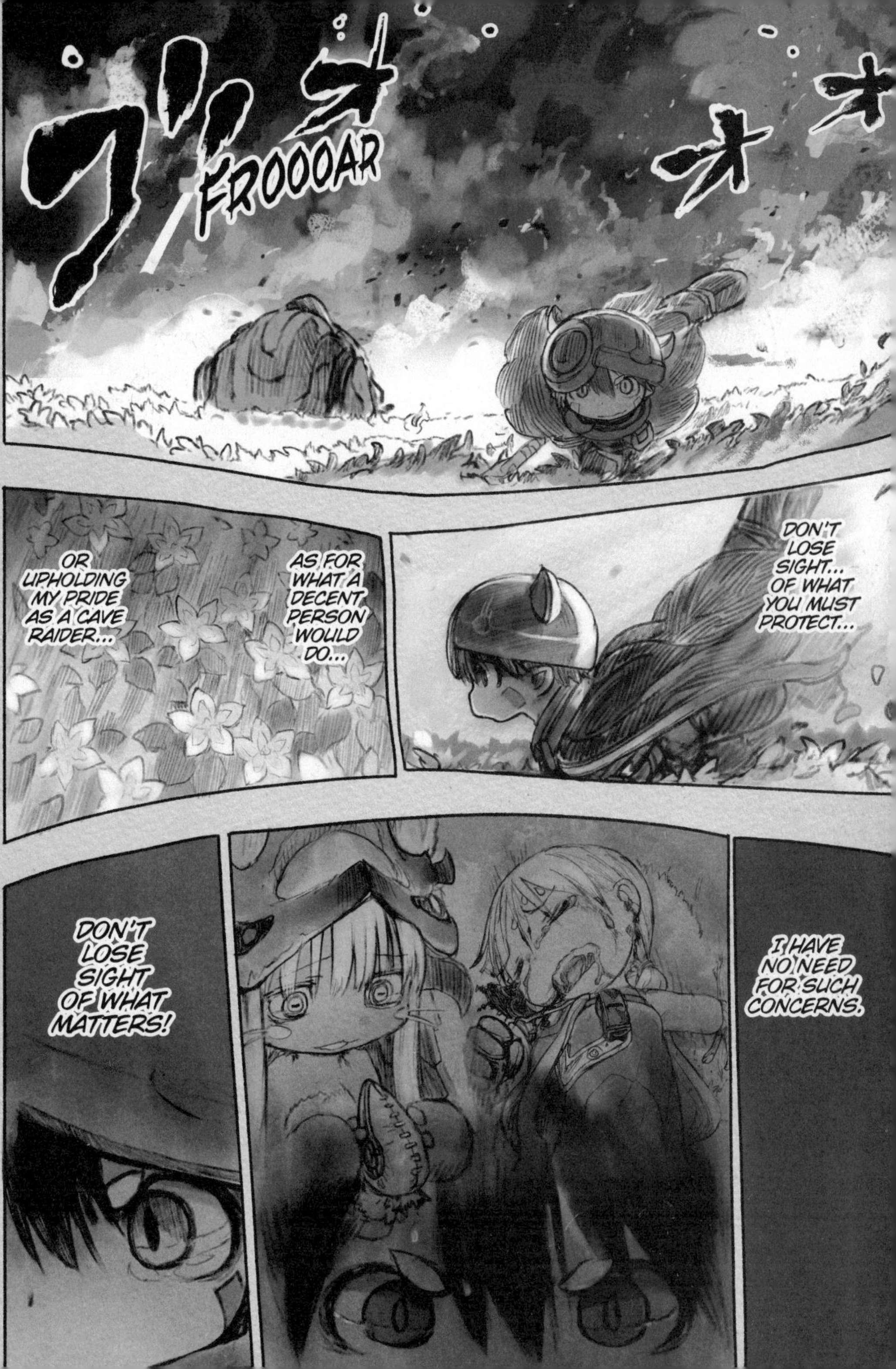
FROOOAR
DON'T LOSE SIGHT... OF WHAT YOU MUST PROTECT...
AS FOR WHAT A DECENT PERSON WOULD DO...
OR UPHOLDING MY PRIDE AS A CAVE RAIDER...
I HAVE NO NEED FOR SUCH CONCERNS.
DON'T LOSE SIGHT OF WHAT MATTERS!

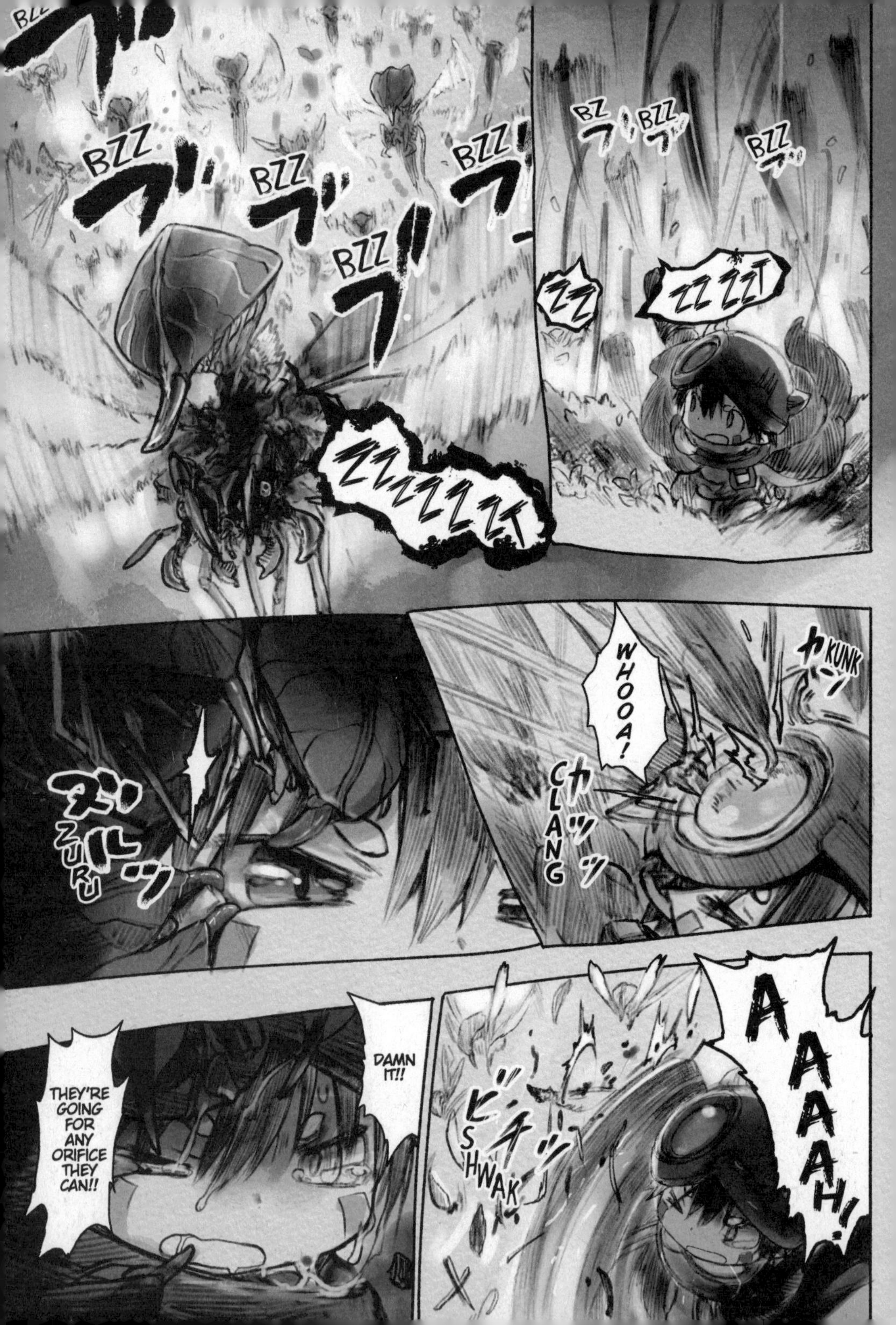

BZ
BZZ
BZZ
ZZ
ZZ ZZT
BZZ
BZZ
BZZ!
BZZ
ZZZZZZZZZT
WHOOA!
KUNK
CLANG
ZURU
AAAAH!
KSHWAK
DAMN IT!!
THEY'RE GOING FOR ANY ORIFICE THEY CAN!!

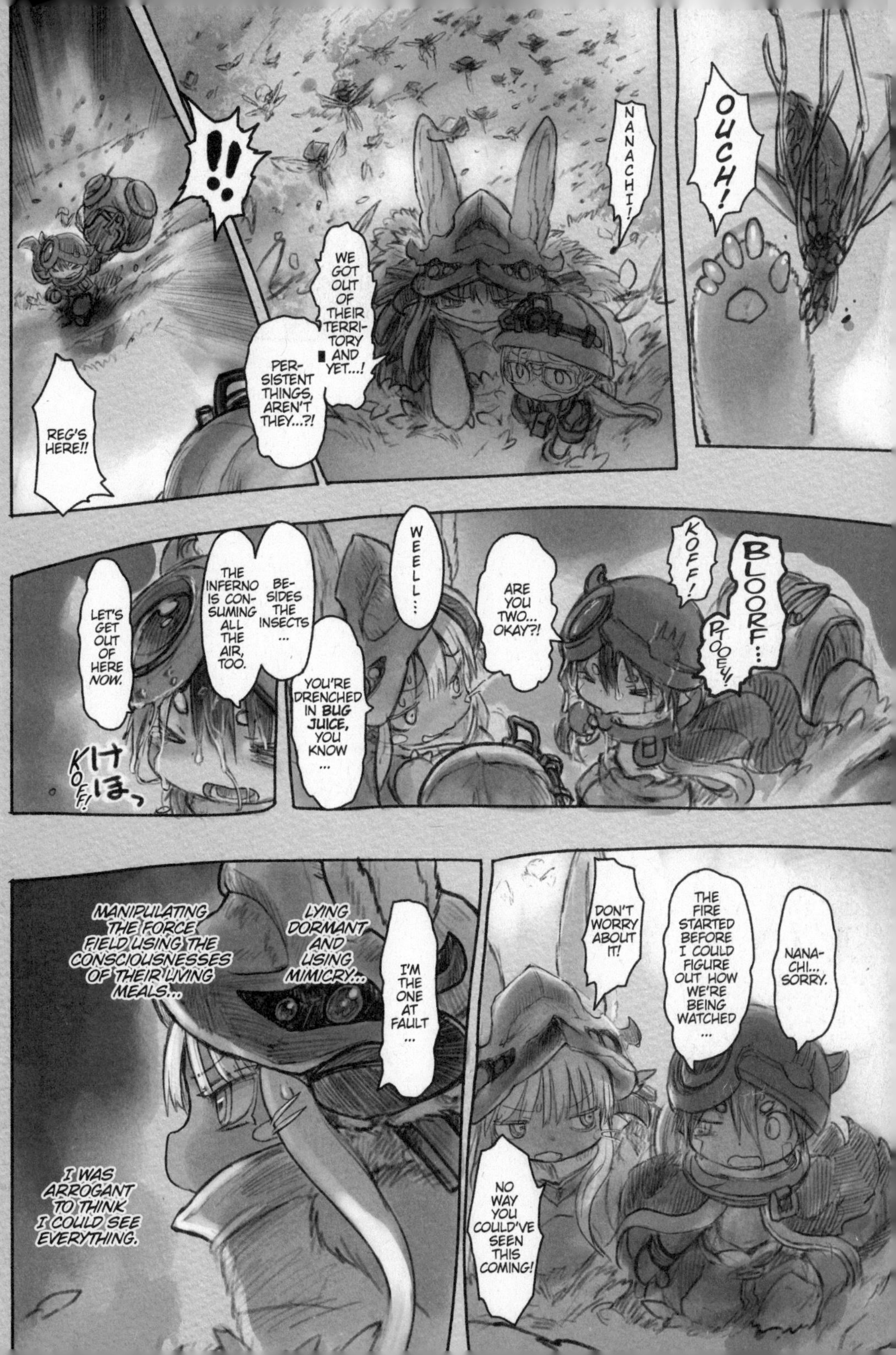
OUCH!
NANACHI!
WE GOT OUT OF THEIR TERRITORY AND YET...!
PERSISTENT THINGS, AREN'T THEY...?!
!!
REG'S HERE!!
BLOORF...
KOFF!
PTOOEY!!
ARE YOU TWO... OKAY?!
WEELL...
YOU'RE DRENCHED IN BUG JUICE, YOU KNOW...
BESIDES THE INSECTS...
THE INFERNO IS CONSUMING ALL THE AIR, TOO.
LET'S GET OUT OF HERE NOW.
けほっ KOFF!
NANACHI... SORRY.
THE FIRE STARTED BEFORE I COULD FIGURE OUT HOW WE'RE BEING WATCHED...
DON'T WORRY ABOUT IT!
NO WAY YOU COULD'VE SEEN THIS COMING!
I'M THE ONE AT FAULT...
LYING DORMANT AND USING MIMICRY...
MANIPULATING THE FORCE FIELD USING THE CONSCIOUSNESSES OF THEIR LIVING MEALS...
I WAS ARROGANT TO THINK I COULD SEE EVERYTHING.

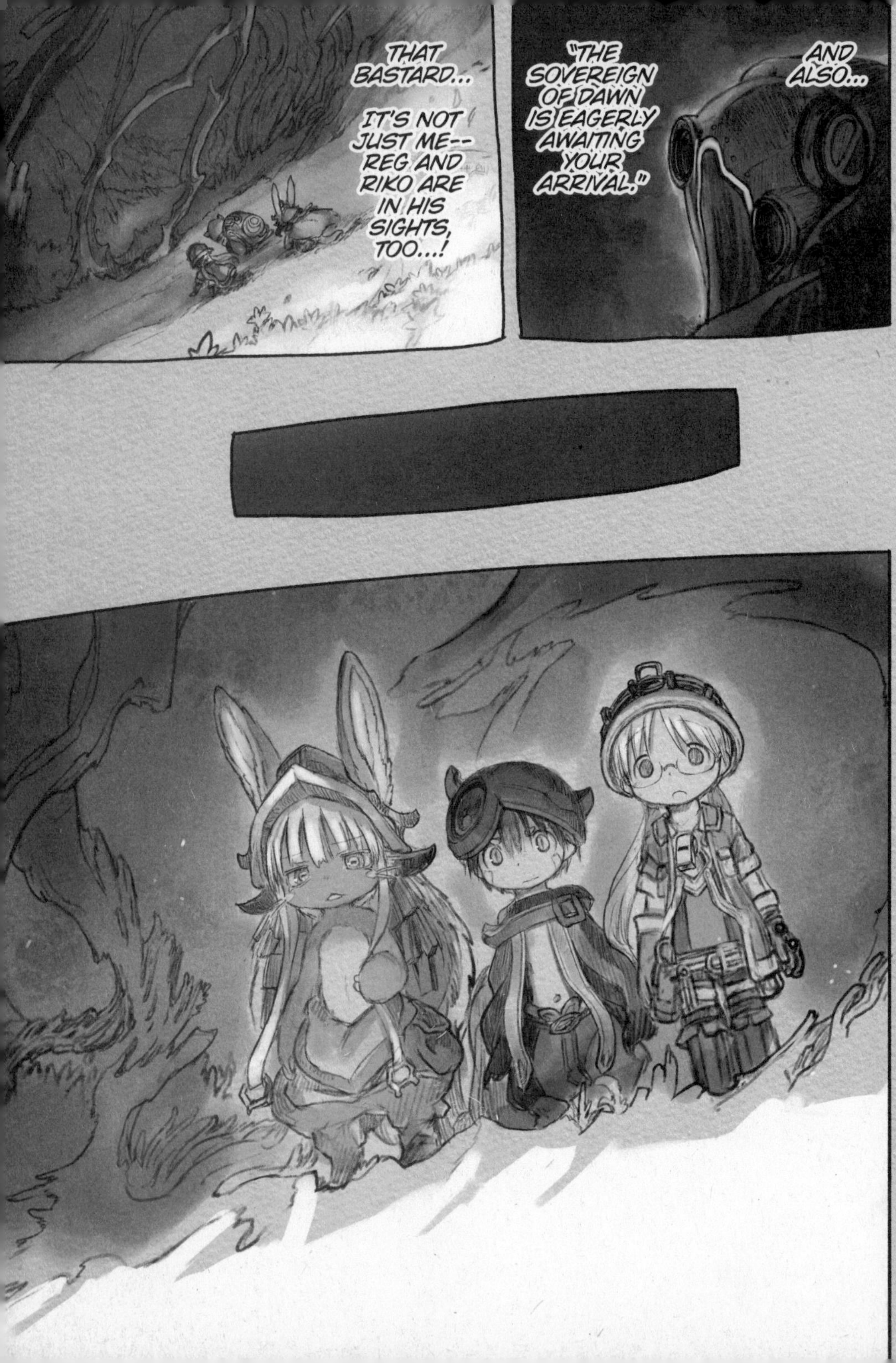
AND ALSO...
"THE SOVEREIGN OF DAWN IS EAGERLY AWAITING YOUR ARRIVAL."
THAT BASTARD...
IT'S NOT JUST ME-- REG AND RIKO ARE IN HIS SIGHTS, TOO...!

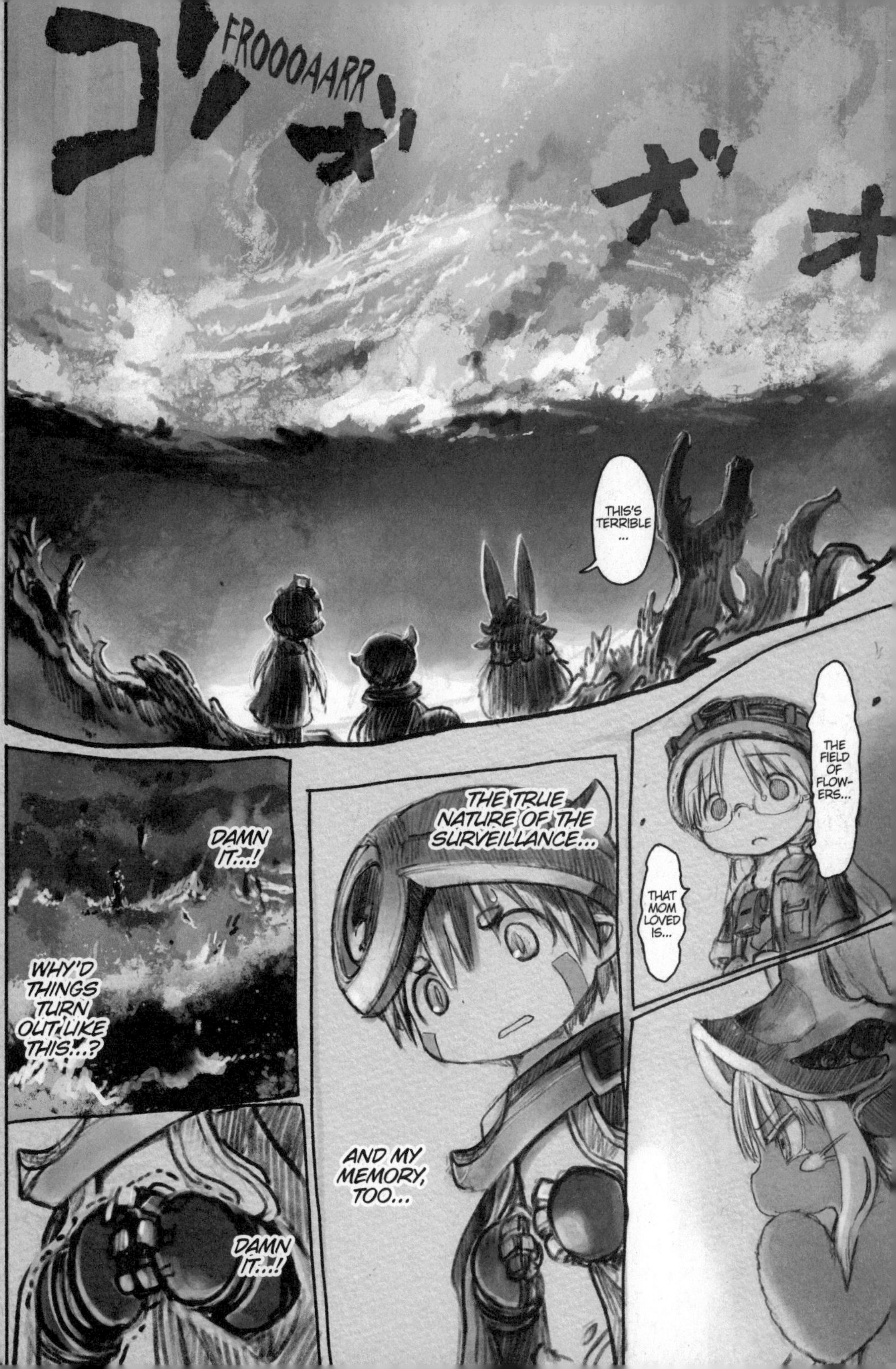

ゴオ゛オ゛オ
FROOOAARR
THIS'S TERRIBLE ...
THE FIELD OF FLOW-ERS...
THAT MOM LOVED IS...
THE TRUE NATURE OF THE SURVEILLANCE...
AND MY MEMORY, TOO...
DAMN IT...!
WHY'D THINGS TURN OUT LIKE THIS...?
DAMN IT...!

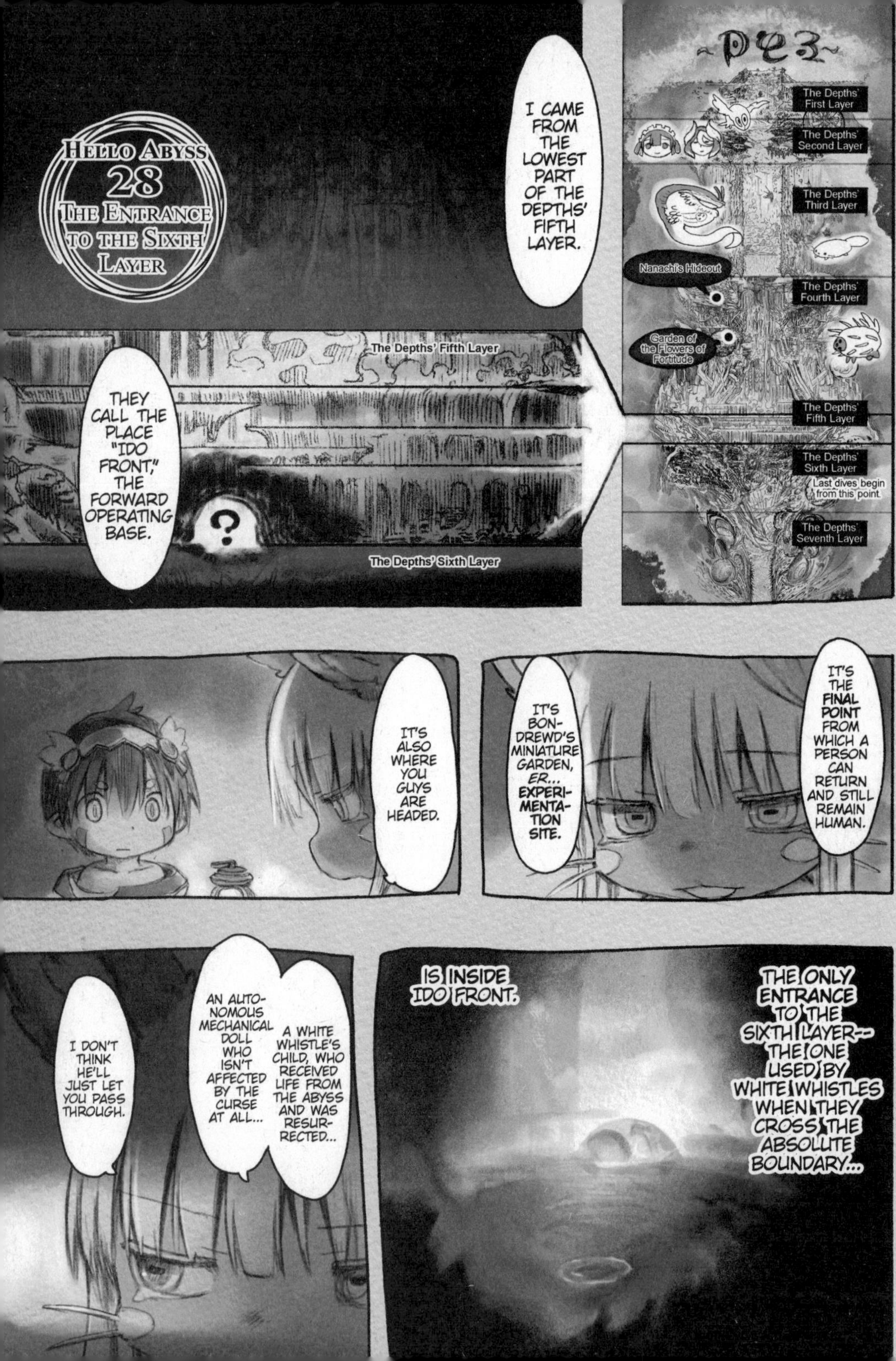

HELLO ABYSS 28 THE ENTRANCE TO THE SIXTH LAYER
I CAME FROM THE LOWEST PART OF THE DEPTHS' FIFTH LAYER.
The Depths' First Layer
The Depths' Second Layer
The Depths' Third Layer
Nanachi's Hideout
The Depths' Fourth Layer
Garden of the Flowers of Fortitude
The Depths' Fifth Layer
The Depths' Sixth Layer
Last dives begin from this point.
The Depths' Seventh Layer
The Depths' Fifth Layer
THEY CALL THE PLACE "IDO FRONT," THE FORWARD OPERATING BASE.
?
The Depths' Sixth Layer
IT'S THE FINAL POINT FROM WHICH A PERSON CAN RETURN AND STILL REMAIN HUMAN.
IT'S BONDREWD'S MINIATURE GARDEN, ER... EXPERIMENTATION SITE.
IT'S ALSO WHERE YOU GUYS ARE HEADED.
THE ONLY ENTRANCE TO THE SIXTH LAYER--THE ONE USED BY WHITE WHISTLES WHEN THEY CROSS THE ABSOLUTE BOUNDARY...
IS INSIDE IDO FRONT.
A WHITE WHISTLE'S CHILD, WHO RECEIVED LIFE FROM THE ABYSS AND WAS RESURRECTED...
AN AUTONOMOUS MECHANICAL DOLL WHO ISN'T AFFECTED BY THE CURSE AT ALL...
I DON'T THINK HE'LL JUST LET YOU PASS THROUGH.

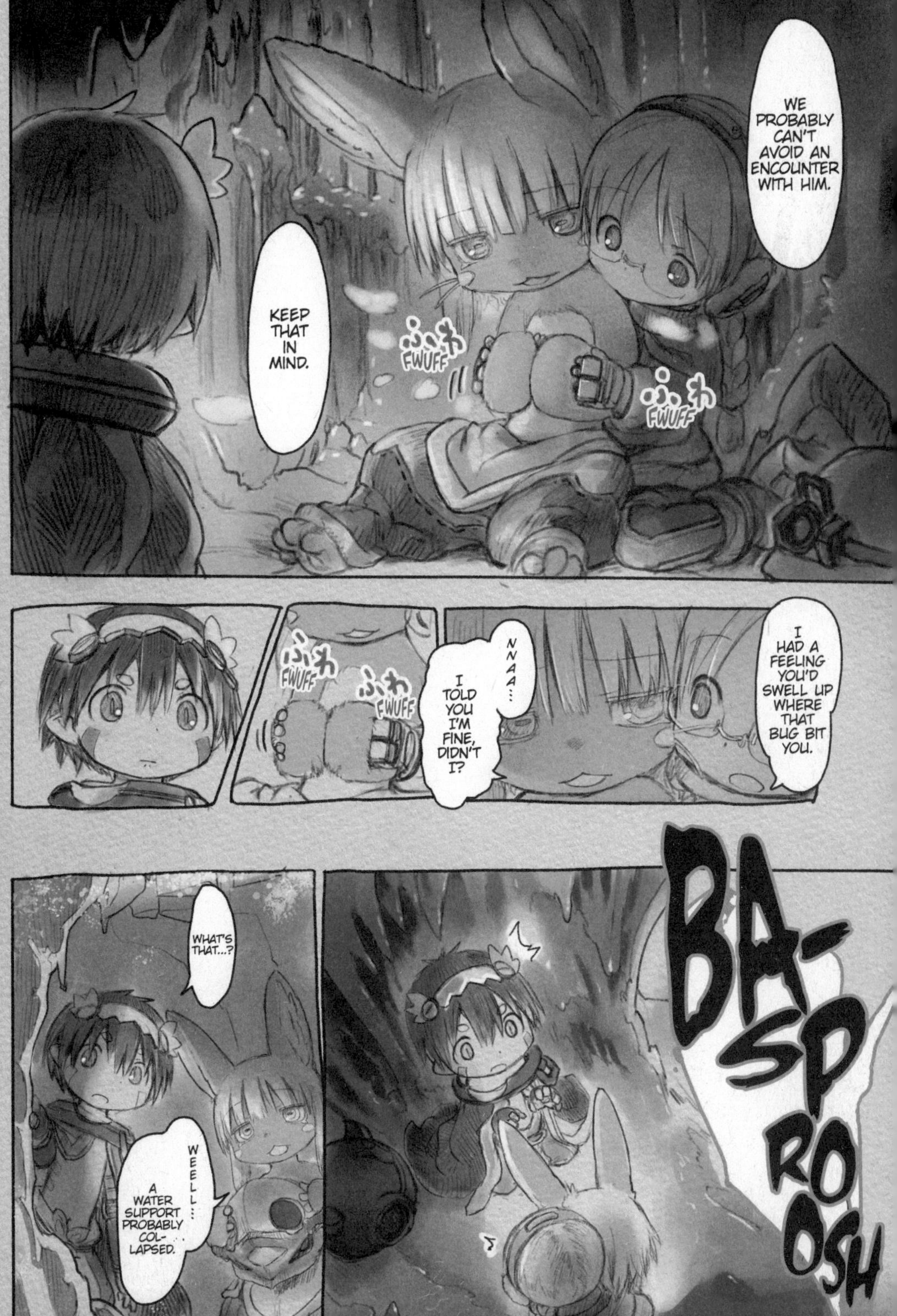
WE PROBABLY CAN'T AVOID AN ENCOUNTER WITH HIM.
KEEP THAT IN MIND.
ふわ FWUFF
ふわ FWUFF
I HAD A FEELING YOU'D SWELL UP WHERE THAT BUG BIT YOU.
NNAA...
I TOLD YOU I'M FINE, DIDN'T I?
ふわ FWUFF
ふわ FWUFF
BA-SPROOSH
WHAT'S THAT...?
WEELL...
A WATER SUPPORT PROBABLY COL-LAPSED.

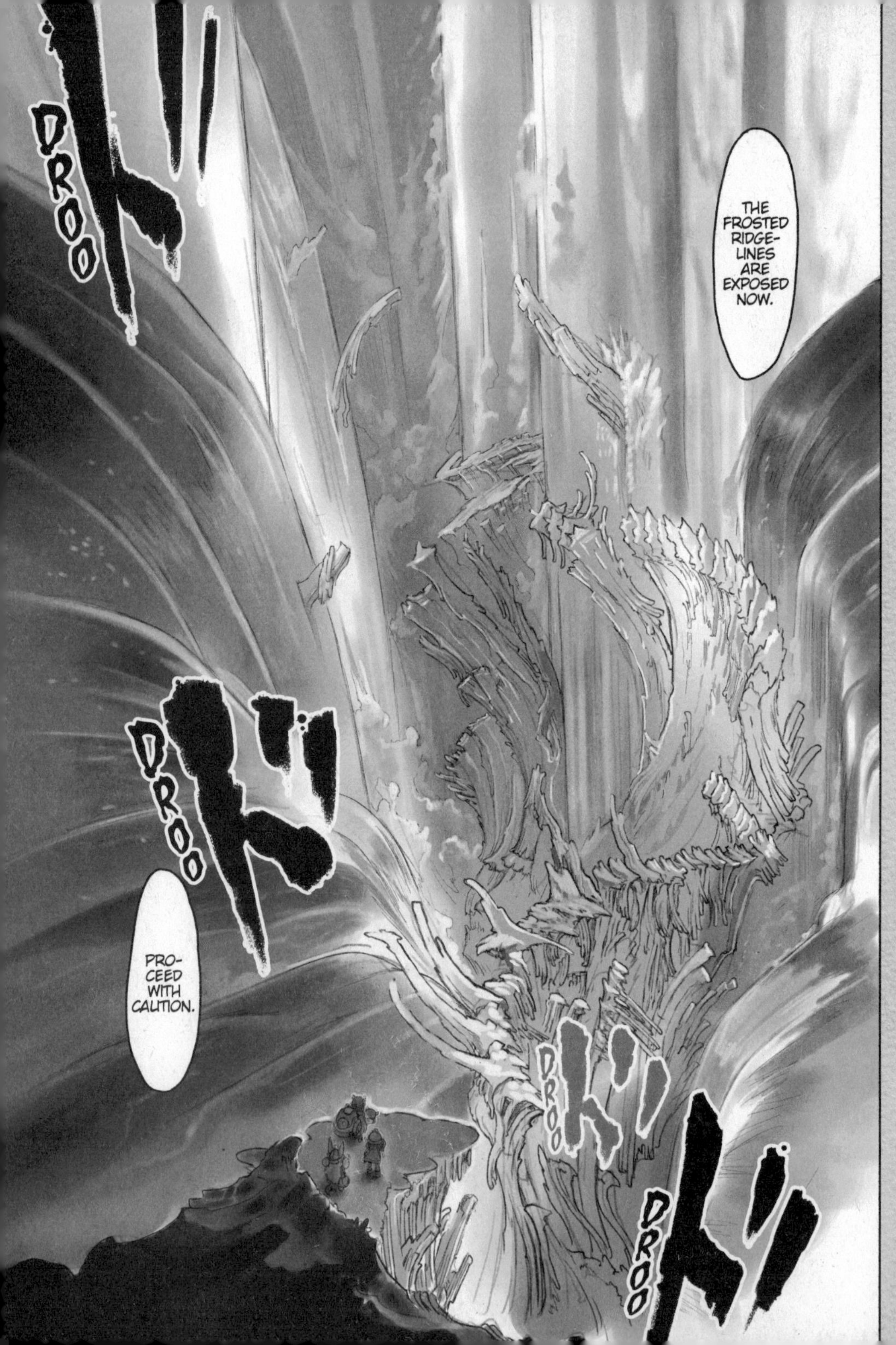
THE FROSTED RIDGE-LINES ARE EXPOSED NOW.
DROO
DROO
PRO-CEED WITH CAUTION.
DROO
DROO

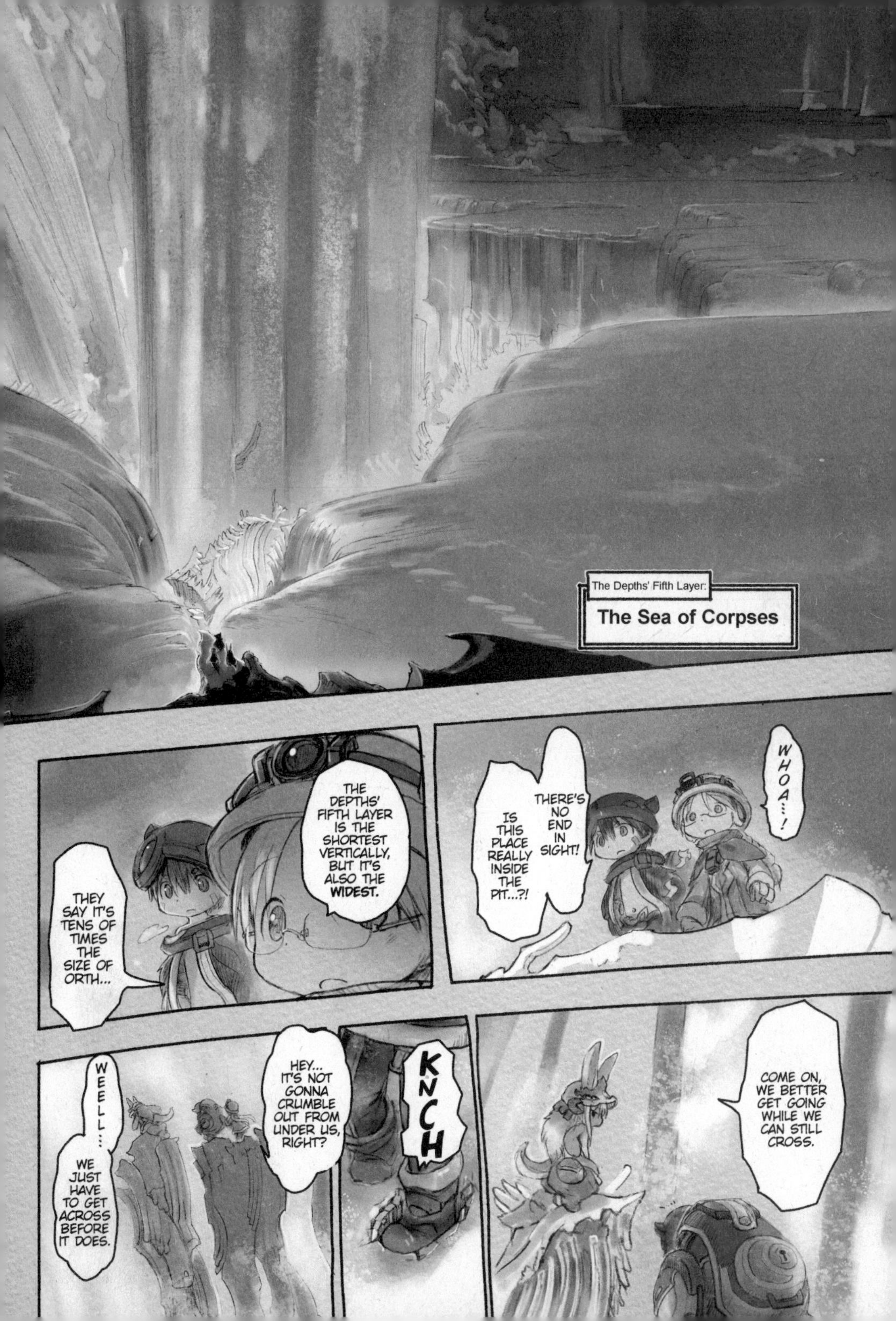
The Depths' Fifth Layer:
The Sea of Corpses
WHOA...!
THERE'S NO END IN SIGHT!
IS THIS PLACE REALLY INSIDE THE PIT...?!
THE DEPTHS' FIFTH LAYER IS THE SHORTEST VERTICALLY, BUT IT'S ALSO THE **WIDEST.**
THEY SAY IT'S TENS OF TIMES THE SIZE OF ORTH...
COME ON, WE BETTER GET GOING WHILE WE CAN STILL CROSS.
KNCH
HEY... IT'S NOT GONNA CRUMBLE OUT FROM UNDER US, RIGHT?
WEELL...
WE JUST HAVE TO GET ACROSS BEFORE IT DOES.

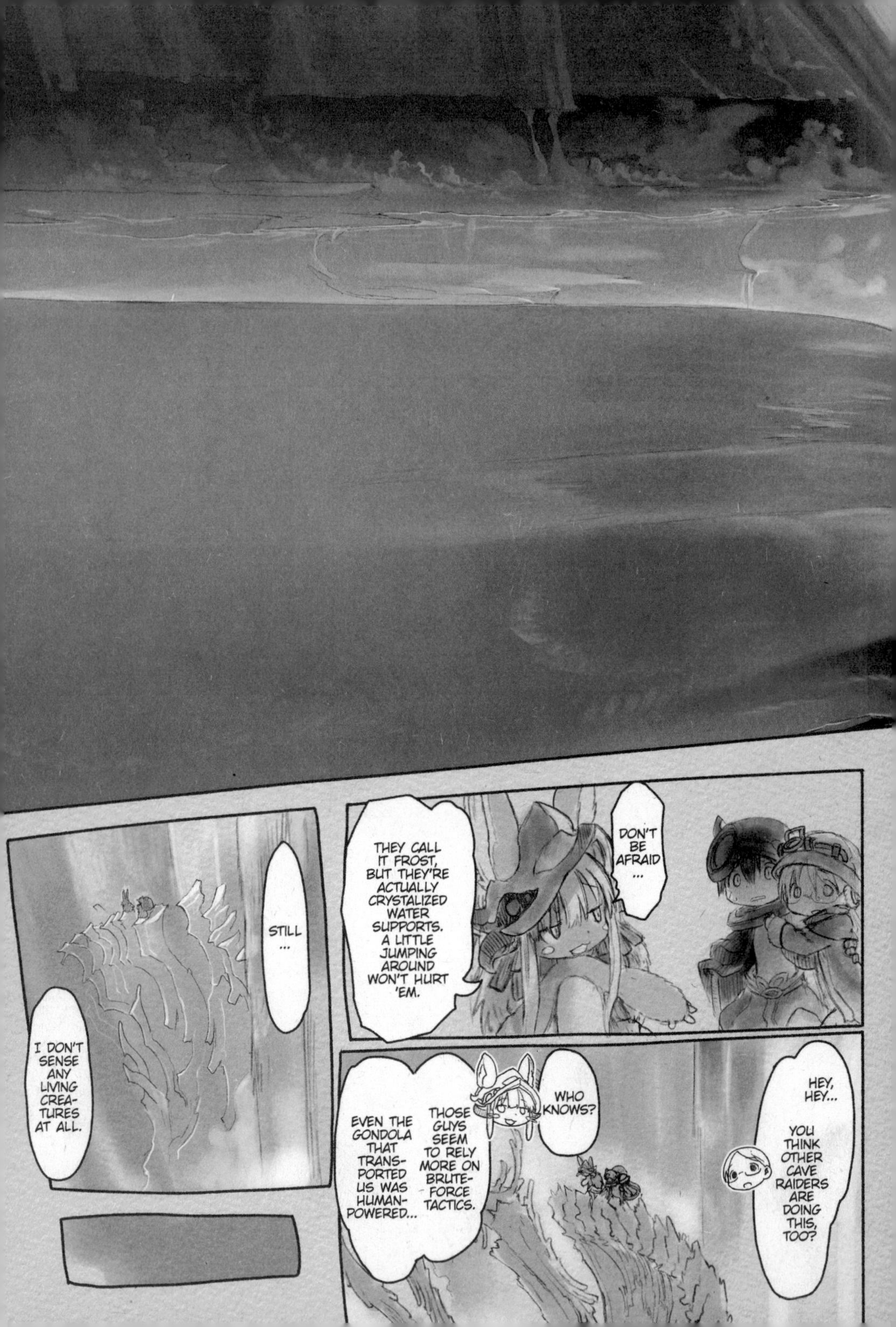
DON'T BE AFRAID ...
THEY CALL IT FROST, BUT THEY'RE ACTUALLY CRYSTALIZED WATER SUPPORTS. A LITTLE JUMPING AROUND WON'T HURT 'EM.
HEY, HEY...
YOU THINK OTHER CAVE RAIDERS ARE DOING THIS, TOO?
WHO KNOWS?
THOSE GUYS SEEM TO RELY MORE ON BRUTE-FORCE TACTICS.
EVEN THE GONDOLA THAT TRANS-PORTED US WAS HUMAN-POWERED...
STILL ...
I DON'T SENSE ANY LIVING CREA-TURES AT ALL.

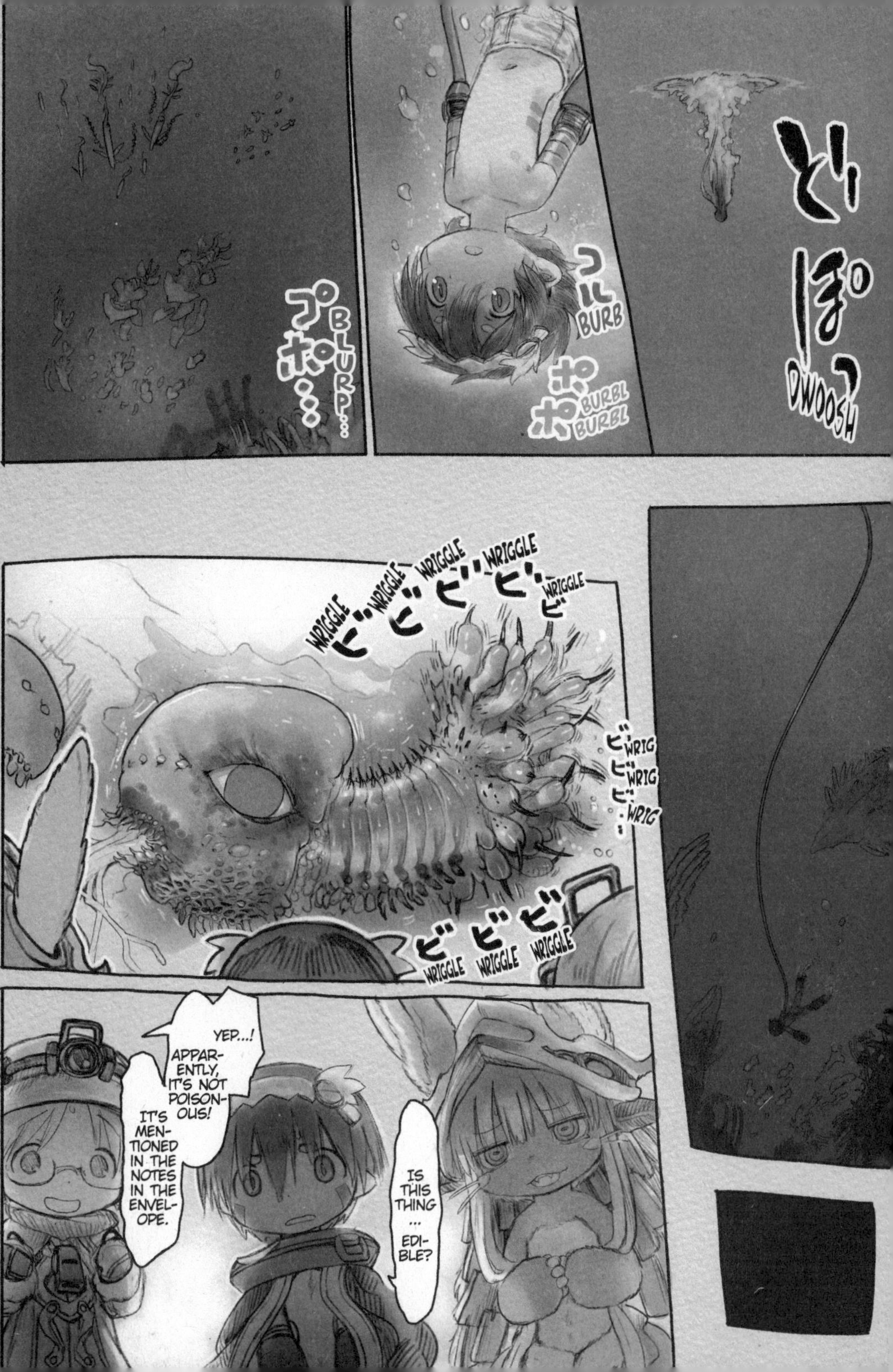

DWOOSH
BURB
BURBL BURBL
BLURP...
WRIGGLE WRIGGLE WRIGGLE WRIGGLE WRIGGLE
WRIG WRIG WRIG
WRIGGLE WRIGGLE WRIGGLE
IS THIS THING... EDIBLE?
YEP...! APPARENTLY, IT'S NOT POISONOUS!
IT'S MENTIONED IN THE NOTES IN THE ENVELOPE.

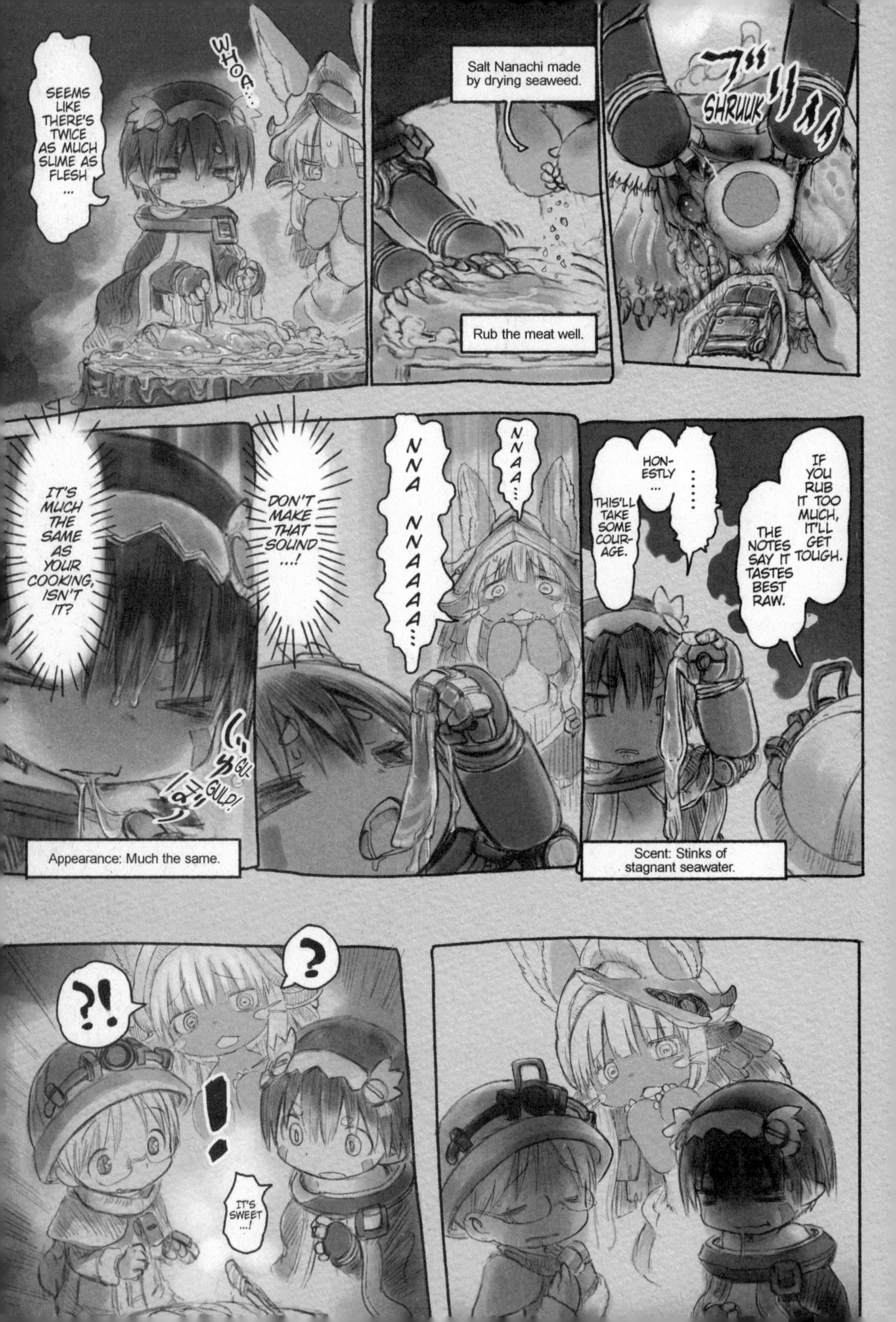
SHRUUK
Salt Nanachi made by drying seaweed.
Rub the meat well.
WHOA...
SEEMS LIKE THERE'S TWICE AS MUCH SLIME AS FLESH...
IF YOU RUB IT TOO MUCH, IT'LL GET TOUGH.
THE NOTES SAY IT TASTES BEST RAW.
......
HON-ESTLY...
THIS'LL TAKE SOME COUR-AGE.
Scent: Stinks of stagnant seawater.
NNAA...
NNA NNAAAAA...
DON'T MAKE THAT SOUND...!
IT'S MUCH THE SAME AS YOUR COOKING, ISN'T IT?
GU... GULP!
Appearance: Much the same.
?!
?
!
IT'S SWEET...!

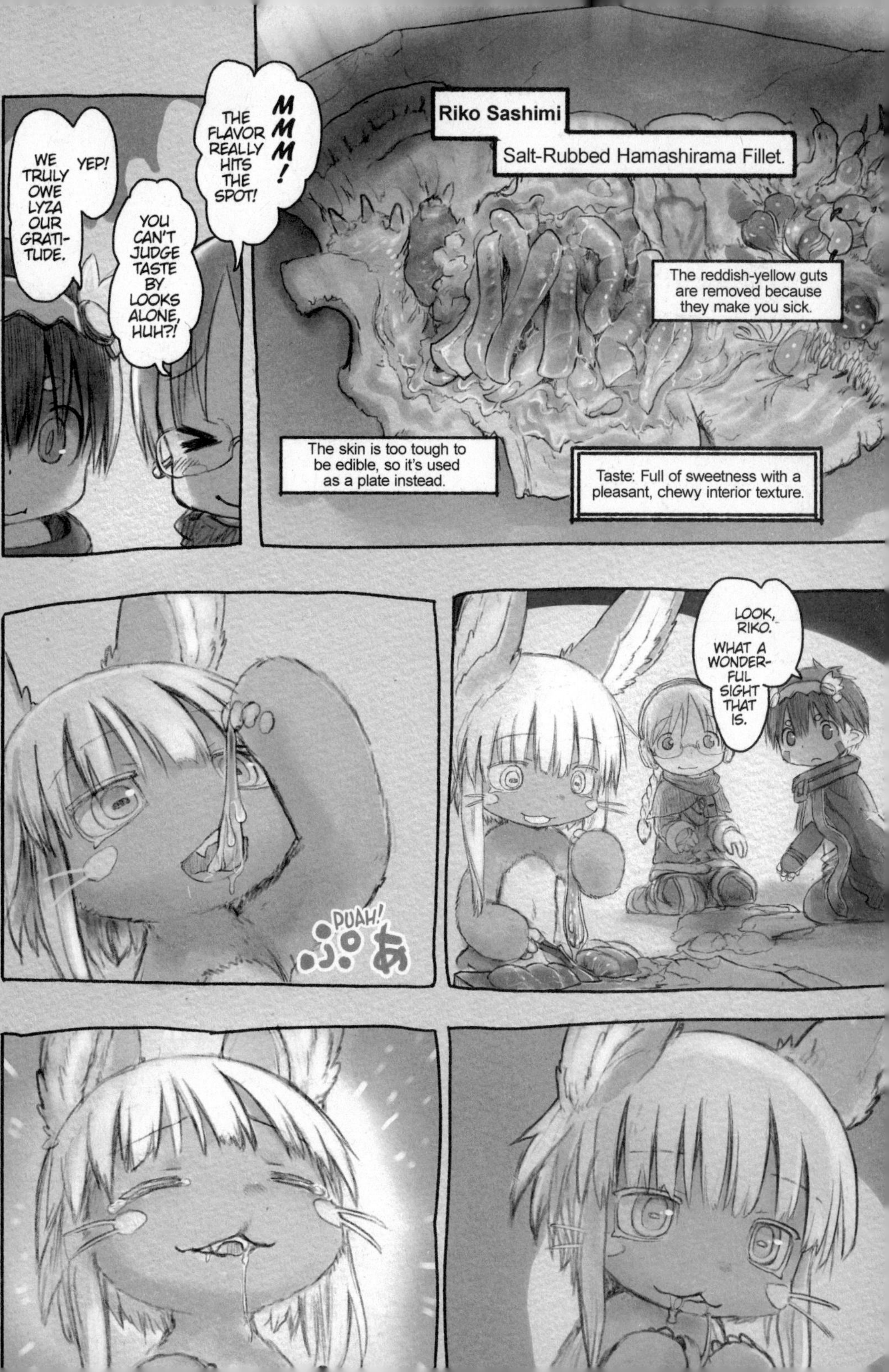
Riko Sashimi
Salt-Rubbed Hamashirama Fillet.
The reddish-yellow guts are removed because they make you sick.
Taste: Full of sweetness with a pleasant, chewy interior texture.
The skin is too tough to be edible, so it's used as a plate instead.
MMM!
THE FLAVOR REALLY HITS THE SPOT!
YOU CAN'T JUDGE TASTE BY LOOKS ALONE, HUH?!
YEP!
WE TRULY OWE LYZA OUR GRATITUDE.
LOOK, RIKO. WHAT A WONDERFUL SIGHT THAT IS.
PUAH!

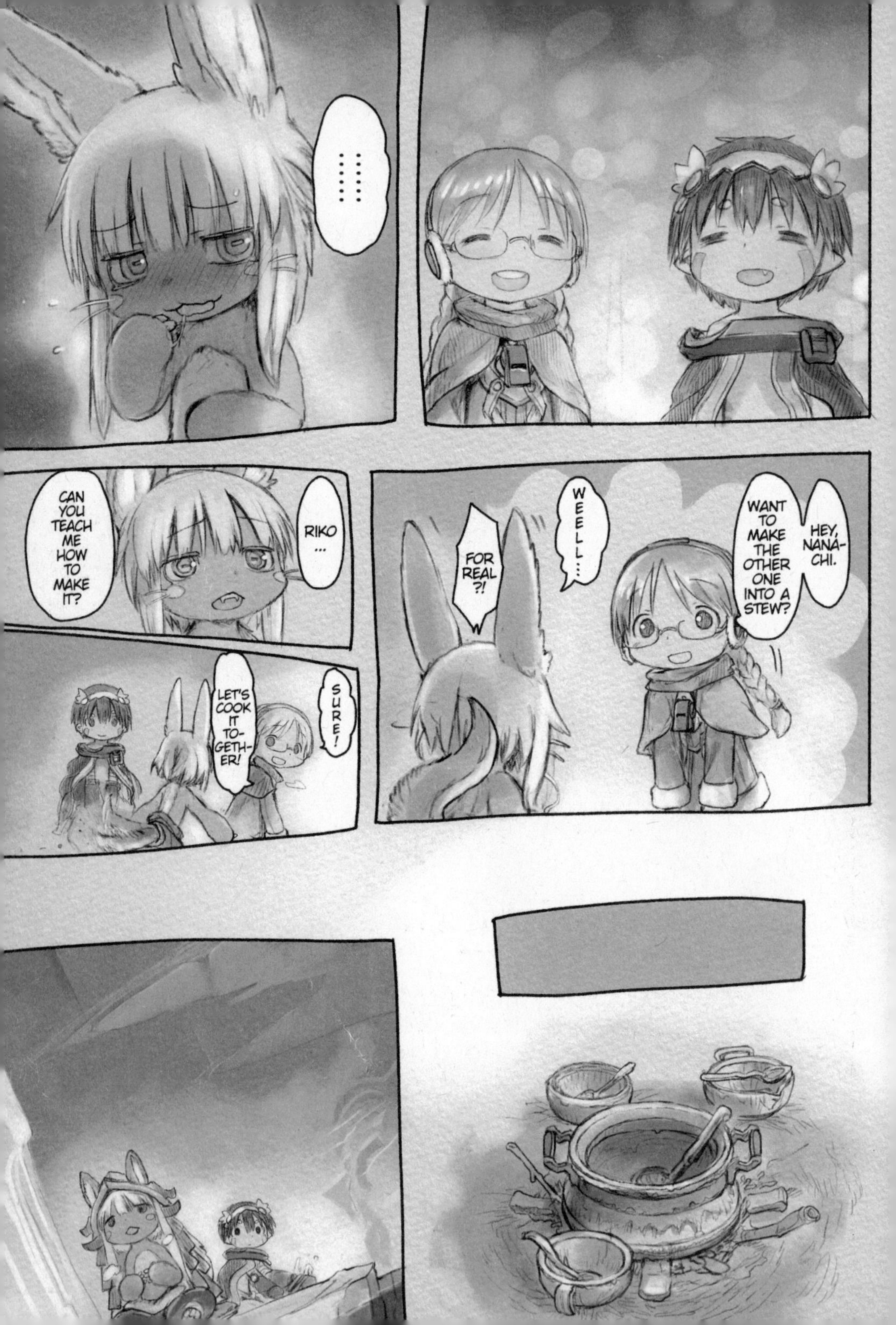
......
HEY, NANÁ-CHI.
WANT TO MAKE THE OTHER ONE INTO A STEW?
WEELL...
FOR REAL?!
RIKO...
CAN YOU TEACH ME HOW TO MAKE IT?
SURE!
LET'S COOK IT TO-GETHER!

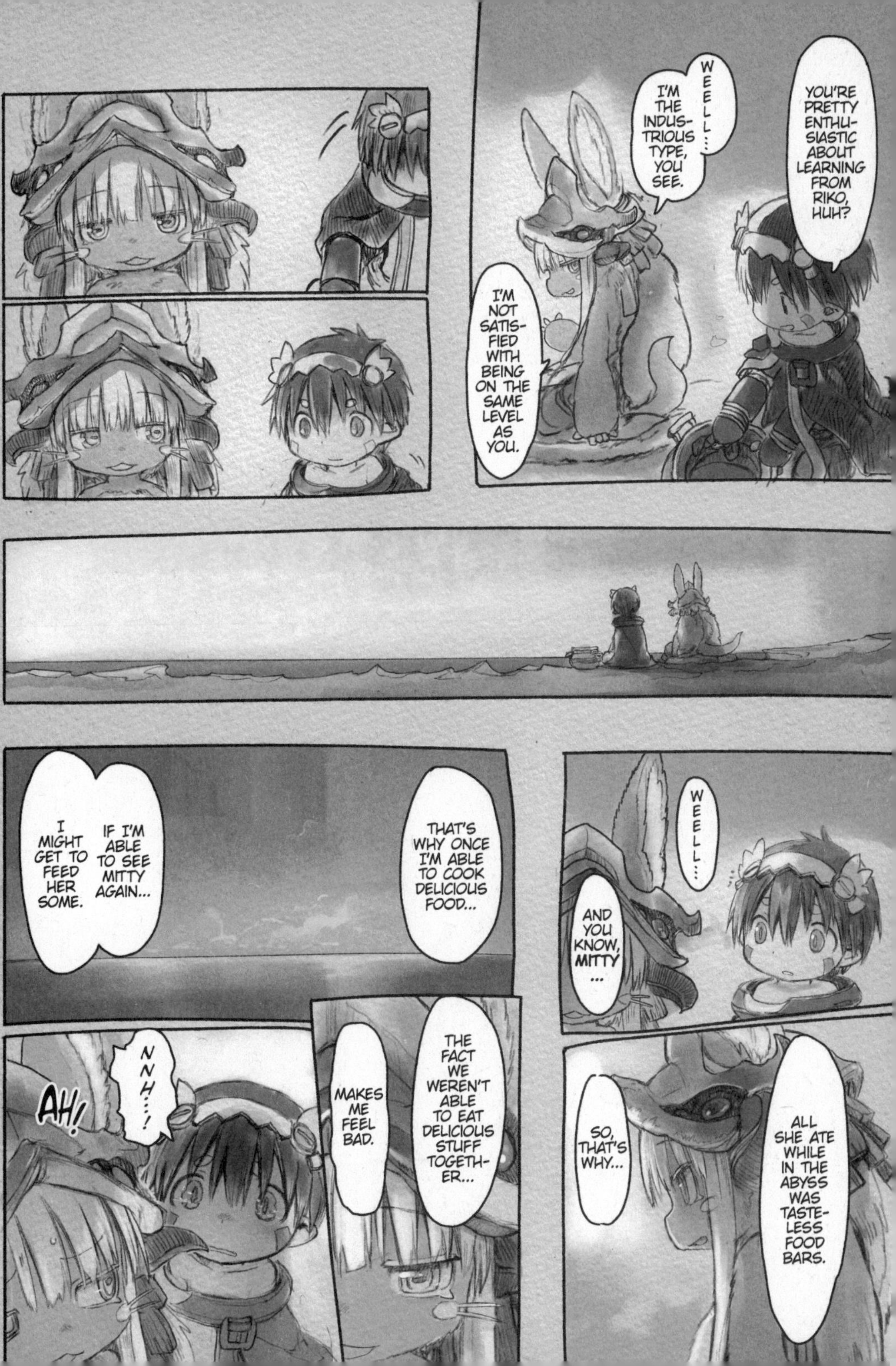

YOU'RE PRETTY ENTHUSIASTIC ABOUT LEARNING FROM RIKO, HUH?
WEELL...
I'M THE INDUSTRIOUS TYPE, YOU SEE.
I'M NOT SATISFIED WITH BEING ON THE SAME LEVEL AS YOU.
WEELL...
AND YOU KNOW, MITTY...
ALL SHE ATE WHILE IN THE ABYSS WAS TASTELESS FOOD BARS.
SO, THAT'S WHY...
THE FACT WE WEREN'T ABLE TO EAT DELICIOUS STUFF TOGETHER...
MAKES ME FEEL BAD.
THAT'S WHY ONCE I'M ABLE TO COOK DELICIOUS FOOD...
IF I'M ABLE TO SEE MITTY AGAIN...
I MIGHT GET TO FEED HER SOME.
NNH...!
AH!

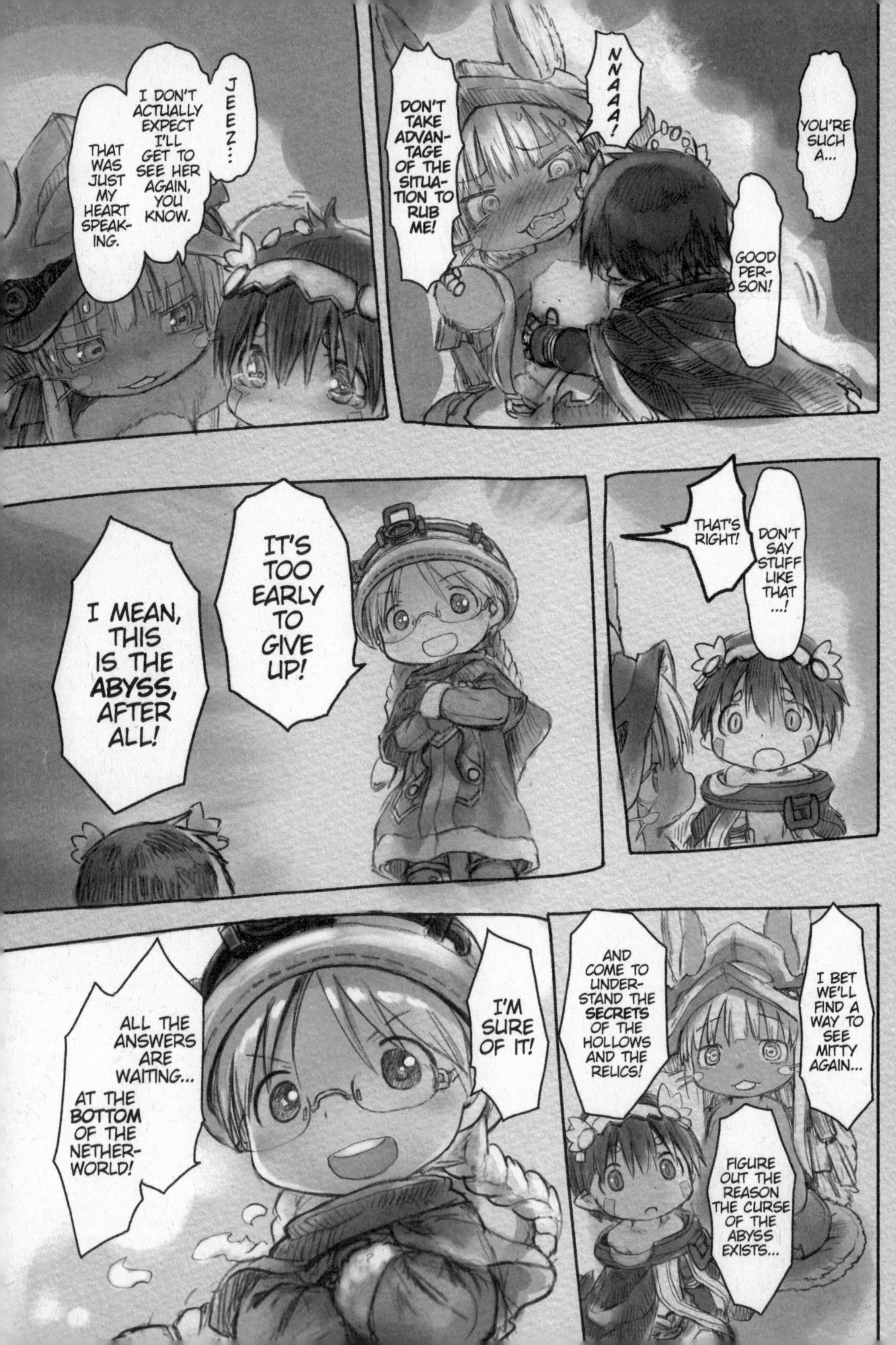
YOU'RE SUCH A...
GOOD PERSON!
NNAAAA!
DON'T TAKE ADVANTAGE OF THE SITUATION TO RUB ME!
JEEZ...
I DON'T ACTUALLY EXPECT I'LL GET TO SEE HER AGAIN, YOU KNOW.
THAT WAS JUST MY HEART SPEAKING.
DON'T SAY STUFF LIKE THAT ...!
THAT'S RIGHT!
IT'S TOO EARLY TO GIVE UP!
I MEAN, THIS IS THE ABYSS, AFTER ALL!
I BET WE'LL FIND A WAY TO SEE MITTY AGAIN...
AND COME TO UNDERSTAND THE SECRETS OF THE HOLLOWS AND THE RELICS!
FIGURE OUT THE REASON THE CURSE OF THE ABYSS EXISTS...
I'M SURE OF IT!
ALL THE ANSWERS ARE WAITING...
AT THE BOTTOM OF THE NETHERWORLD!

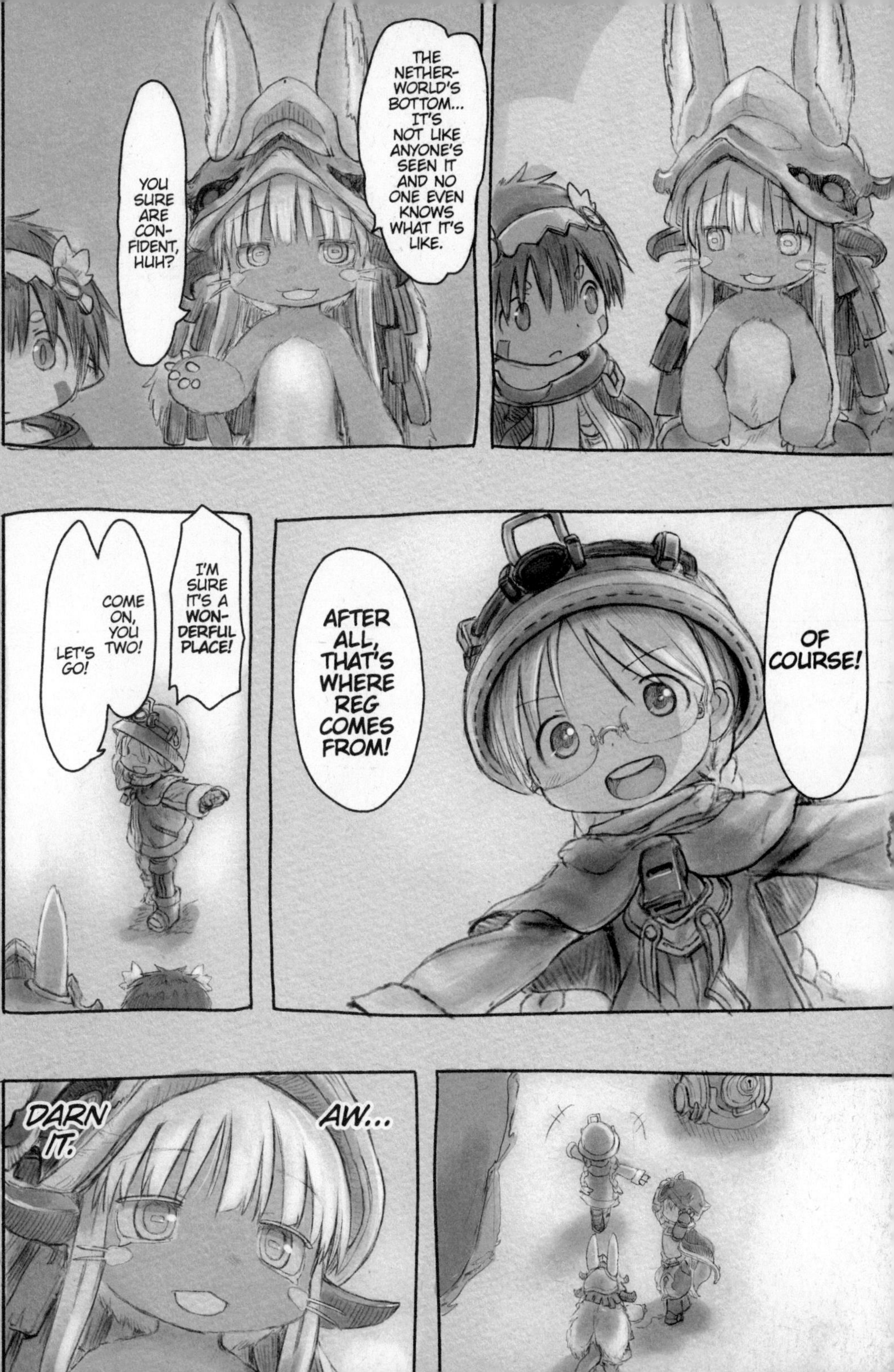
THE NETHER-WORLD'S BOTTOM... IT'S NOT LIKE ANYONE'S SEEN IT AND NO ONE EVEN KNOWS WHAT IT'S LIKE.
YOU SURE ARE CON-FIDENT, HUH?
OF COURSE!
AFTER ALL, THAT'S WHERE REG COMES FROM!
I'M SURE IT'S A WON-DERFUL PLACE!
COME ON, YOU TWO!
LET'S GO!
AW...
DARN IT.

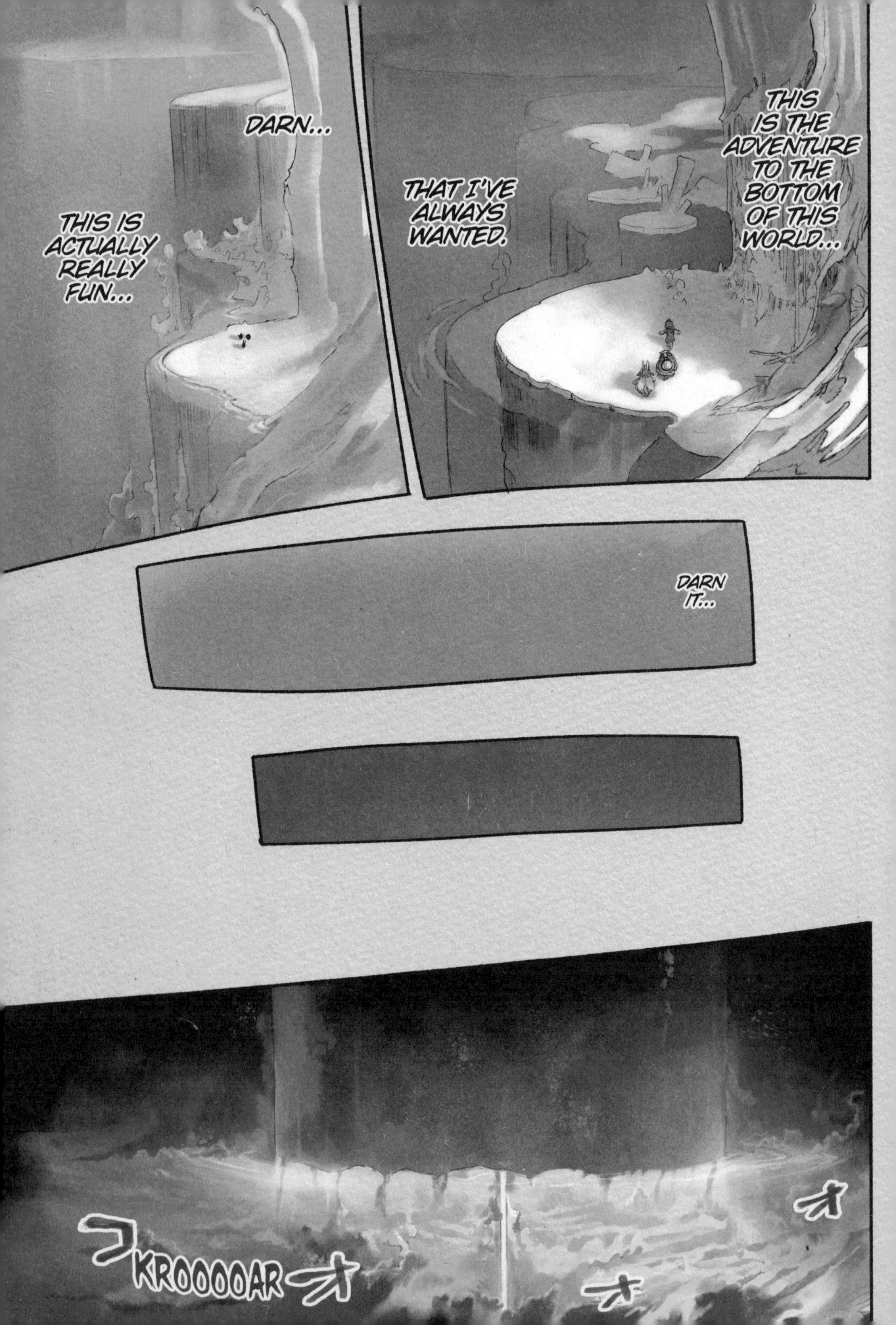
THIS IS THE ADVENTURE TO THE BOTTOM OF THIS WORLD...
THAT I'VE ALWAYS WANTED.
DARN...
THIS IS ACTUALLY REALLY FUN...
DARN IT...
KROOOOAR

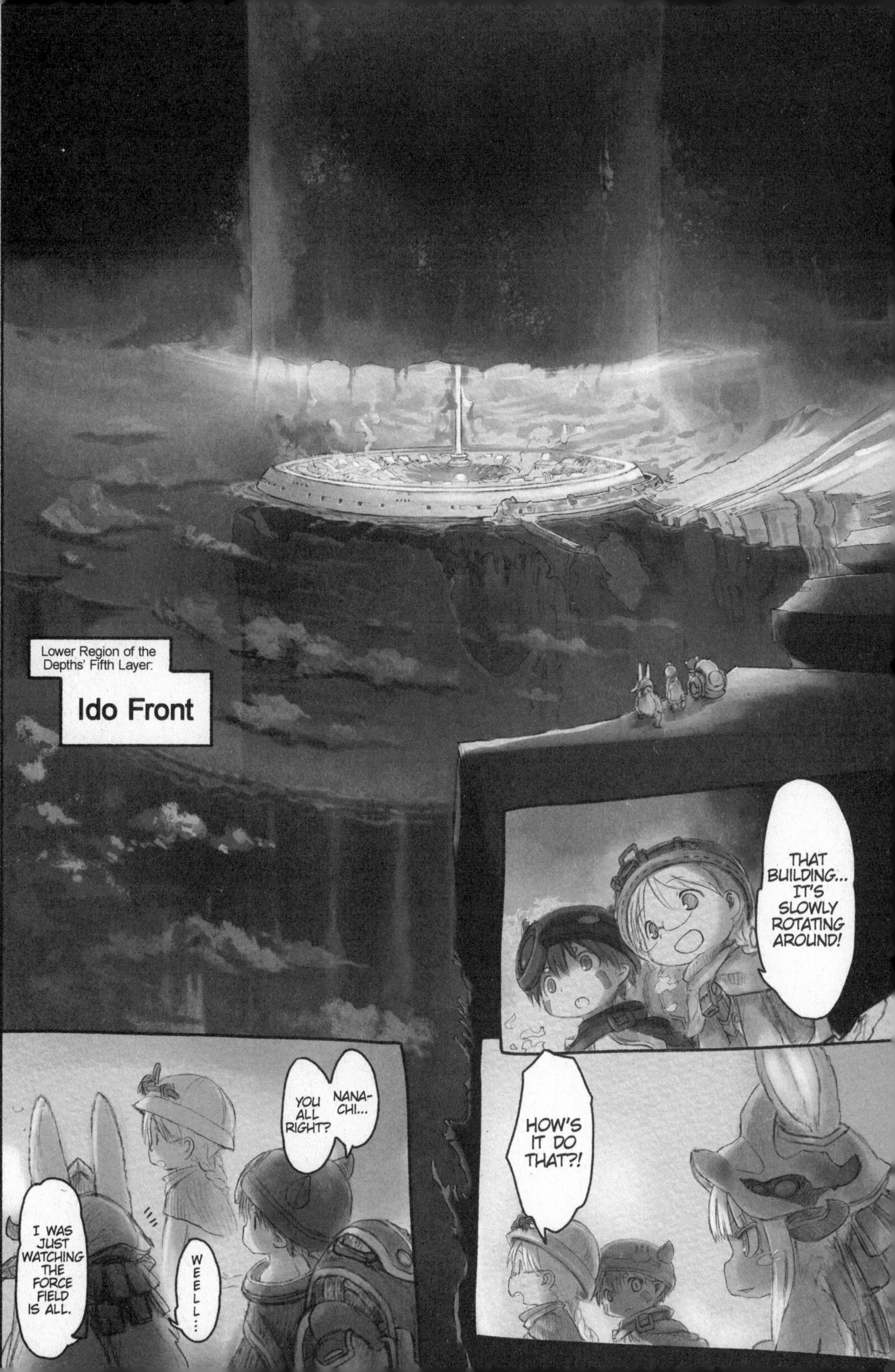
Lower Region of the Depths' Fifth Layer:
Ido Front
THAT BUILDING... IT'S SLOWLY ROTATING AROUND!
HOW'S IT DO THAT?!
NANA-CHI... YOU ALL RIGHT?
WEELL...
I WAS JUST WATCHING THE FORCE FIELD IS ALL.

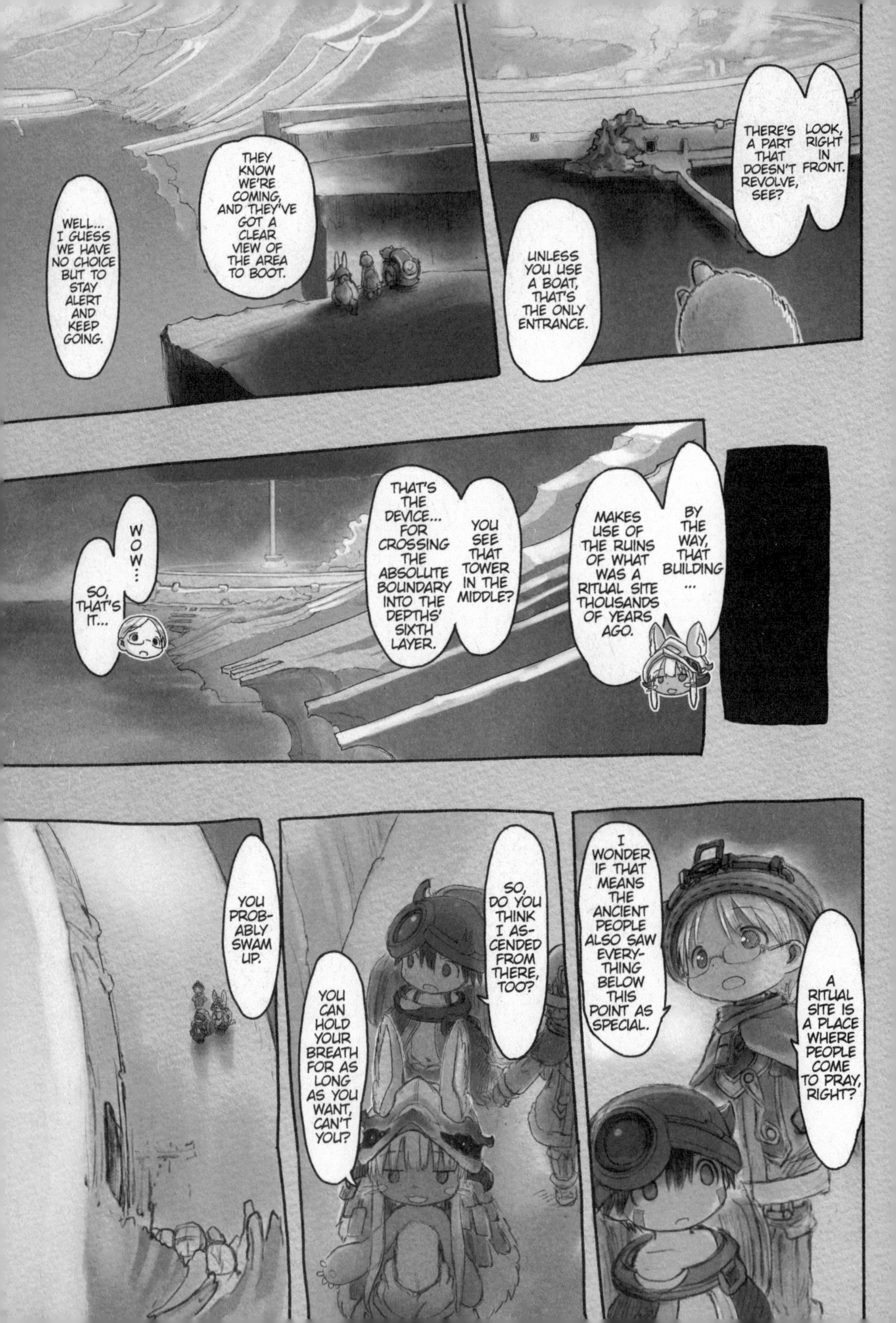
LOOK, RIGHT IN FRONT.
THERE'S A PART THAT DOESN'T REVOLVE, SEE?
UNLESS YOU USE A BOAT, THAT'S THE ONLY ENTRANCE.
THEY KNOW WE'RE COMING, AND THEY'VE GOT A CLEAR VIEW OF THE AREA TO BOOT.
WELL... I GUESS WE HAVE NO CHOICE BUT TO STAY ALERT AND KEEP GOING.
BY THE WAY, THAT BUILDING...
MAKES USE OF THE RUINS OF WHAT WAS A RITUAL SITE THOUSANDS OF YEARS AGO.
YOU SEE THAT TOWER IN THE MIDDLE?
THAT'S THE DEVICE... FOR CROSSING THE ABSOLUTE BOUNDARY INTO THE DEPTHS' SIXTH LAYER.
WOW...
SO, THAT'S IT...
A RITUAL SITE IS A PLACE WHERE PEOPLE COME TO PRAY, RIGHT?
I WONDER IF THAT MEANS THE ANCIENT PEOPLE ALSO SAW EVERYTHING BELOW THIS POINT AS SPECIAL.
SO, DO YOU THINK I ASCENDED FROM THERE, TOO?
YOU CAN HOLD YOUR BREATH FOR AS LONG AS YOU WANT, CAN'T YOU?
YOU PROBABLY SWAM UP.

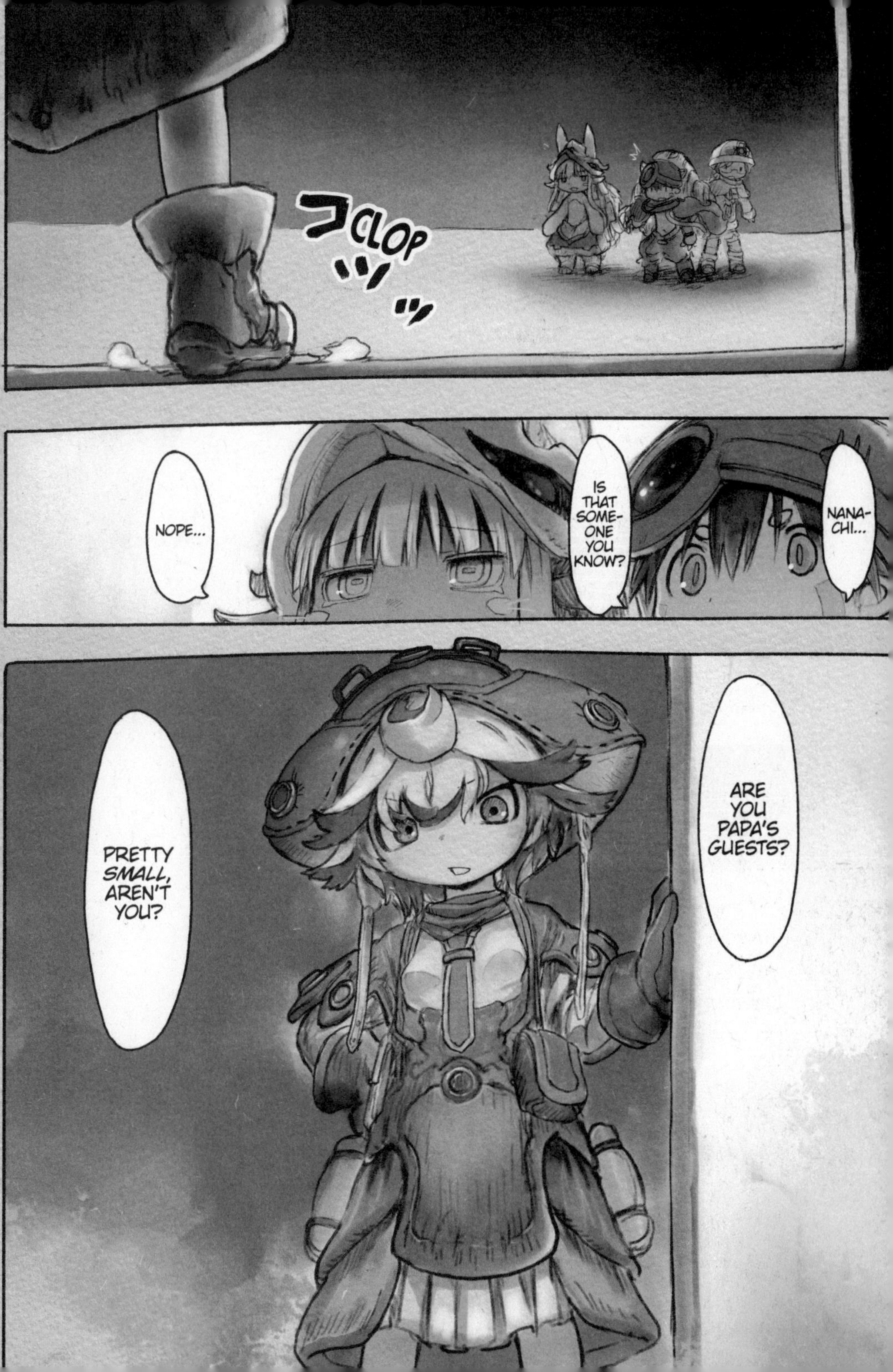
CLOP
NANA-CHI...
IS THAT SOME-ONE YOU KNOW?
NOPE...
ARE YOU PAPA'S GUESTS?
PRETTY SMALL, AREN'T YOU?

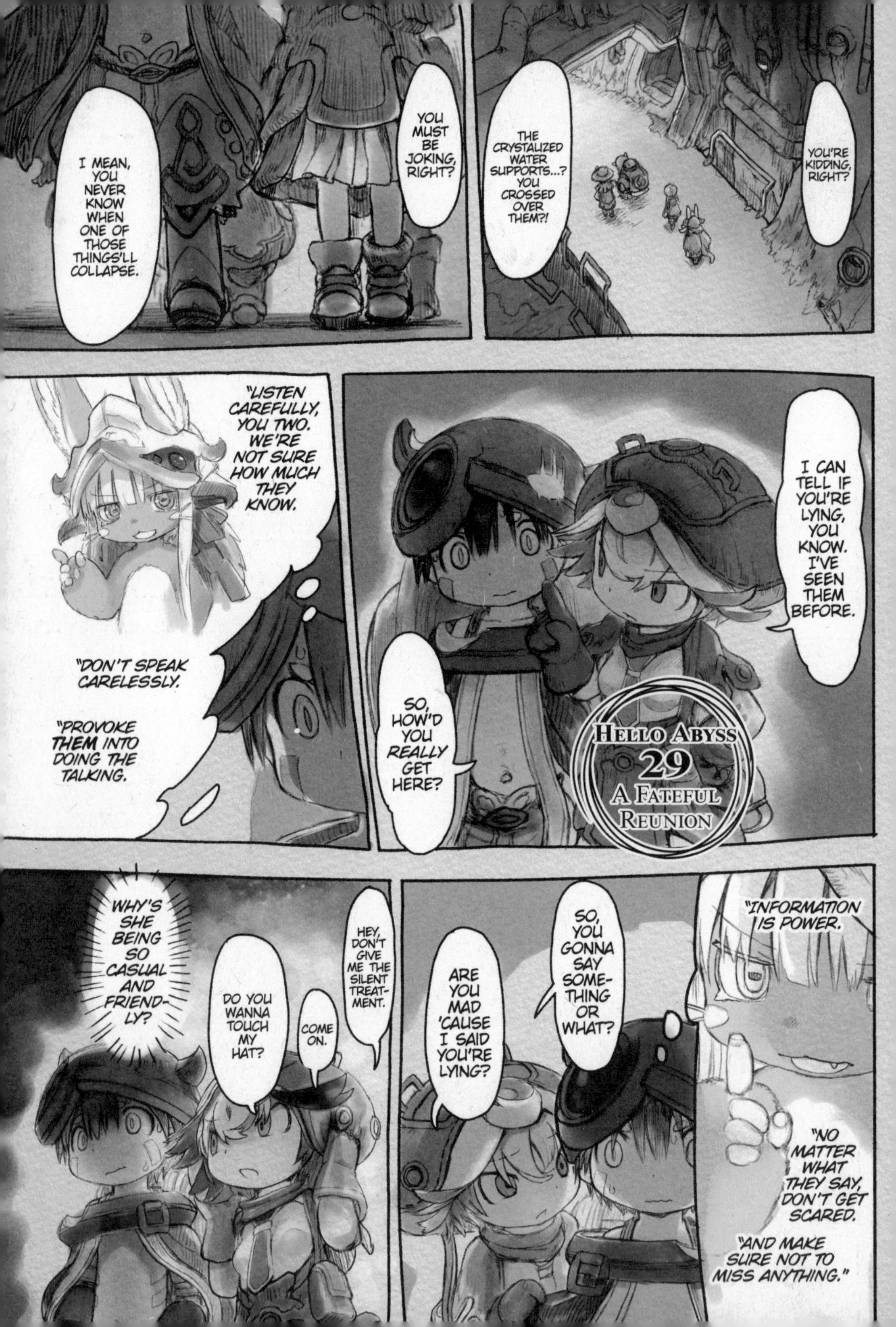
YOU'RE KIDDING, RIGHT?
THE CRYSTALIZED WATER SUPPORTS...? YOU CROSSED OVER THEM?!
YOU MUST BE JOKING, RIGHT?
I MEAN, YOU NEVER KNOW WHEN ONE OF THOSE THINGS'LL COLLAPSE.
I CAN TELL IF YOU'RE LYING, YOU KNOW. I'VE SEEN THEM BEFORE.
SO, HOW'D YOU REALLY GET HERE?
HELLO ABYSS 29 A FATEFUL REUNION
"LISTEN CAREFULLY, YOU TWO. WE'RE NOT SURE HOW MUCH THEY KNOW.
"DON'T SPEAK CARELESSLY.
"PROVOKE THEM INTO DOING THE TALKING.
"INFORMATION IS POWER.
"NO MATTER WHAT THEY SAY, DON'T GET SCARED.
"AND MAKE SURE NOT TO MISS ANYTHING."
SO, YOU GONNA SAY SOME-THING OR WHAT?
ARE YOU MAD 'CAUSE I SAID YOU'RE LYING?
HEY, DON'T GIVE ME THE SILENT TREAT-MENT.
COME ON.
DO YOU WANNA TOUCH MY HAT?
WHY'S SHE BEING SO CASUAL AND FRIEND-LY?

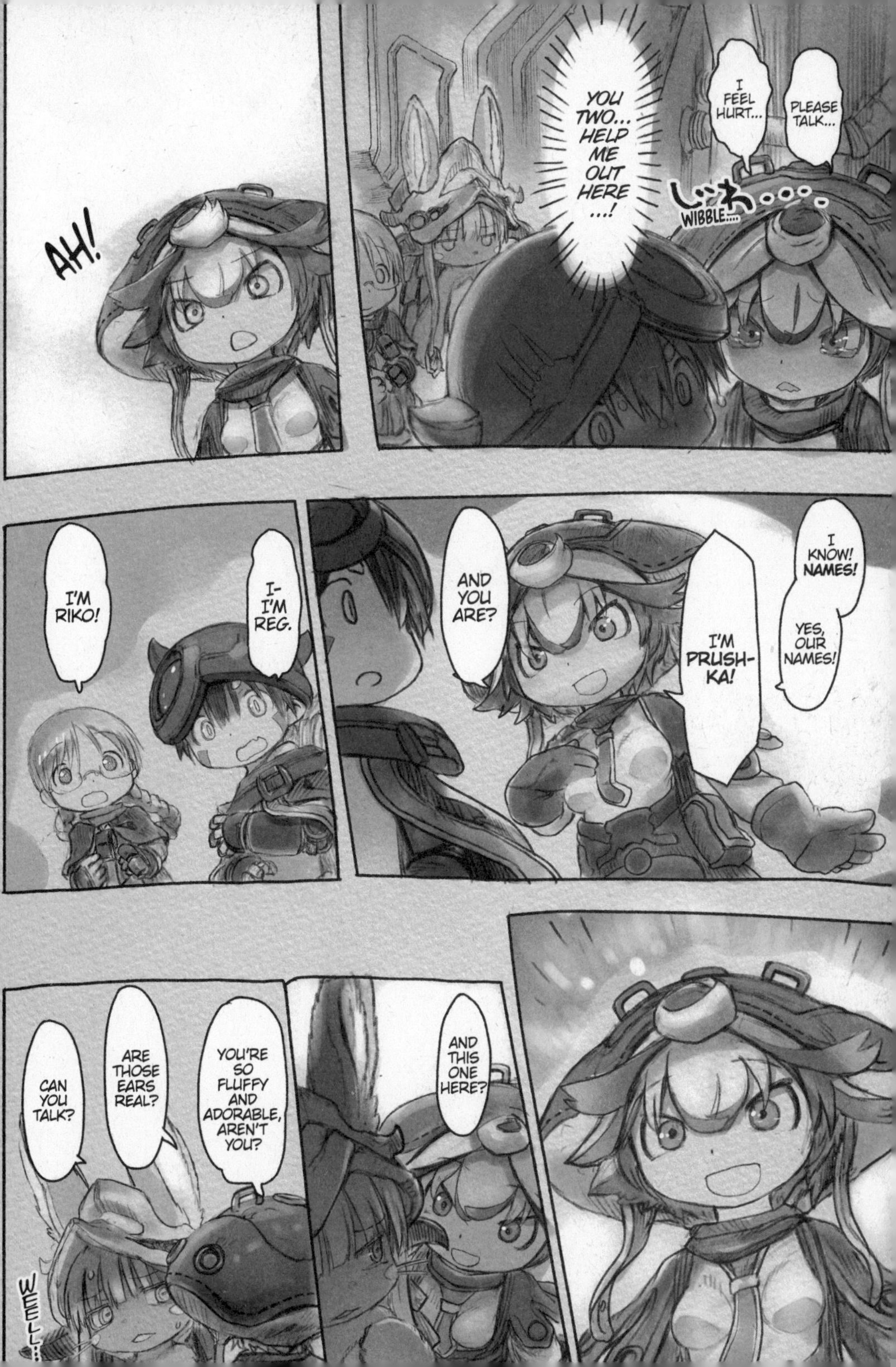
PLEASE TALK...
I FEEL HURT...
WIBBLE....
YOU TWO... HELP ME OUT HERE...!
AH!
I KNOW! NAMES!
YES, OUR NAMES!
I'M PRUSHKA!
AND YOU ARE?
I- I'M REG.
I'M RIKO!
AND THIS ONE HERE?
YOU'RE SO FLUFFY AND ADORABLE, AREN'T YOU?
ARE THOSE EARS REAL?
CAN YOU TALK?
WEELL...

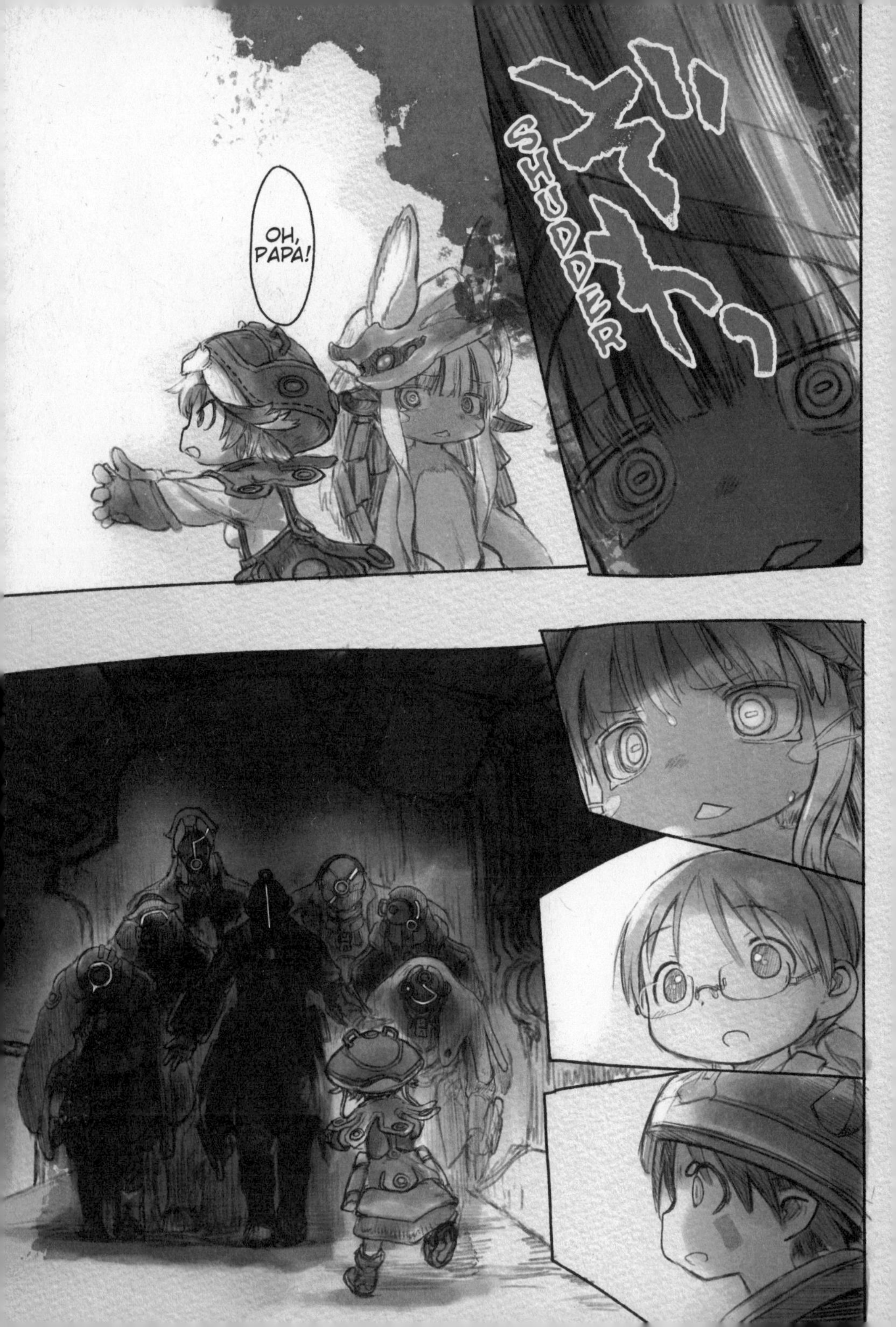
SHUDDER
OH, PAPA!

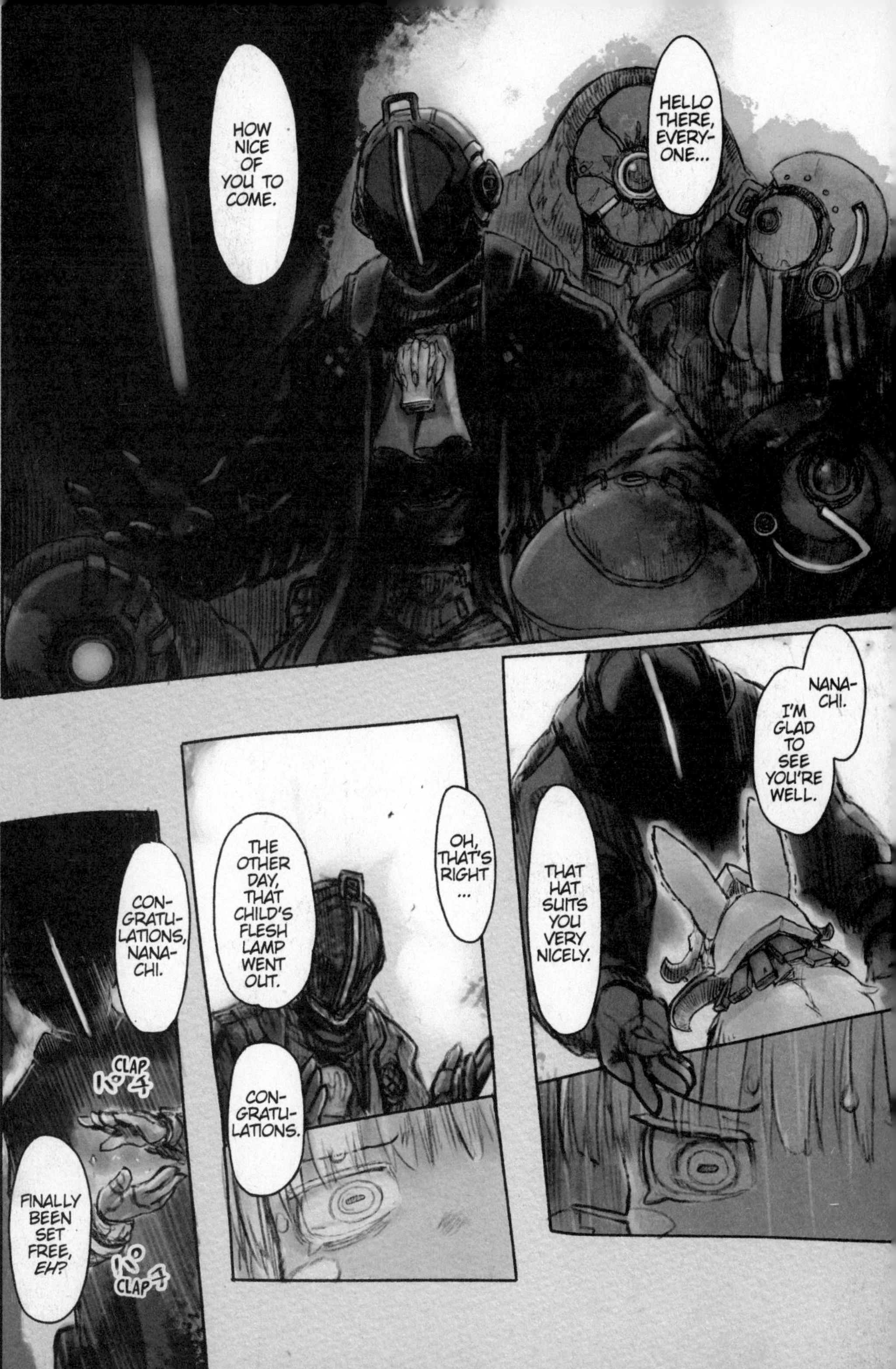
HELLO THERE, EVERY-ONE...
HOW NICE OF YOU TO COME.
NANA-CHI. I'M GLAD TO SEE YOU'RE WELL.
THAT HAT SUITS YOU VERY NICELY.
OH, THAT'S RIGHT...
THE OTHER DAY, THAT CHILD'S FLESH LAMP WENT OUT.
CON-GRATU-LATIONS.
CON-GRATU-LATIONS, NANA-CHI.
CLAP
FINALLY BEEN SET FREE, EH?
CLAP

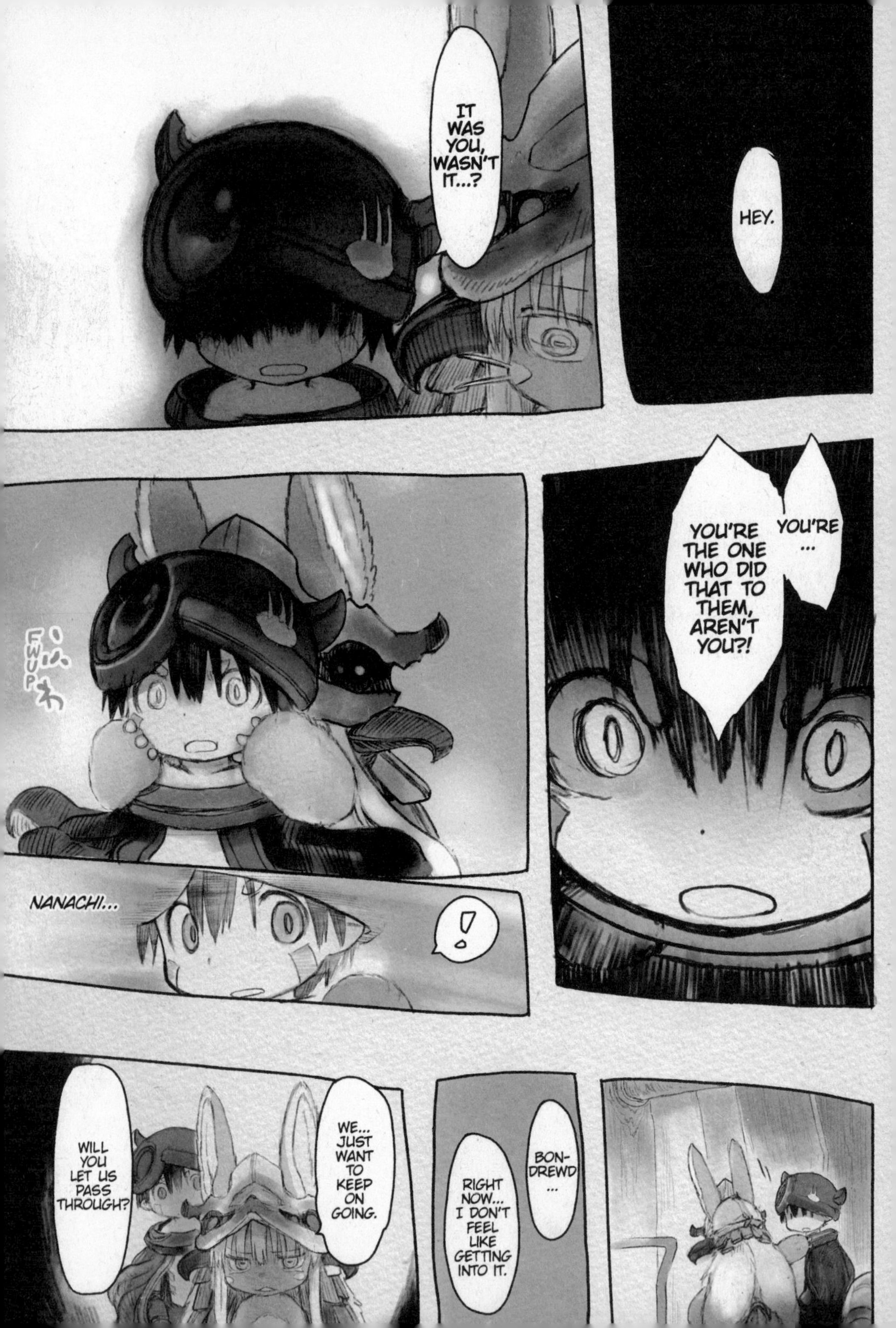
HEY.
IT WAS YOU, WASN'T IT...?
YOU'RE...
YOU'RE THE ONE WHO DID THAT TO THEM, AREN'T YOU?!
ふわ
FWUP
!
NANACHI...
BONDREWD...
RIGHT NOW... I DON'T FEEL LIKE GETTING INTO IT.
WE... JUST WANT TO KEEP ON GOING.
WILL YOU LET US PASS THROUGH?

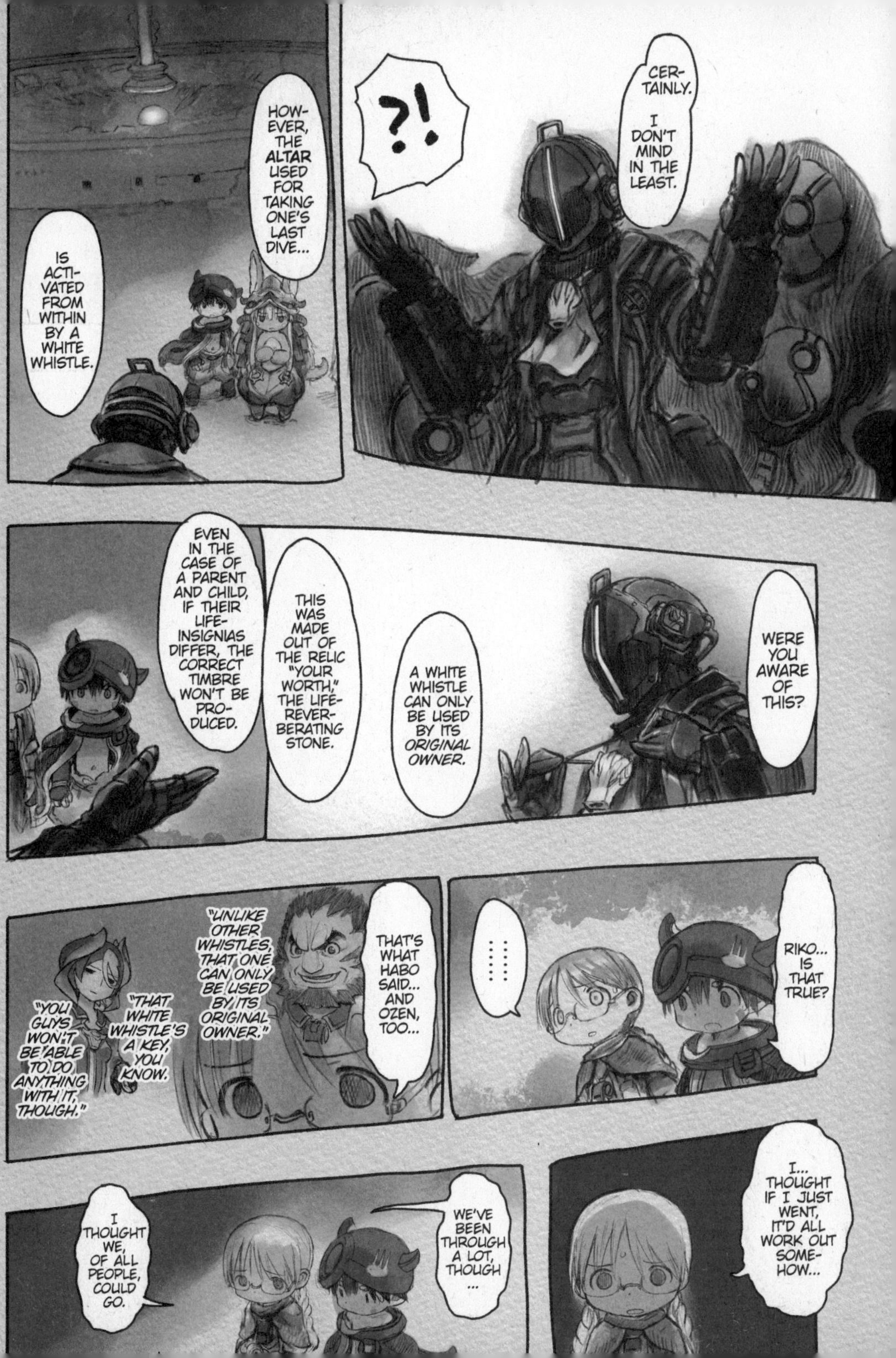
CERTAINLY.
I DON'T MIND IN THE LEAST.
?!
HOWEVER, THE ALTAR USED FOR TAKING ONE'S LAST DIVE...
IS ACTIVATED FROM WITHIN BY A WHITE WHISTLE.
WERE YOU AWARE OF THIS?
A WHITE WHISTLE CAN ONLY BE USED BY ITS ORIGINAL OWNER.
THIS WAS MADE OUT OF THE RELIC "YOUR WORTH," THE LIFE-REVERBERATING STONE.
EVEN IN THE CASE OF A PARENT AND CHILD, IF THEIR LIFE-INSIGNIAS DIFFER, THE CORRECT TIMBRE WON'T BE PRODUCED.
RIKO... IS THAT TRUE?
......
THAT'S WHAT HABO SAID... AND OZEN, TOO...
"UNLIKE OTHER WHISTLES, THAT ONE CAN ONLY BE USED BY ITS ORIGINAL OWNER."
"THAT WHITE WHISTLE'S A KEY, YOU KNOW.
"YOU GUYS WON'T BE ABLE TO DO ANYTHING WITH IT, THOUGH."
I... THOUGHT IF I JUST WENT, IT'D ALL WORK OUT SOMEHOW...
WE'VE BEEN THROUGH A LOT, THOUGH...
I THOUGHT WE, OF ALL PEOPLE, COULD GO.

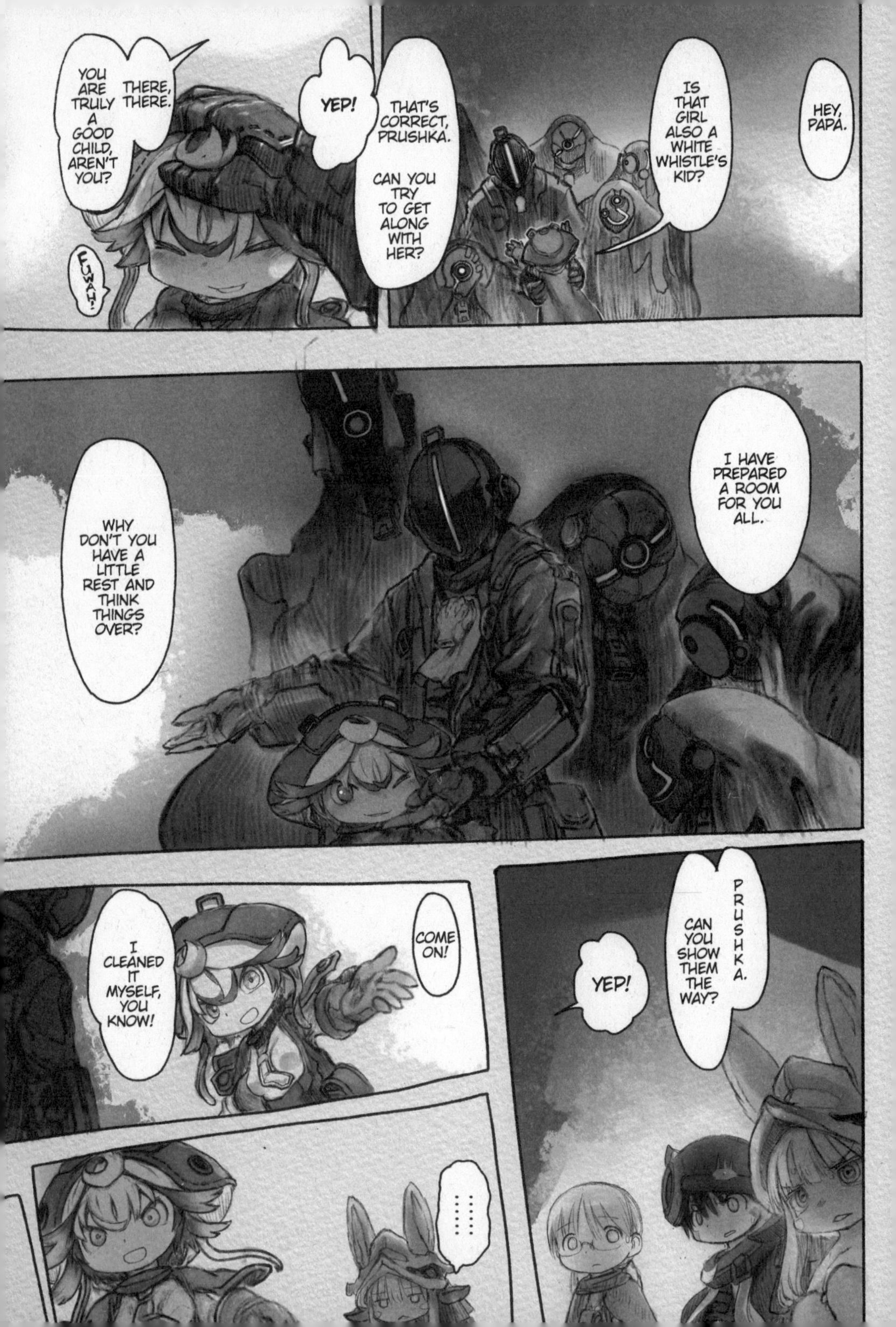
HEY, PAPA.
IS THAT GIRL ALSO A WHITE WHISTLE'S KID?
THAT'S CORRECT, PRUSHKA. CAN YOU TRY TO GET ALONG WITH HER?
YEP!
THERE, THERE.
YOU ARE TRULY A GOOD CHILD, AREN'T YOU?
FUWAH!
I HAVE PREPARED A ROOM FOR YOU ALL.
WHY DON'T YOU HAVE A LITTLE REST AND THINK THINGS OVER?
PRUSHKA.
CAN YOU SHOW THEM THE WAY?
YEP!
COME ON!
I CLEANED IT MYSELF, YOU KNOW!
……

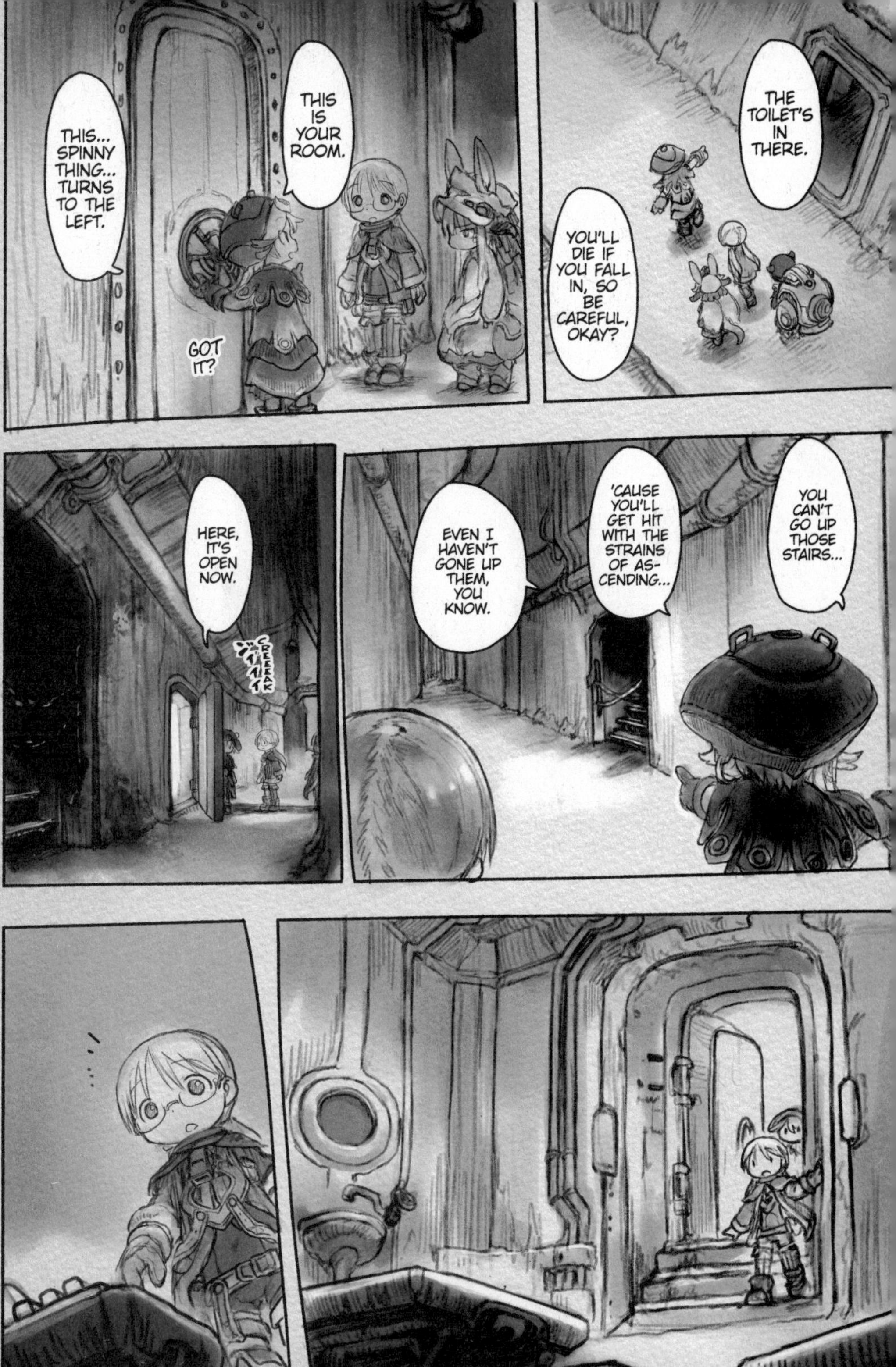
THE TOILET'S IN THERE.
YOU'LL DIE IF YOU FALL IN, SO BE CAREFUL, OKAY?
THIS IS YOUR ROOM.
THIS... SPINNY THING... TURNS TO THE LEFT.
GOT IT?
YOU CAN'T GO UP THOSE STAIRS...
'CAUSE YOU'LL GET HIT WITH THE STRAINS OF AS-CENDING...
EVEN I HAVEN'T GONE UP THEM, YOU KNOW.
HERE, IT'S OPEN NOW.
CREEEAK

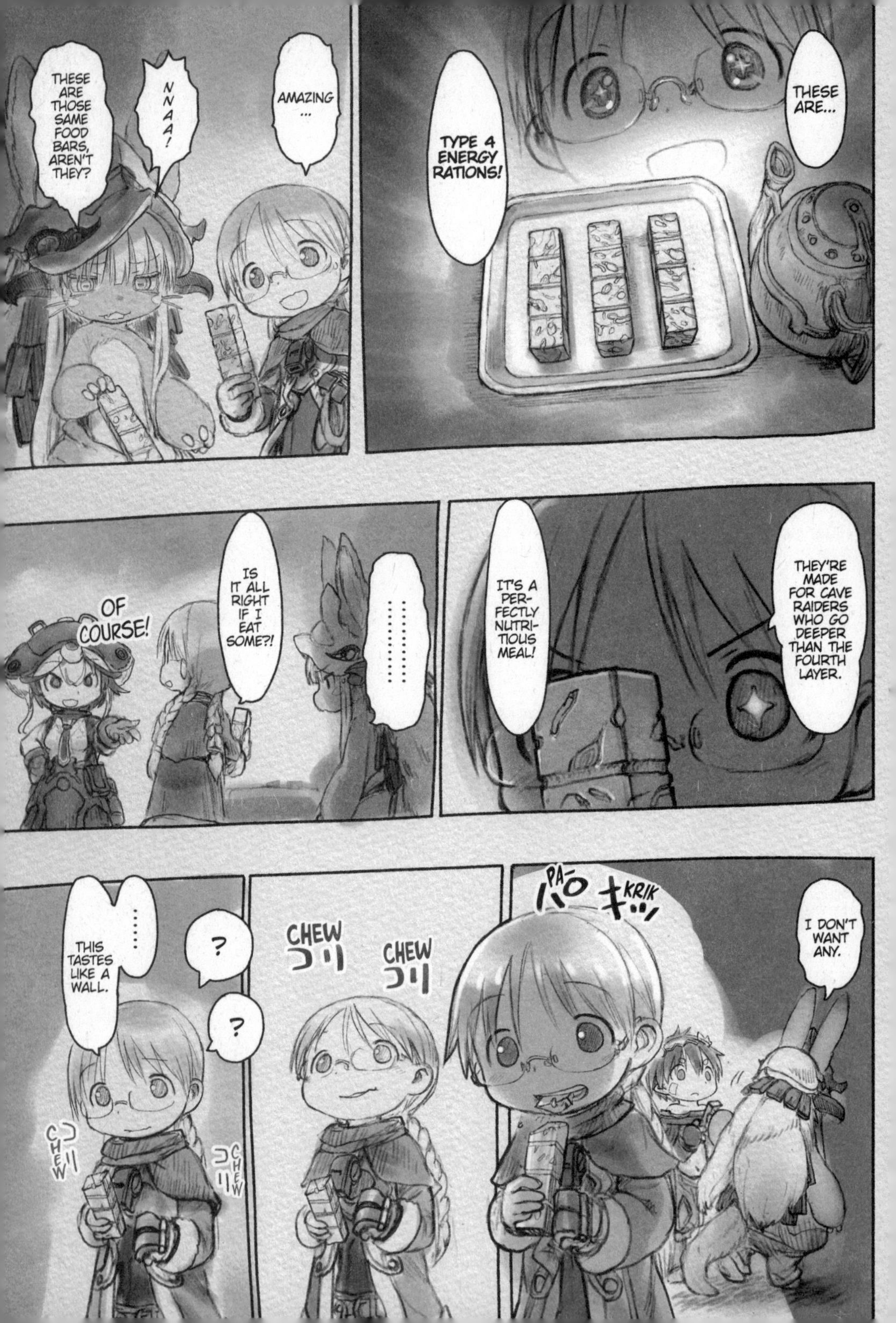
THESE ARE...
TYPE 4 ENERGY RATIONS!
AMAZING...
NNAAA!
THESE ARE THOSE SAME FOOD BARS, AREN'T THEY?
THEY'RE MADE FOR CAVE RAIDERS WHO GO DEEPER THAN THE FOURTH LAYER.
IT'S A PERFECTLY NUTRITIOUS MEAL!
....
IS IT ALL RIGHT IF I EAT SOME?!
OF COURSE!
I DON'T WANT ANY.
PA- パ
KRIK キッ
CHEW コリ
CHEW コリ
?
?
......
THIS TASTES LIKE A WALL.
CHEW コリ
CHEW コリ

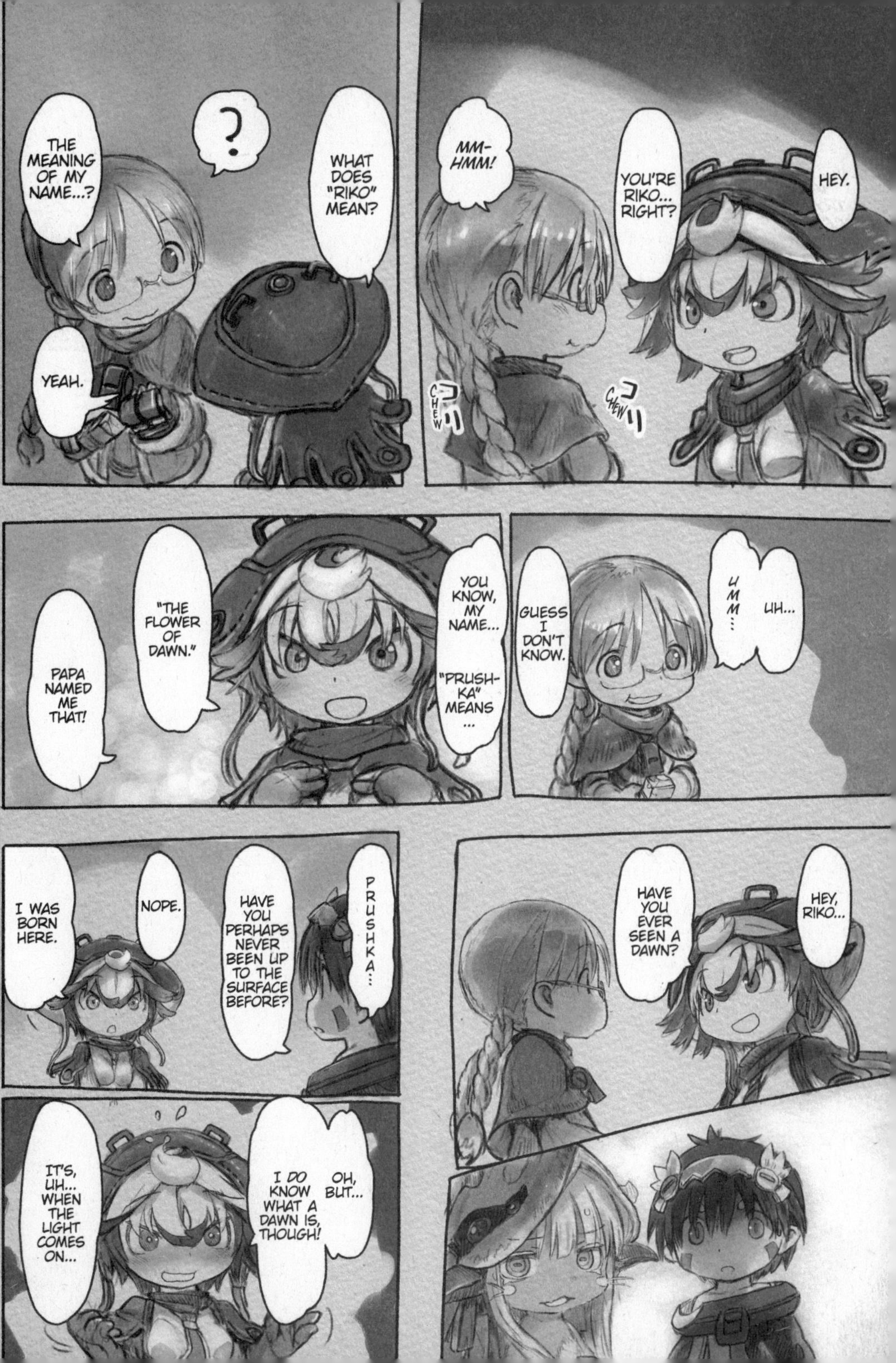
HEY.
YOU'RE RIKO... RIGHT?
MM-HMM!
CHEW
CHEW
WHAT DOES "RIKO" MEAN?
?
THE MEANING OF MY NAME...?
YEAH.
UH...
UMM...
GUESS I DON'T KNOW.
YOU KNOW, MY NAME...
"PRUSHKA" MEANS...
"THE FLOWER OF DAWN."
PAPA NAMED ME THAT!
HEY, RIKO...
HAVE YOU EVER SEEN A DAWN?
PRUSHKA...
HAVE YOU PERHAPS NEVER BEEN UP TO THE SURFACE BEFORE?
NOPE.
I WAS BORN HERE.
OH, BUT...
I DO KNOW WHAT A DAWN IS, THOUGH!
IT'S, UH... WHEN THE LIGHT COMES ON...

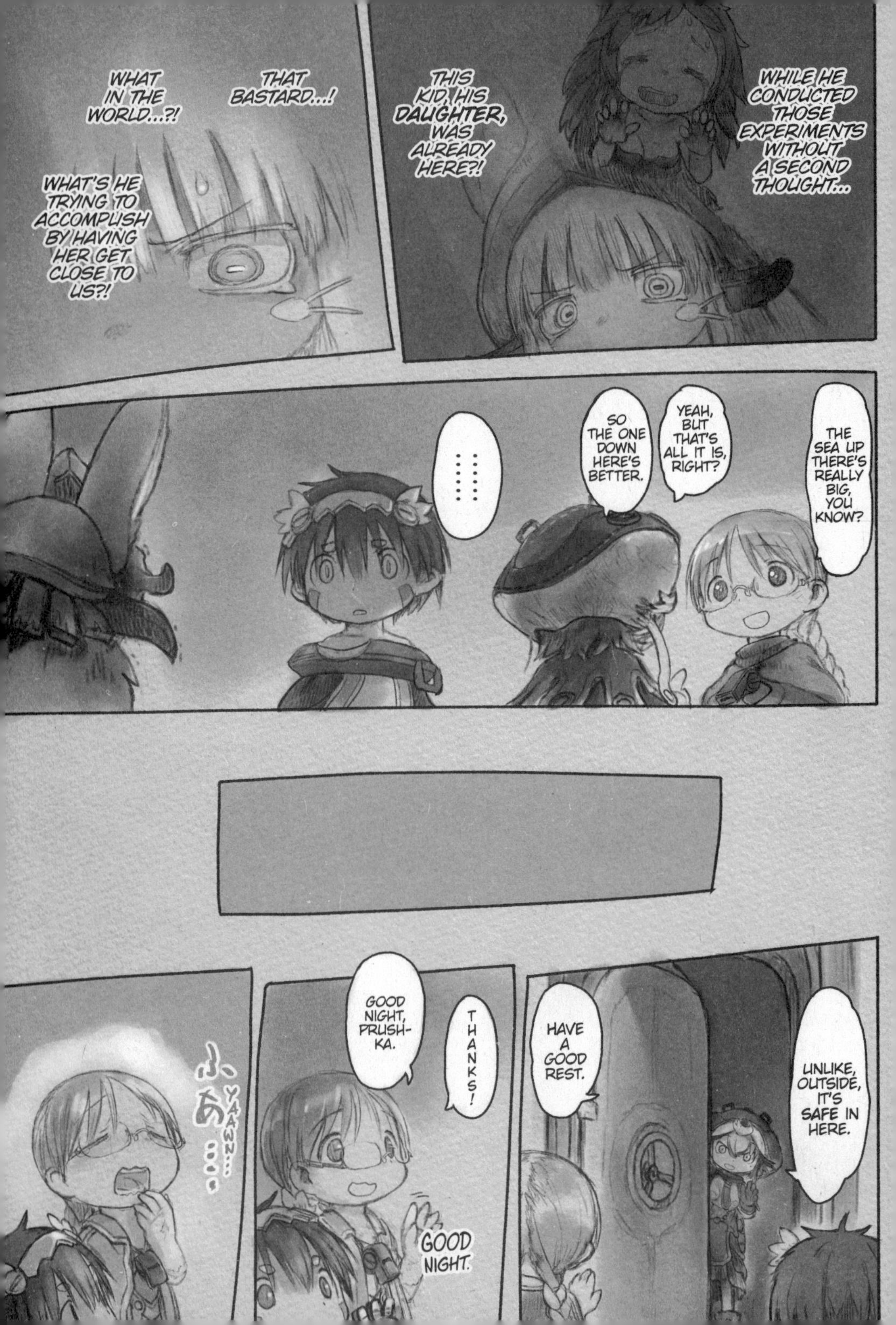
WHILE HE CONDUCTED THOSE EXPERIMENTS WITHOUT A SECOND THOUGHT...
THIS KID, HIS DAUGHTER, WAS ALREADY HERE?!
THAT BASTARD...!
WHAT IN THE WORLD...?!
WHAT'S HE TRYING TO ACCOMPLISH BY HAVING HER GET CLOSE TO US?!
THE SEA UP THERE'S REALLY BIG, YOU KNOW?
YEAH, BUT THAT'S ALL IT IS, RIGHT?
SO THE ONE DOWN HERE'S BETTER.
......
UNLIKE, OUTSIDE, IT'S SAFE IN HERE.
HAVE A GOOD REST.
THANKS!
GOOD NIGHT, PRUSHKA.
GOOD NIGHT.
ふあ…
YAAWN...

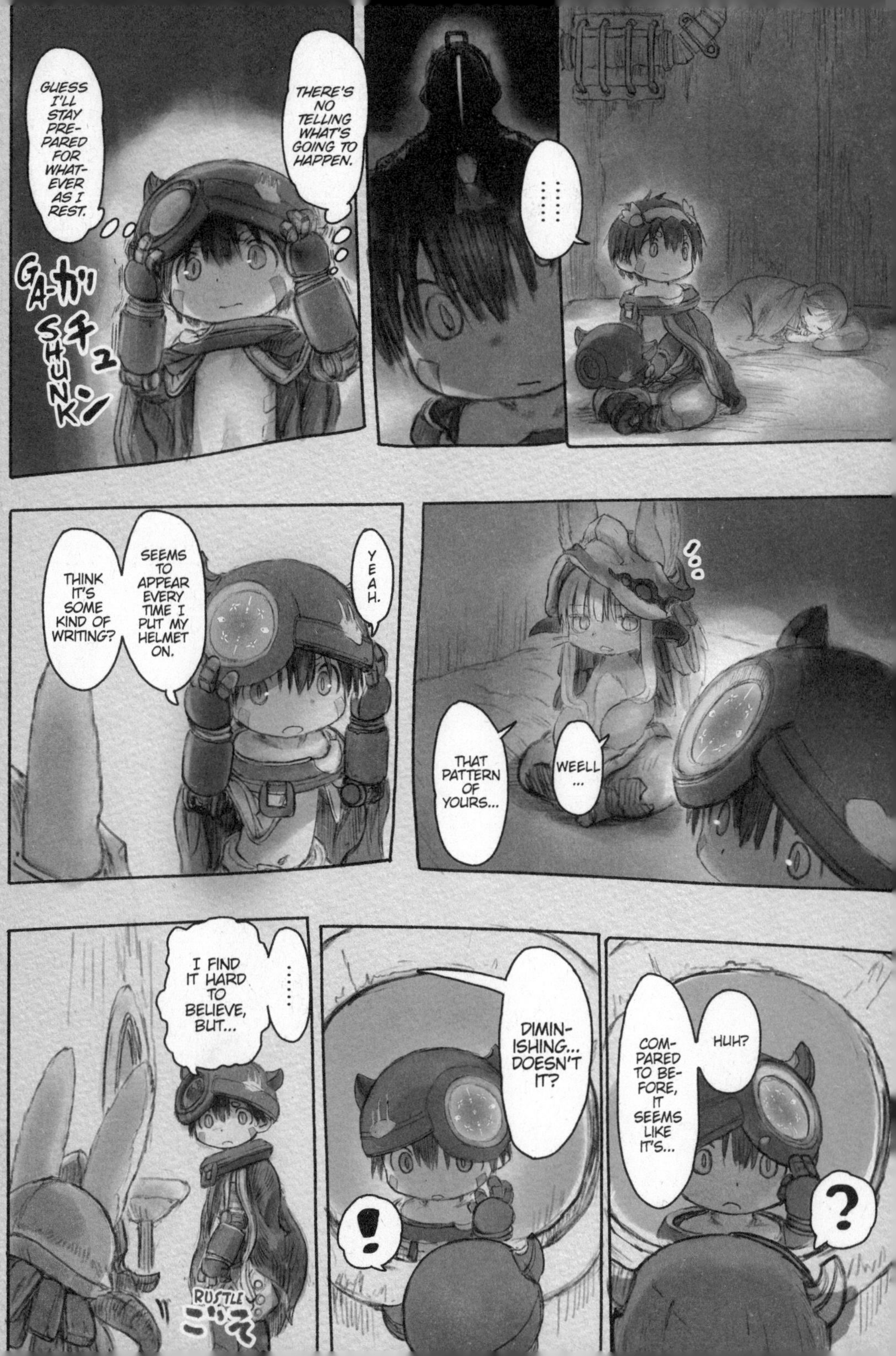
......
THERE'S NO TELLING WHAT'S GOING TO HAPPEN.
GUESS I'LL STAY PREPARED FOR WHATEVER AS I REST.
GA-SHUNK
WEELL...
THAT PATTERN OF YOURS...
YEAH.
SEEMS TO APPEAR EVERY TIME I PUT MY HELMET ON.
THINK IT'S SOME KIND OF WRITING?
HUH?
COMPARED TO BEFORE, IT SEEMS LIKE IT'S...
?
DIMINISHING... DOESN'T IT?
!
......
I FIND IT HARD TO BELIEVE, BUT...
RUSTLE

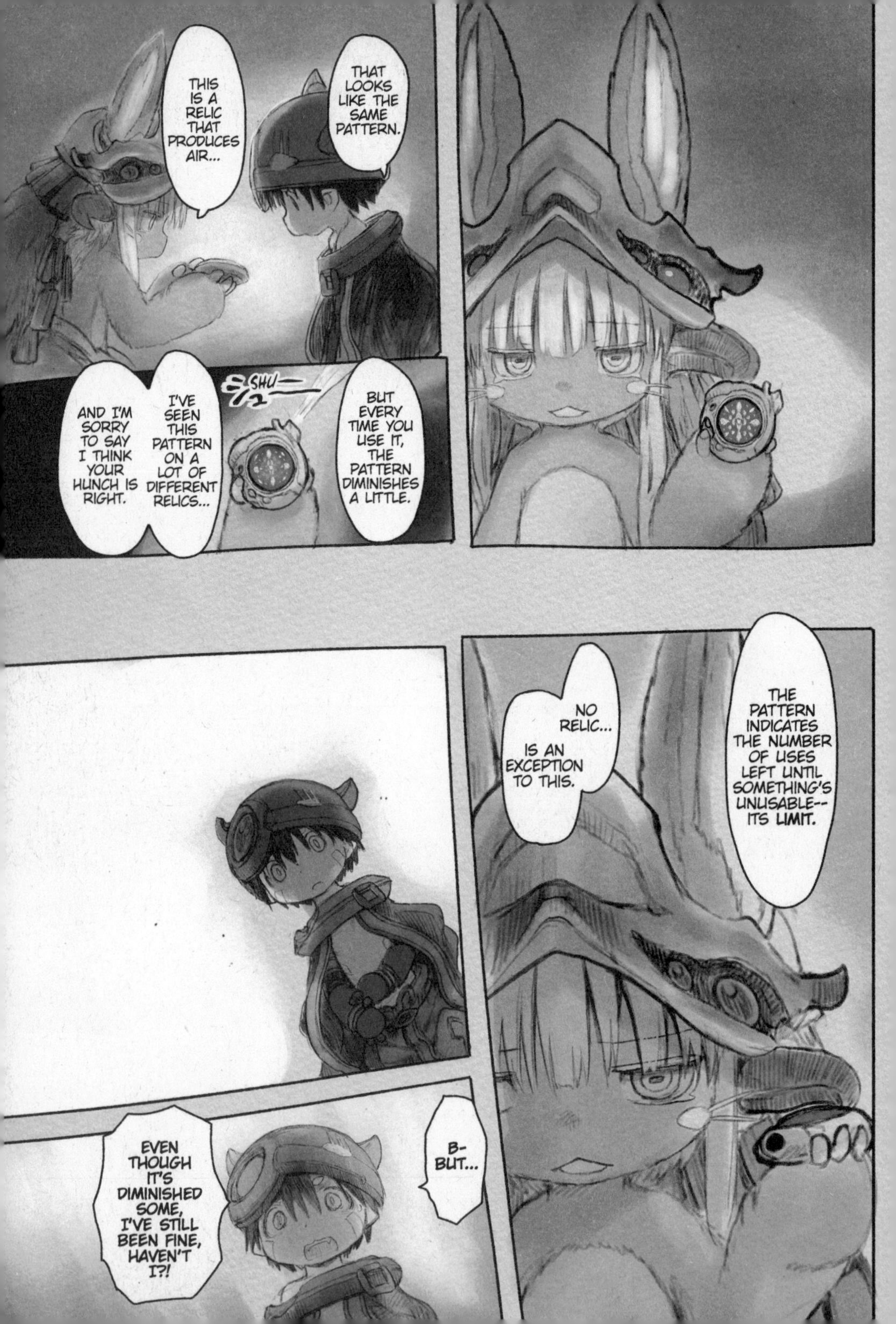
THAT LOOKS LIKE THE SAME PATTERN.
THIS IS A RELIC THAT PRODUCES AIR...
BUT EVERY TIME YOU USE IT, THE PATTERN DIMINISHES A LITTLE.
SHU--
I'VE SEEN THIS PATTERN ON A LOT OF DIFFERENT RELICS...
AND I'M SORRY TO SAY I THINK YOUR HUNCH IS RIGHT.
THE PATTERN INDICATES THE NUMBER OF USES LEFT UNTIL SOMETHING'S UNUSABLE-- ITS LIMIT.
NO RELIC...
IS AN EXCEPTION TO THIS.
B-BUT...
EVEN THOUGH IT'S DIMINISHED SOME, I'VE STILL BEEN FINE, HAVEN'T I?!

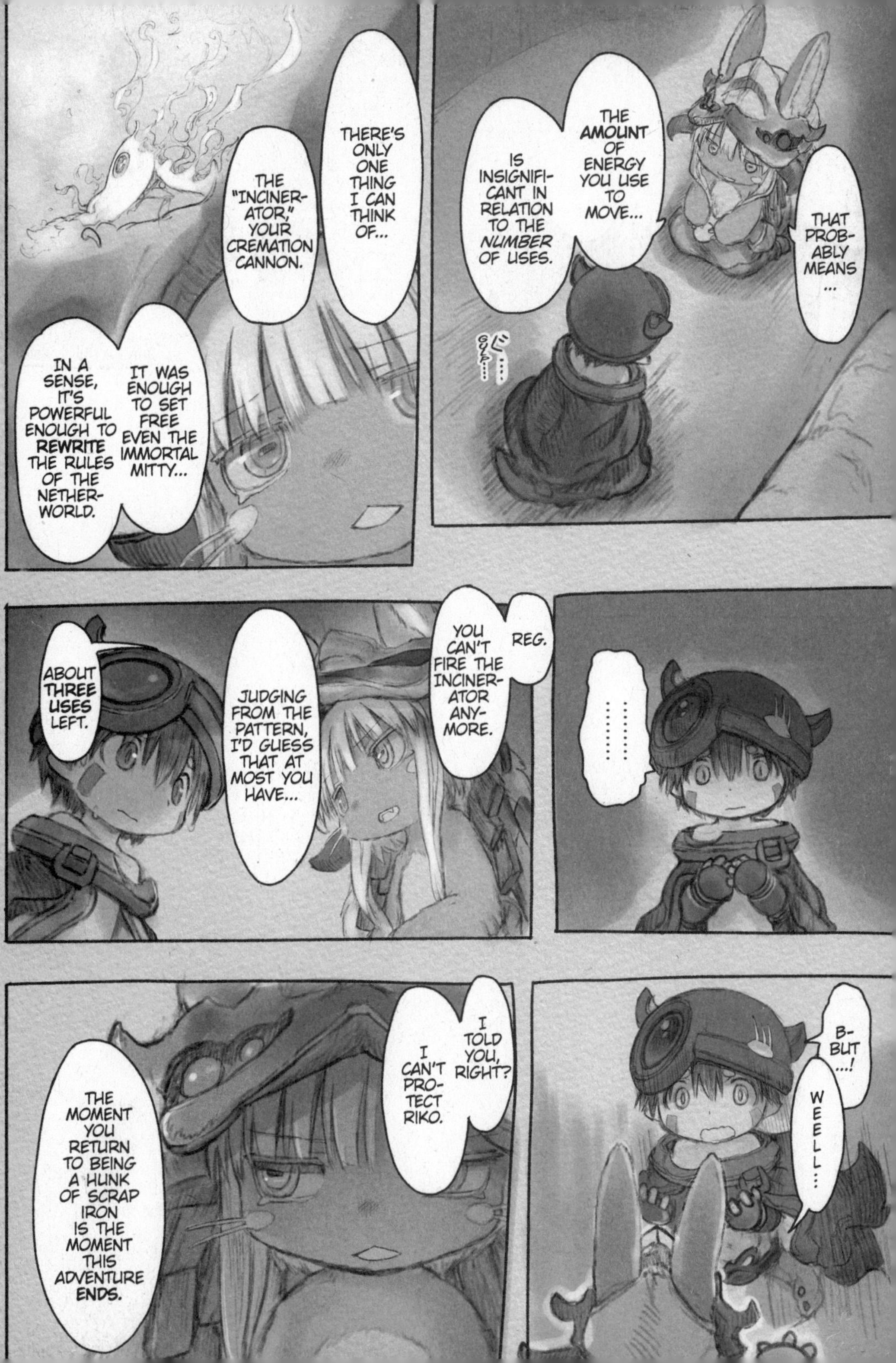
THAT PROBABLY MEANS ...
THE AMOUNT OF ENERGY YOU USE TO MOVE...
IS INSIGNIFICANT IN RELATION TO THE NUMBER OF USES.
じ...
GULP...
THERE'S ONLY ONE THING I CAN THINK OF...
THE "INCINERATOR," YOUR CREMATION CANNON.
IT WAS ENOUGH TO SET FREE EVEN THE IMMORTAL MITTY...
IN A SENSE, IT'S POWERFUL ENOUGH TO REWRITE THE RULES OF THE NETHERWORLD.
......
REG.
YOU CAN'T FIRE THE INCINERATOR ANYMORE.
JUDGING FROM THE PATTERN, I'D GUESS THAT AT MOST YOU HAVE...
ABOUT THREE USES LEFT.
B-BUT...!
WEELL...
I TOLD YOU, RIGHT?
I CAN'T PROTECT RIKO.
THE MOMENT YOU RETURN TO BEING A HUNK OF SCRAP IRON IS THE MOMENT THIS ADVENTURE ENDS.

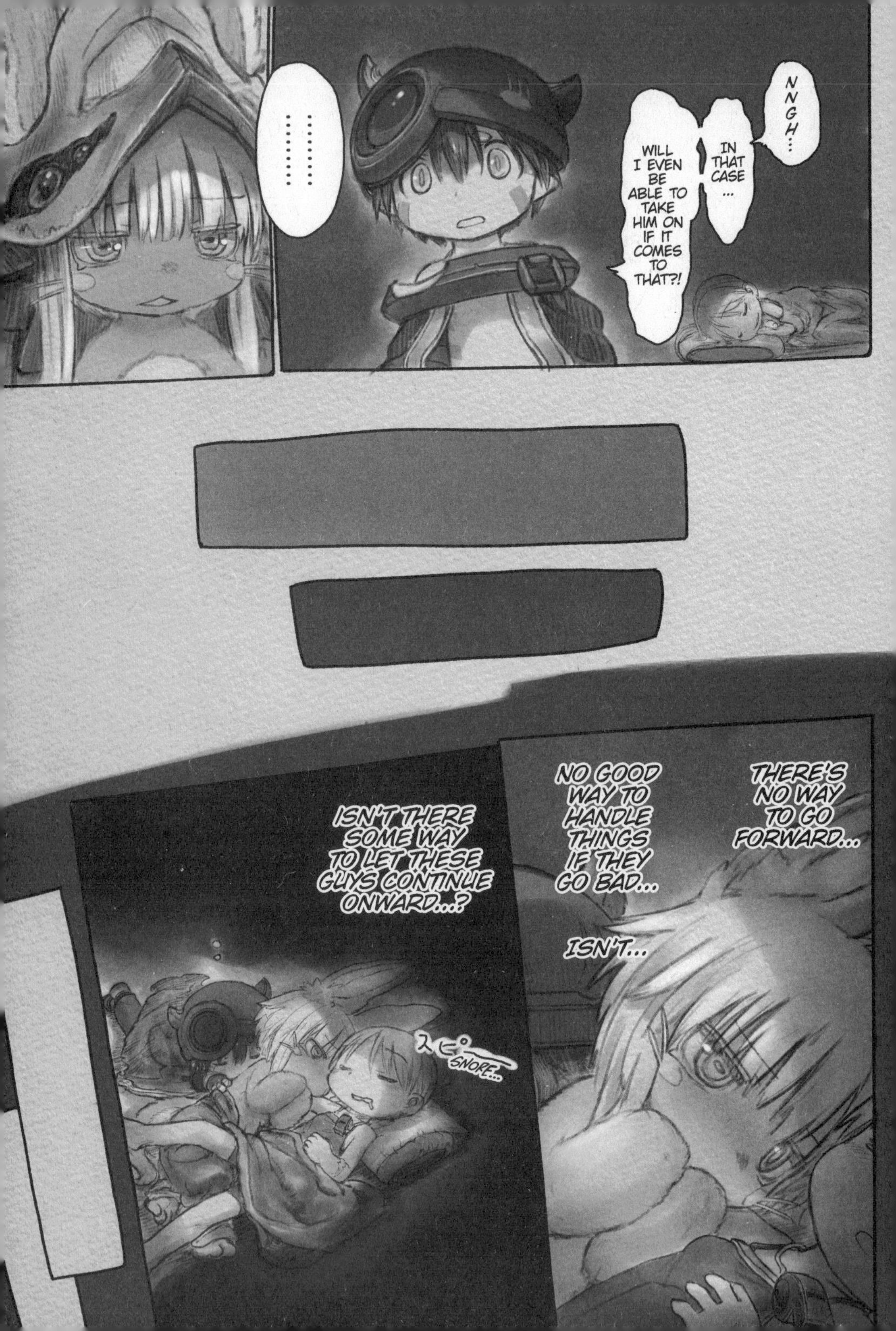
NNGH...
IN THAT CASE...
WILL I EVEN BE ABLE TO TAKE HIM ON IF IT COMES TO THAT?!
......
THERE'S NO WAY TO GO FORWARD...
NO GOOD WAY TO HANDLE THINGS IF THEY GO BAD...
ISN'T...
ISN'T THERE SOME WAY TO LET THESE GUYS CONTINUE ONWARD...?
スピー
SNORE...

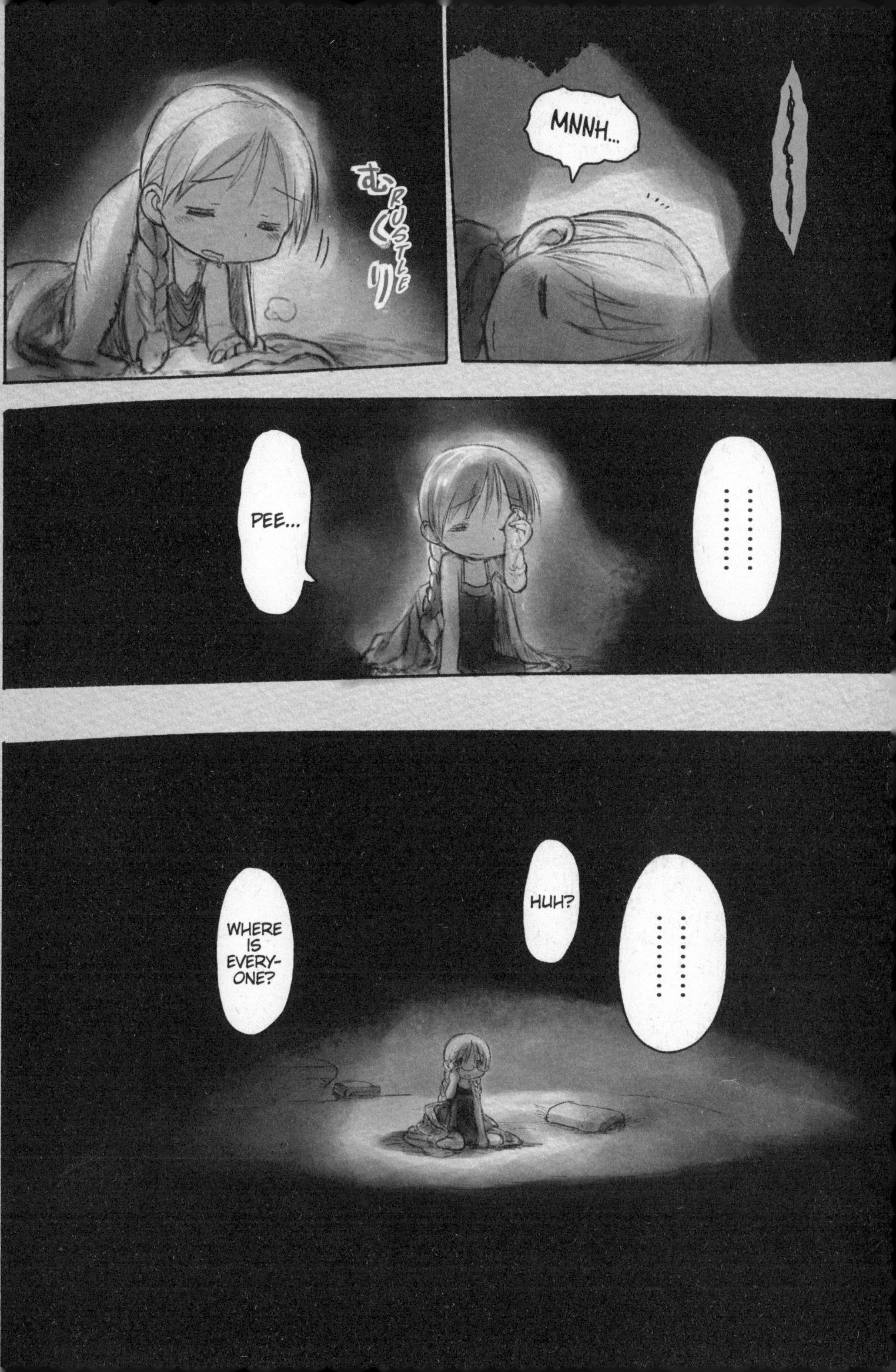
MNNH...
RUSTLE
......
PEE...
......
HUH?
WHERE IS EVERY-ONE?

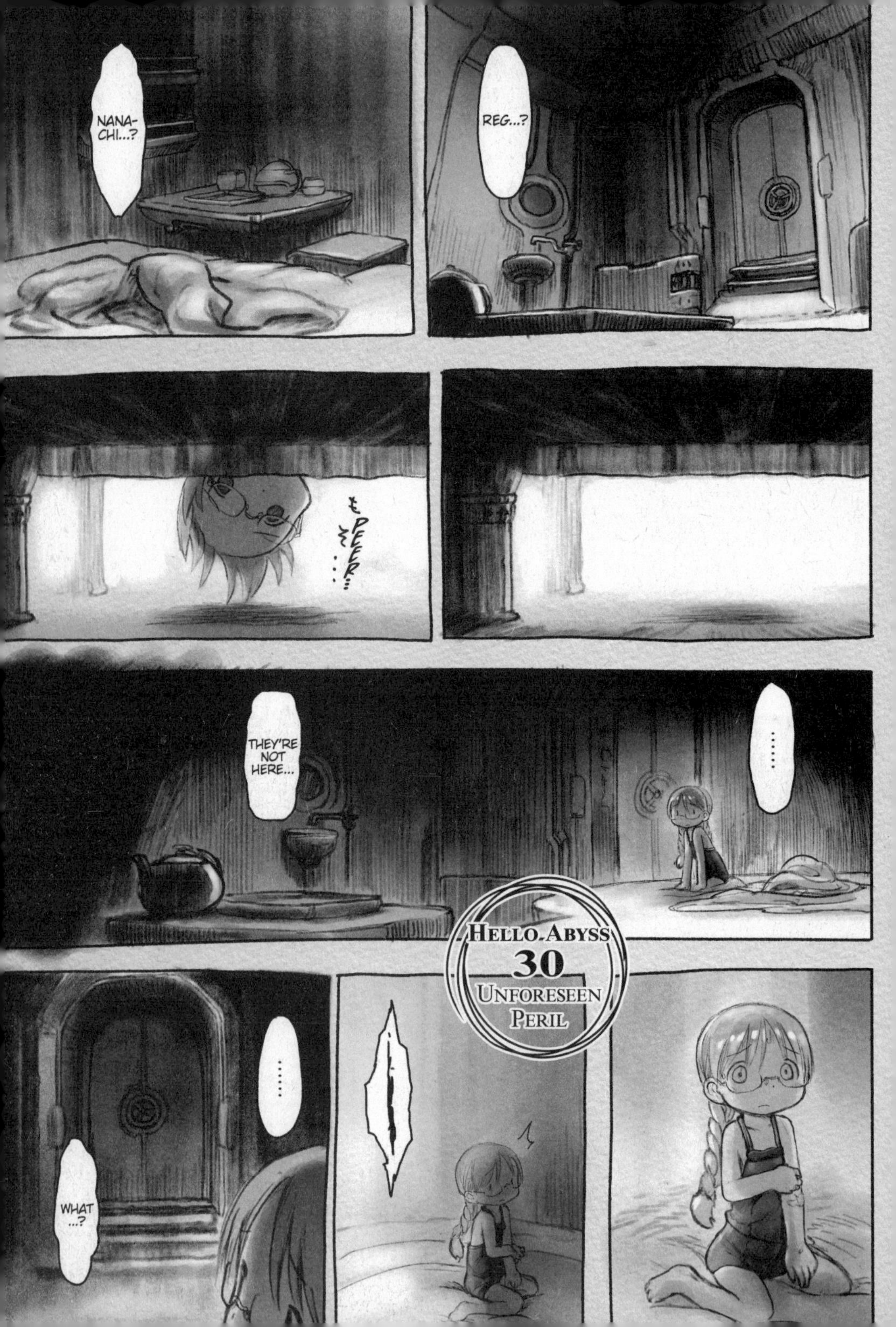
REG...?
NANA-CHI...?
PEEER..
......
THEY'RE NOT HERE...
HELLO ABYSS
30
UNFORESEEN PERIL
!
......
WHAT ...?

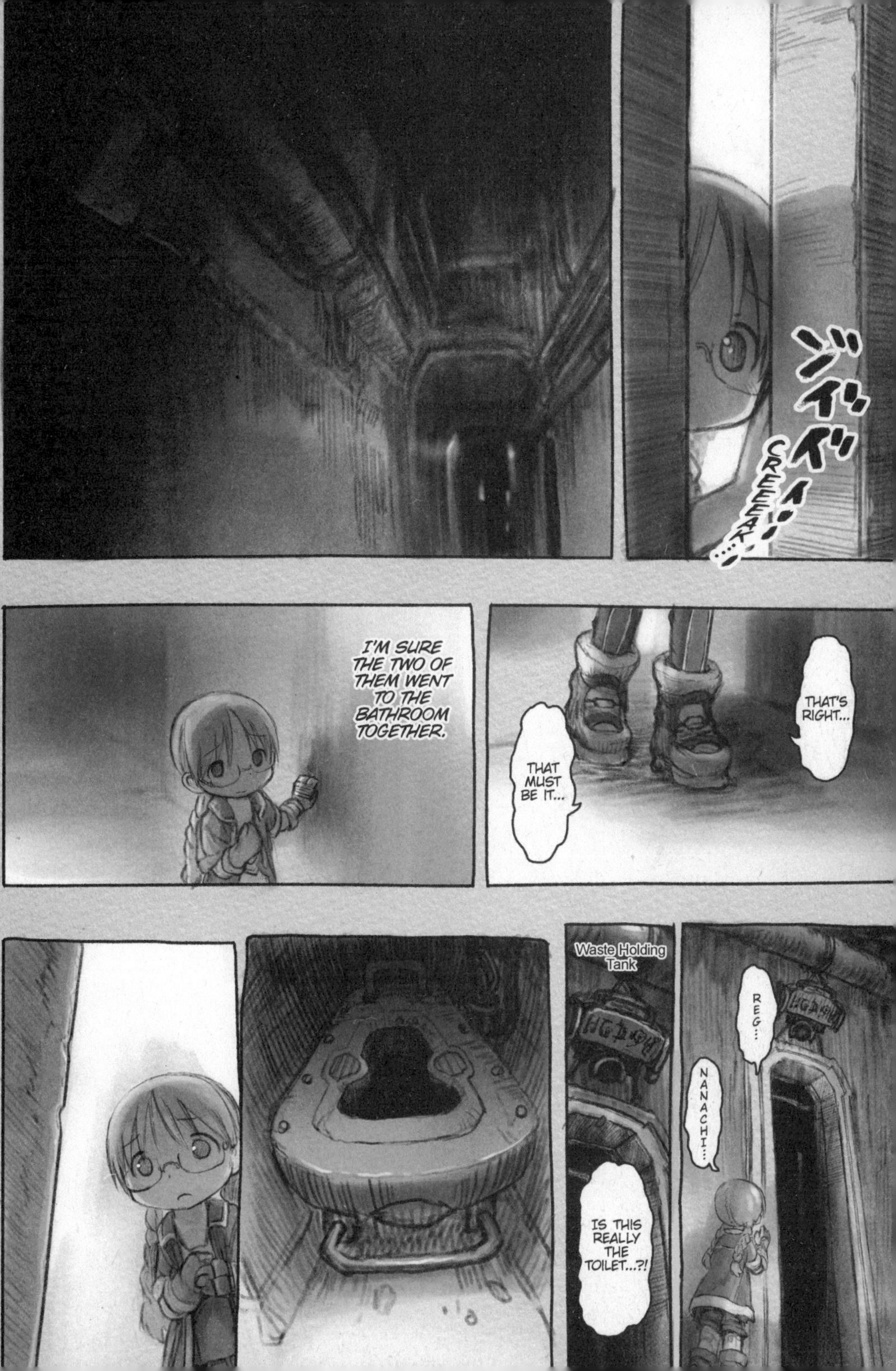
CREEEAK...
THAT'S RIGHT...
THAT MUST BE IT...
I'M SURE THE TWO OF THEM WENT TO THE BATHROOM TOGETHER.
REG...
NANACHI...
IS THIS REALLY THE TOILET...?!
Waste Holding Tank

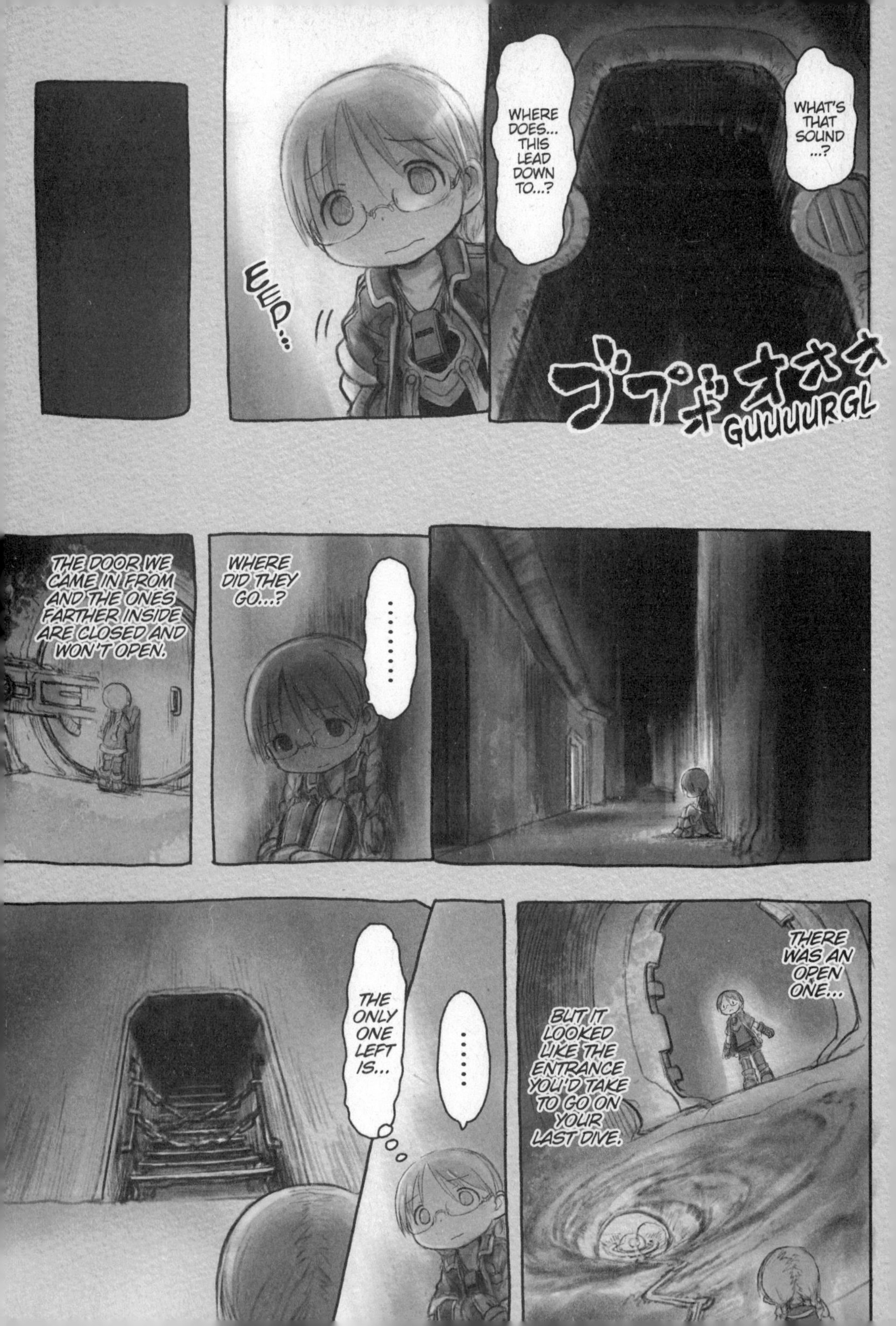
WHAT'S THAT SOUND ...?
WHERE DOES... THIS LEAD DOWN TO...?
GUUUURGL
EEP...
WHERE DID THEY GO...?
......
THE DOOR WE CAME IN FROM AND THE ONES FARTHER INSIDE ARE CLOSED AND WON'T OPEN.
THERE WAS AN OPEN ONE...
BUT IT LOOKED LIKE THE ENTRANCE YOU'D TAKE TO GO ON YOUR LAST DIVE.
......
THE ONLY ONE LEFT IS...

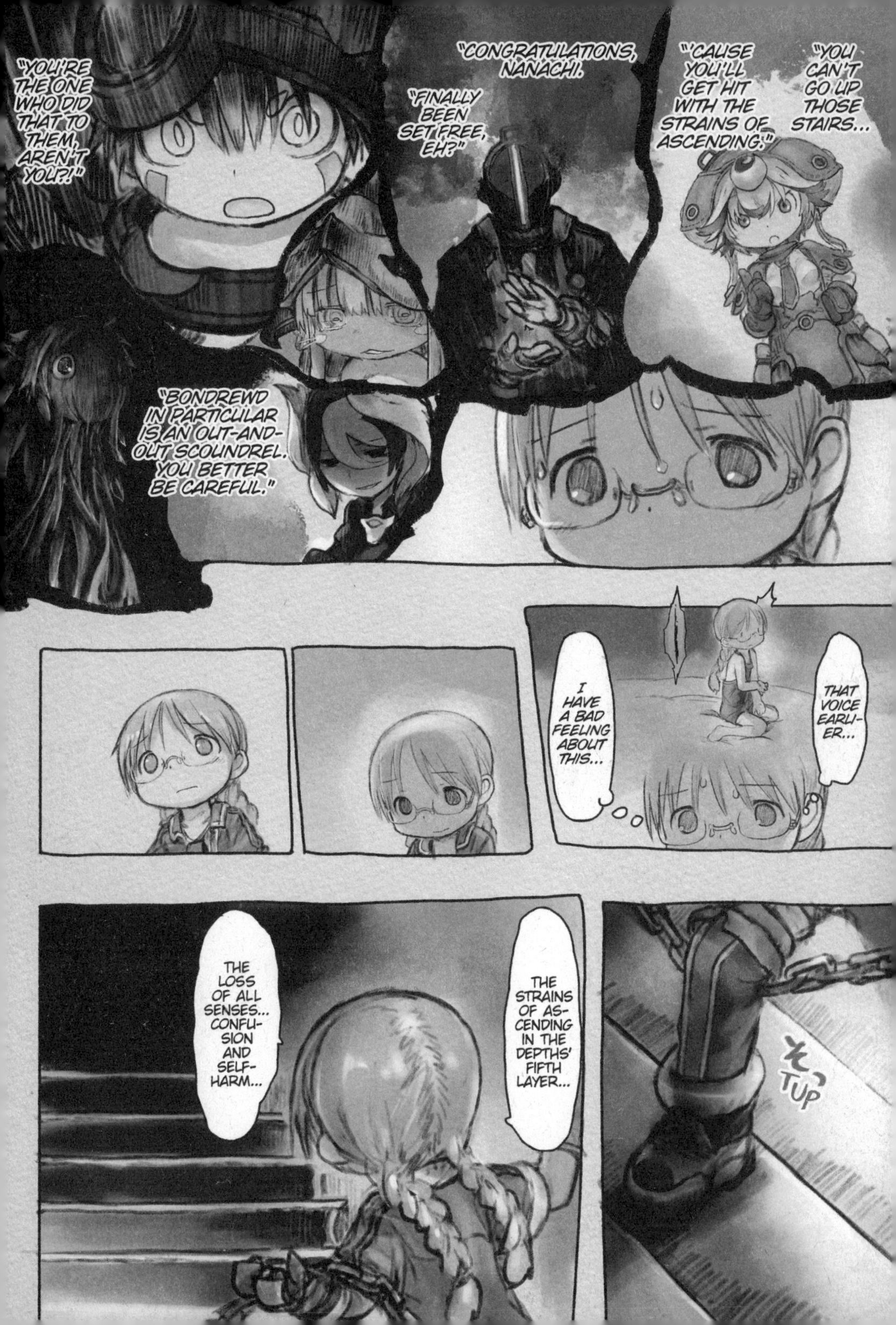
"YOU CAN'T GO UP THOSE STAIRS...
'CAUSE YOU'LL GET HIT WITH THE STRAINS OF ASCENDING."
"CONGRATULATIONS, NANACHI.
"FINALLY BEEN SET FREE, EH?"
"YOU'RE THE ONE WHO DID THAT TO THEM, AREN'T YOU?!"
"BONDREWD IN PARTICULAR IS AN OUT-AND-OUT SCOUNDREL. YOU BETTER BE CAREFUL."
THAT VOICE EARLI-ER...
I HAVE A BAD FEELING ABOUT THIS...
そっ
TUP
THE STRAINS OF AS-CENDING IN THE DEPTHS' FIFTH LAYER...
THE LOSS OF ALL SENSES... CONFU-SION AND SELF-HARM...

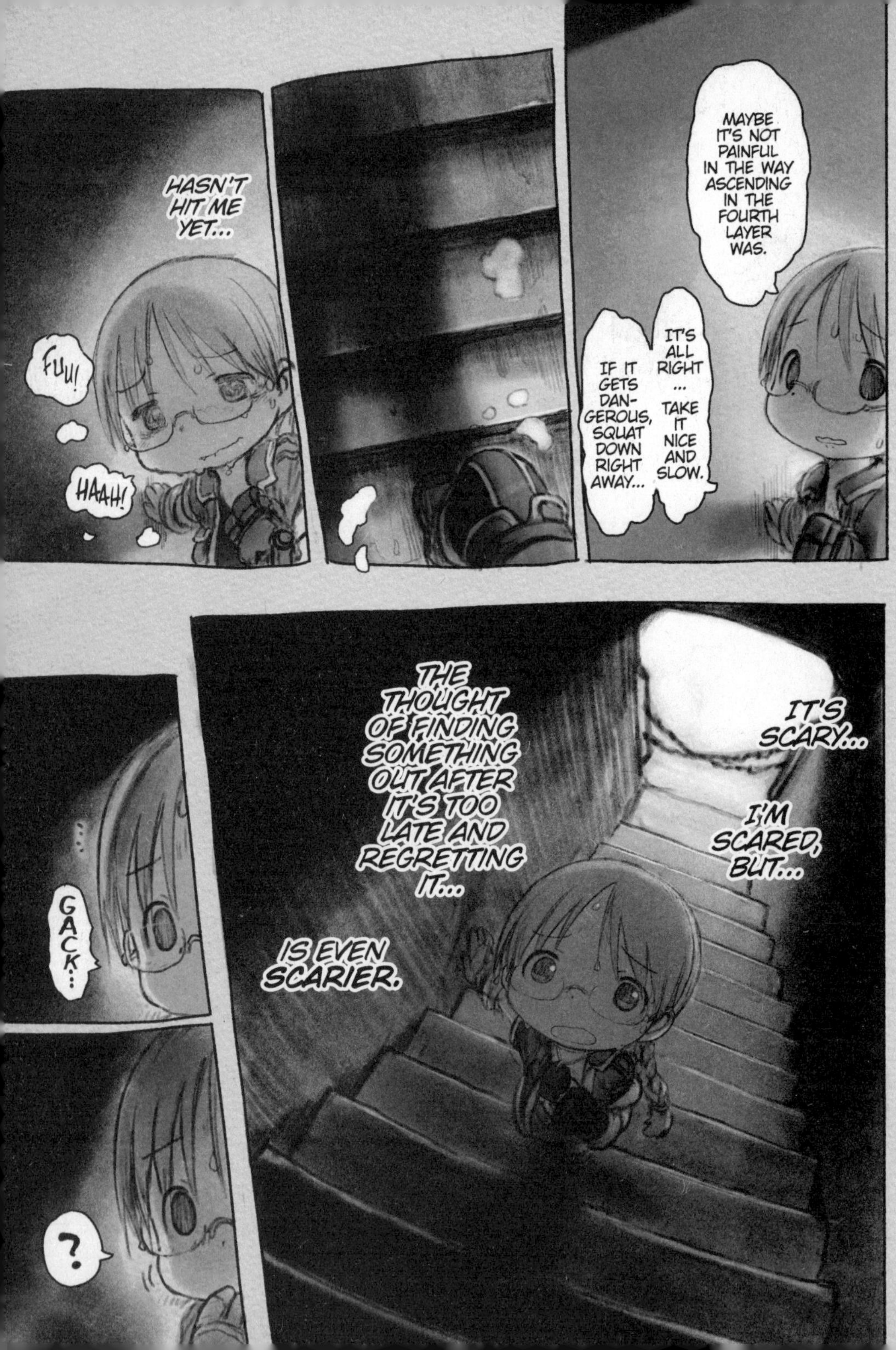
MAYBE IT'S NOT PAINFUL IN THE WAY ASCENDING IN THE FOURTH LAYER WAS.
IT'S ALL RIGHT... TAKE IT NICE AND SLOW.
IF IT GETS DAN-GEROUS, SQUAT DOWN RIGHT AWAY...
HASN'T HIT ME YET...
FUU!
HAAH!
IT'S SCARY...
I'M SCARED, BUT...
THE THOUGHT OF FINDING SOMETHING OUT AFTER IT'S TOO LATE AND REGRETTING IT...
IS EVEN SCARIER.
...
GACK...
?

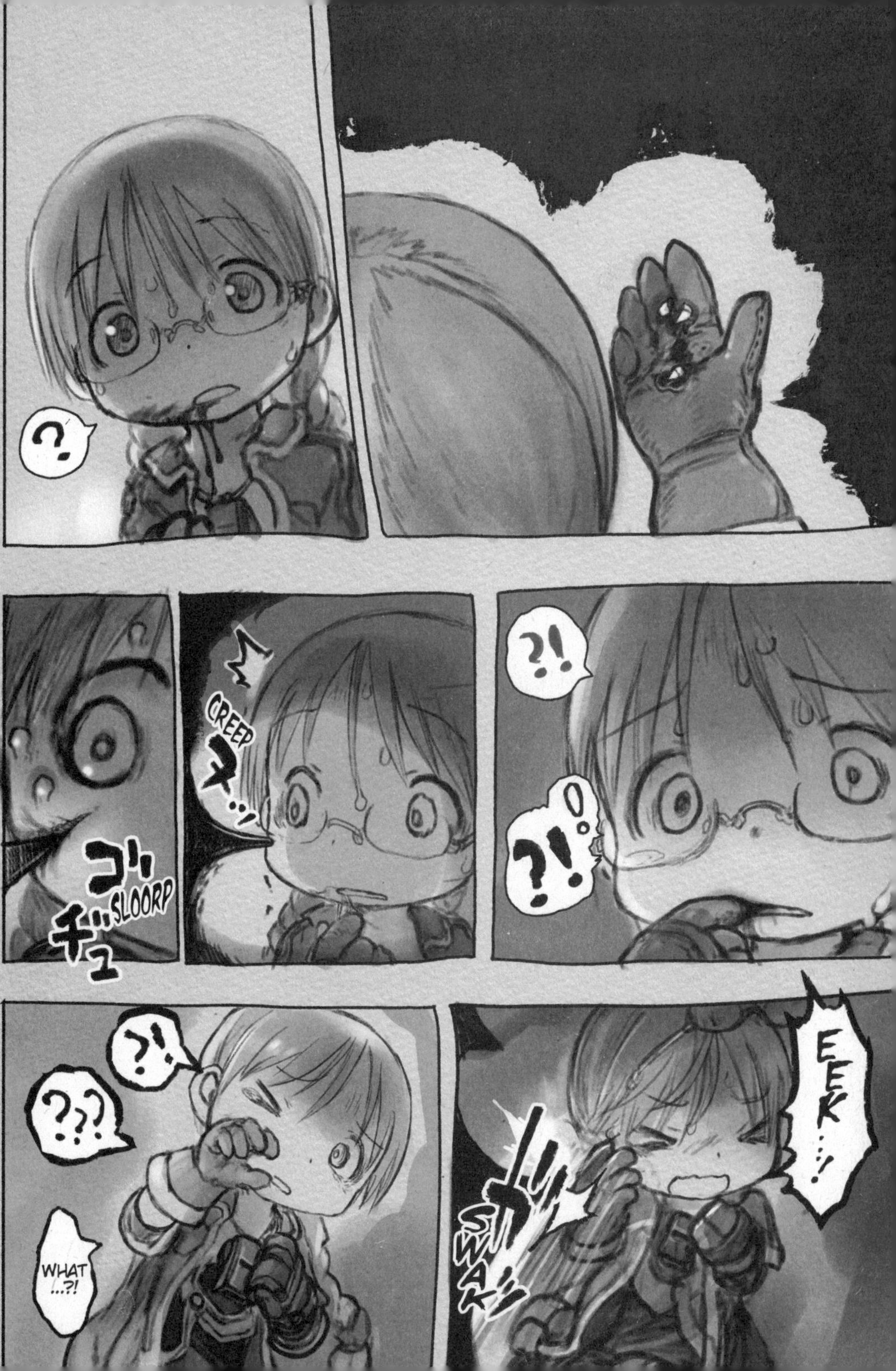
?
?!
?!
CREEP
SLOORP
EEK...!
SWAK!!
?!
???
WHAT ...?!

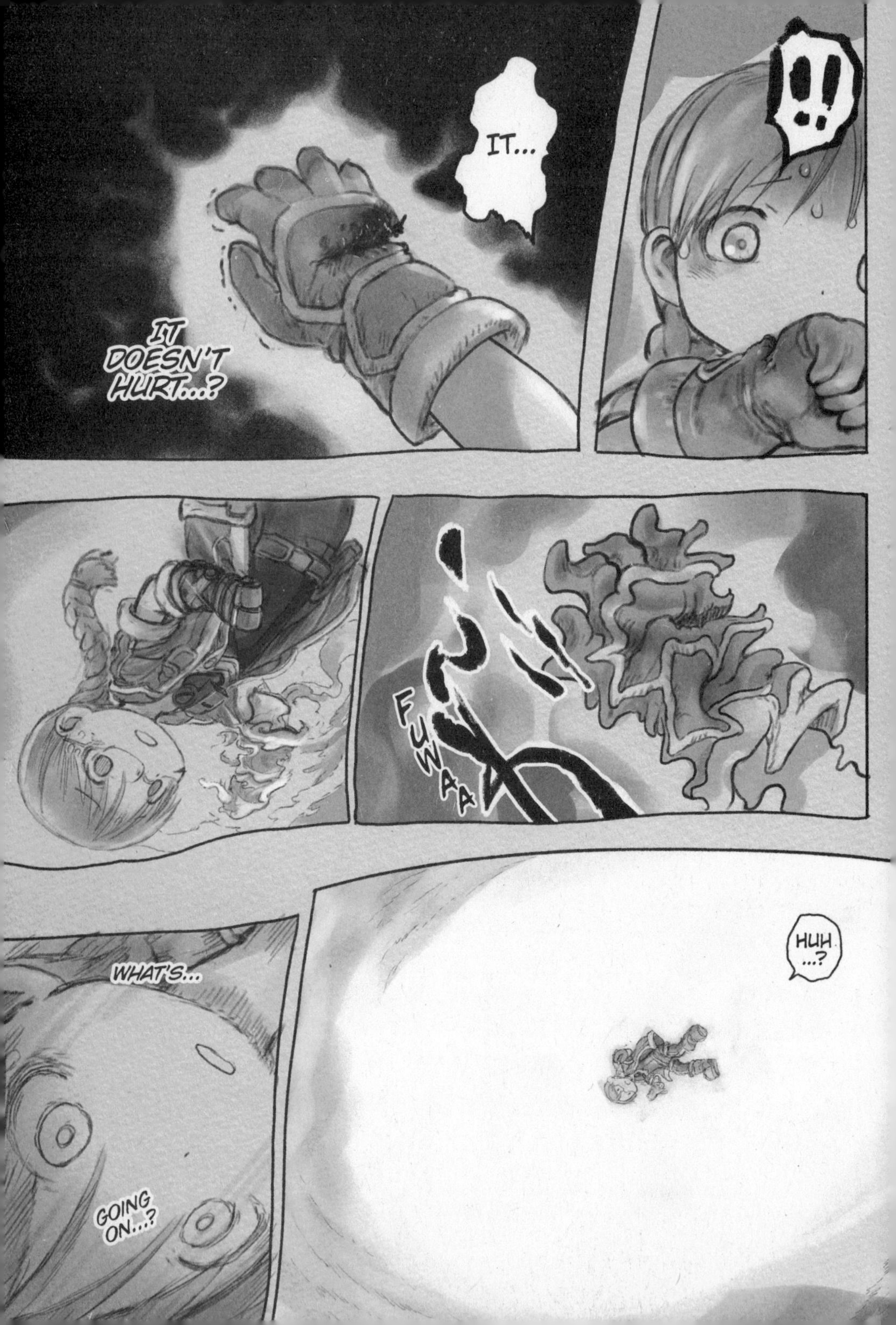
!!
IT...
IT DOESN'T HURT...?
FUWAA
HUH ...?
WHAT'S...
GOING ON...?

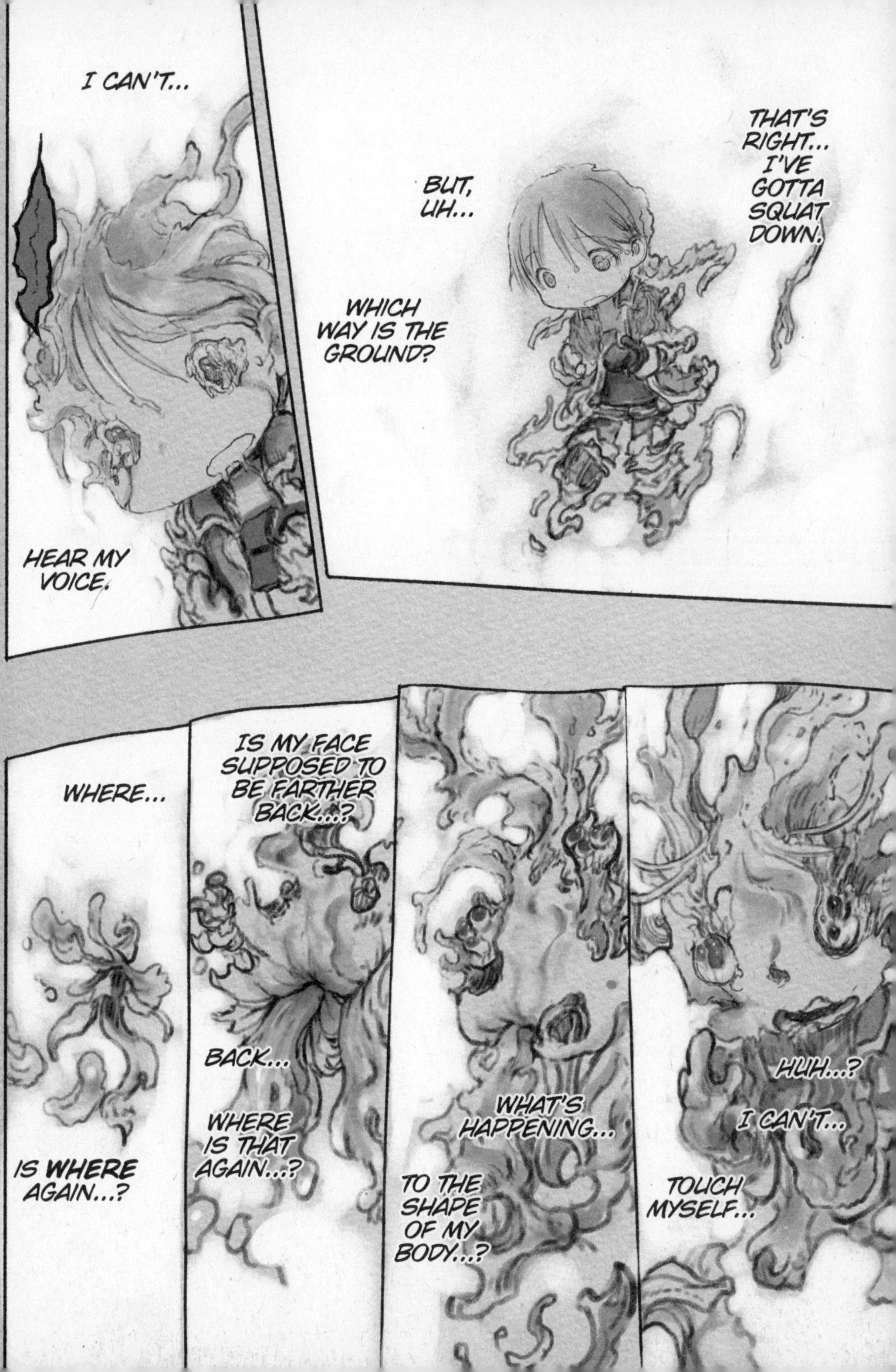
THAT'S RIGHT... I'VE GOTTA SQUAT DOWN.
BUT, UH...
WHICH WAY IS THE GROUND?
I CAN'T...
HEAR MY VOICE.
HUH...?
I CAN'T...
TOUCH MYSELF...
WHAT'S HAPPENING...
TO THE SHAPE OF MY BODY...?
IS MY FACE SUPPOSED TO BE FARTHER BACK...?
BACK...
WHERE IS THAT AGAIN...?
WHERE...
IS **WHERE** AGAIN...?

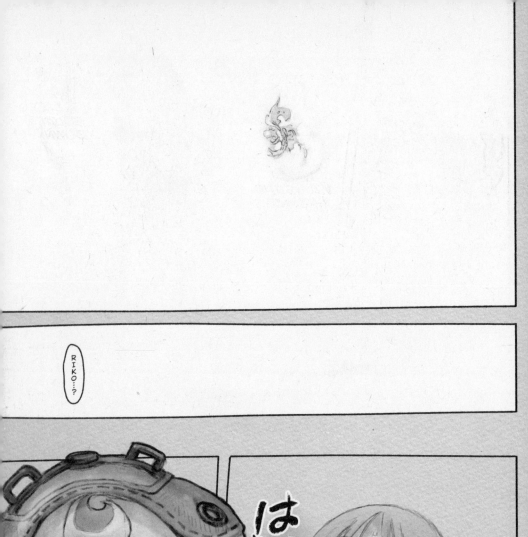

RIKO...!?

は
HAH!?

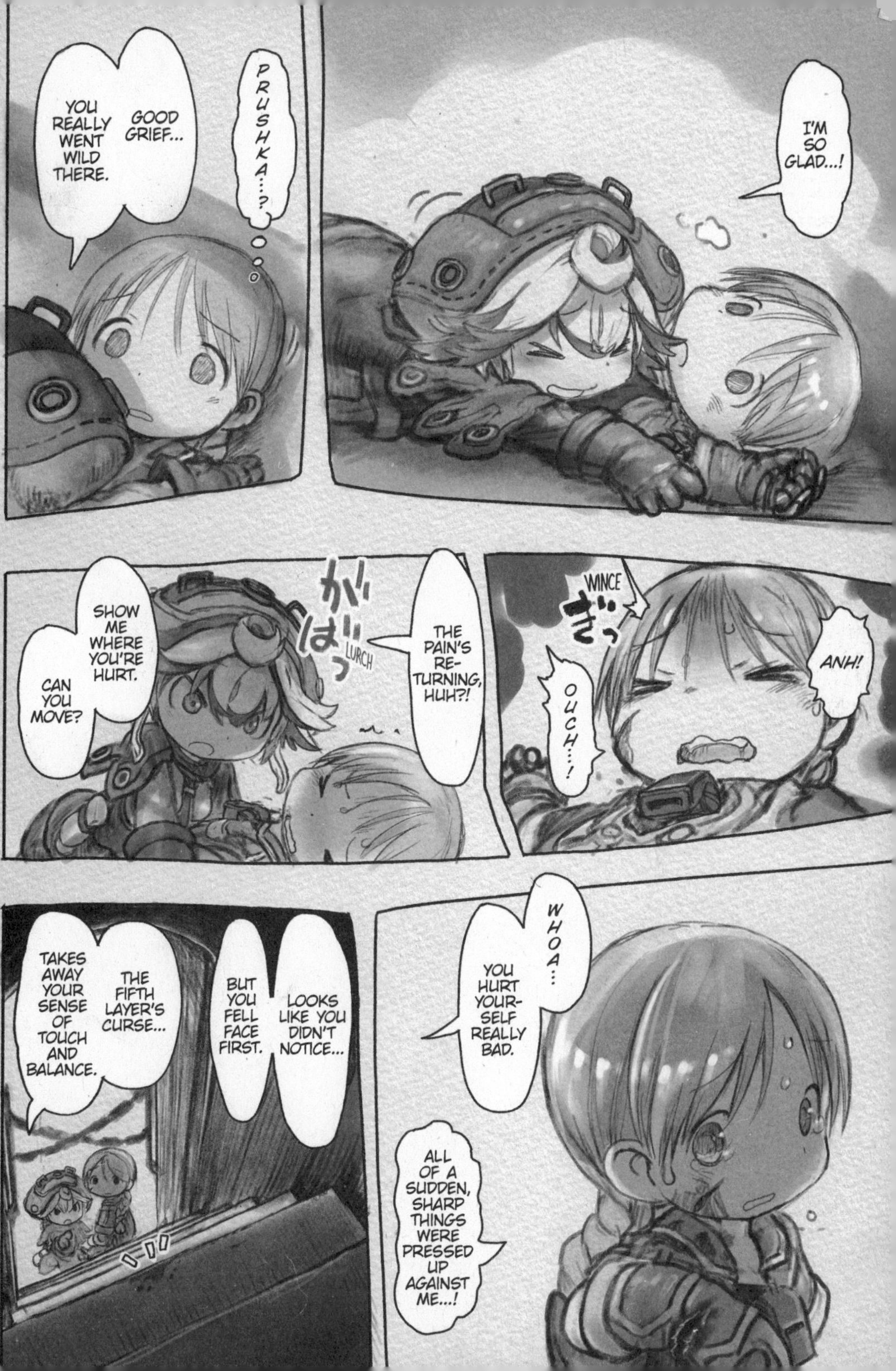
I'M SO GLAD...!
PRUSHKA...?
GOOD GRIEF...
YOU REALLY WENT WILD THERE.
WINCE
ぎっ
ANH!
OUCH...!
THE PAIN'S RE-TURNING, HUH?!
がばっ
LURCH
SHOW ME WHERE YOU'RE HURT.
CAN YOU MOVE?
WHOA...
YOU HURT YOUR-SELF REALLY BAD.
ALL OF A SUDDEN, SHARP THINGS WERE PRESSED UP AGAINST ME...!
LOOKS LIKE YOU DIDN'T NOTICE...
BUT YOU FELL FACE FIRST.
THE FIFTH LAYER'S CURSE...
TAKES AWAY YOUR SENSE OF TOUCH AND BALANCE.

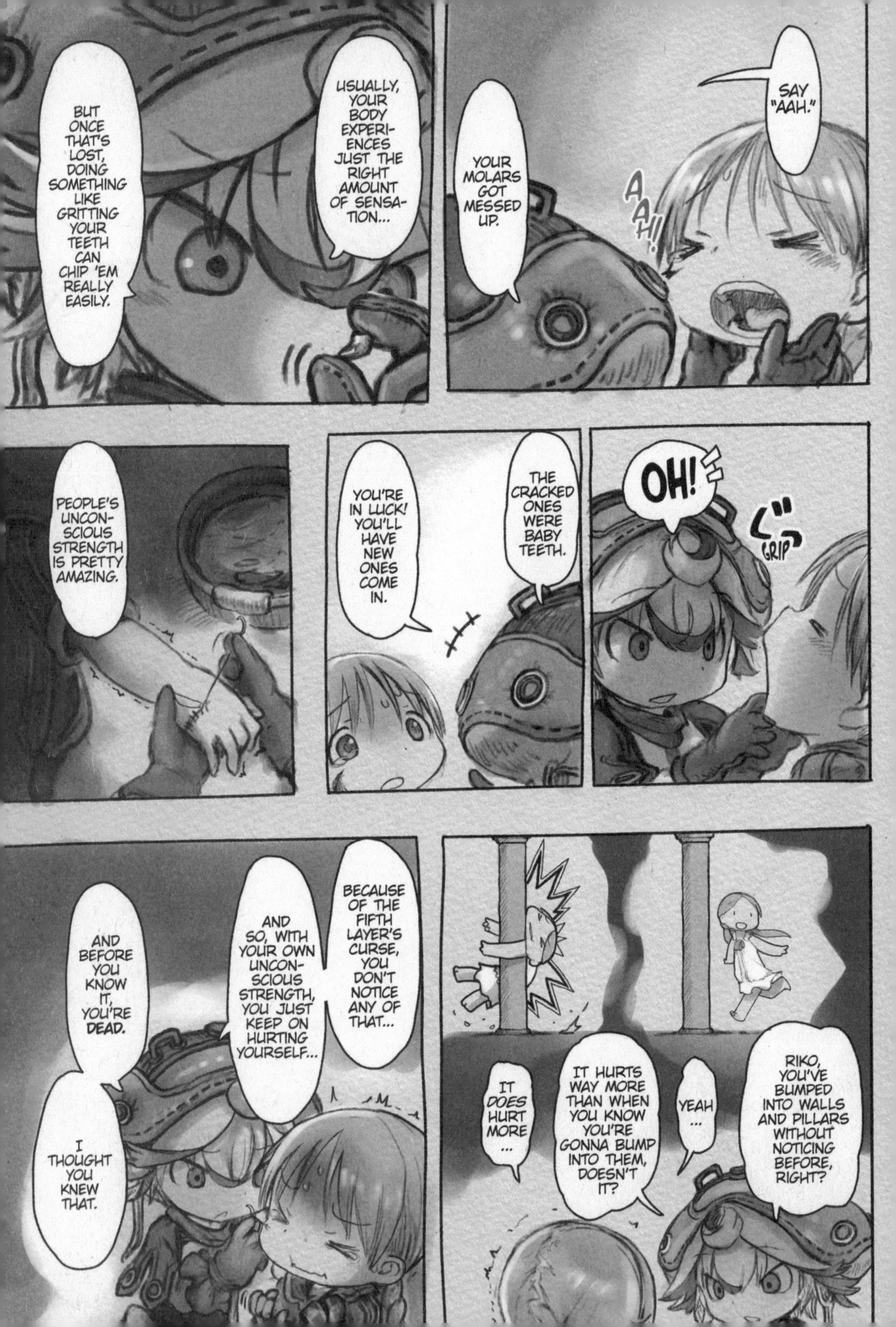
SAY "AAH."
AAH!!
YOUR MOLARS GOT MESSED UP.
USUALLY, YOUR BODY EXPERIENCES JUST THE RIGHT AMOUNT OF SENSATION...
BUT ONCE THAT'S LOST, DOING SOMETHING LIKE GRITTING YOUR TEETH CAN CHIP 'EM REALLY EASILY.
OH!
GRIP
THE CRACKED ONES WERE BABY TEETH.
YOU'RE IN LUCK! YOU'LL HAVE NEW ONES COME IN.
PEOPLE'S UNCONSCIOUS STRENGTH IS PRETTY AMAZING.
RIKO, YOU'VE BUMPED INTO WALLS AND PILLARS WITHOUT NOTICING BEFORE, RIGHT?
YEAH...
IT HURTS WAY MORE THAN WHEN YOU KNOW YOU'RE GONNA BUMP INTO THEM, DOESN'T IT?
IT *DOES* HURT MORE...
BECAUSE OF THE FIFTH LAYER'S CURSE, YOU DON'T NOTICE ANY OF THAT...
AND SO, WITH YOUR OWN UNCONSCIOUS STRENGTH, YOU JUST KEEP ON HURTING YOURSELF...
AND BEFORE YOU KNOW IT, YOU'RE **DEAD.**
I THOUGHT YOU KNEW THAT.

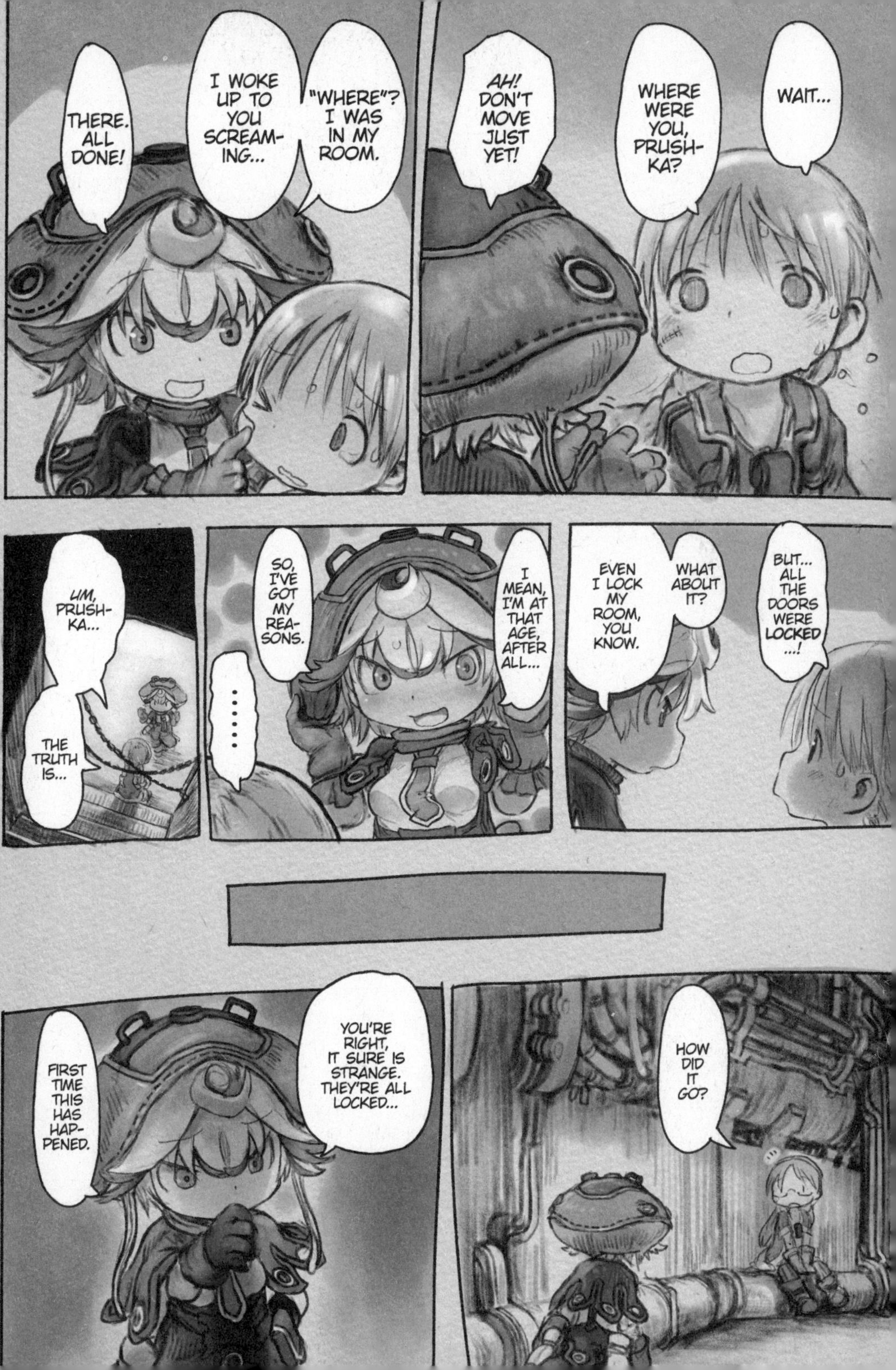
WAIT...
WHERE WERE YOU, PRUSHKA?
AH! DON'T MOVE JUST YET!
"WHERE"? I WAS IN MY ROOM.
I WOKE UP TO YOU SCREAMING...
THERE. ALL DONE!
BUT... ALL THE DOORS WERE LOCKED...!
WHAT ABOUT IT?
EVEN I LOCK MY ROOM, YOU KNOW.
I MEAN, I'M AT THAT AGE, AFTER ALL...
SO, I'VE GOT MY REASONS.
......
UM, PRUSHKA...
THE TRUTH IS...
HOW DID IT GO?
YOU'RE RIGHT, IT SURE IS STRANGE. THEY'RE ALL LOCKED...
FIRST TIME THIS HAS HAPPENED.

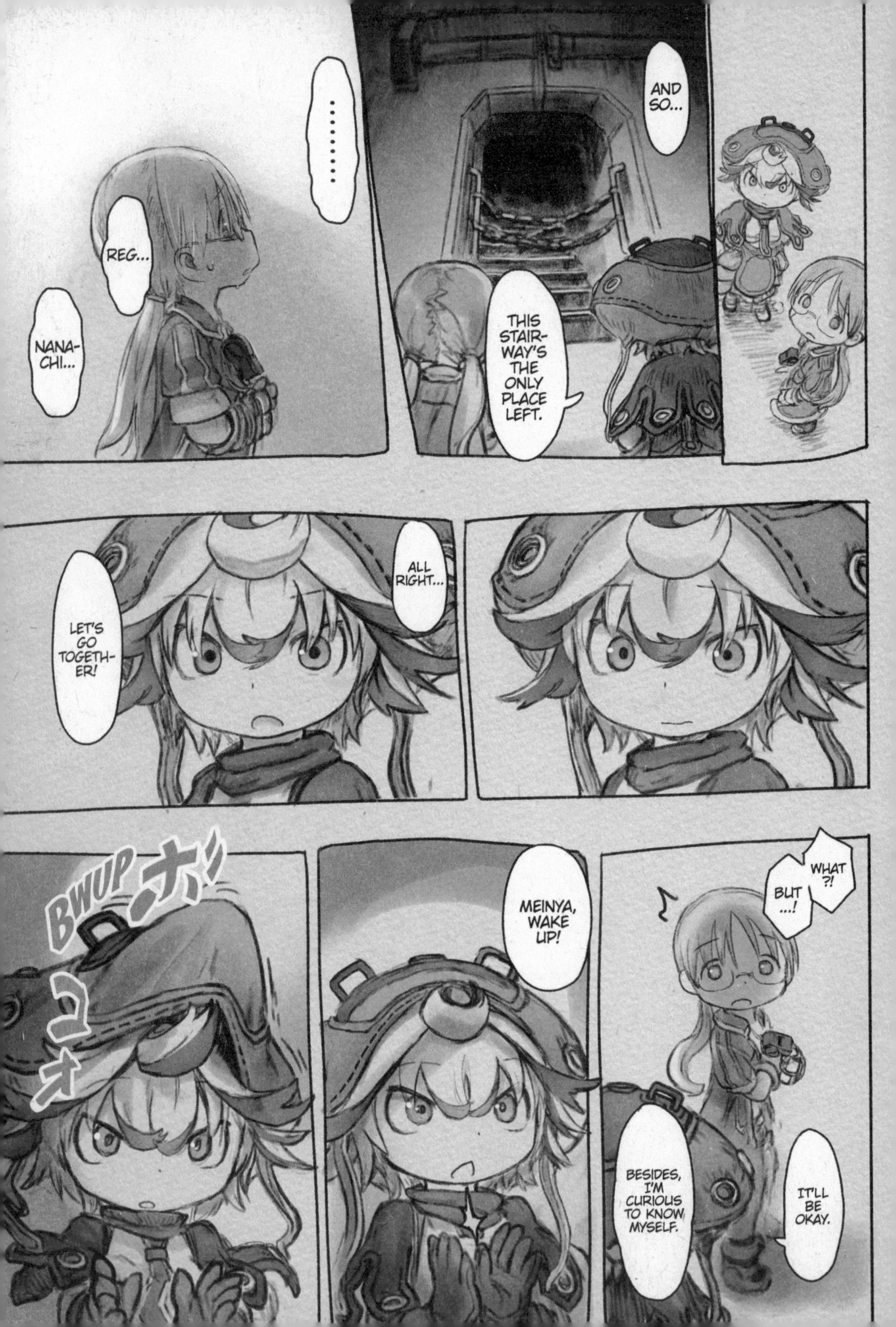
AND SO...
THIS STAIR-WAY'S THE ONLY PLACE LEFT.
......
REG...
NANA-CHI...
ALL RIGHT...
LET'S GO TOGETH-ER!
WHAT ?!
BUT ...!
IT'LL BE OKAY.
BESIDES, I'M CURIOUS TO KNOW MYSELF.
MEINYA, WAKE UP!
BWUP

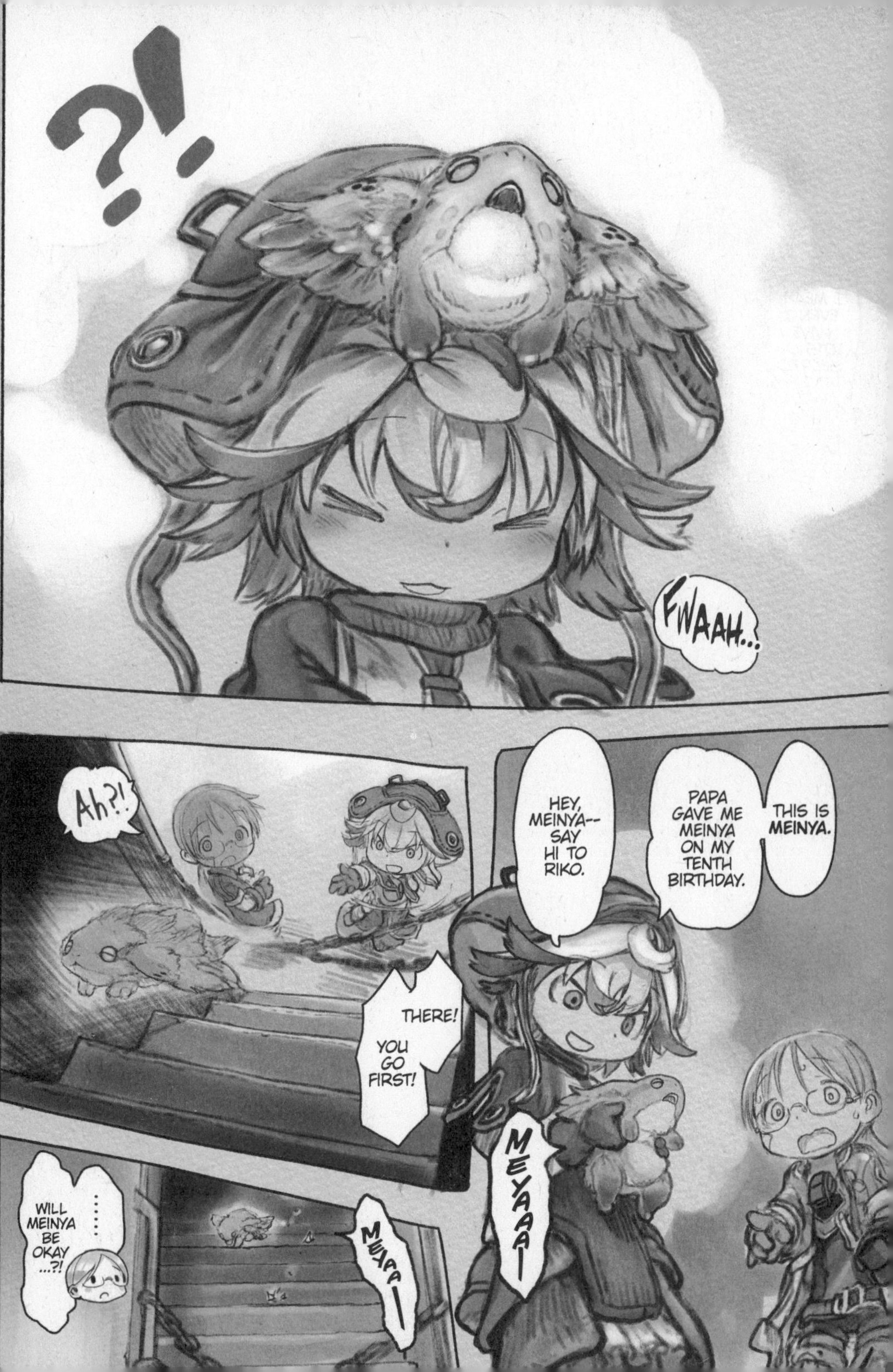
?!
FWAAH...
THIS IS MEINYA.
PAPA GAVE ME MEINYA ON MY TENTH BIRTHDAY.
HEY, MEINYA-- SAY HI TO RIKO.
THERE! YOU GO FIRST!
MEYAAA!
Ah?!
MEYAA!
......
WILL MEINYA BE OKAY ...?!

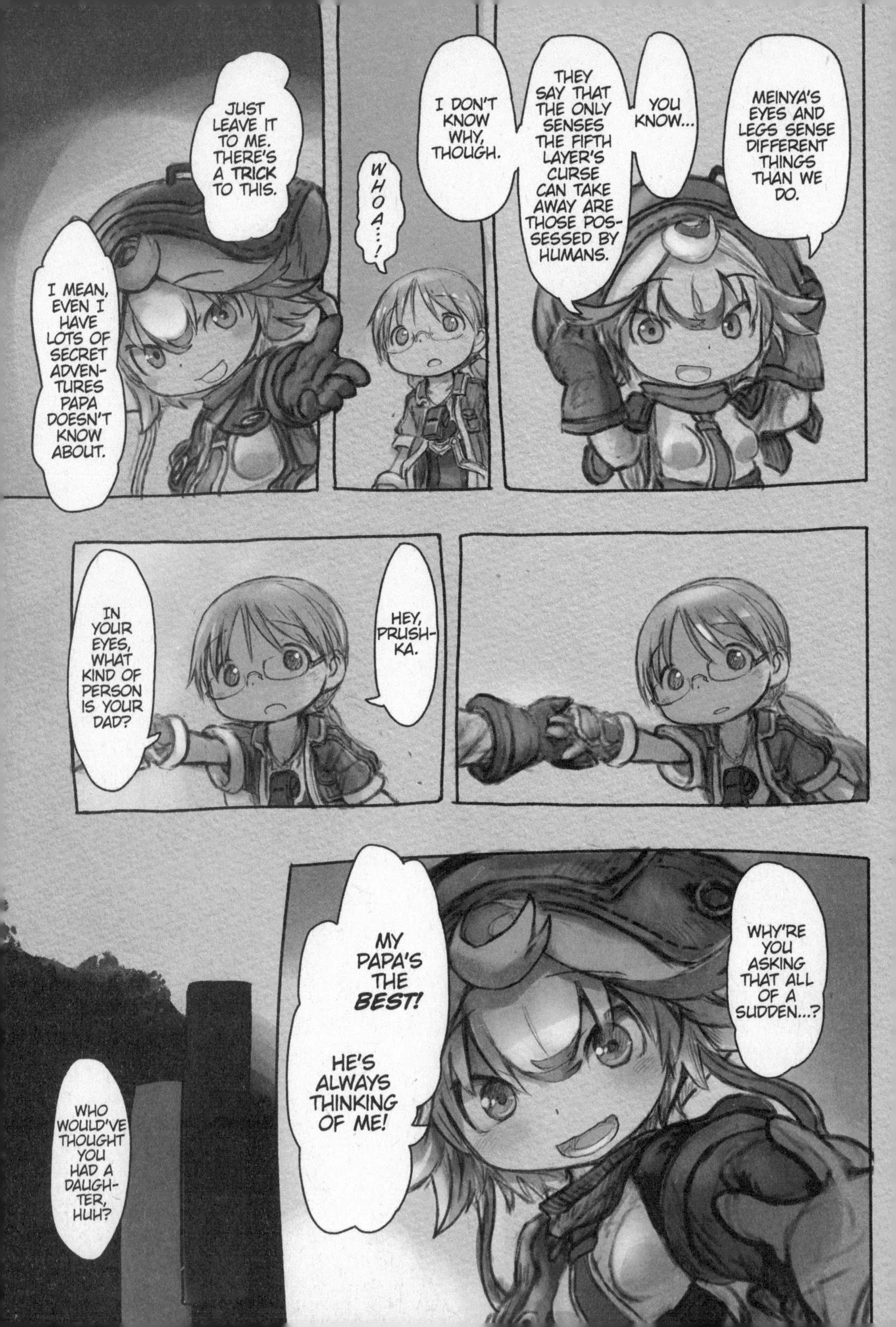
MEINYA'S EYES AND LEGS SENSE DIFFERENT THINGS THAN WE DO.
YOU KNOW...
THEY SAY THAT THE ONLY SENSES THE FIFTH LAYER'S CURSE CAN TAKE AWAY ARE THOSE POSSESSED BY HUMANS.
I DON'T KNOW WHY, THOUGH.
WHOA...!
JUST LEAVE IT TO ME. THERE'S A TRICK TO THIS.
I MEAN, EVEN I HAVE LOTS OF SECRET ADVENTURES PAPA DOESN'T KNOW ABOUT.
HEY, PRUSHKA.
IN YOUR EYES, WHAT KIND OF PERSON IS YOUR DAD?
WHY'RE YOU ASKING THAT ALL OF A SUDDEN...?
MY PAPA'S THE *BEST!*
HE'S ALWAYS THINKING OF ME!
WHO WOULD'VE THOUGHT YOU HAD A DAUGHTER, HUH?

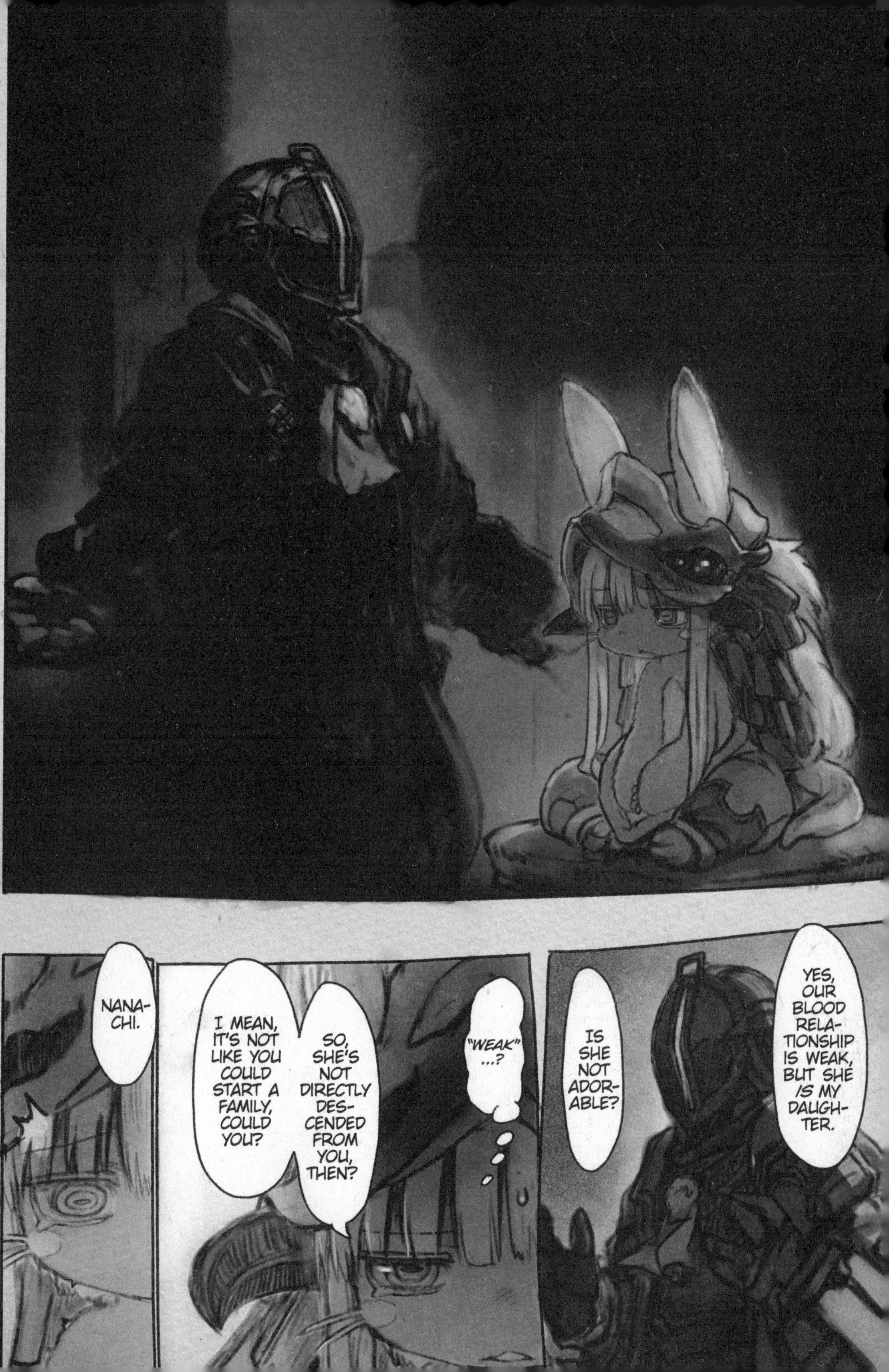
YES, OUR BLOOD RELATIONSHIP IS WEAK, BUT SHE IS MY DAUGHTER.
IS SHE NOT ADORABLE?
"WEAK" ...?
SO, SHE'S NOT DIRECTLY DESCENDED FROM YOU, THEN?
I MEAN, IT'S NOT LIKE YOU COULD START A FAMILY, COULD YOU?
NANACHI.

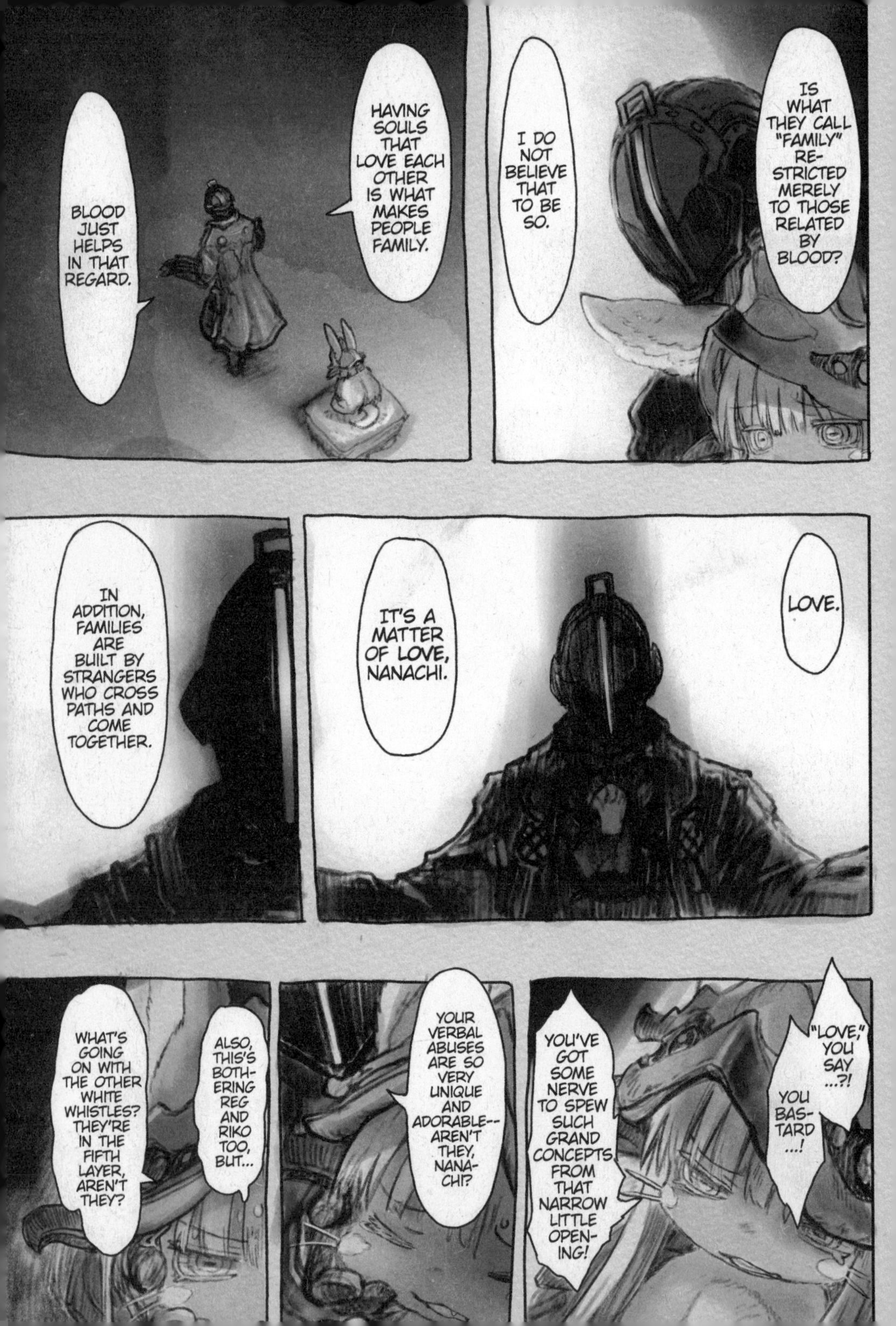
IS WHAT THEY CALL "FAMILY" RESTRICTED MERELY TO THOSE RELATED BY BLOOD?
I DO NOT BELIEVE THAT TO BE SO.
HAVING SOULS THAT LOVE EACH OTHER IS WHAT MAKES PEOPLE FAMILY.
BLOOD JUST HELPS IN THAT REGARD.
LOVE.
IT'S A MATTER OF LOVE, NANACHI.
IN ADDITION, FAMILIES ARE BUILT BY STRANGERS WHO CROSS PATHS AND COME TOGETHER.
"LOVE," YOU SAY ...?!
YOU BASTARD ...!
YOU'VE GOT SOME NERVE TO SPEW SUCH GRAND CONCEPTS FROM THAT NARROW LITTLE OPENING!
YOUR VERBAL ABUSES ARE SO VERY UNIQUE AND ADORABLE--AREN'T THEY, NANACHI?
ALSO, THIS'S BOTHERING REG AND RIKO TOO, BUT...
WHAT'S GOING ON WITH THE OTHER WHITE WHISTLES? THEY'RE IN THE FIFTH LAYER, AREN'T THEY?

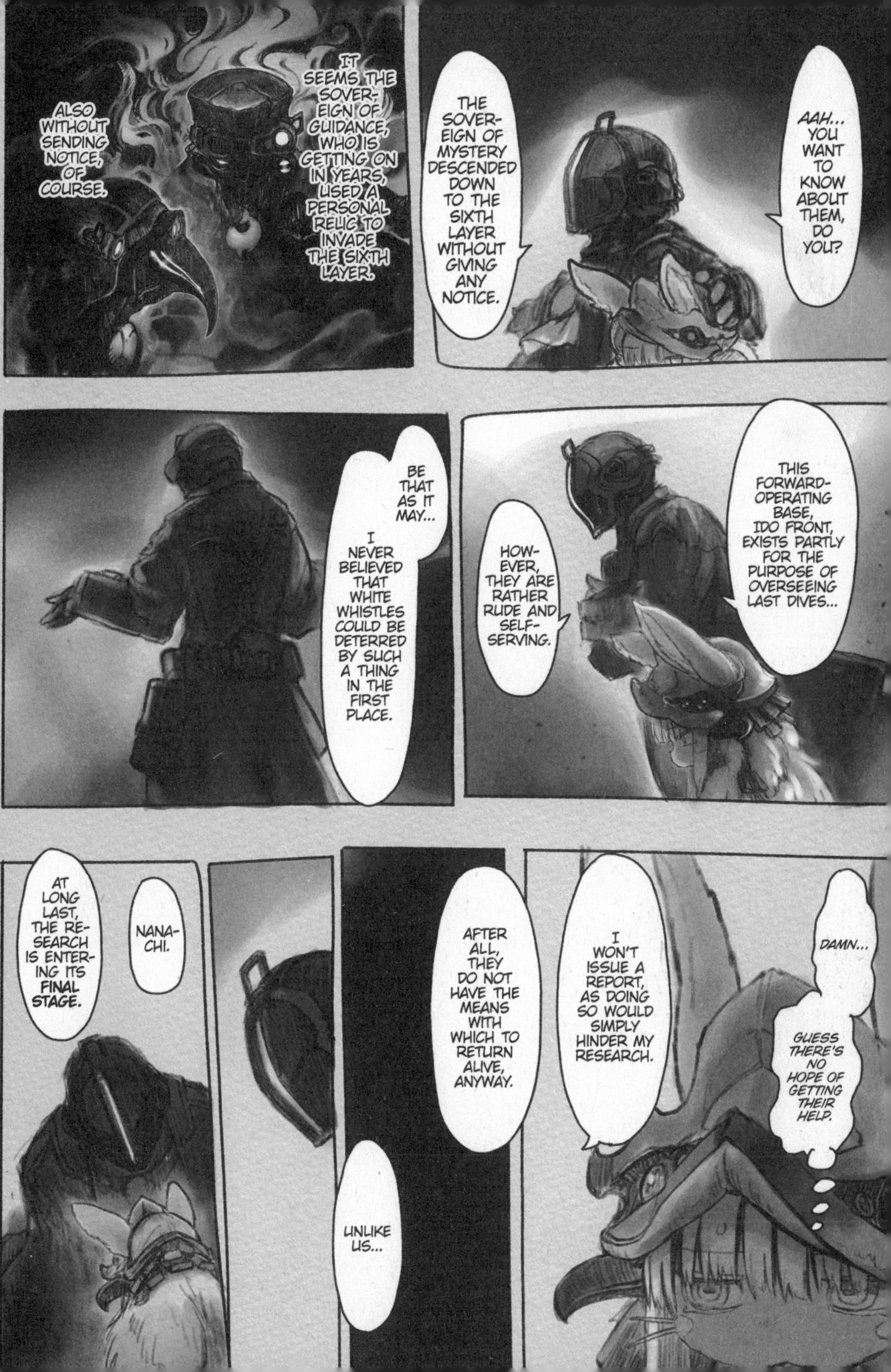
AAH... YOU WANT TO KNOW ABOUT THEM, DO YOU?
THE SOVER-EIGN OF MYSTERY DESCENDED DOWN TO THE SIXTH LAYER WITHOUT GIVING ANY NOTICE.
IT SEEMS, THE SOVER-EIGN OF GUIDANCE, WHO IS GETTING ON IN YEARS, USED A PERSONAL RELIC TO INVADE THE SIXTH LAYER.
ALSO WITHOUT SENDING NOTICE, OF COURSE.
THIS FORWARD-OPERATING BASE, IDO FRONT, EXISTS PARTLY FOR THE PURPOSE OF OVERSEEING LAST DIVES...
HOW-EVER, THEY ARE RATHER RUDE AND SELF-SERVING.
BE THAT AS IT MAY...
I NEVER BELIEVED THAT WHITE WHISTLES COULD BE DETERRED BY SUCH A THING IN THE FIRST PLACE.
DAMN...
GUESS THERE'S NO HOPE OF GETTING THEIR HELP.
I WON'T ISSUE A REPORT, AS DOING SO WOULD SIMPLY HINDER MY RESEARCH.
AFTER ALL, THEY DO NOT HAVE THE MEANS WITH WHICH TO RETURN ALIVE, ANYWAY.
UNLIKE US...
NANA-CHI.
AT LONG LAST, THE RE-SEARCH IS ENTER-ING ITS FINAL STAGE.

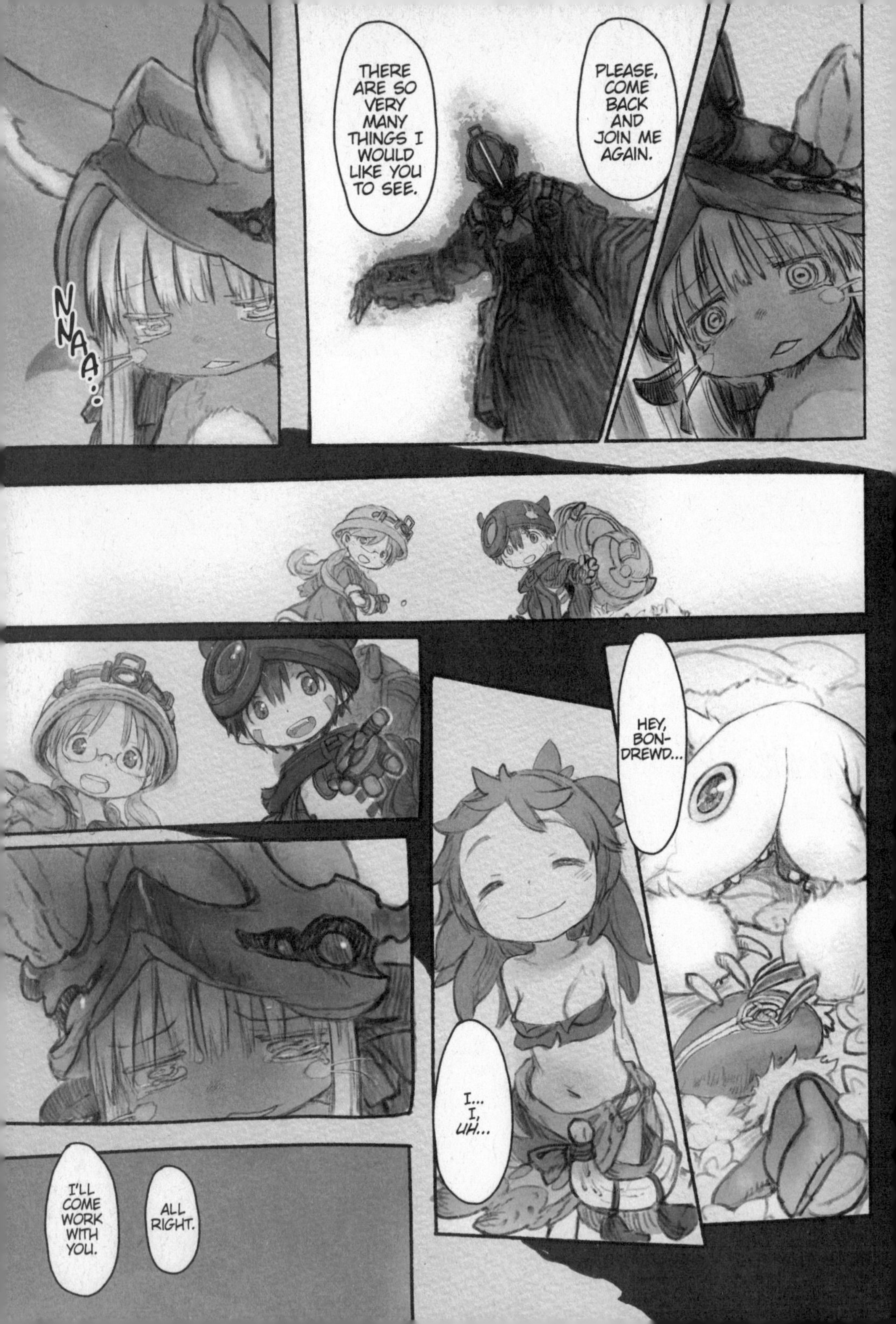
PLEASE, COME BACK AND JOIN ME AGAIN.
THERE ARE SO VERY MANY THINGS I WOULD LIKE YOU TO SEE.
NNAA..
HEY, BON-DREWD...
I... I, UH...
ALL RIGHT.
I'LL COME WORK WITH YOU.

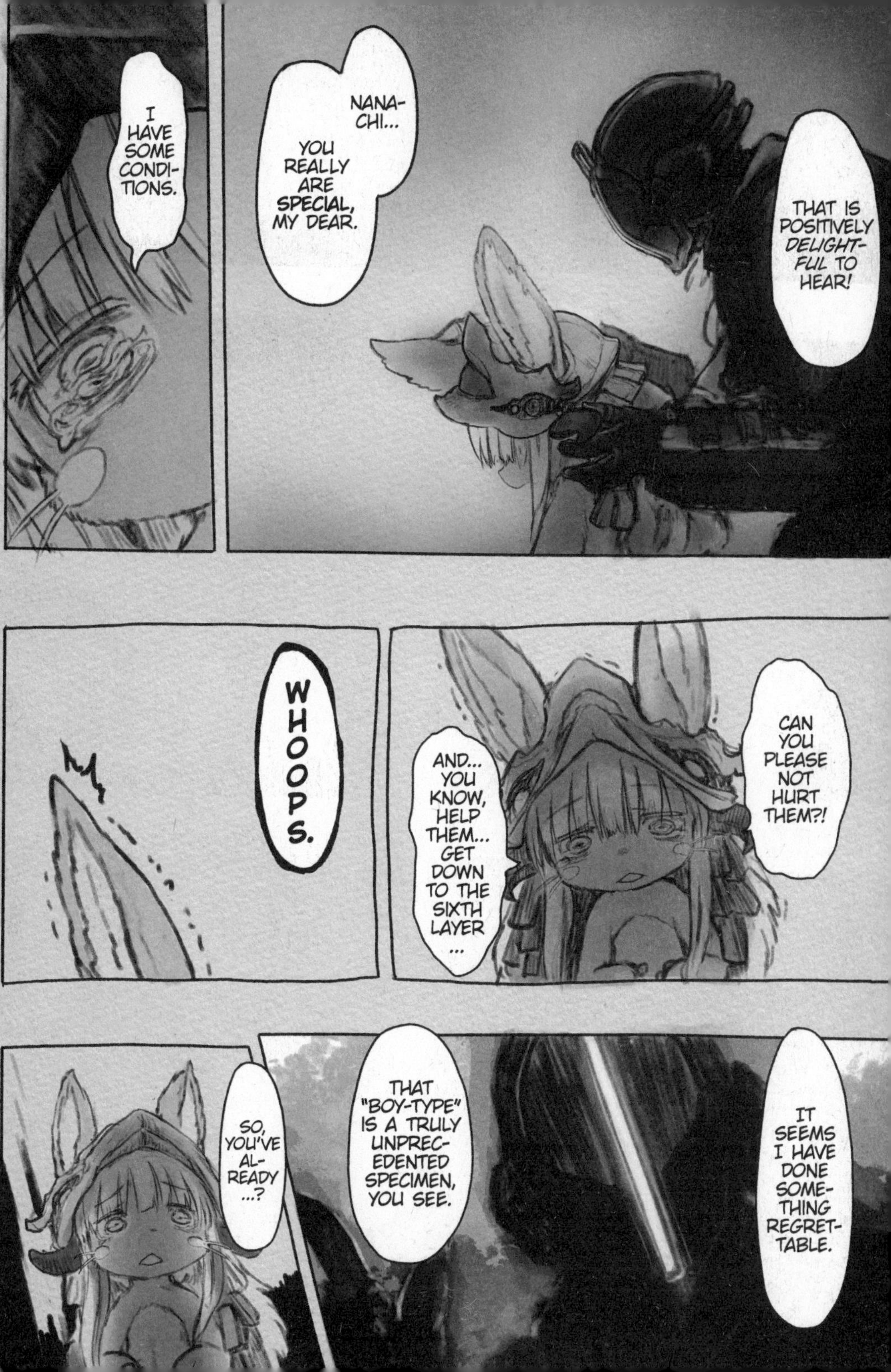

THAT IS POSITIVELY DELIGHTFUL TO HEAR!
NANACHI... YOU REALLY ARE SPECIAL, MY DEAR.
I HAVE SOME CONDITIONS.
CAN YOU PLEASE NOT HURT THEM?!
AND... YOU KNOW, HELP THEM... GET DOWN TO THE SIXTH LAYER ...
WHOOPS.
IT SEEMS I HAVE DONE SOMETHING REGRETTABLE.
THAT "BOY-TYPE" IS A TRULY UNPRECEDENTED SPECIMEN, YOU SEE.
SO, YOU'VE ALREADY ...?

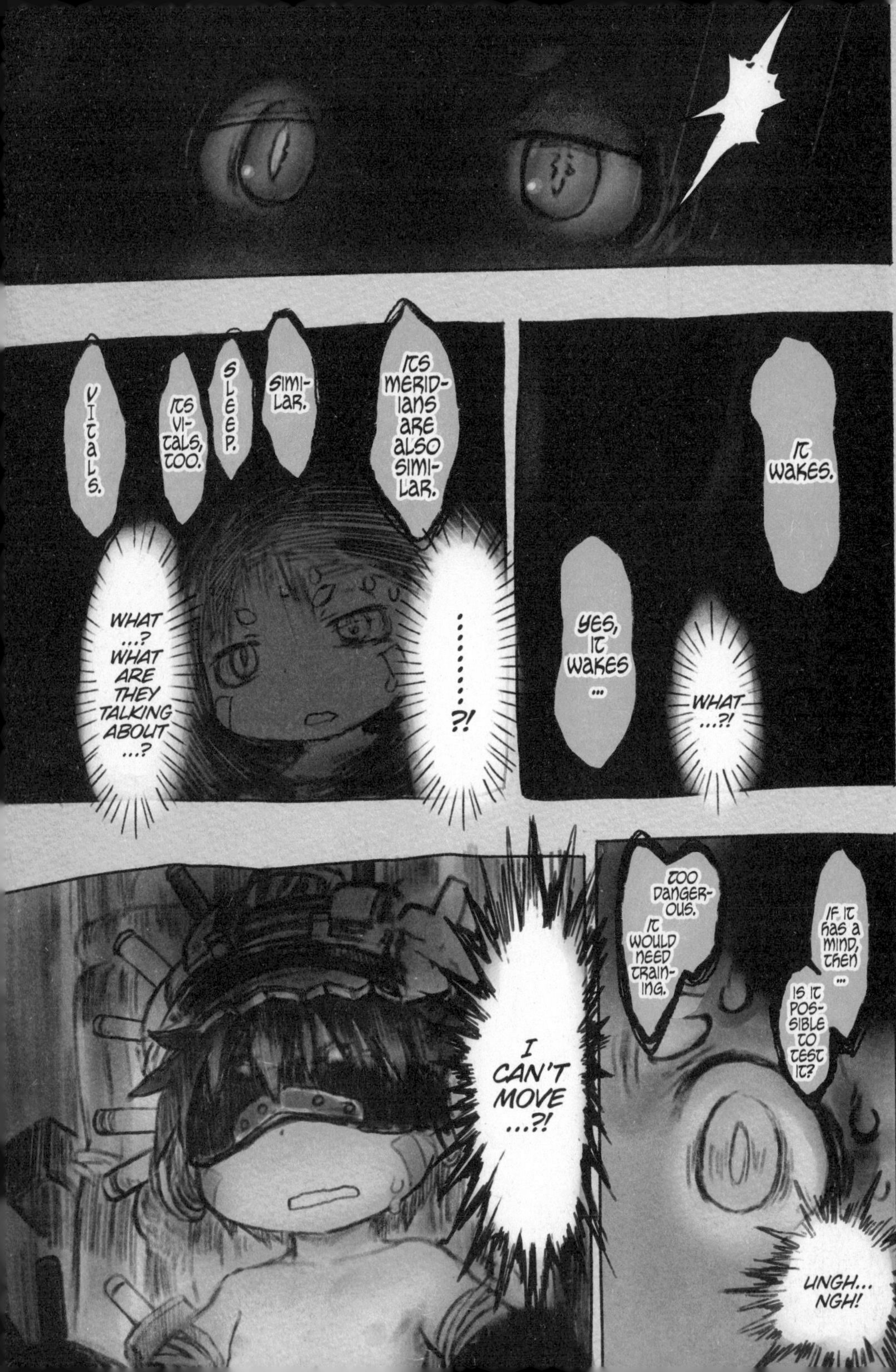
IT WAKES.
YES, IT WAKES...
WHAT...?!
ITS MERIDIANS ARE ALSO SIMILAR.
SIMILAR.
SLEEP.
ITS VITALS, TOO.
VITALS.
......?!
WHAT...? WHAT ARE THEY TALKING ABOUT...?
IF IT HAS A MIND, THEN...
TOO DANGEROUS. IT WOULD NEED TRAINING.
IS IT POSSIBLE TO TEST IT?
UNGH... NGH!
I CAN'T MOVE...?!

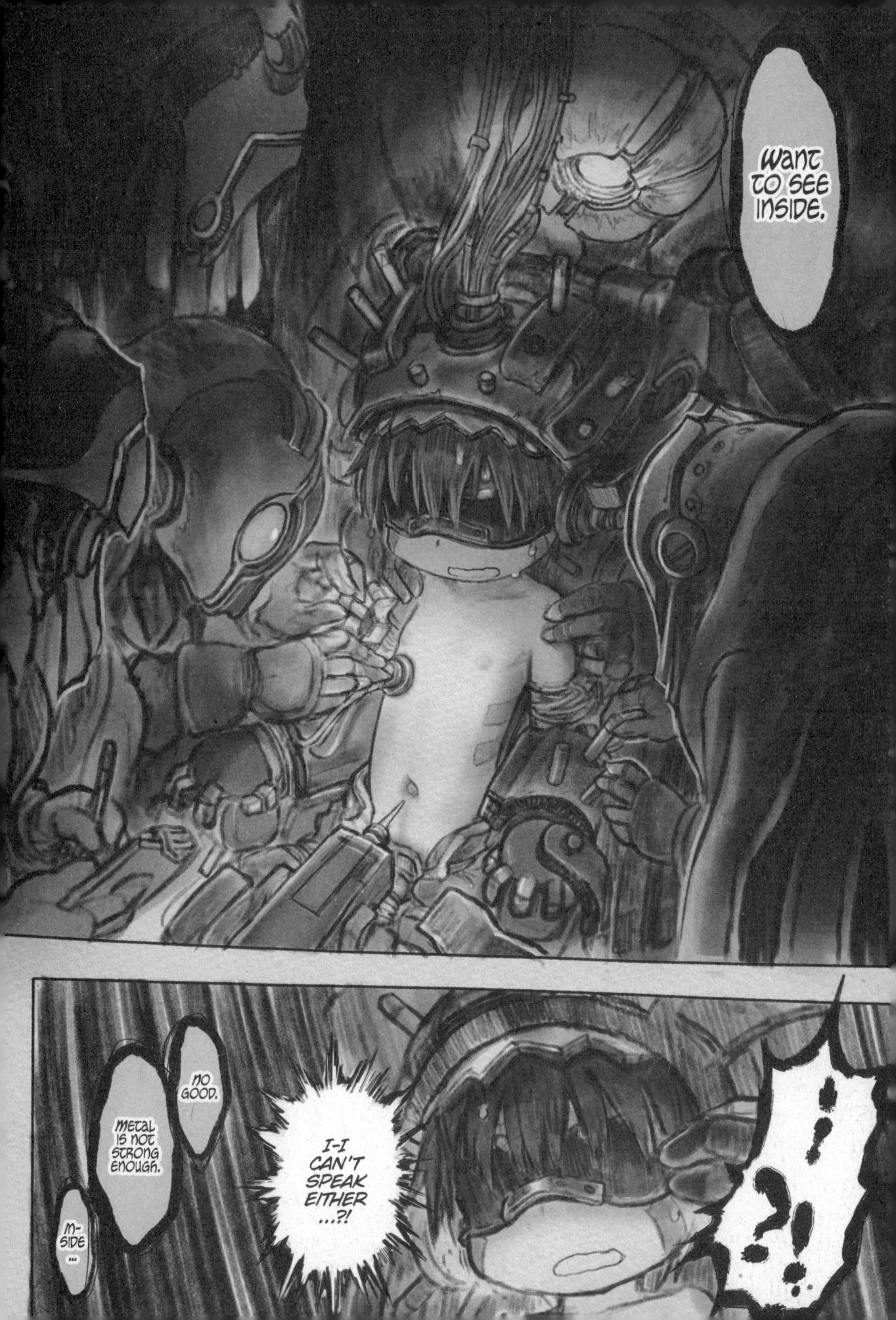
WANT TO SEE INSIDE.
!?!?
I-I CAN'T SPEAK EITHER ...?!
NO GOOD.
METAL IS NOT STRONG ENOUGH.
M-SIDE ...

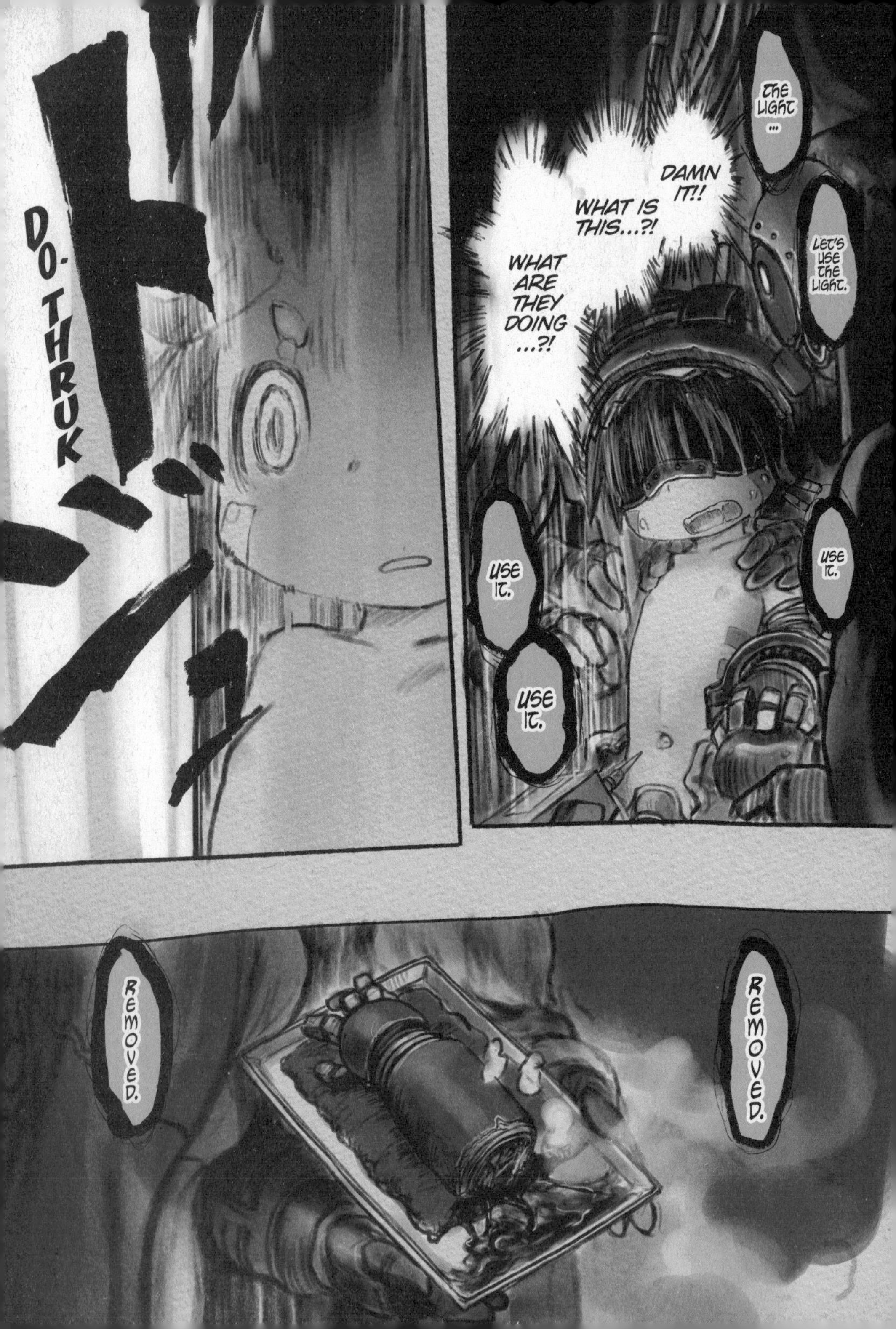
THE LIGHT ...
LET'S USE THE LIGHT.
DAMN IT!!
WHAT IS THIS...?!
WHAT ARE THEY DOING ...?!
USE IT.
USE IT.
USE IT.
DO-THRUK
REMOVED.
REMOVED.

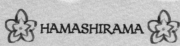

HAMASHIRAMA

THESE STRANGE-LOOKING, FREE-SWIMMING AQUATIC CREATURES ARE WIDESPREAD IN THE FLOATING SEA OF THE DEPTHS' FIFTH LAYER. THEY ARE SAID TO EAT THE DETRITUS OF AQUATIC CREATURES.

DANGER LEVEL: ★ (INSIGNIFICANT)

HOWEVER, THIS ONLY APPLIES WHEN FISHING FOR THEM FROM THE WATER'S SURFACE. DIVING DEEP INTO THE WATERS OF THE DEPTHS' FIFTH LAYER IS SYNONYMOUS WITH SUICIDE.

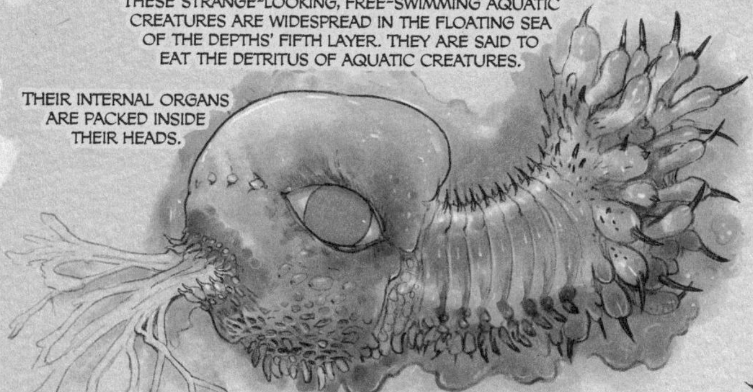

THEIR INTERNAL ORGANS ARE PACKED INSIDE THEIR HEADS.

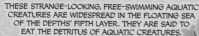

MANY OF THE AQUATIC CREATURES OF THE FIFTH LAYER, INCLUDING THE HAMASHIRAMA, ARE SAID TO BE UNAFFECTED BY THE STRAINS OF ASCENDING. THESE CREATURES POSSESS MANY SENSORY ORGANS THAT THE ORGANISMS OF THE SURFACE DO NOT.

THEY HAVE BEEN REPORTED TO SPEW THEIR VISCOUS LIQUID INNARDS TO IMMOBILIZE PREDATORS AND THEN USE THEM AS LIVING SHIELDS.

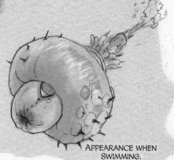

APPEARANCE WHEN SWIMMING.

AMARANTHINE-DECEPTOR

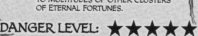

THESE WINGED INSECTS ARE SAID TO LIVE IN THE IMPENETRABLE TERRITORY THAT IS THE DEPTHS' SIXTH LAYER. THEIR EXISTENCE IS KNOWN ONLY THROUGH A VERY SMALL NUMBER OF REPORTS PROVIDED BY WHITE WHISTLES.

THE DECIDING FACTOR WAS LYZA'S DETAILED SKETCHES AND ROUGH ECOLOGICAL SURVEYS.

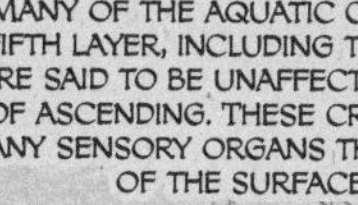

THE STRING OF DISAPPEARANCES IN THE FOURTH LAYER'S "GARDEN OF THE FLOWERS OF FORTITUDE" BORE A CLOSE RESEMBLANCE TO THE REPORTS WRITTEN BY LYZA, THE SOVEREIGN OF ANNIHILATION, SO IT WAS CONCLUDED THE SAME SPECIES, THE AMARANTHINE-DECEPTOR, WAS RESPONSIBLE IN BOTH CASES.

THE CAVE RAIDER GUILD REQUESTED THAT BONDREWD, THE SOVEREIGN OF DAWN, IMMEDIATELY INVESTIGATE AND REMEDY THE SITUATION.

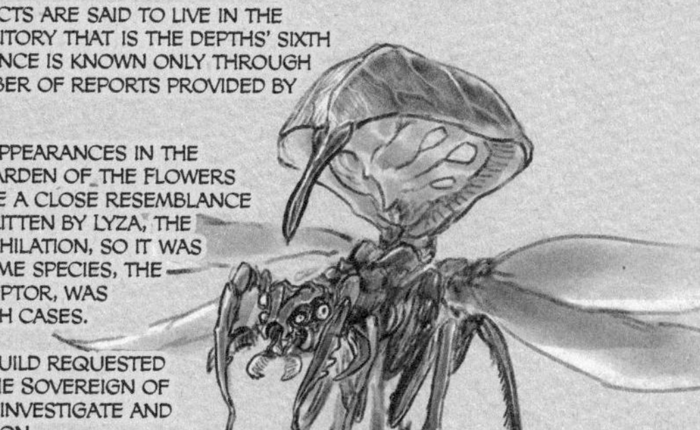

THE REASON FOR THEIR ASCENSION TO THE FOURTH LAYER IS UNKNOWN. IT IS FEARED THAT THEY WILL SPREAD TO MULTITUDES OF OTHER CLUSTERS OF ETERNAL FORTUNES.

DANGER LEVEL: ★★★★★ (ABSURD)

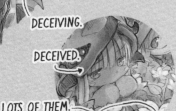

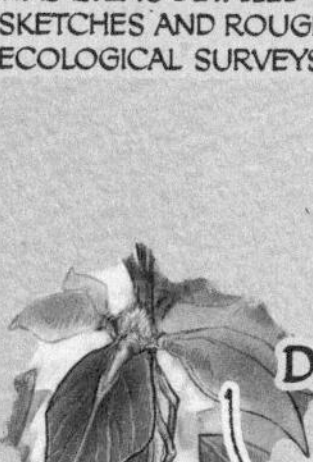

DECEIVING.
DECEIVED.
LOTS OF THEM.

ETERNAL FORTUNES, THE "FLOWERS OF FORTITUDE" THAT ARE THE SYMBOL OF THE ABYSS, ALSO TURN UP AS FOSSILS FROM TENS OF THOUSANDS OF YEARS AGO. THESE GUYS TURN ETERNAL FORTUNES, WHICH BLOOM JUST ABOUT EVERYWHERE, INTO DEATH TRAPS. THEY'RE HORRIBLE BADDIES THAT ETERNALLY DECEIVE.

WHEN CAMOUFLAGED, THEY'RE IN A DORMANT STATE AND CAN DECEIVE EVEN THOSE THAT "READ CONSCIOUSNESSES BASED ON THE FLOW OF THE FORCE FIELD," SUCH AS PREDATORS FROM THE DEEP LAYERS AND ME.

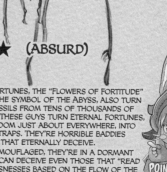

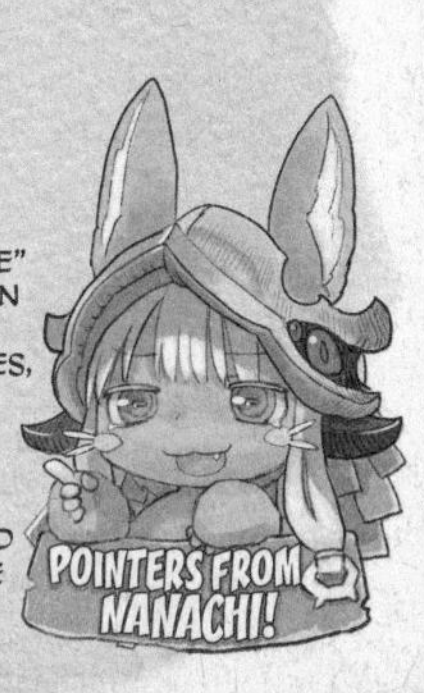

POINTERS FROM NANACHI!

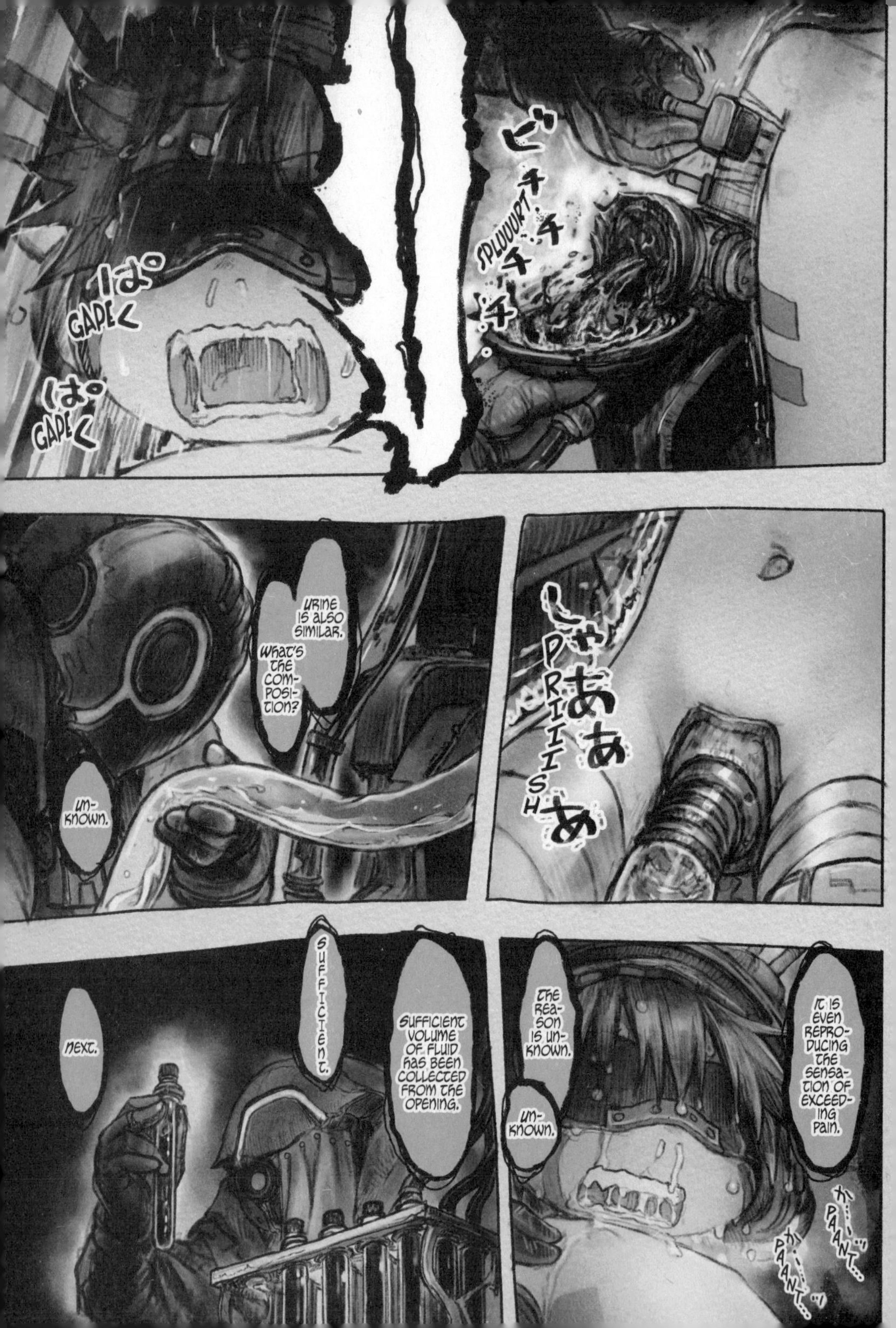
ビチチチチ
SPLUUURT.
はぱ
GAPE
はぱ
GAPE
しゃあああ
SPRIIISH
Urine is also similar.
What's the composition?
Unknown.
It is even reproducing the sensation of exceeding pain.
The reason is unknown.
Unknown.
パ……
PAANT...
パ……
PAANT...
Sufficient volume of fluid has been collected from the opening.
Sufficient.
Next.

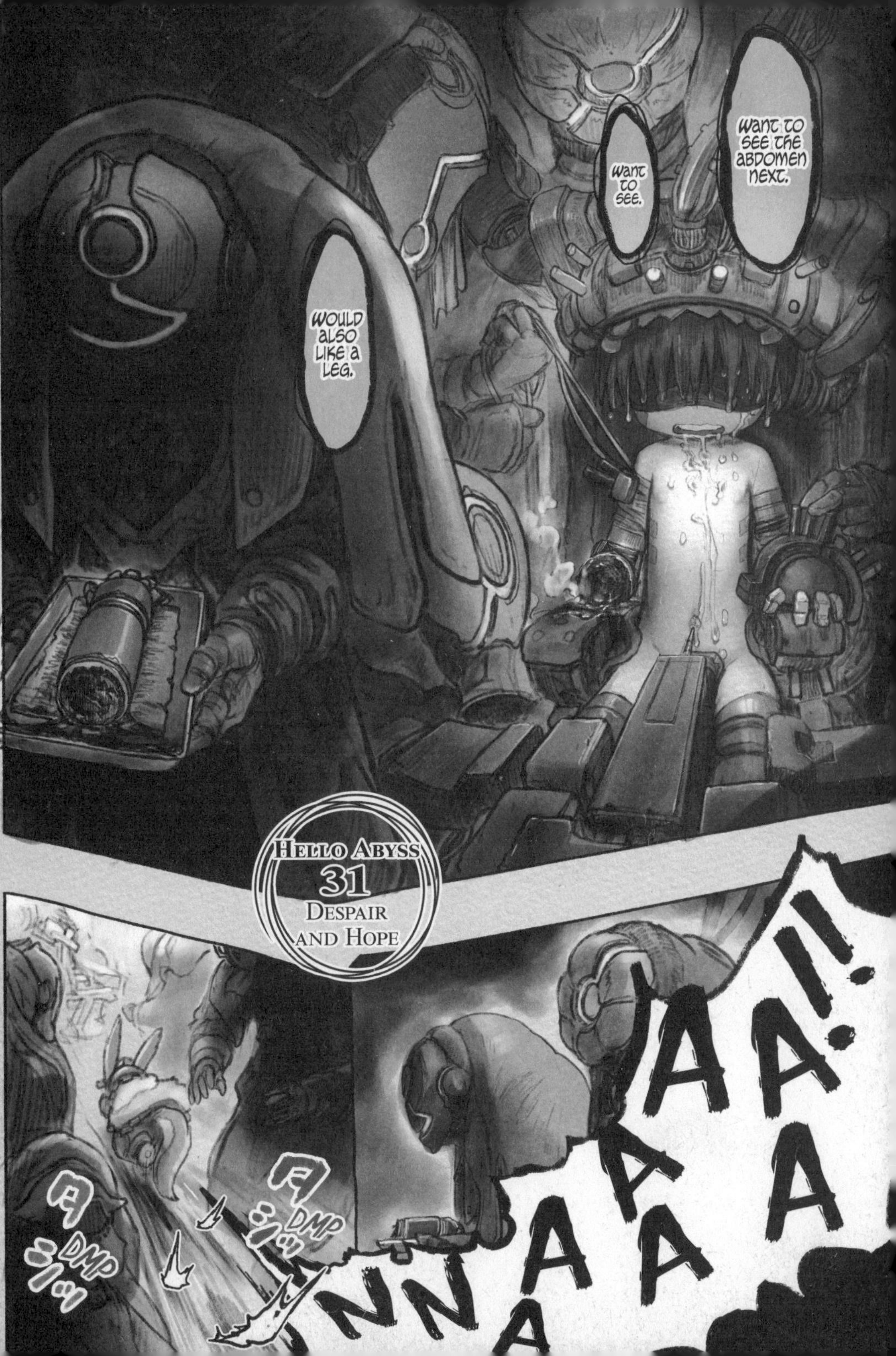
Want to see the abdomen next.
Want to see.
Would also like a leg.
Hello Abyss
31
Despair and Hope
NNAAAAAAAAAA!!
DMP
DMP

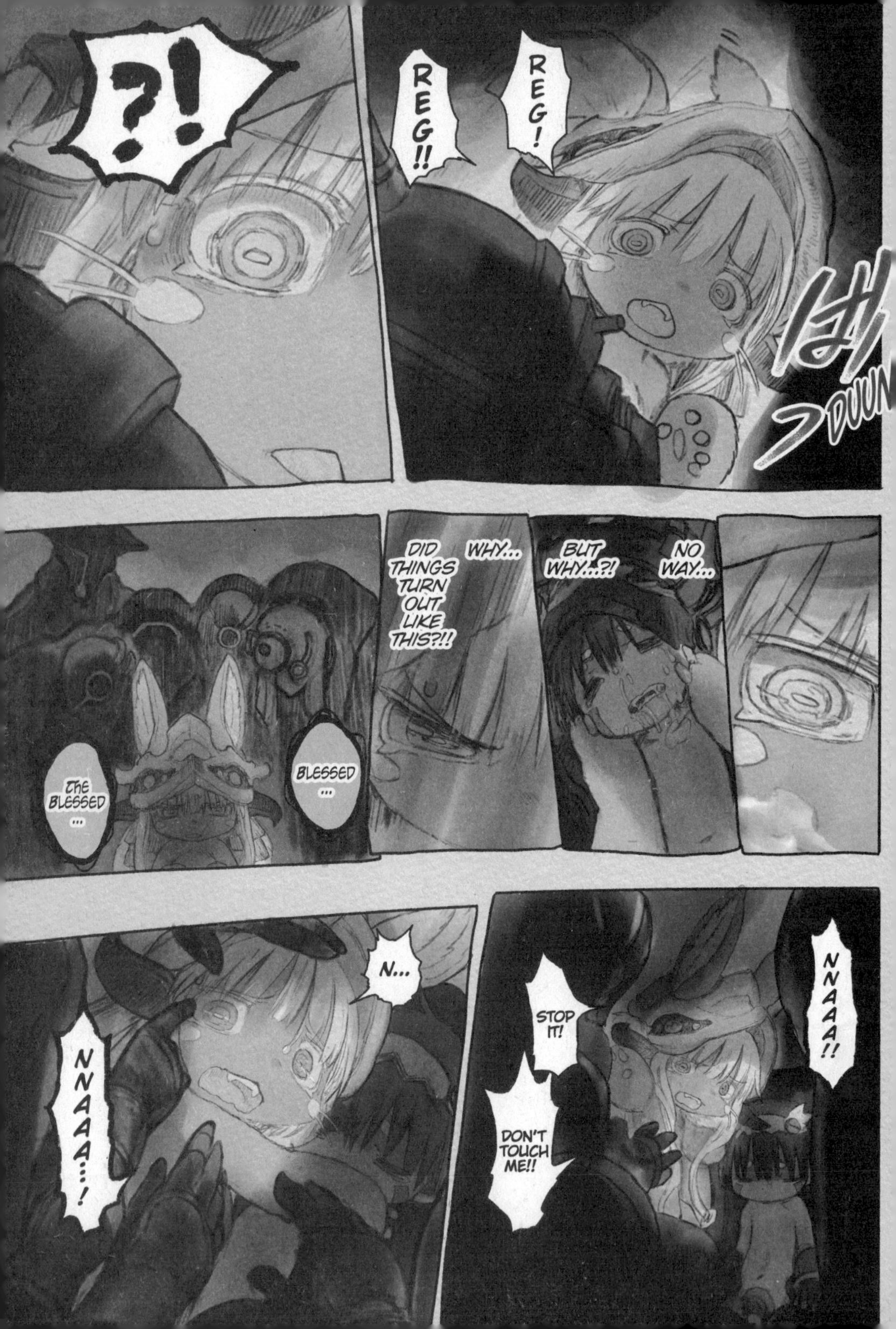
REG!
REG!!
はっ
DUUN
?!
NO WAY...
BUT WHY...?!
WHY...
DID THINGS TURN OUT LIKE THIS?!!
BLESSED...
THE BLESSED...
NNAAAA!!
STOP IT!
DON'T TOUCH ME!!
N...
NNAAAA...!

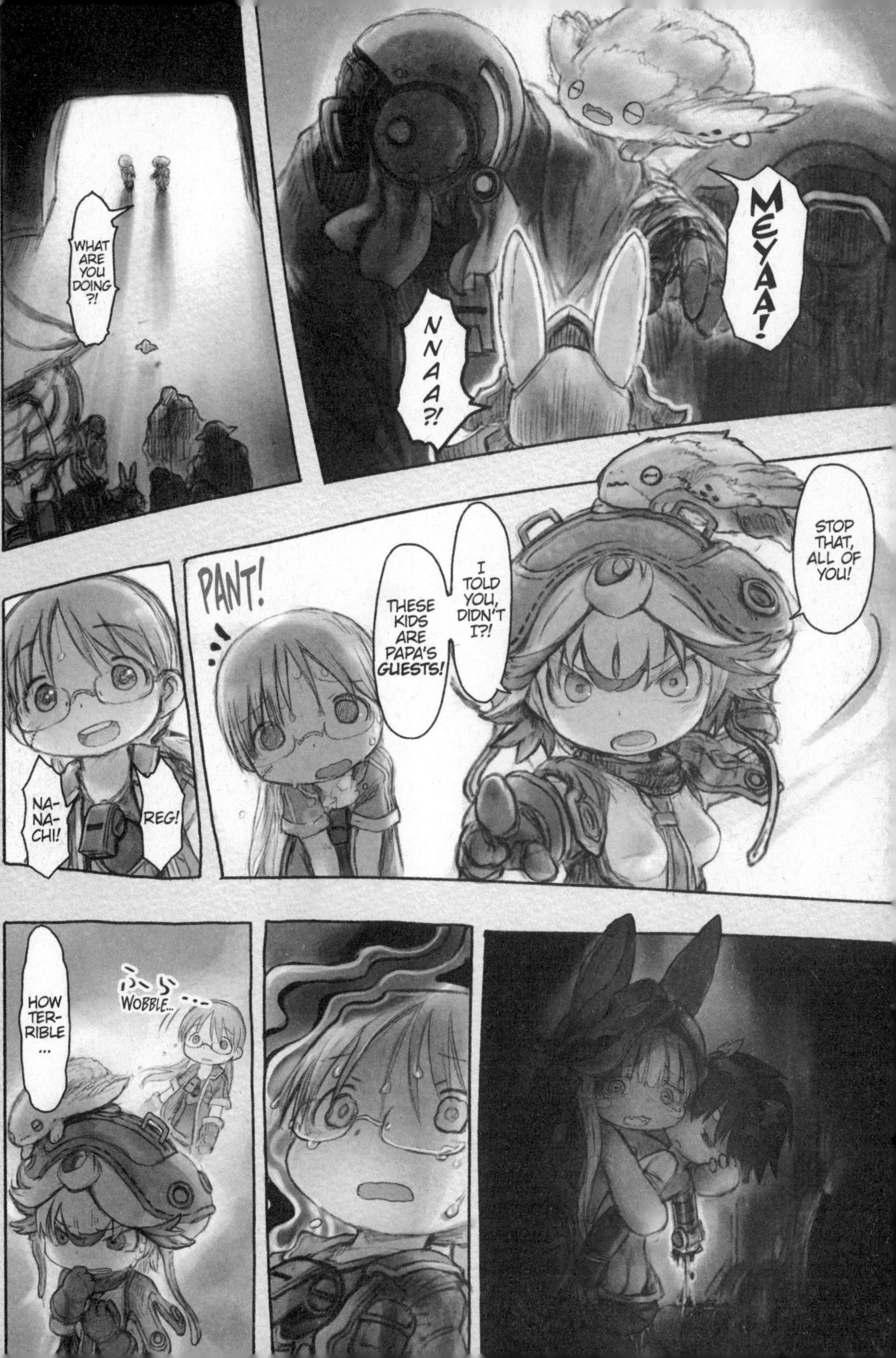
MEYAA!
NNAAA?!
WHAT ARE YOU DOING?!
STOP THAT, ALL OF YOU!
I TOLD YOU, DIDN'T I?!
THESE KIDS ARE PAPA'S GUESTS!
PANT!
REG!
NANACHI!
ふら…
WOBBLE...
HOW TERRIBLE...

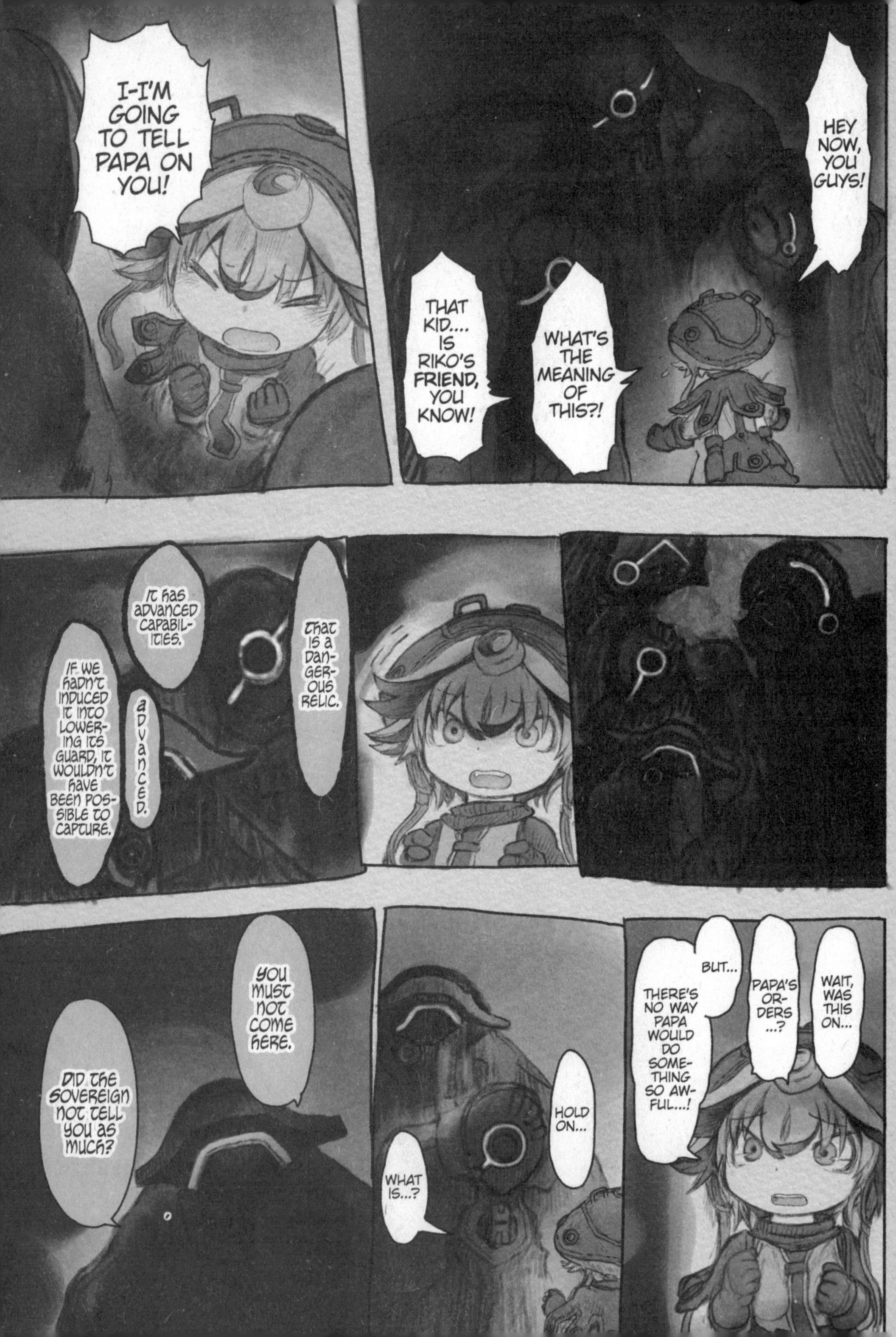
HEY NOW, YOU GUYS!
WHAT'S THE MEANING OF THIS?!
THAT KID.... IS RIKO'S FRIEND, YOU KNOW!
I-I'M GOING TO TELL PAPA ON YOU!
That is a DANGEROUS RELIC.
It has advanced capabilities.
advanced.
If we hadn't induced it into lowering its guard, it wouldn't have been possible to capture.
WAIT, WAS THIS ON...
PAPA'S ORDERS...?
BUT...
THERE'S NO WAY PAPA WOULD DO SOMETHING SO AWFUL...!
HOLD ON...
WHAT IS...?
You must not come here.
Did the Sovereign not tell you as much?

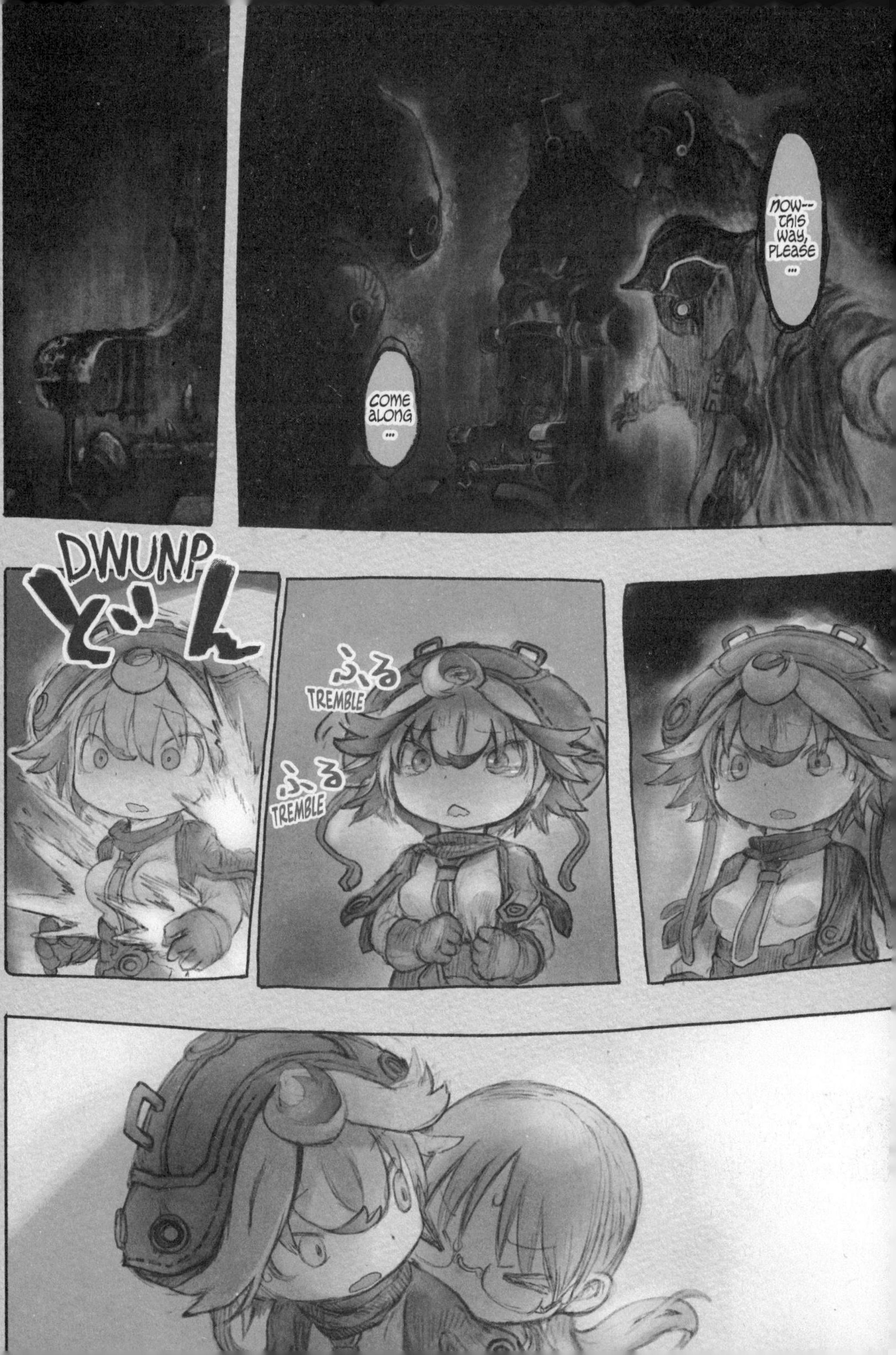
Now--this way, please...
Come along...
ふる
TREMBLE
ふる
TREMBLE
DWUNP
どーん

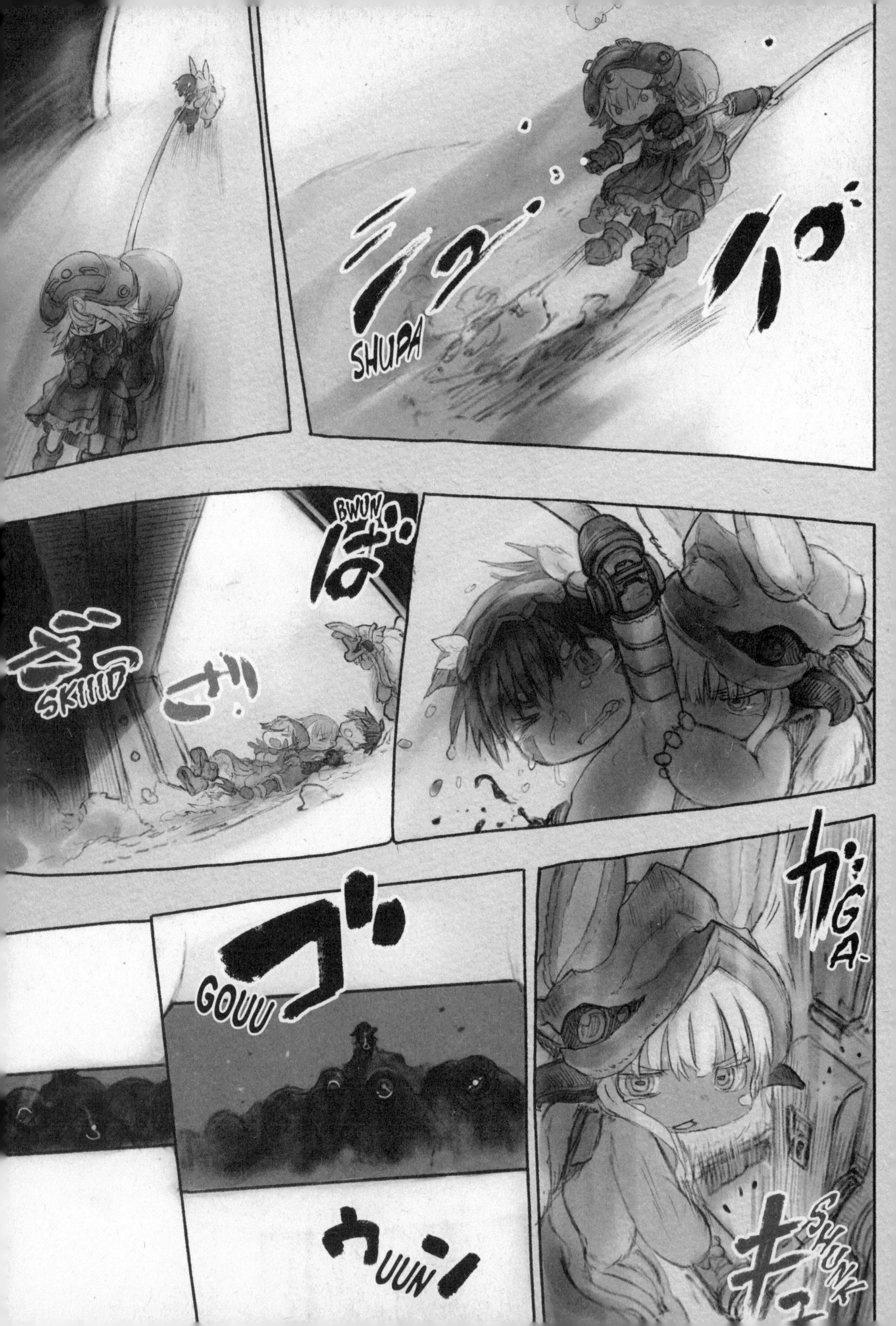

SHUPA
BWUN
SKIIID
GA-
SHUNK
GOUU
UUUN

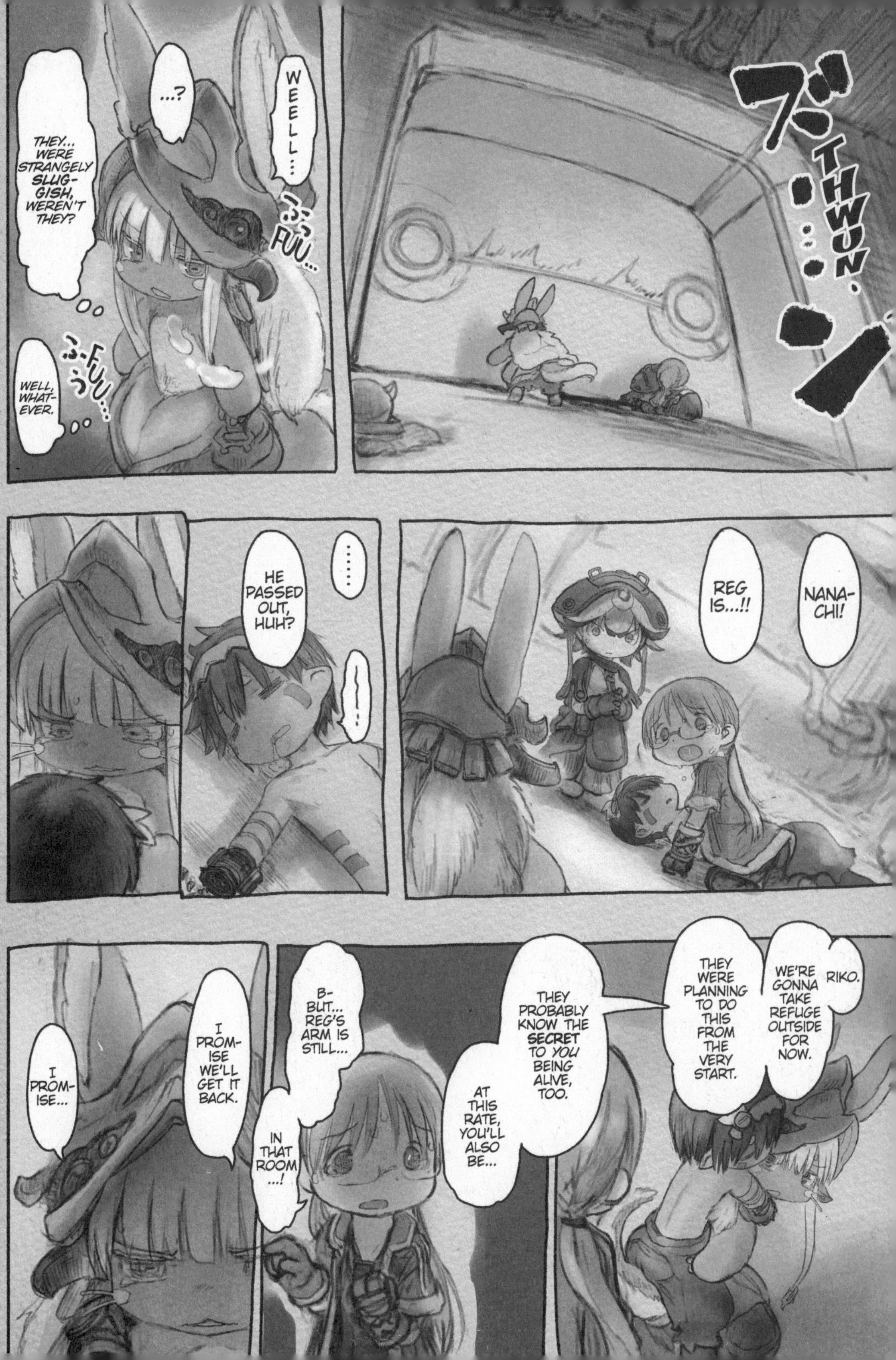
ブ
THWUN...
ン
WEELL...
...?
ふぅ FUU...
THEY... WERE STRANGELY **SLUG-GISH**, WEREN'T THEY?
ふぅ FUU...
WELL, WHATEVER.
NANA-CHI!
REG IS...!!
......
HE PASSED OUT, HUH?
...!
RIKO.
WE'RE GONNA TAKE REFUGE OUTSIDE FOR NOW.
THEY WERE PLANNING TO DO THIS FROM THE VERY START.
THEY PROBABLY KNOW THE **SECRET** TO *YOU* BEING ALIVE, TOO.
AT THIS RATE, YOU'LL ALSO BE...
B-BUT... REG'S ARM IS STILL...
IN THAT ROOM...!
I PROM-ISE WE'LL GET IT BACK.
I PROM-ISE...

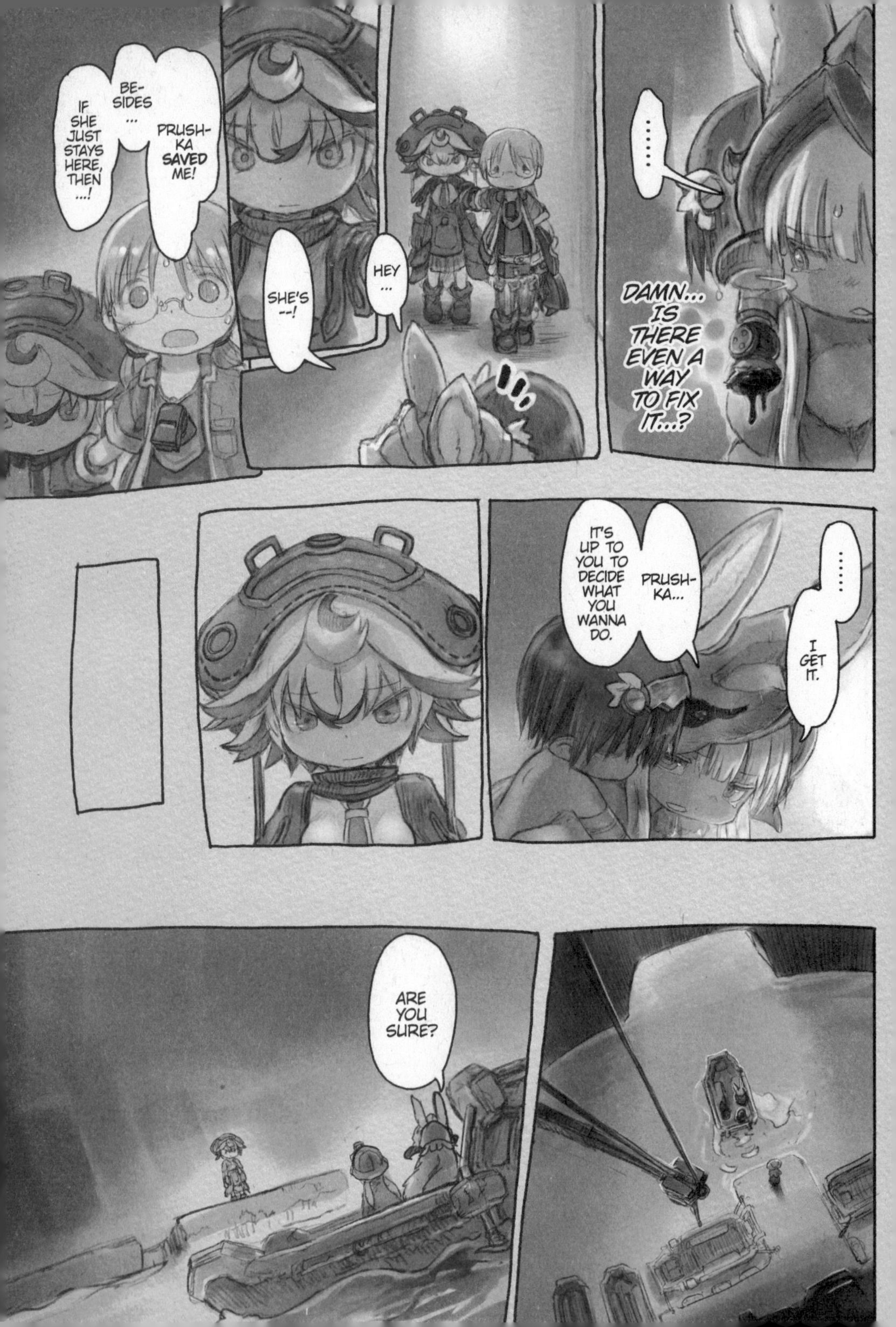
......
DAMN... IS THERE EVEN A WAY TO FIX IT...?
HEY...
SHE'S--!
!!
PRUSH-KA SAVED ME!
BE-SIDES...
IF SHE JUST STAYS HERE, THEN...!
......
I GET IT.
PRUSH-KA...
IT'S UP TO YOU TO DECIDE WHAT YOU WANNA DO.
ARE YOU SURE?

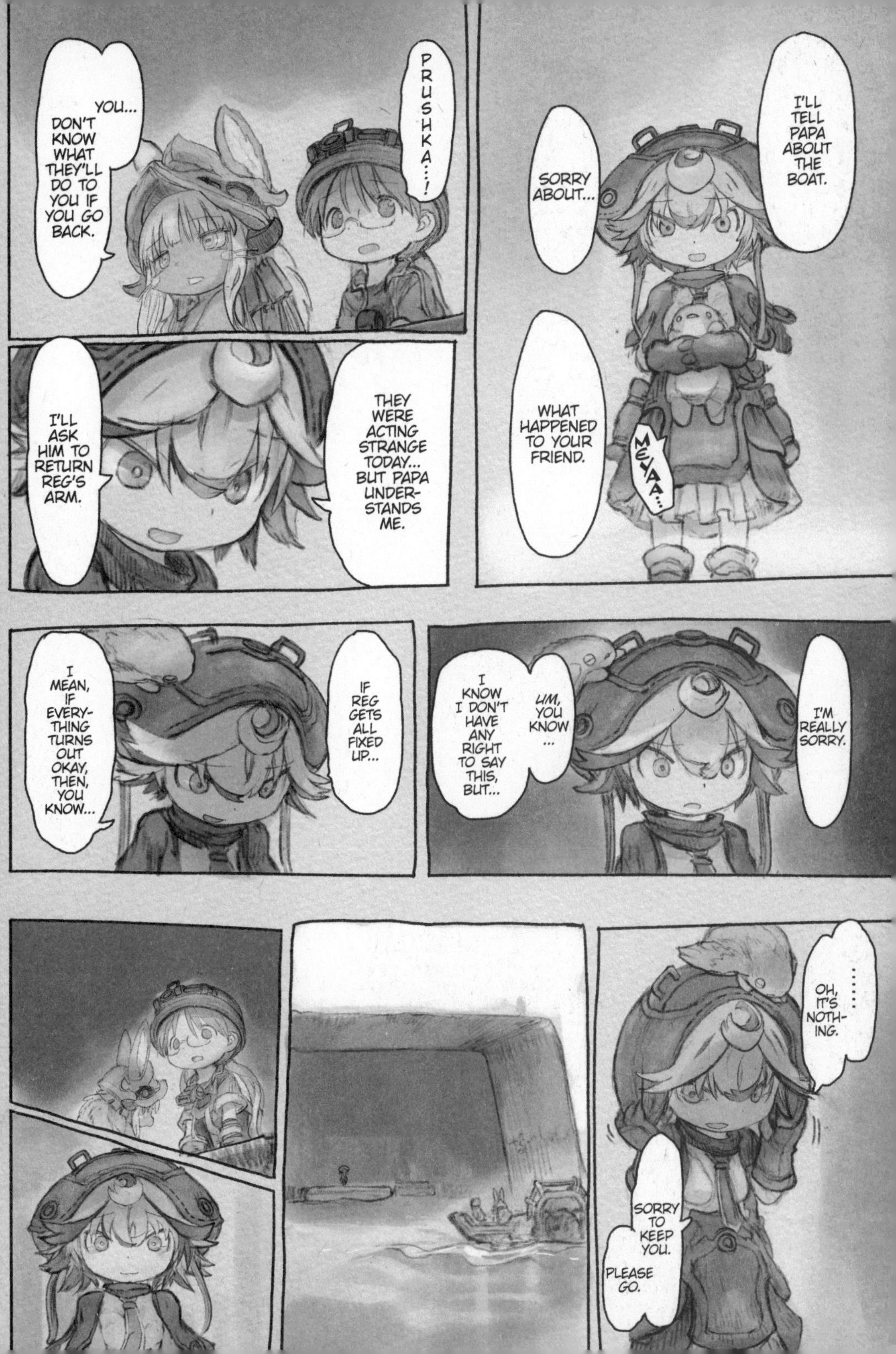
I'LL TELL PAPA ABOUT THE BOAT.
SORRY ABOUT...
WHAT HAPPENED TO YOUR FRIEND.
MEYAA...
PRUSHKA...!
YOU... DON'T KNOW WHAT THEY'LL DO TO YOU IF YOU GO BACK.
THEY WERE ACTING STRANGE TODAY... BUT PAPA UNDERSTANDS ME.
I'LL ASK HIM TO RETURN REG'S ARM.
I'M REALLY SORRY.
UM, YOU KNOW...
I KNOW I DON'T HAVE ANY RIGHT TO SAY THIS, BUT...
IF REG GETS ALL FIXED UP...
I MEAN, IF EVERYTHING TURNS OUT OKAY, THEN, YOU KNOW...
......
OH, IT'S NOTHING.
SORRY TO KEEP YOU.
PLEASE GO.

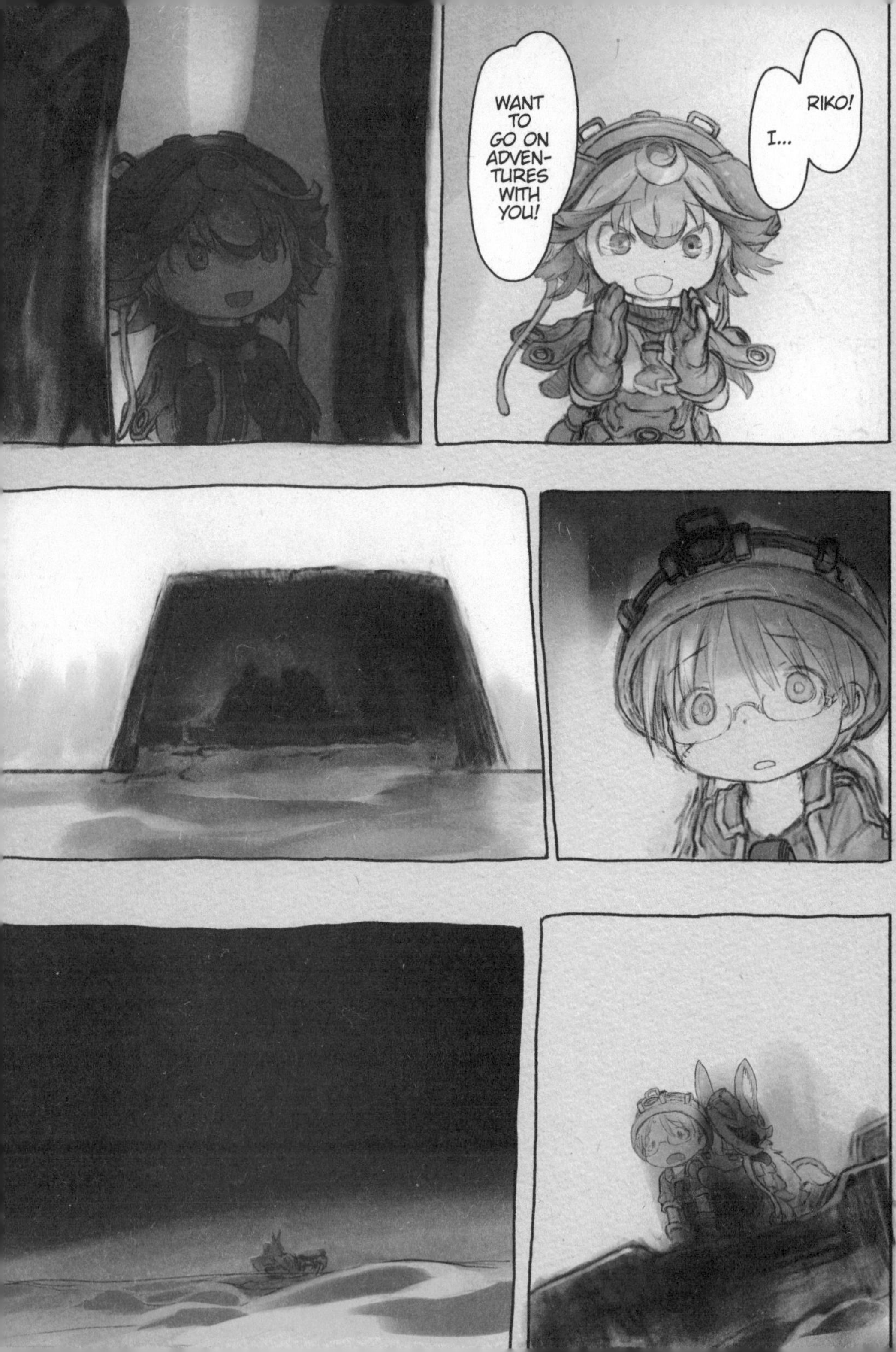
RIKO! I...
WANT TO GO ON ADVENTURES WITH YOU!

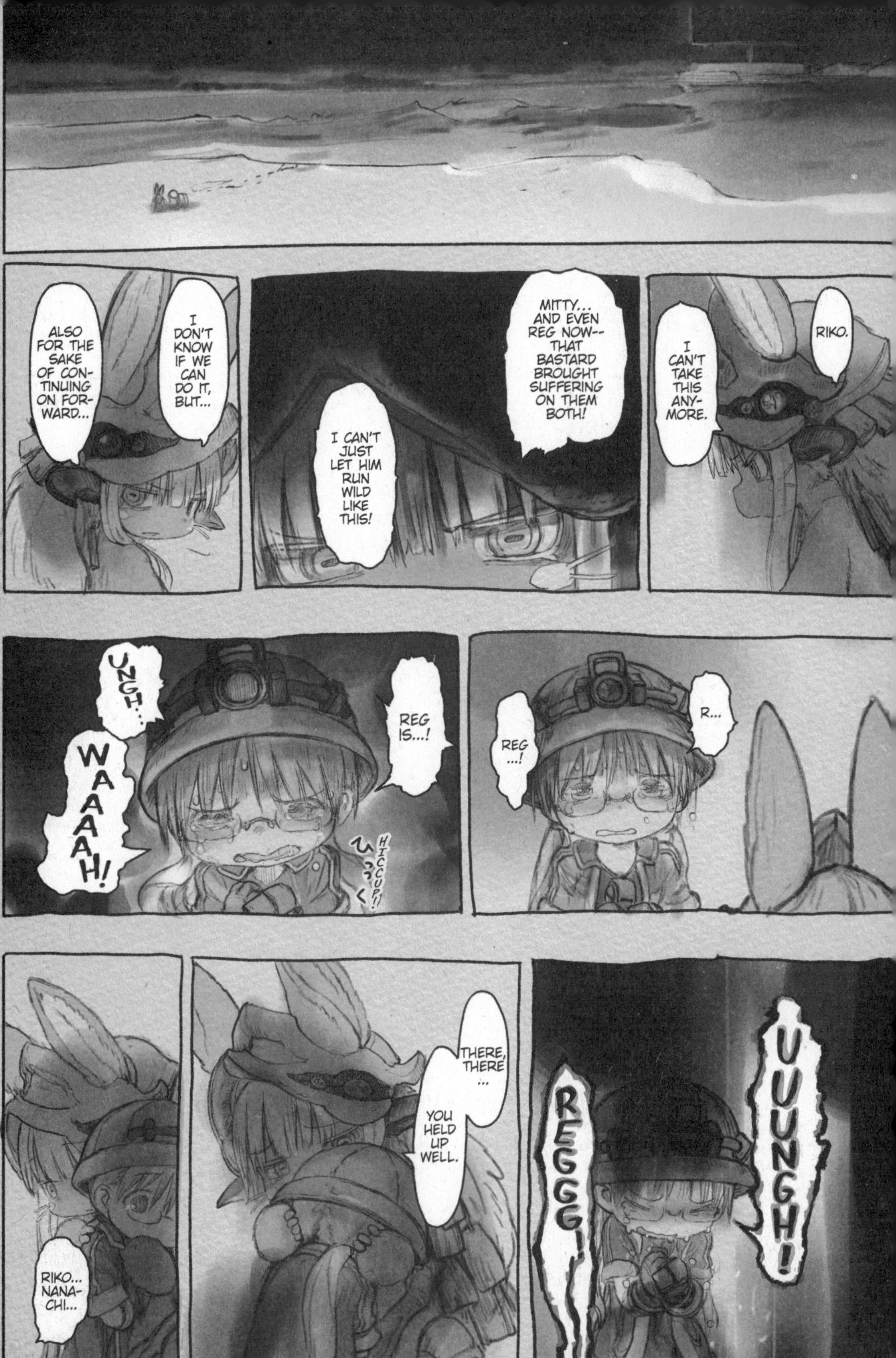
RIKO.
I CAN'T TAKE THIS ANYMORE.
MITTY... AND EVEN REG NOW--THAT BASTARD BROUGHT SUFFERING ON THEM BOTH!
I CAN'T JUST LET HIM RUN WILD LIKE THIS!
I DON'T KNOW IF WE CAN DO IT, BUT...
ALSO FOR THE SAKE OF CONTINUING ON FORWARD...
R...
REG ...!
REG IS...!
UNGH...
WAAAAH!
HICCUP!!
UUUNGH!
REGGG!
THERE, THERE ...
YOU HELD UP WELL.
RIKO... NANACHI...

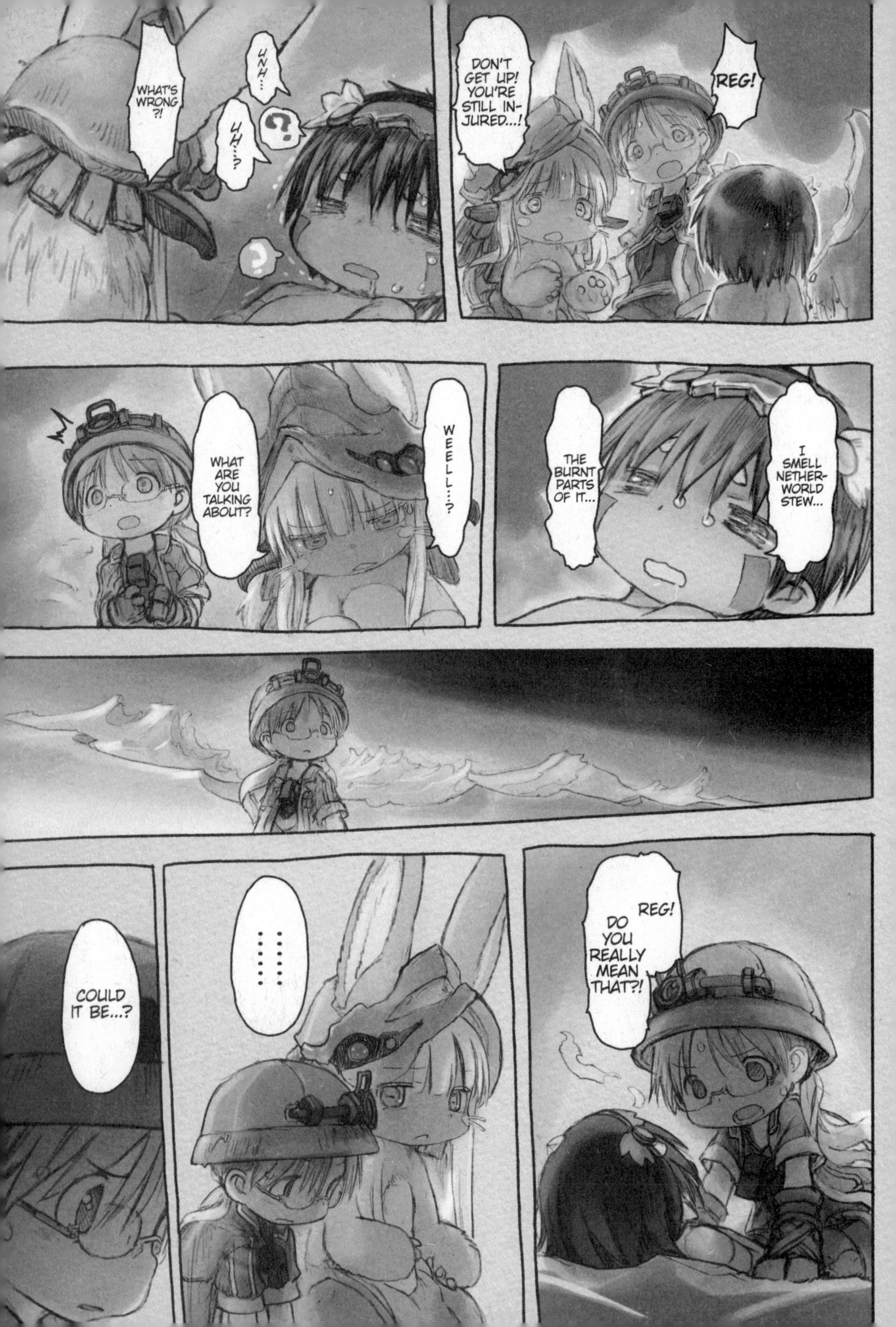
REG!
DON'T GET UP! YOU'RE STILL INJURED...!
UNH...
UH...?
WHAT'S WRONG ?!
I SMELL NETHER-WORLD STEW...
THE BURNT PARTS OF IT...
WEELL...?
WHAT ARE YOU TALKING ABOUT?
REG! DO YOU REALLY MEAN THAT?!
......
COULD IT BE...?

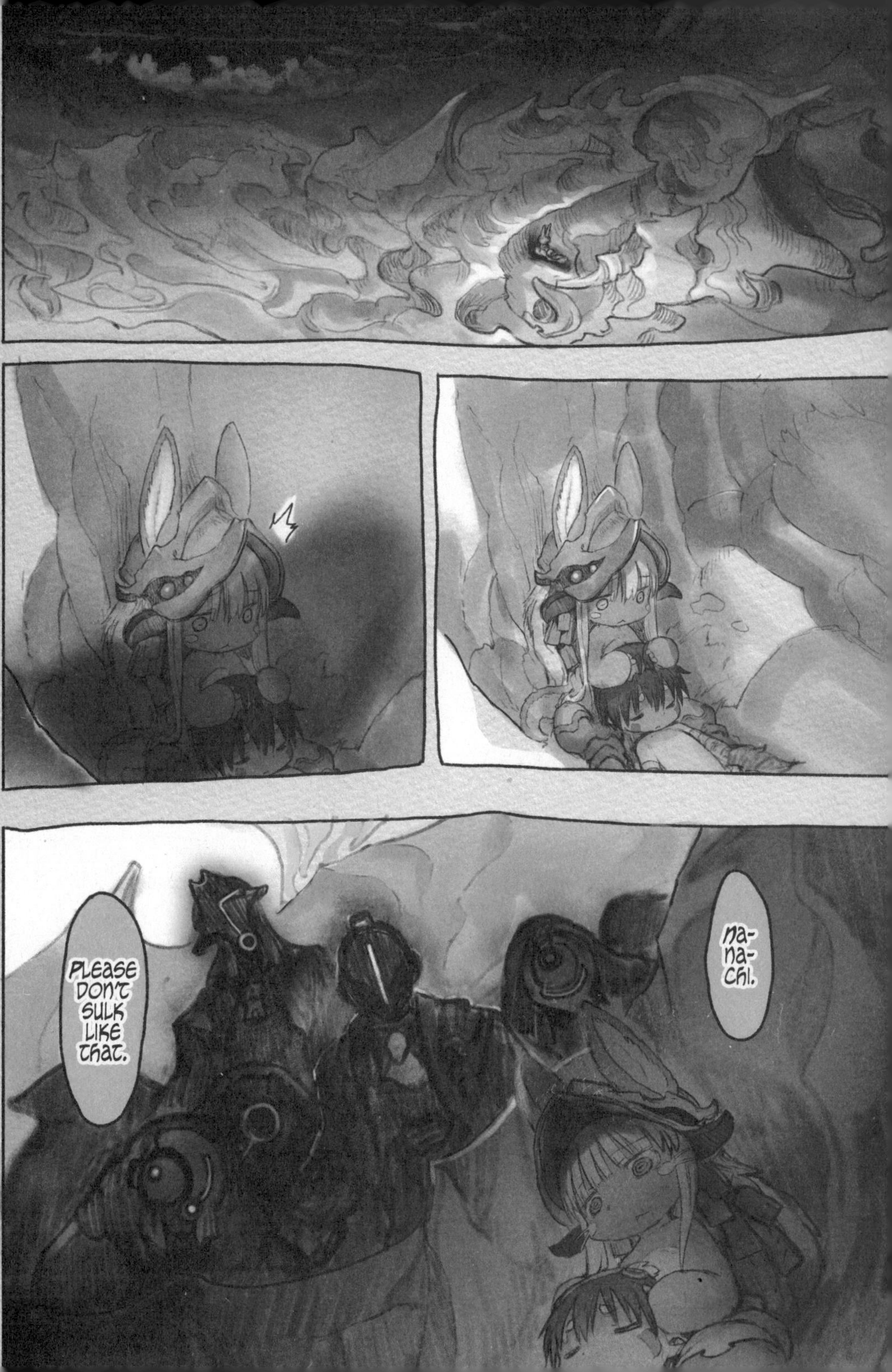
NA-NA-CHI.
PLEASE DON'T SULK LIKE THAT.

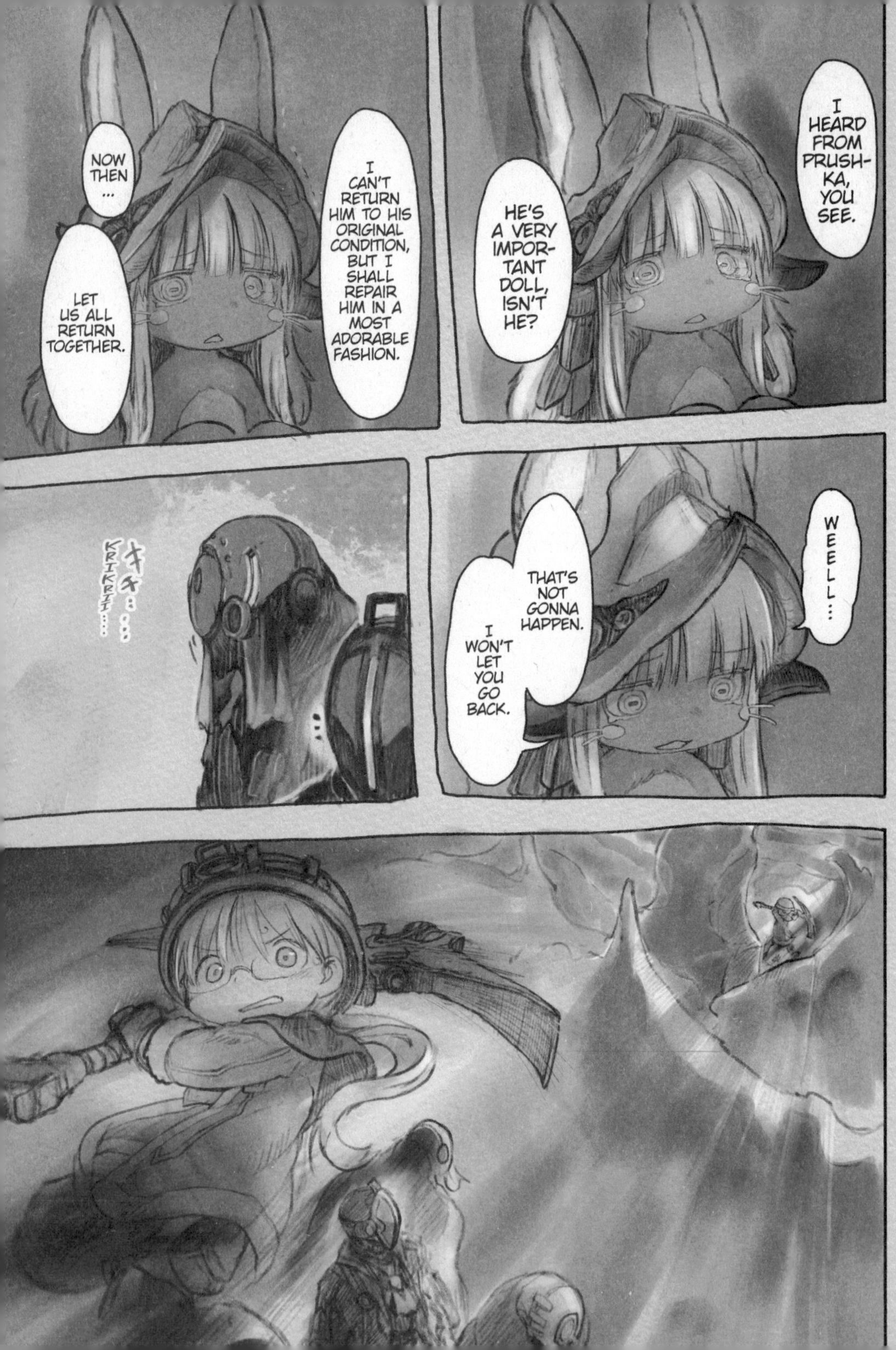
I HEARD FROM PRUSH-KA, YOU SEE.
HE'S A VERY IMPOR-TANT DOLL, ISN'T HE?
I CAN'T RETURN HIM TO HIS ORIGINAL CONDITION, BUT I SHALL REPAIR HIM IN A MOST ADORABLE FASHION.
NOW THEN ...
LET US ALL RETURN TOGETHER.
WEELL...
THAT'S NOT GONNA HAPPEN.
I WON'T LET YOU GO BACK.
キキ…
KRIKRII...

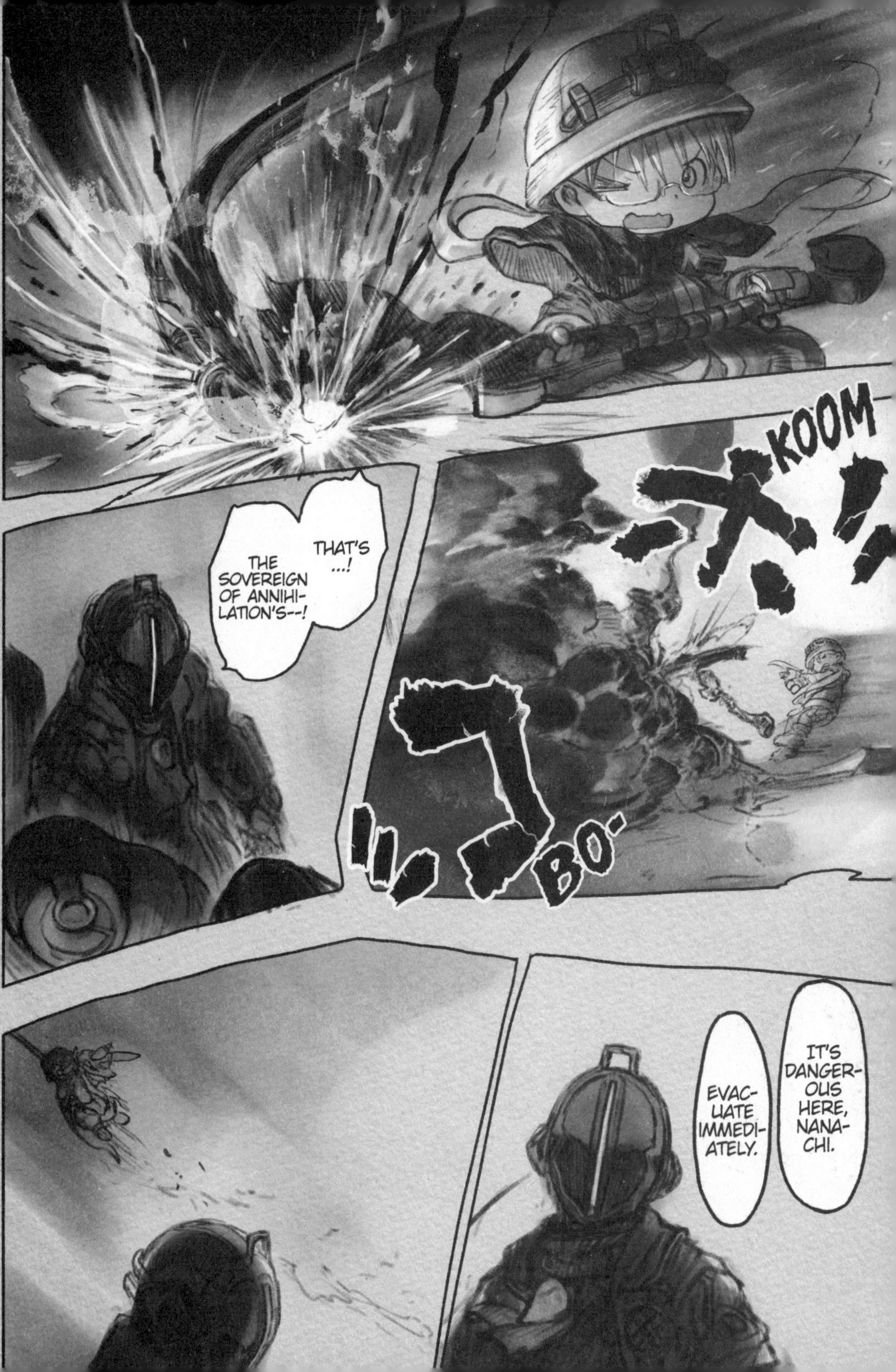
KOOM
BO-
THAT'S ...! THE SOVEREIGN OF ANNIHILATION'S--!
IT'S DANGEROUS HERE, NANACHI.
EVACUATE IMMEDIATELY.

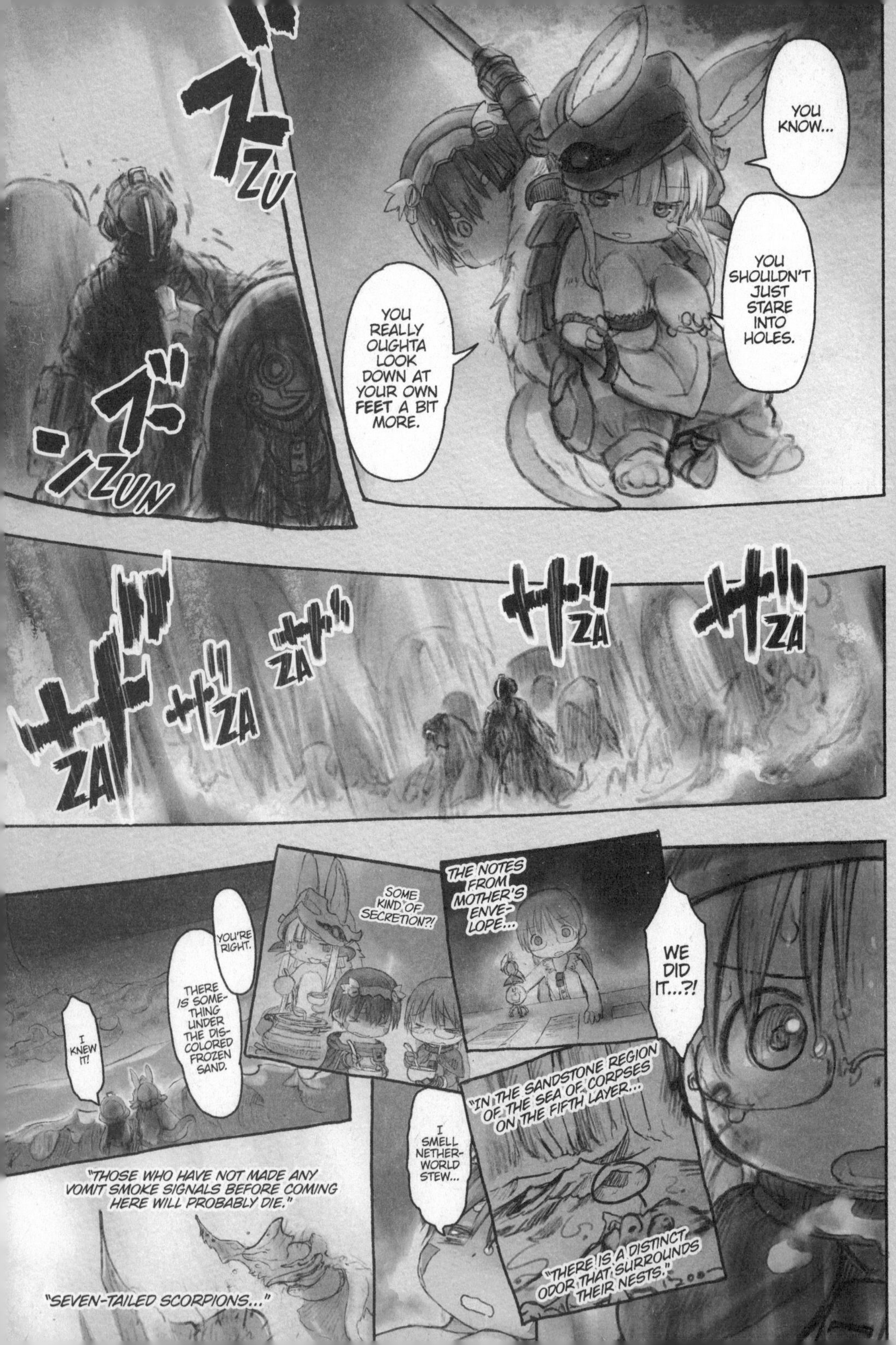
YOU KNOW...
YOU SHOULDN'T JUST STARE INTO HOLES.
YOU REALLY OUGHTA LOOK DOWN AT YOUR OWN FEET A BIT MORE.
ZU
ZUN
ZA
ZA
ZA
ZA
ZA
WE DID IT...?!
THE NOTES FROM MOTHER'S ENVE-LOPE...
SOME KIND OF SECRETION?!
YOU'RE RIGHT.
THERE IS SOME-THING UNDER THE DIS-COLORED FROZEN SAND.
I KNEW IT!
"IN THE SANDSTONE REGION OF THE SEA OF CORPSES ON THE FIFTH LAYER...
I SMELL NETHER-WORLD STEW...
"THERE IS A DISTINCT ODOR THAT SURROUNDS THEIR NESTS."
"THOSE WHO HAVE NOT MADE ANY VOMIT SMOKE SIGNALS BEFORE COMING HERE WILL PROBABLY DIE."
"SEVEN-TAILED SCORPIONS..."

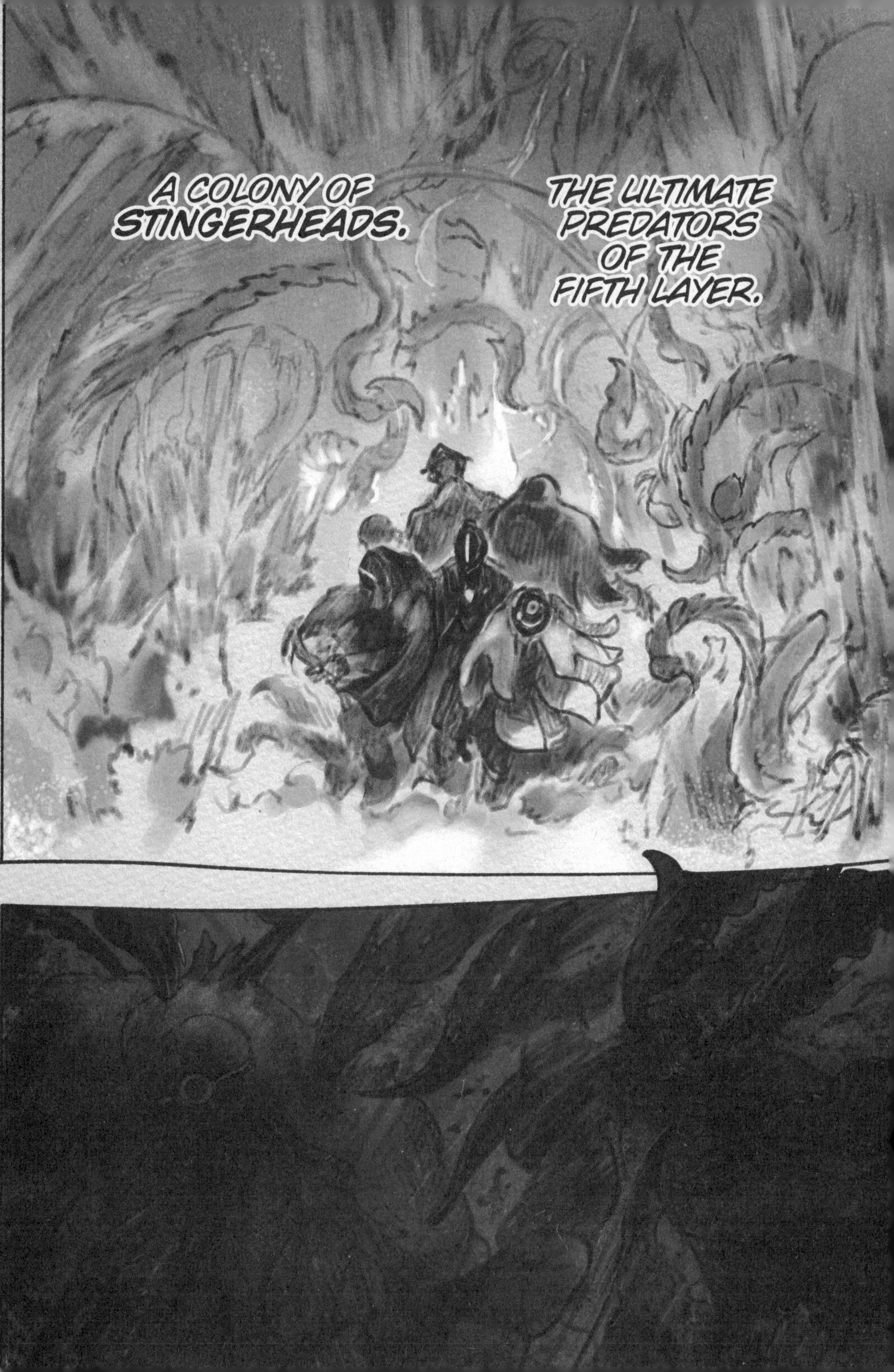
THE ULTIMATE PREDATORS OF THE FIFTH LAYER.
A COLONY OF STINGERHEADS.

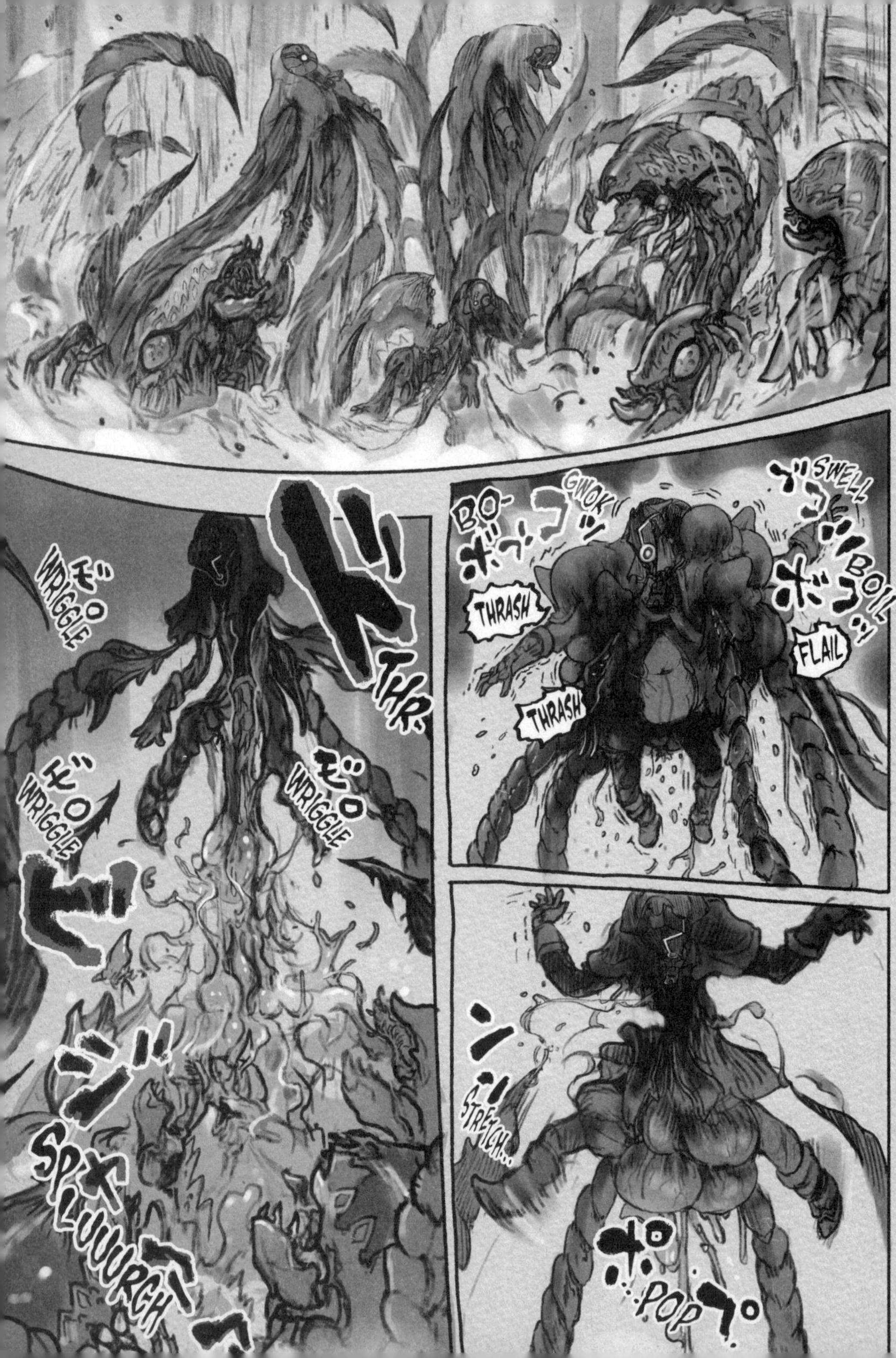
SWELL
GWOK
BO-
BOIL
THRASH
FLAIL
THRASH
STRETCH...
POP
WRIGGLE
THR.
WRIGGLE
WRIGGLE
SPLUUURGH

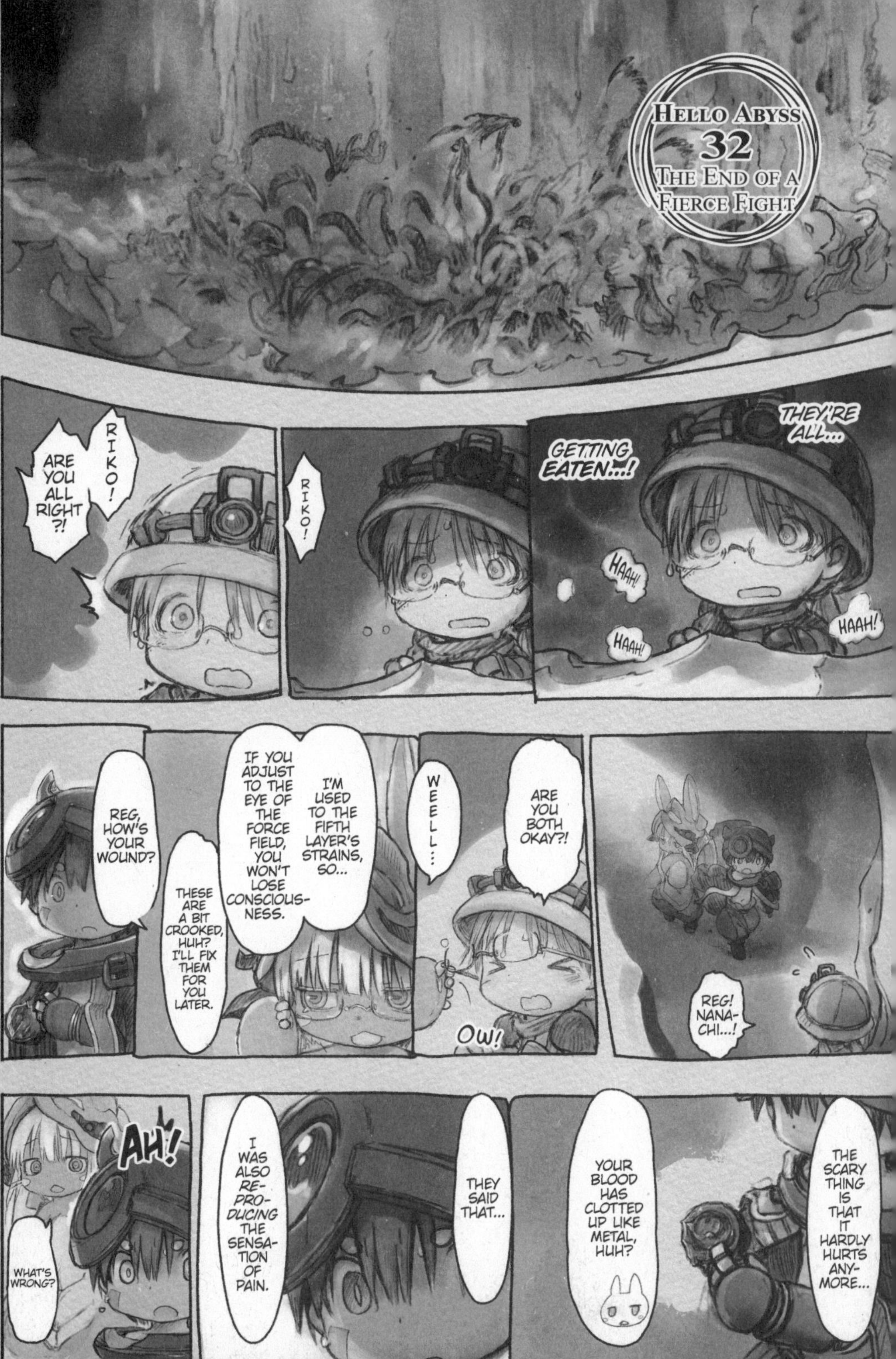
HELLO ABYSS 32
THE END OF A FIERCE FIGHT
THEY'RE ALL...
GETTING EATEN...!
HAAH!
HAAH!
HAAH!
RIKO!
RIKO!
ARE YOU ALL RIGHT?!
REG! NANACHI...!
ARE YOU BOTH OKAY?!
WEELL...
OW!
I'M USED TO THE FIFTH LAYER'S STRAINS, SO...
IF YOU ADJUST TO THE EYE OF THE FORCE FIELD, YOU WON'T LOSE CONSCIOUSNESS.
THESE ARE A BIT CROOKED, HUH? I'LL FIX THEM FOR YOU LATER.
REG, HOW'S YOUR WOUND?
THE SCARY THING IS THAT IT HARDLY HURTS ANYMORE...
YOUR BLOOD HAS CLOTTED UP LIKE METAL, HUH?
THEY SAID THAT...
I WAS ALSO REPRODUCING THE SENSATION OF PAIN.
AH!
WHAT'S WRONG?

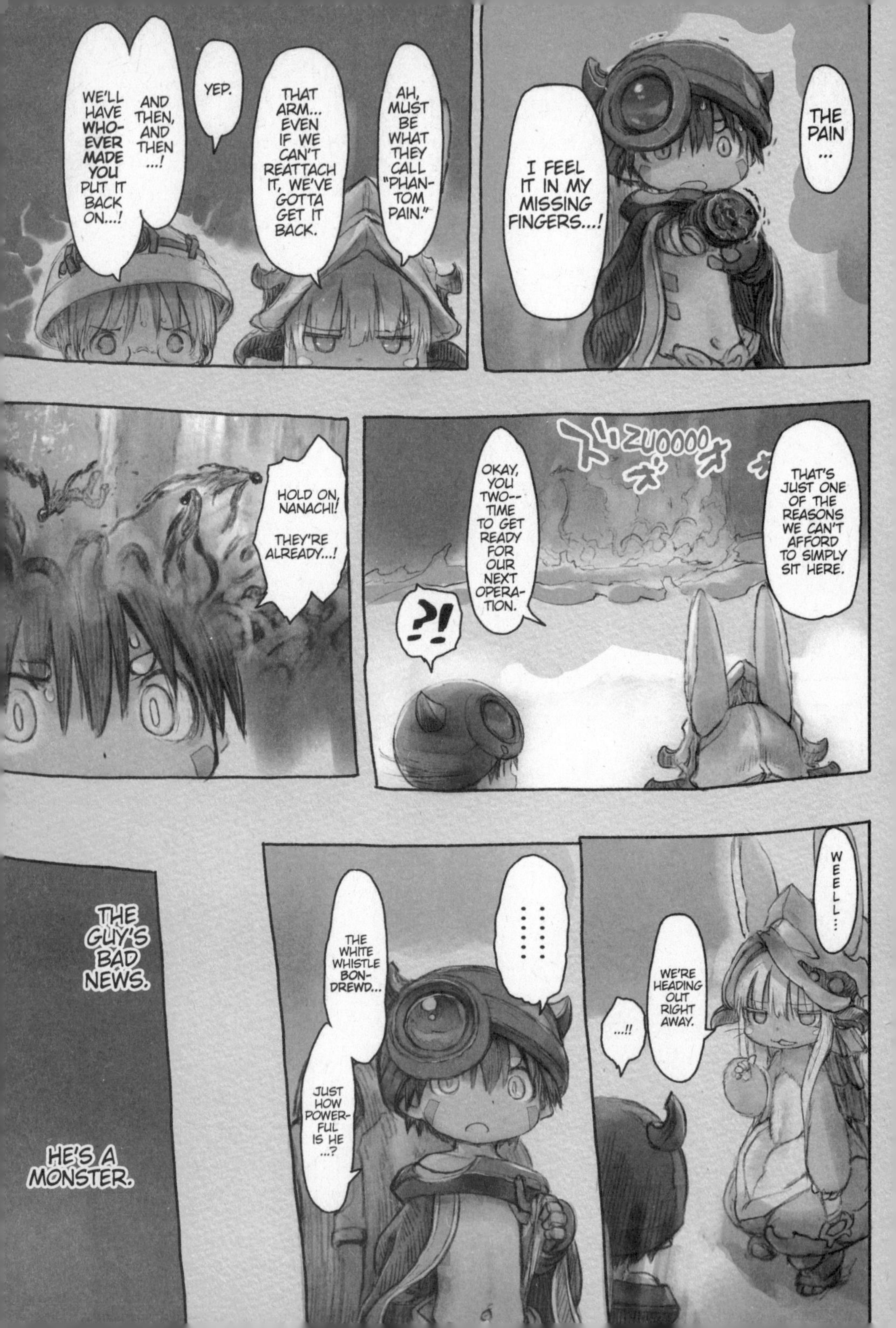
THE PAIN ...
I FEEL IT IN MY MISSING FINGERS...!
AH, MUST BE WHAT THEY CALL "PHANTOM PAIN."
THAT ARM... EVEN IF WE CAN'T REATTACH IT, WE'VE GOTTA GET IT BACK.
YEP.
AND THEN, AND THEN ...!
WE'LL HAVE WHOEVER MADE YOU PUT IT BACK ON...!
ZUOOOO
THAT'S JUST ONE OF THE REASONS WE CAN'T AFFORD TO SIMPLY SIT HERE.
OKAY, YOU TWO--TIME TO GET READY FOR OUR NEXT OPERATION.
?!
HOLD ON, NANACHI!
THEY'RE ALREADY...!
WEELL...
WE'RE HEADING OUT RIGHT AWAY.
...!!
......
THE WHITE WHISTLE BONDREWD...
JUST HOW POWERFUL IS HE ...?
THE GUY'S BAD NEWS.
HE'S A MONSTER.

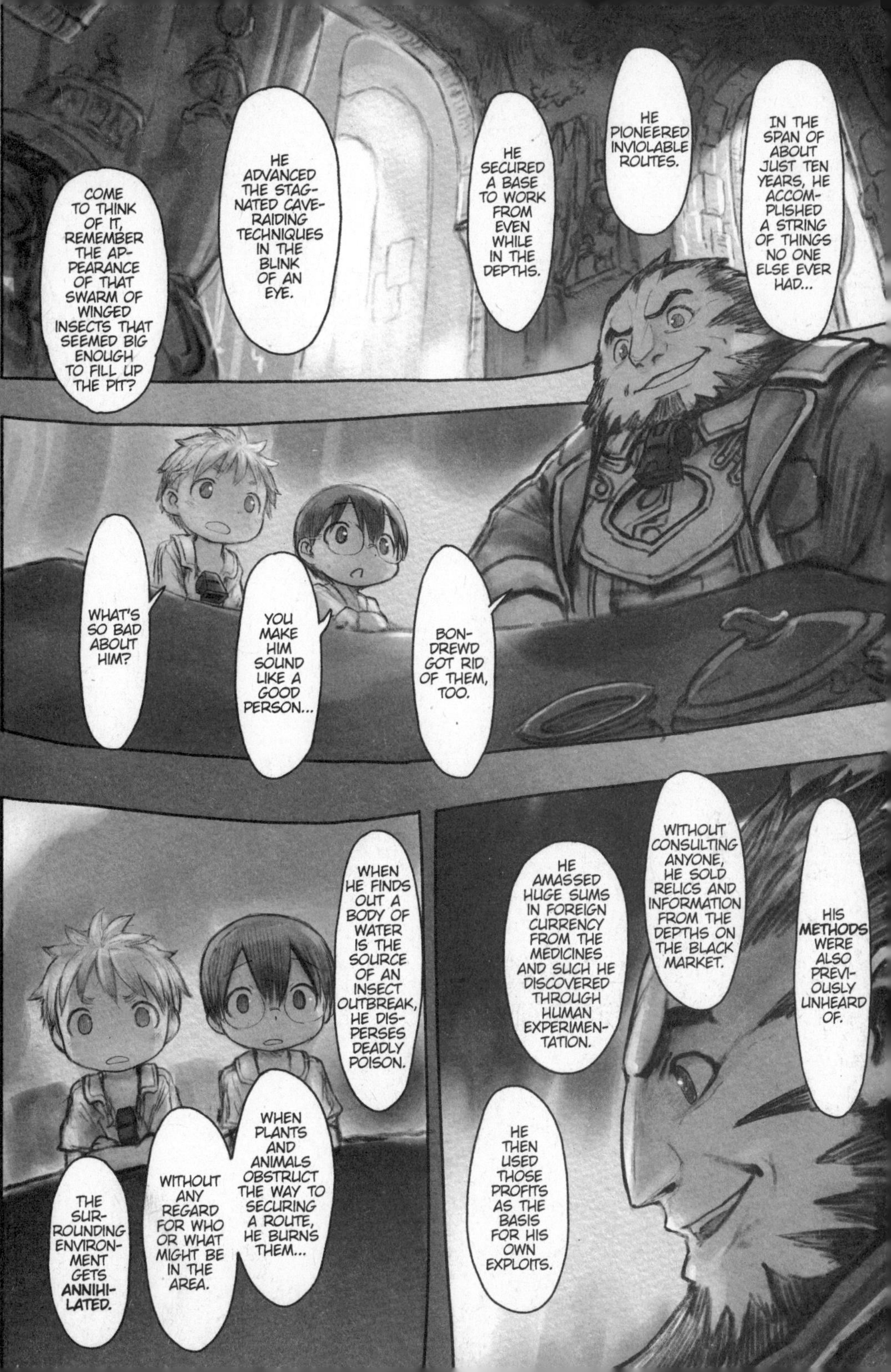
IN THE SPAN OF ABOUT JUST TEN YEARS, HE ACCOMPLISHED A STRING OF THINGS NO ONE ELSE EVER HAD...
HE PIONEERED INVIOLABLE ROUTES.
HE SECURED A BASE TO WORK FROM EVEN WHILE IN THE DEPTHS.
HE ADVANCED THE STAGNATED CAVE-RAIDING TECHNIQUES IN THE BLINK OF AN EYE.
COME TO THINK OF IT, REMEMBER THE APPEARANCE OF THAT SWARM OF WINGED INSECTS THAT SEEMED BIG ENOUGH TO FILL UP THE PIT?
BONDREWD GOT RID OF THEM, TOO.
YOU MAKE HIM SOUND LIKE A GOOD PERSON...
WHAT'S SO BAD ABOUT HIM?
HIS **METHODS** WERE ALSO PREVIOUSLY UNHEARD OF.
WITHOUT CONSULTING ANYONE, HE SOLD RELICS AND INFORMATION FROM THE DEPTHS ON THE BLACK MARKET.
HE AMASSED HUGE SUMS IN FOREIGN CURRENCY FROM THE MEDICINES AND SUCH HE DISCOVERED THROUGH HUMAN EXPERIMENTATION.
HE THEN USED THOSE PROFITS AS THE BASIS FOR HIS OWN EXPLOITS.
WHEN HE FINDS OUT A BODY OF WATER IS THE SOURCE OF AN INSECT OUTBREAK, HE DISPERSES DEADLY POISON.
WHEN PLANTS AND ANIMALS OBSTRUCT THE WAY TO SECURING A ROUTE, HE BURNS THEM...
WITHOUT ANY REGARD FOR WHO OR WHAT MIGHT BE IN THE AREA.
THE SURROUNDING ENVIRONMENT GETS **ANNIHILATED.**

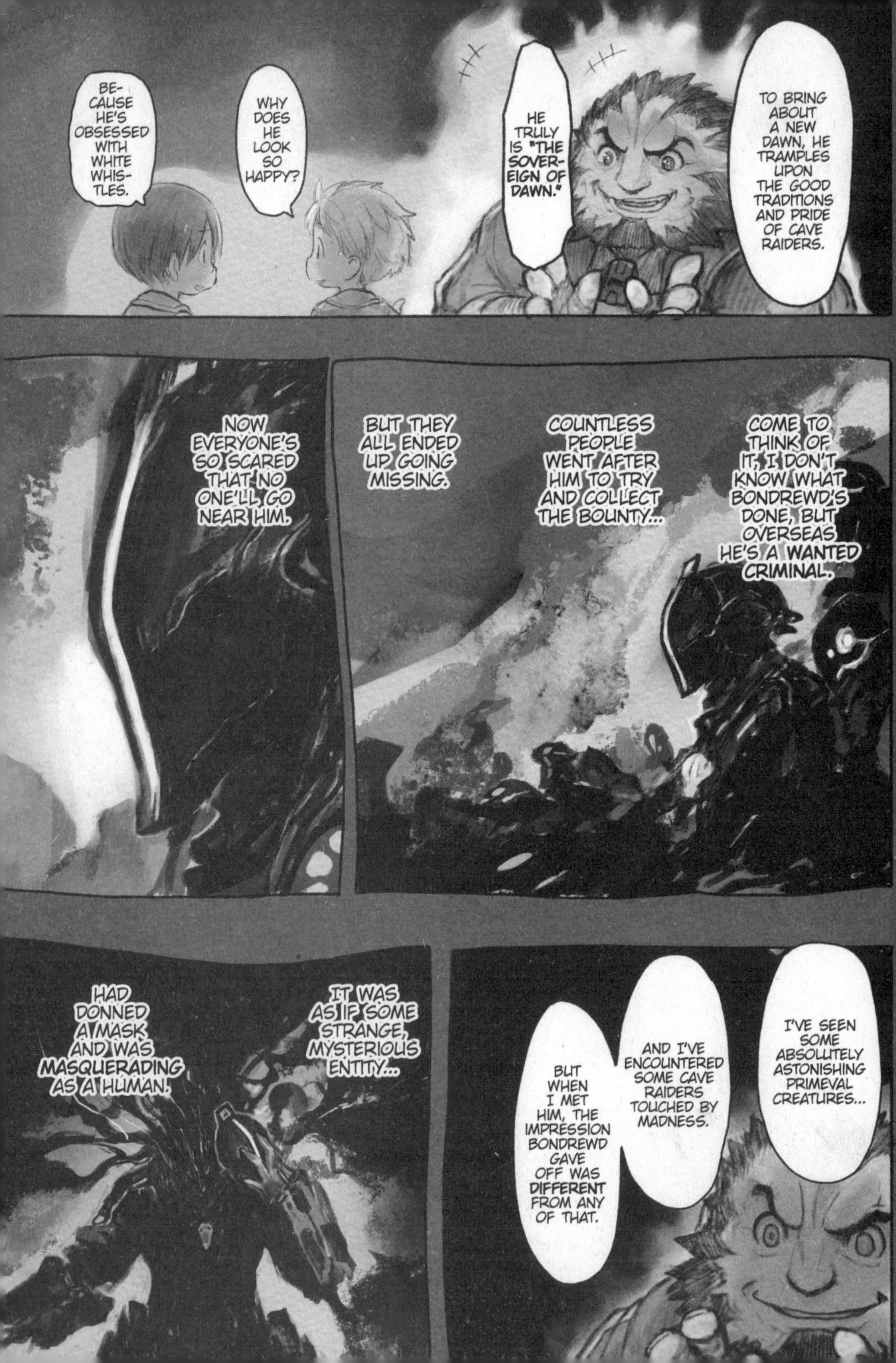
TO BRING ABOUT A NEW DAWN, HE TRAMPLES UPON THE GOOD TRADITIONS AND PRIDE OF CAVE RAIDERS.
HE TRULY IS "THE SOVEREIGN OF DAWN."
WHY DOES HE LOOK SO HAPPY?
BECAUSE HE'S OBSESSED WITH WHITE WHISTLES.
COME TO THINK OF IT, I DON'T KNOW WHAT BONDREWD'S DONE, BUT OVERSEAS HE'S A WANTED CRIMINAL.
COUNTLESS PEOPLE WENT AFTER HIM TO TRY AND COLLECT THE BOUNTY...
BUT THEY ALL ENDED UP GOING MISSING.
NOW EVERYONE'S SO SCARED THAT NO ONE'LL GO NEAR HIM.
I'VE SEEN SOME ABSOLUTELY ASTONISHING PRIMEVAL CREATURES...
AND I'VE ENCOUNTERED SOME CAVE RAIDERS TOUCHED BY MADNESS.
BUT WHEN I MET HIM, THE IMPRESSION BONDREWD GAVE OFF WAS DIFFERENT FROM ANY OF THAT.
IT WAS AS IF SOME STRANGE, MYSTERIOUS ENTITY...
HAD DONNED A MASK AND WAS MASQUERADING AS A HUMAN.

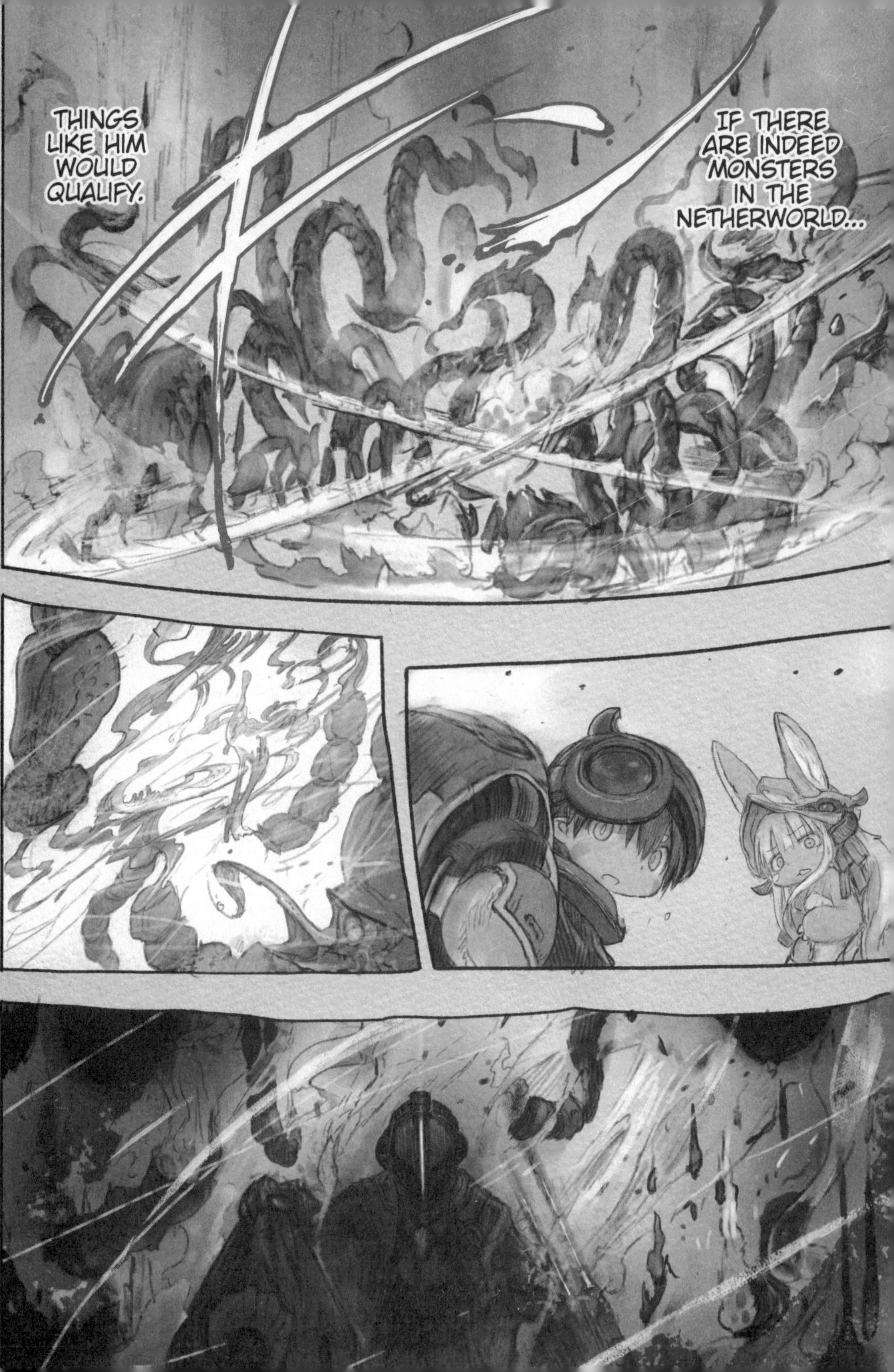
IF THERE ARE INDEED MONSTERS IN THE NETHERWORLD...
THINGS LIKE HIM WOULD QUALIFY.

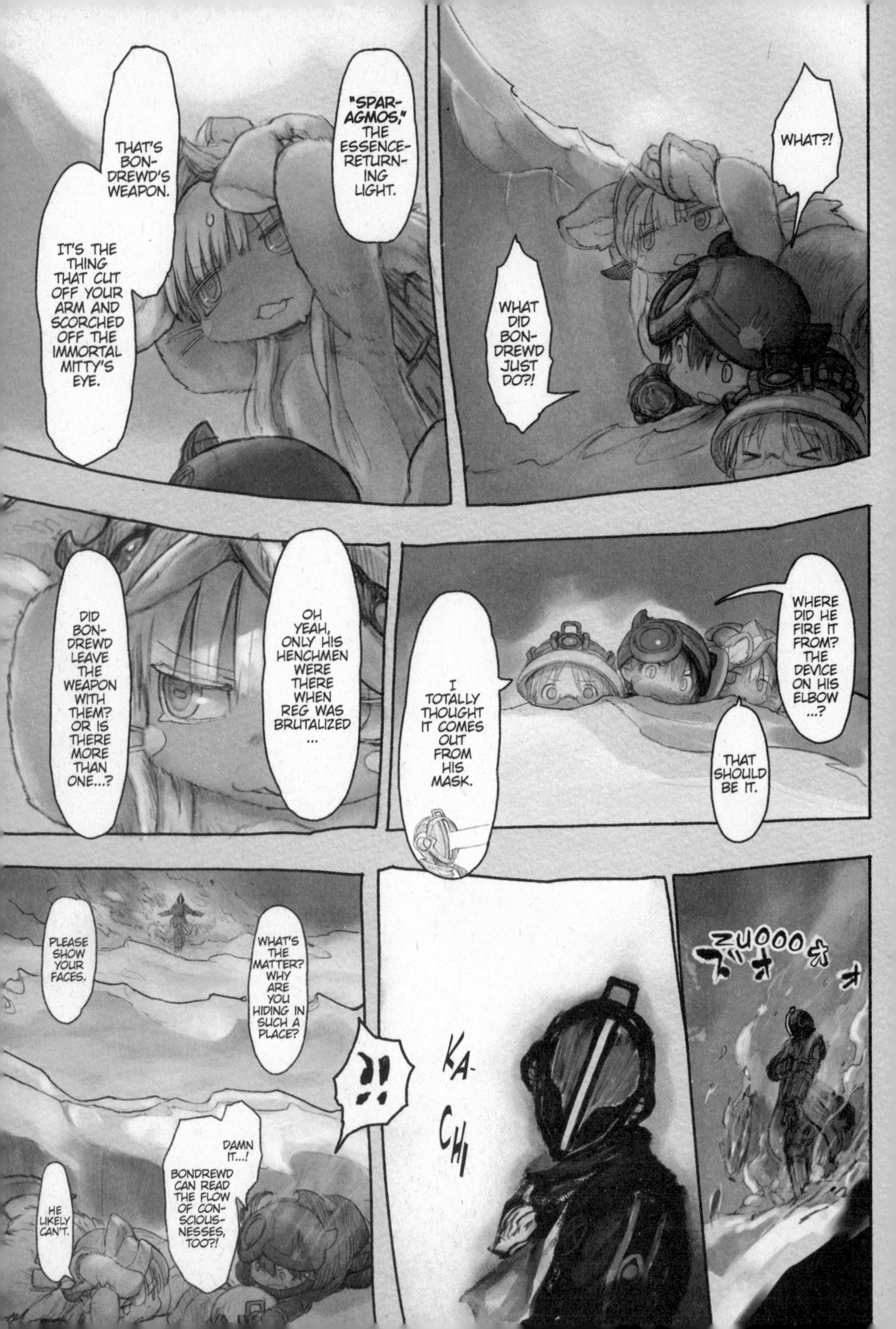

WHAT?!
WHAT DID BONDREWD JUST DO?!
"SPARAGMOS," THE ESSENCE-RETURNING LIGHT.
THAT'S BONDREWD'S WEAPON.
IT'S THE THING THAT CUT OFF YOUR ARM AND SCORCHED OFF THE IMMORTAL MITTY'S EYE.
WHERE DID HE FIRE IT FROM? THE DEVICE ON HIS ELBOW ...?
THAT SHOULD BE IT.
I TOTALLY THOUGHT IT COMES OUT FROM HIS MASK.
OH YEAH, ONLY HIS HENCHMEN WERE THERE WHEN REG WAS BRUTALIZED ...
DID BONDREWD LEAVE THE WEAPON WITH THEM? OR IS THERE MORE THAN ONE...?
ZUOOO
KA-CHI
WHAT'S THE MATTER? WHY ARE YOU HIDING IN SUCH A PLACE?
PLEASE SHOW YOUR FACES.
?!
DAMN IT...!
BONDREWD CAN READ THE FLOW OF CONSCIOUSNESSES, TOO?!
HE LIKELY CAN'T.

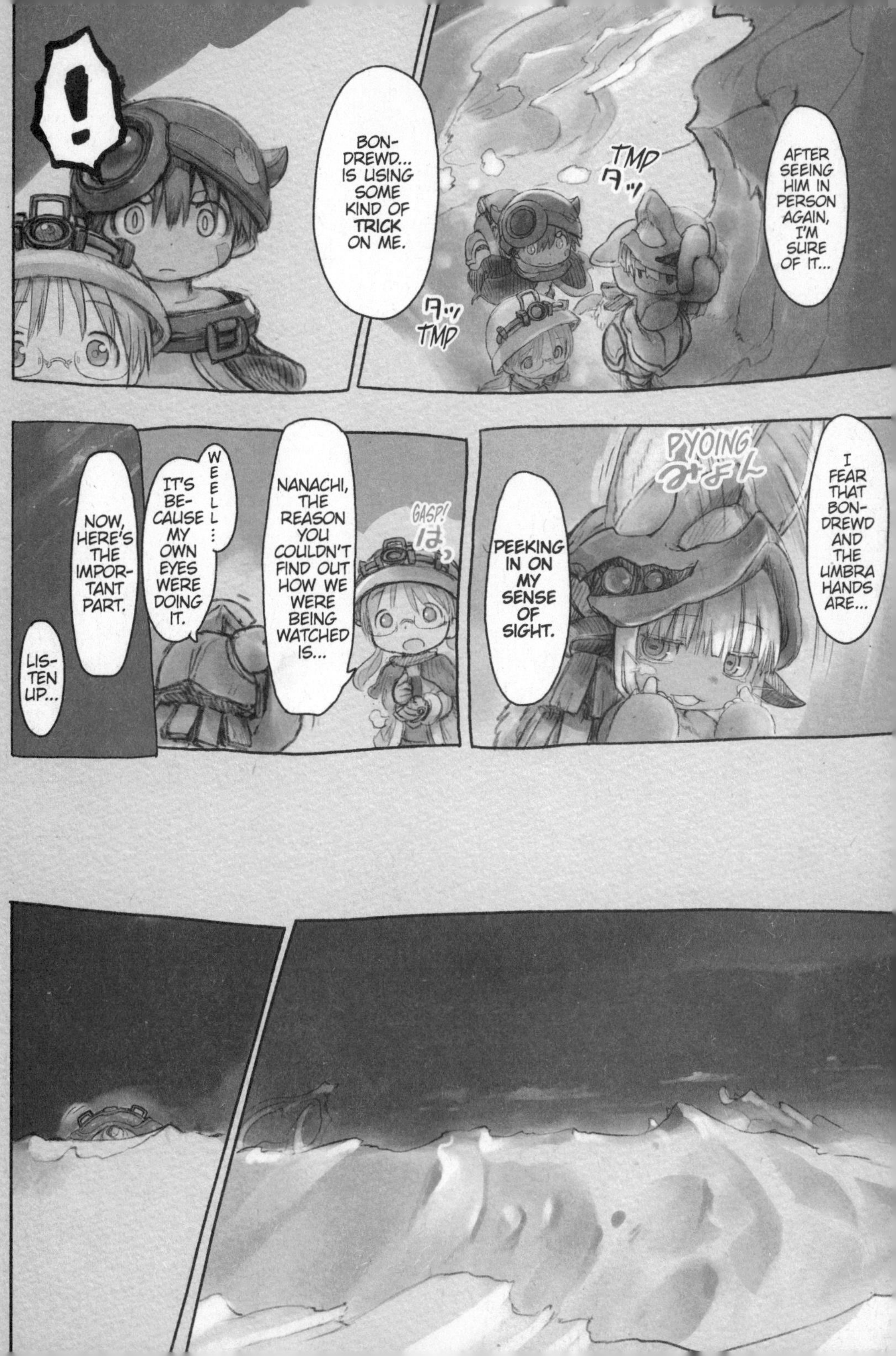
AFTER SEEING HIM IN PERSON AGAIN, I'M SURE OF IT...
TMP タッ
BON-DREWD... IS USING SOME KIND OF TRICK ON ME.
タッ TMP
!
I FEAR THAT BON-DREWD AND THE UMBRA HANDS ARE...
PYOING みょん
PEEKING IN ON MY SENSE OF SIGHT.
GASP! は,
NANACHI, THE REASON YOU COULDN'T FIND OUT HOW WE WERE BEING WATCHED IS...
WEELL...
IT'S BE-CAUSE MY OWN EYES WERE DOING IT.
NOW, HERE'S THE IMPOR-TANT PART.
LIS-TEN UP...

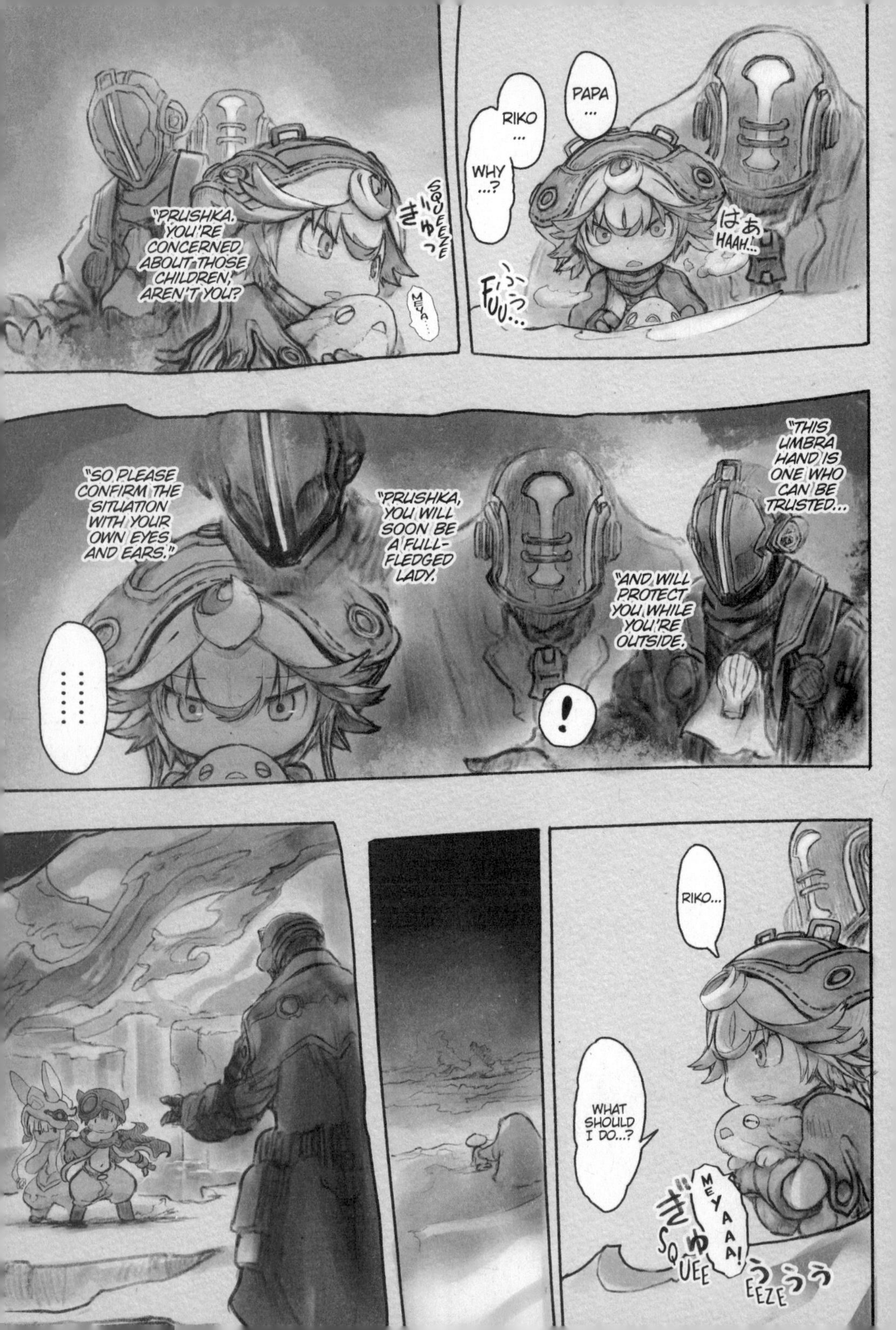
PAPA ...
RIKO ...
WHY ...?
はあ
HAAH...
ふうっ
FUUU...
"PRUSHKA. YOU'RE CONCERNED ABOUT THOSE CHILDREN, AREN'T YOU?
ぎゅっ
SQUEEZE
MEYA...
"THIS UMBRA HAND IS ONE WHO CAN BE TRUSTED...
"AND WILL PROTECT YOU WHILE YOU'RE OUTSIDE.
"PRUSHKA, YOU WILL SOON BE A FULL-FLEDGED LADY.
!
"SO PLEASE CONFIRM THE SITUATION WITH YOUR OWN EYES AND EARS."
......
RIKO...
WHAT SHOULD I DO...?
MEYAAA!
ぎゅうううう
SQUEEEZE

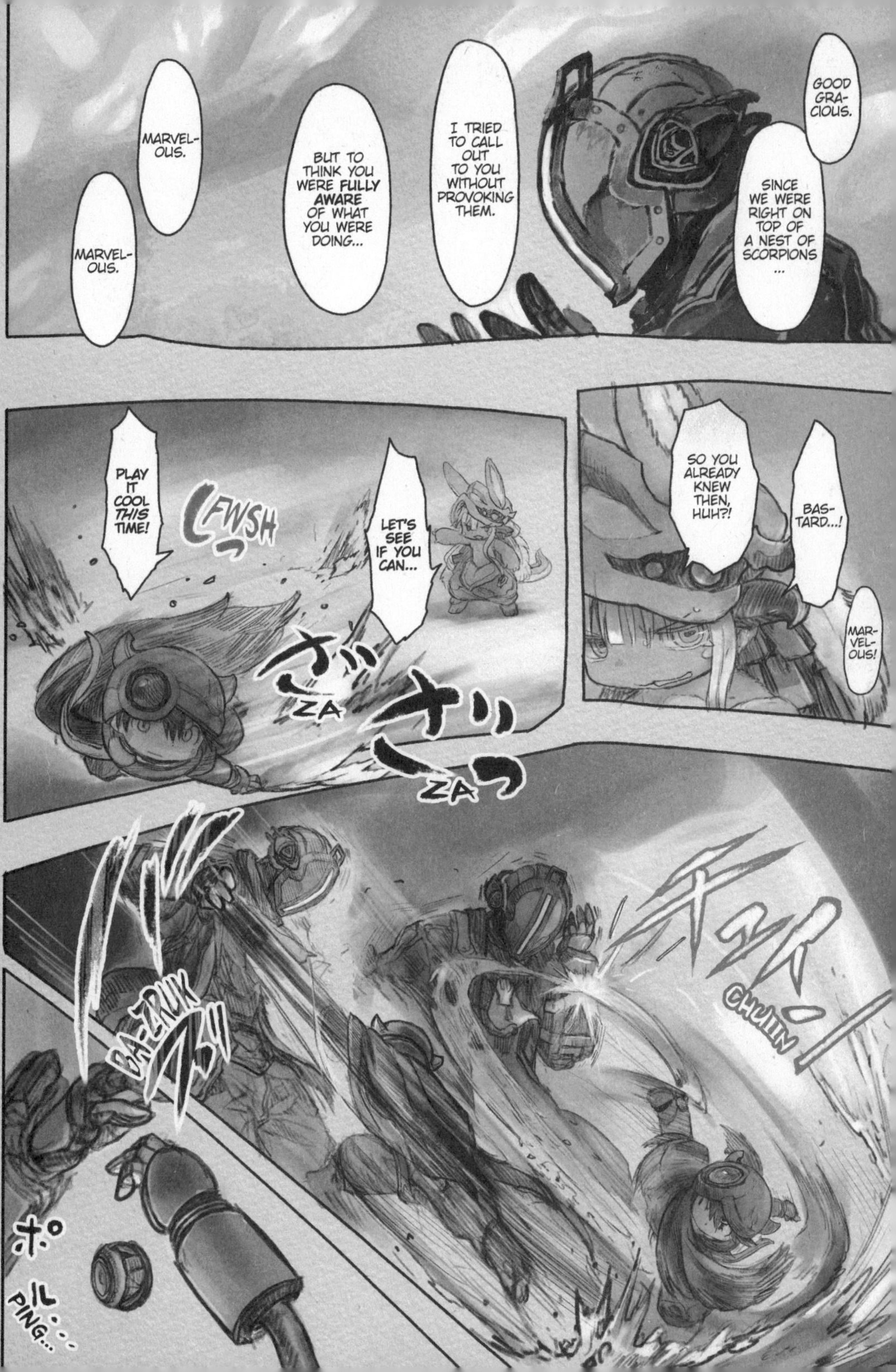
GOOD GRACIOUS.
SINCE WE WERE RIGHT ON TOP OF A NEST OF SCORPIONS ...
I TRIED TO CALL OUT TO YOU WITHOUT PROVOKING THEM.
BUT TO THINK YOU WERE **FULLY AWARE** OF WHAT YOU WERE DOING...
MARVELOUS.
MARVELOUS.
BASTARD...!
SO YOU ALREADY KNEW THEN, HUH?!
MARVELOUS!
LET'S SEE IF YOU CAN...
PLAY IT COOL *THIS* TIME!
FWSH
ZA
ZA
CHUIIN
BA-ZRUK
PING...

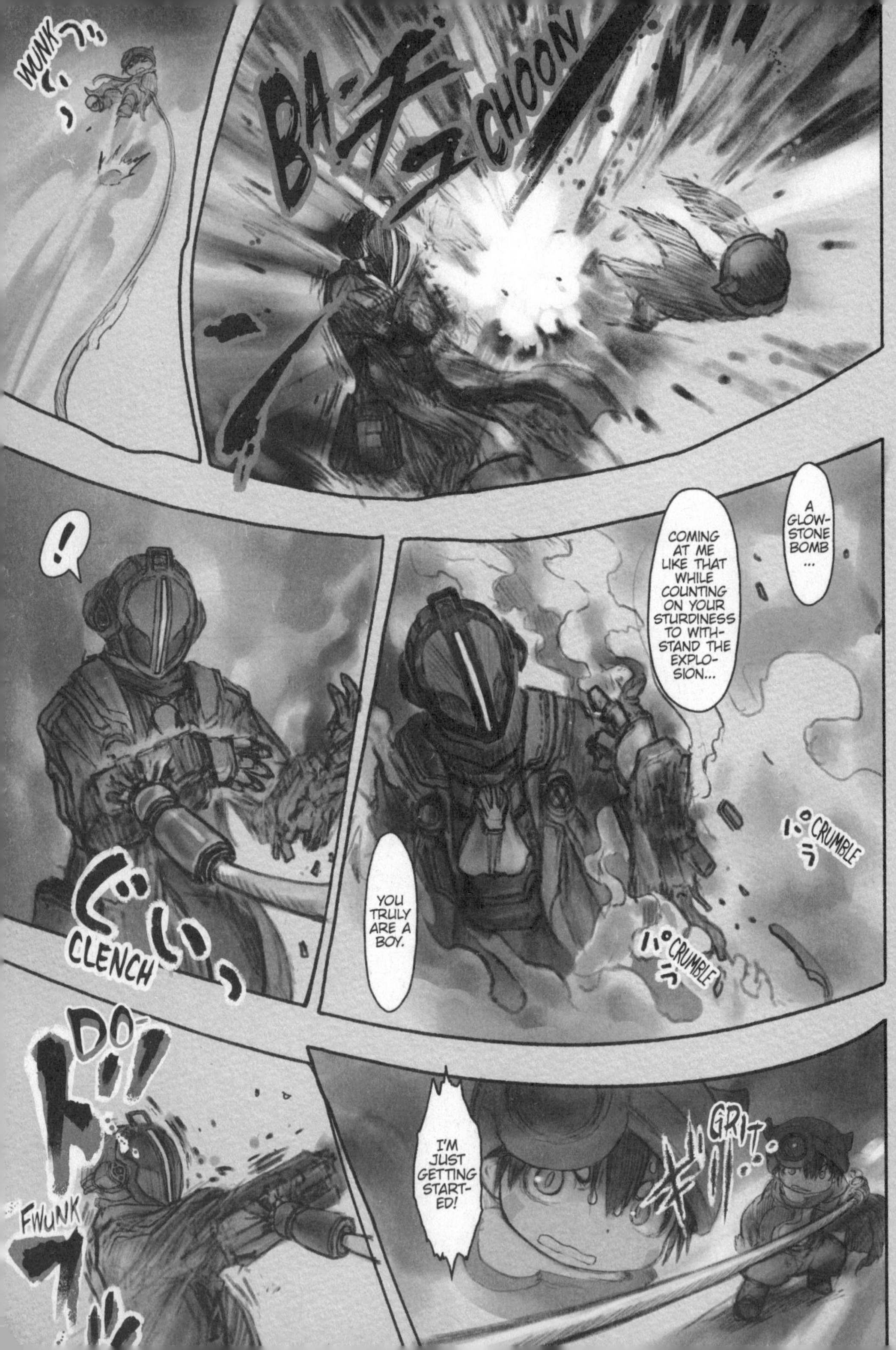
BA-CHOON
WUNK
A GLOW-STONE BOMB...
COMING AT ME LIKE THAT WHILE COUNTING ON YOUR STURDINESS TO WITHSTAND THE EXPLOSION...
YOU TRULY ARE A BOY.
CRUMBLE
CRUMBLE
!
CLENCH
GRIT
I'M JUST GETTING STARTED!
DO
FWUNK

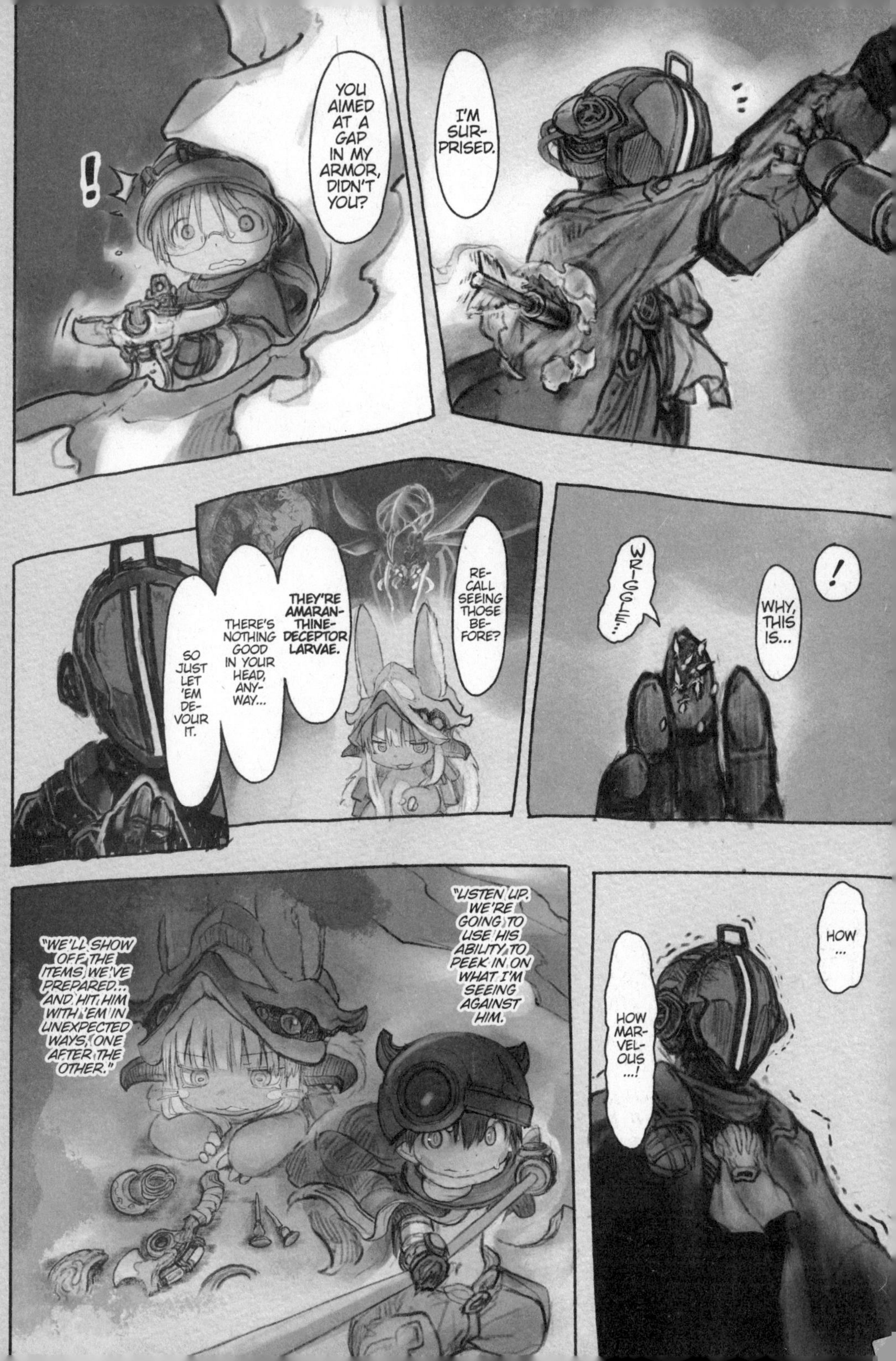
I'M SURPRISED.
YOU AIMED AT A GAP IN MY ARMOR, DIDN'T YOU?
!
!
WHY, THIS IS...
WRIGGLE...
RECALL SEEING THOSE BEFORE?
THEY'RE AMARANTHINE-DECEPTOR LARVAE.
THERE'S NOTHING GOOD IN YOUR HEAD, ANYWAY...
SO JUST LET 'EM DEVOUR IT.
HOW ...
HOW MARVELOUS ...!
"LISTEN UP. WE'RE GOING TO USE HIS ABILITY TO PEEK IN ON WHAT I'M SEEING AGAINST HIM.
"WE'LL SHOW OFF THE ITEMS WE'VE PREPARED... AND HIT HIM WITH 'EM IN UNEXPECTED WAYS, ONE AFTER THE OTHER."

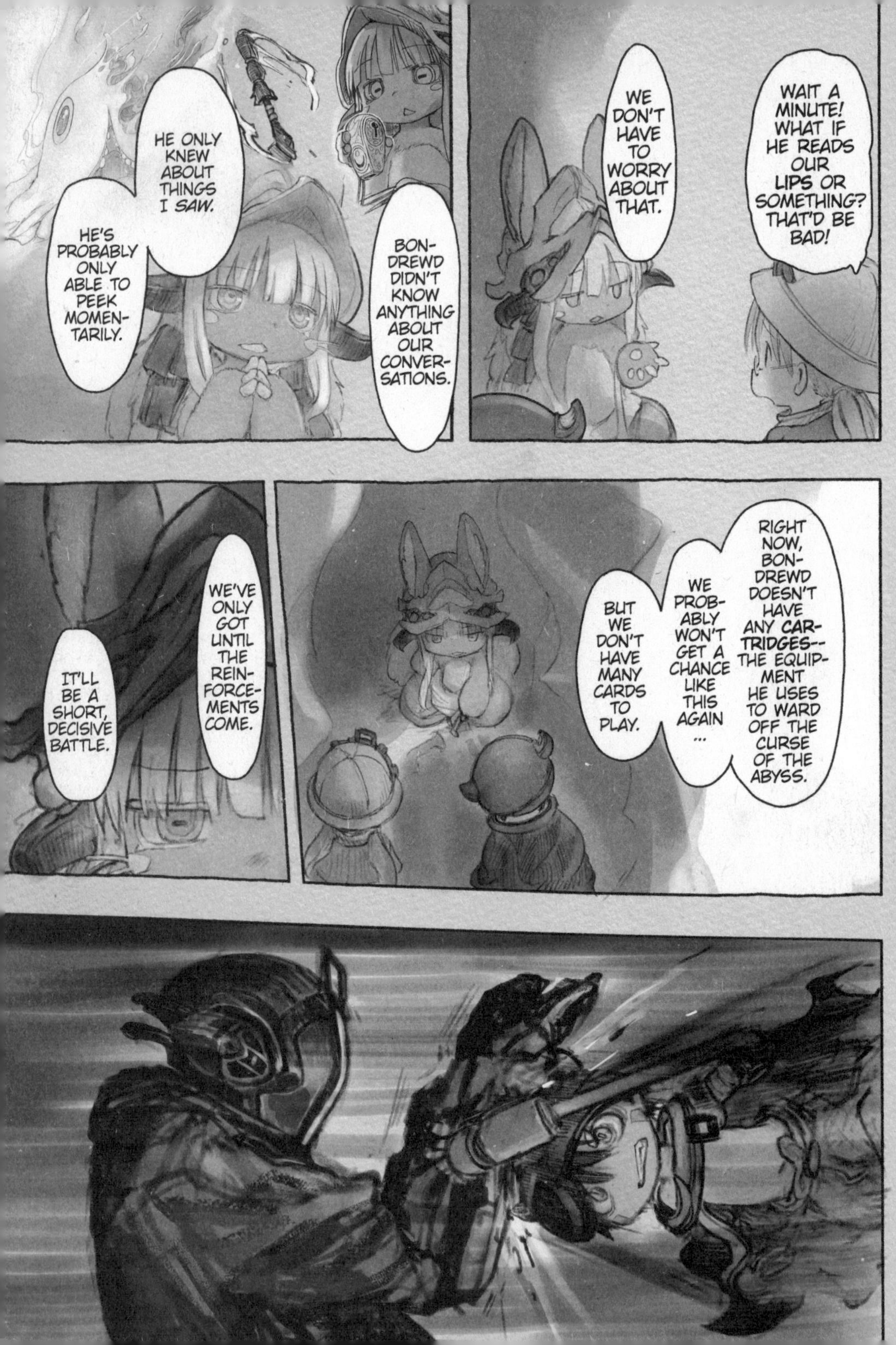
WAIT A MINUTE! WHAT IF HE READS OUR LIPS OR SOMETHING? THAT'D BE BAD!
WE DON'T HAVE TO WORRY ABOUT THAT.
BONDREWD DIDN'T KNOW ANYTHING ABOUT OUR CONVERSATIONS.
HE ONLY KNEW ABOUT THINGS I SAW.
HE'S PROBABLY ONLY ABLE TO PEEK MOMENTARILY.
RIGHT NOW, BONDREWD DOESN'T HAVE ANY CARTRIDGES-- THE EQUIPMENT HE USES TO WARD OFF THE CURSE OF THE ABYSS.
WE PROBABLY WON'T GET A CHANCE LIKE THIS AGAIN...
BUT WE DON'T HAVE MANY CARDS TO PLAY.
WE'VE ONLY GOT UNTIL THE REINFORCEMENTS COME.
IT'LL BE A SHORT, DECISIVE BATTLE.

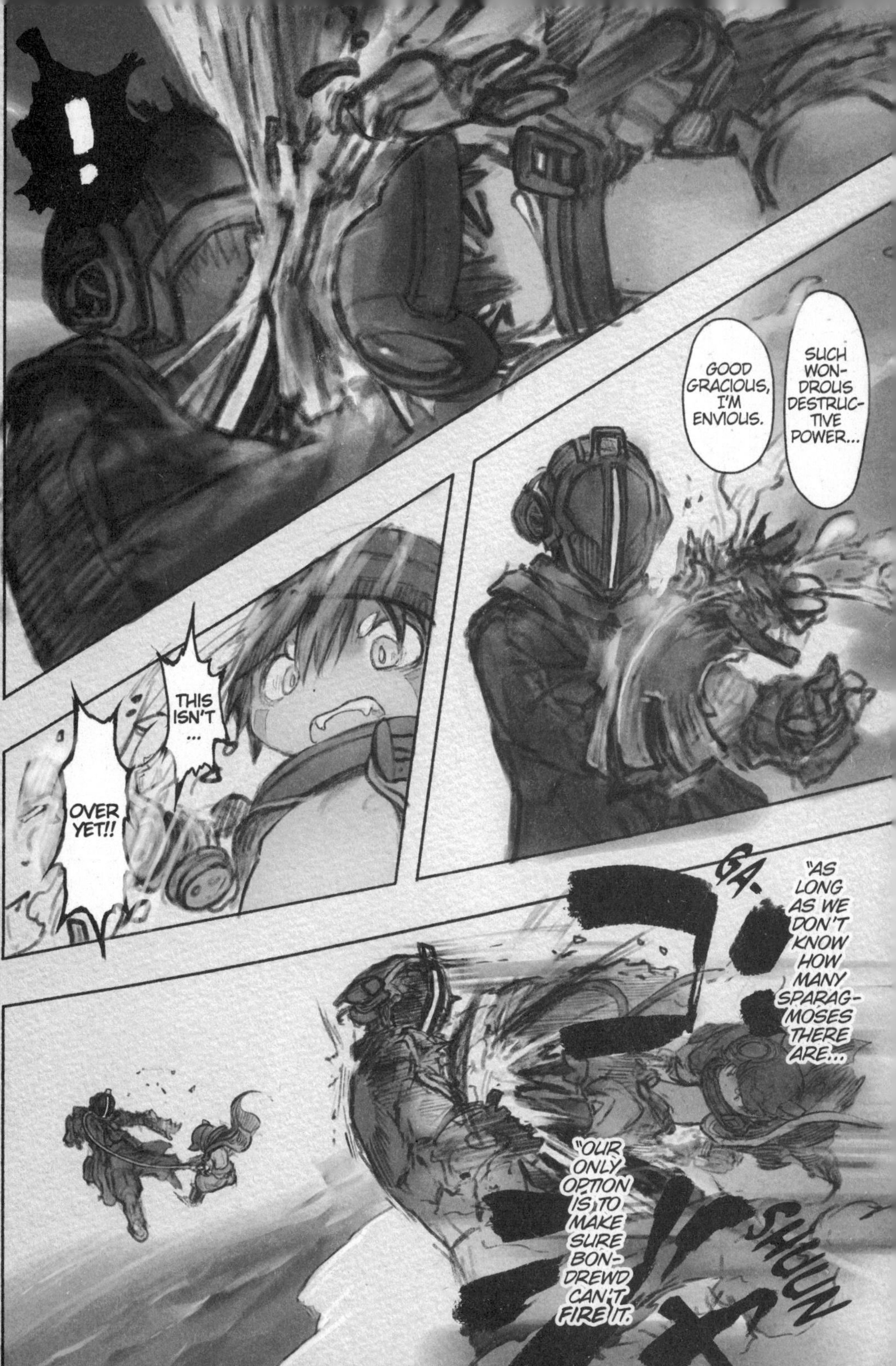
!
SUCH WONDROUS DESTRUCTIVE POWER...
GOOD GRACIOUS, I'M ENVIOUS.
THIS ISN'T ...
OVER YET!!
GA-
"AS LONG AS WE DON'T KNOW HOW MANY SPARAGMOSES THERE ARE...
SHUUN
"OUR ONLY OPTION IS TO MAKE SURE BONDREWD CAN'T FIRE IT.

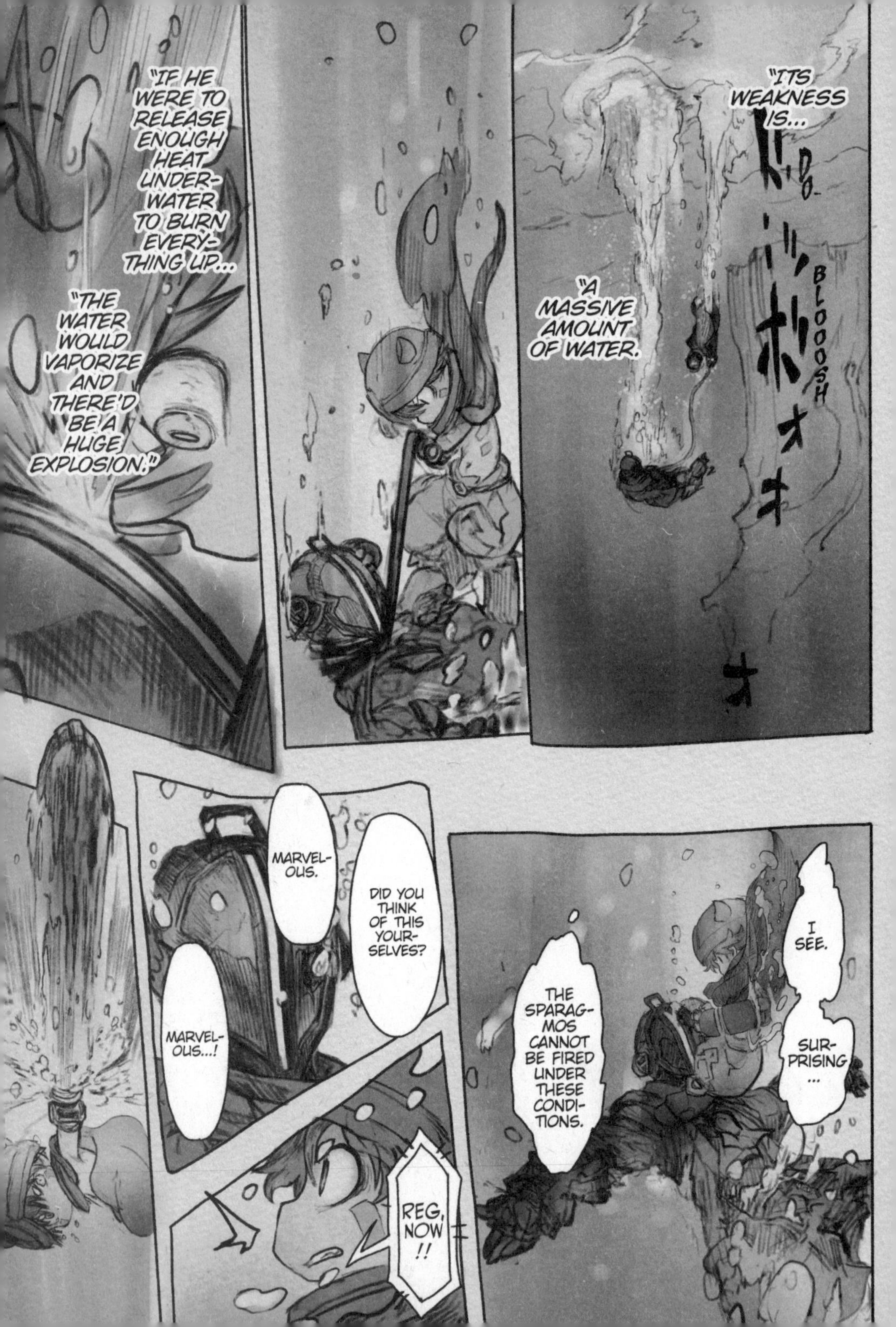
"ITS WEAKNESS IS...
"A MASSIVE AMOUNT OF WATER.
BLOOOSH
"IF HE WERE TO RELEASE ENOUGH HEAT UNDER-WATER TO BURN EVERY-THING UP...
"THE WATER WOULD VAPORIZE AND THERE'D BE A HUGE EXPLOSION."
I SEE.
SUR-PRISING...
THE SPARAG-MOS CANNOT BE FIRED UNDER THESE CONDI-TIONS.
MARVEL-OUS.
DID YOU THINK OF THIS YOUR-SELVES?
MARVEL-OUS...!
REG, NOW!!

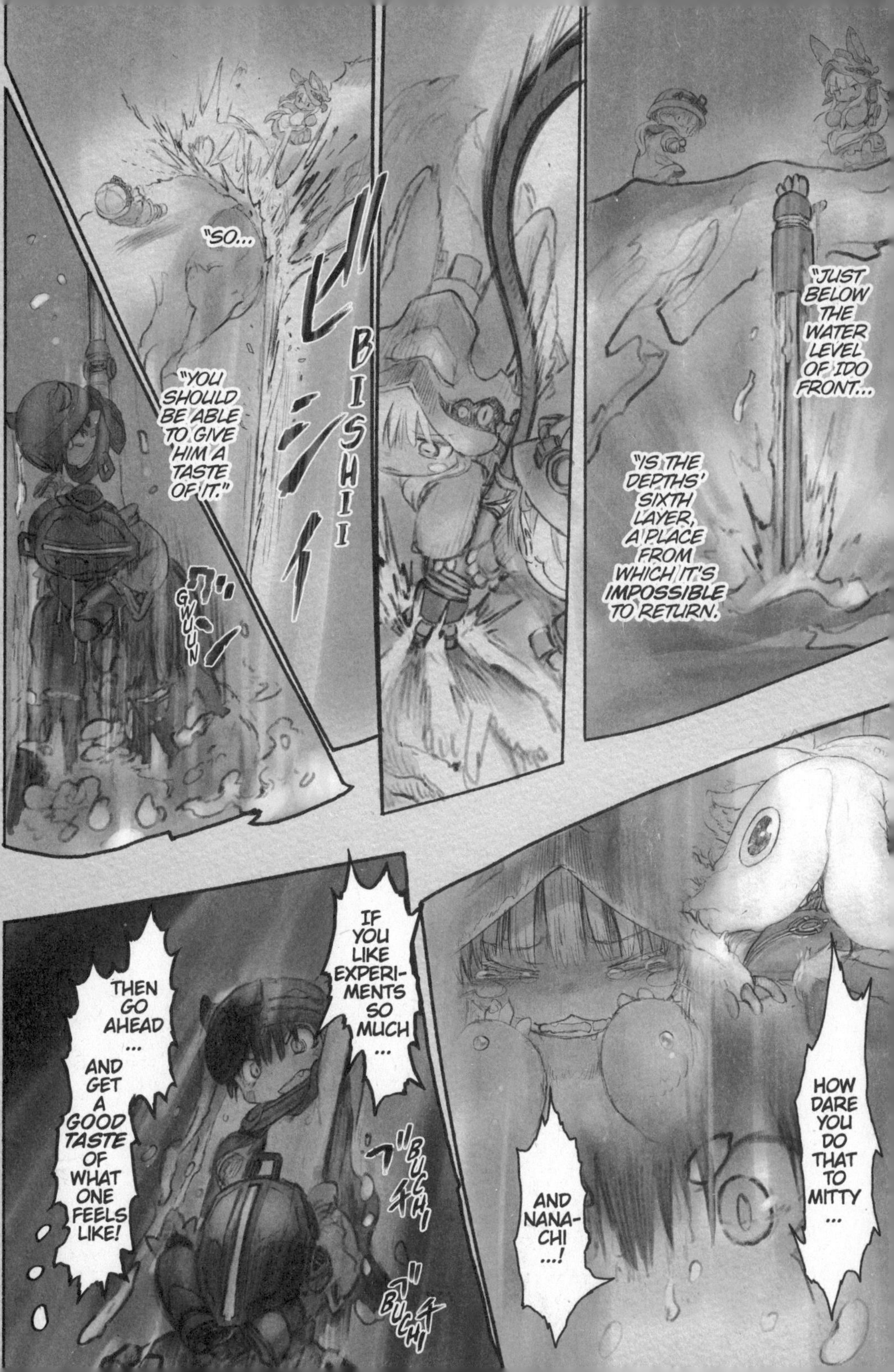
"JUST BELOW THE WATER LEVEL OF IDO FRONT...
"IS THE DEPTHS' SIXTH LAYER, A PLACE FROM WHICH IT'S IMPOSSIBLE TO RETURN.
BISHIII
"SO...
"YOU SHOULD BE ABLE TO GIVE HIM A TASTE OF IT."
GWUUUN
HOW DARE YOU DO THAT TO MITTY...
AND NANACHI...!
IF YOU LIKE EXPERIMENTS SO MUCH...
THEN GO AHEAD... AND GET A GOOD TASTE OF WHAT ONE FEELS LIKE!
BUCHI
BUCHI

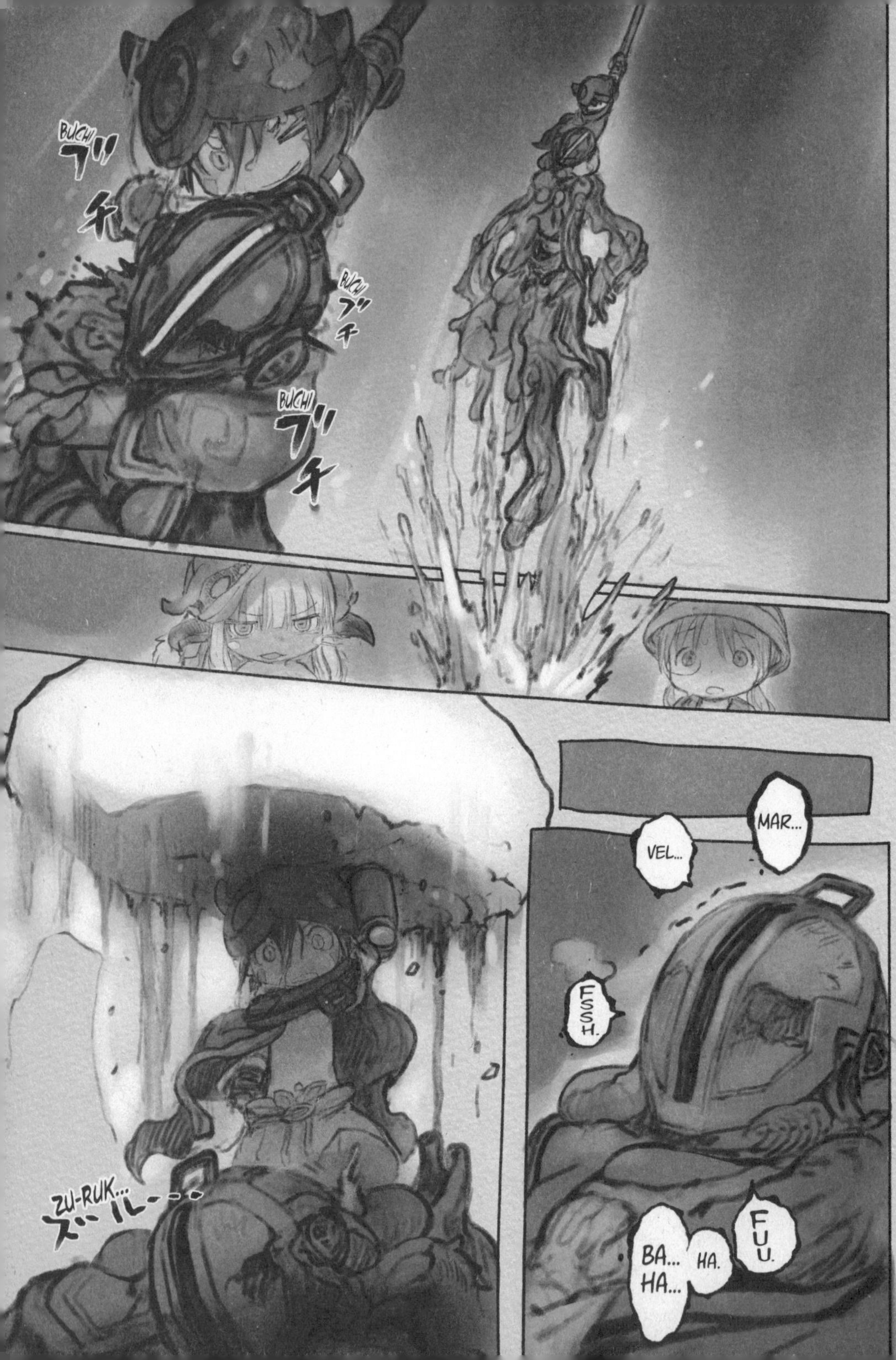
BUCHI
ブチ
BUCHI
ブチ
BUCHI
ブチ
MAR...
VEL...
FSSH.
FUU.
HA.
BA... HA...
ZU-RUK...
ズルー…

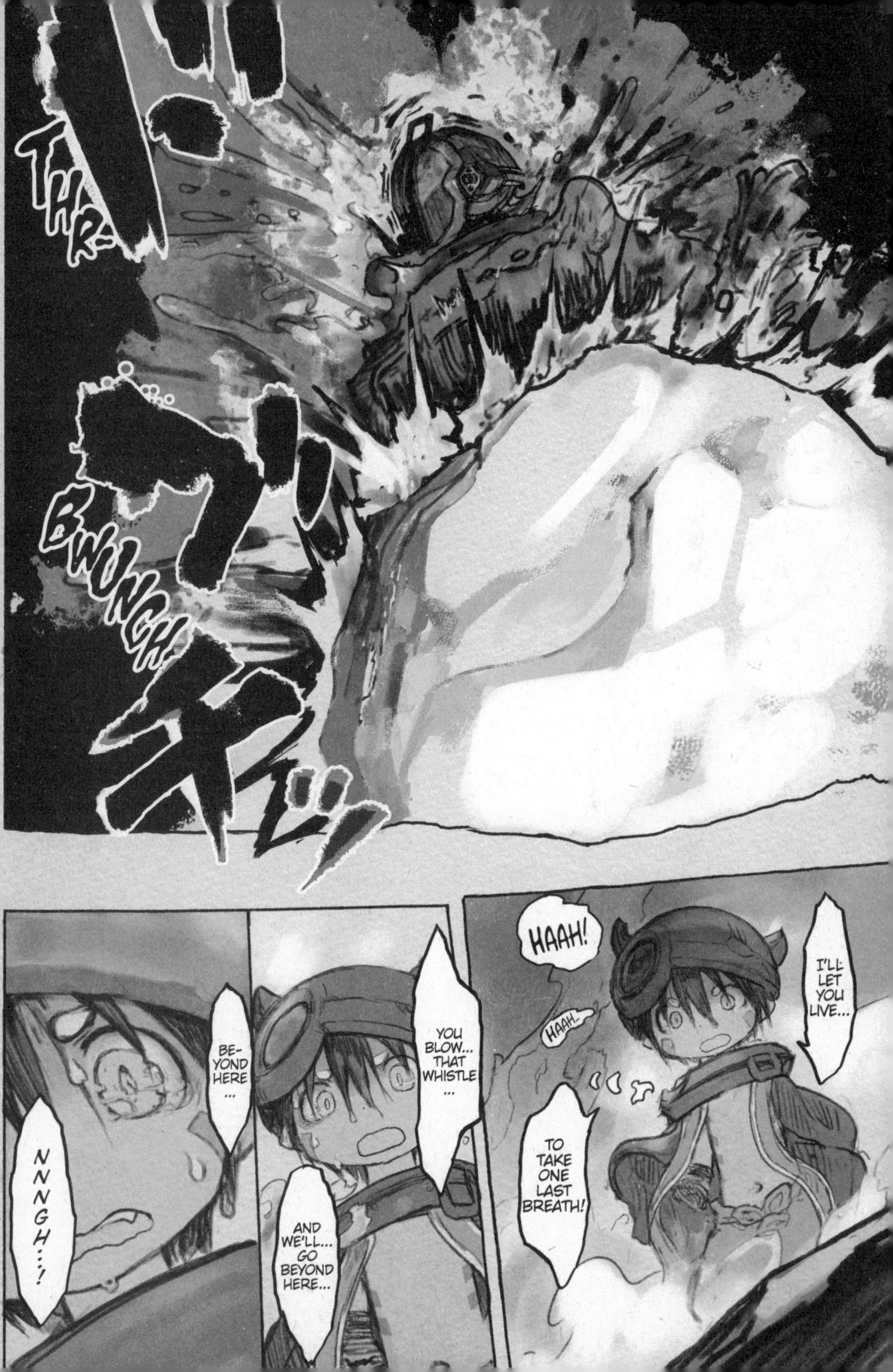
THR-
BWUNCH
I'LL LET YOU LIVE...
HAAH!
HAAH...
TO TAKE ONE LAST BREATH!
YOU BLOW... THAT WHISTLE...
AND WE'LL... GO BEYOND HERE...
BE-YOND HERE...
NNNGH...!

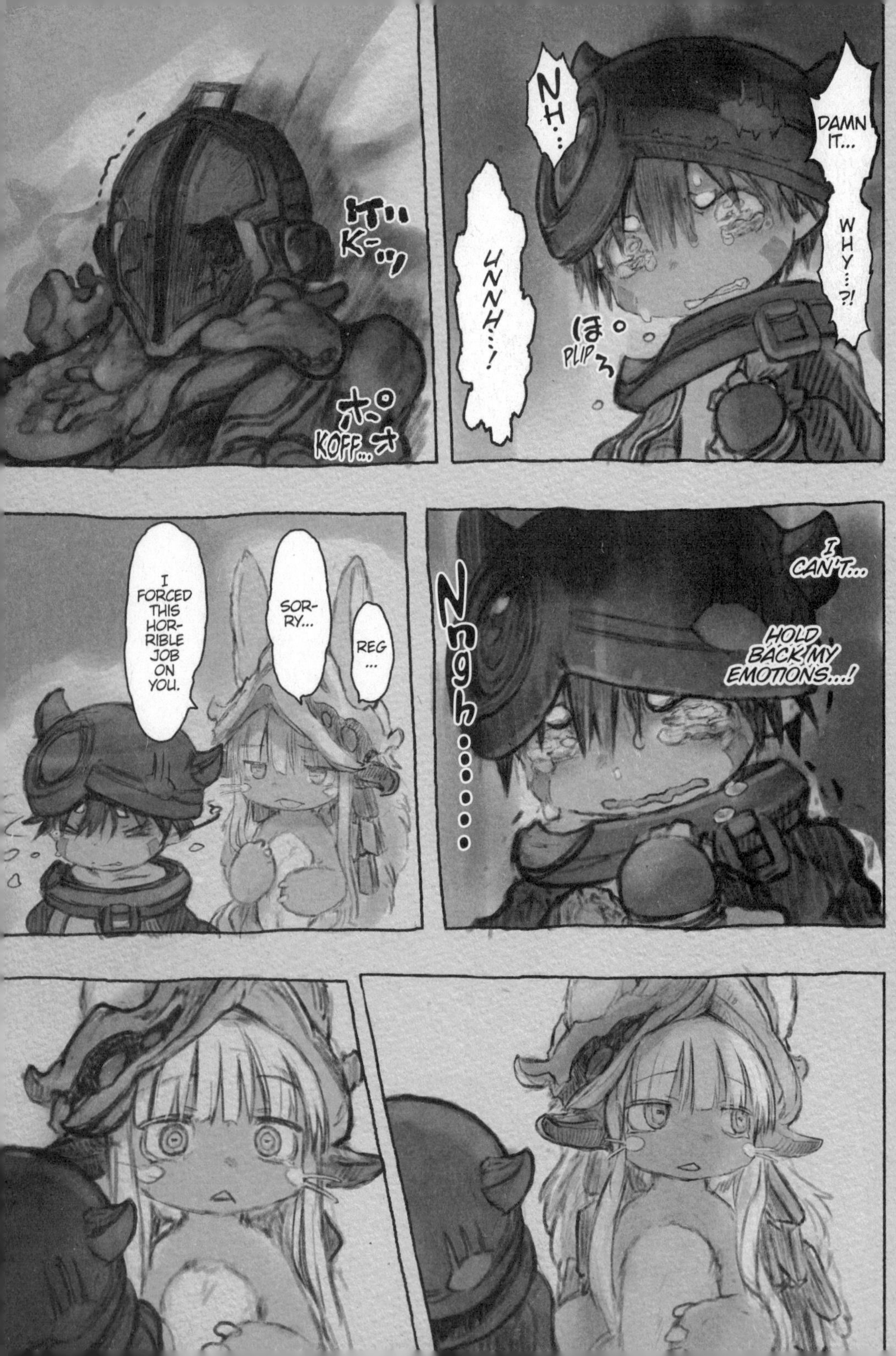
DAMN IT...
WHY...?!
NH...
UNNH...!
ほろ
PLIP
KOFF...
I CAN'T...
HOLD BACK MY EMOTIONS...!
Nngh......
REG...
SORRY...
I FORCED THIS HORRIBLE JOB ON YOU.

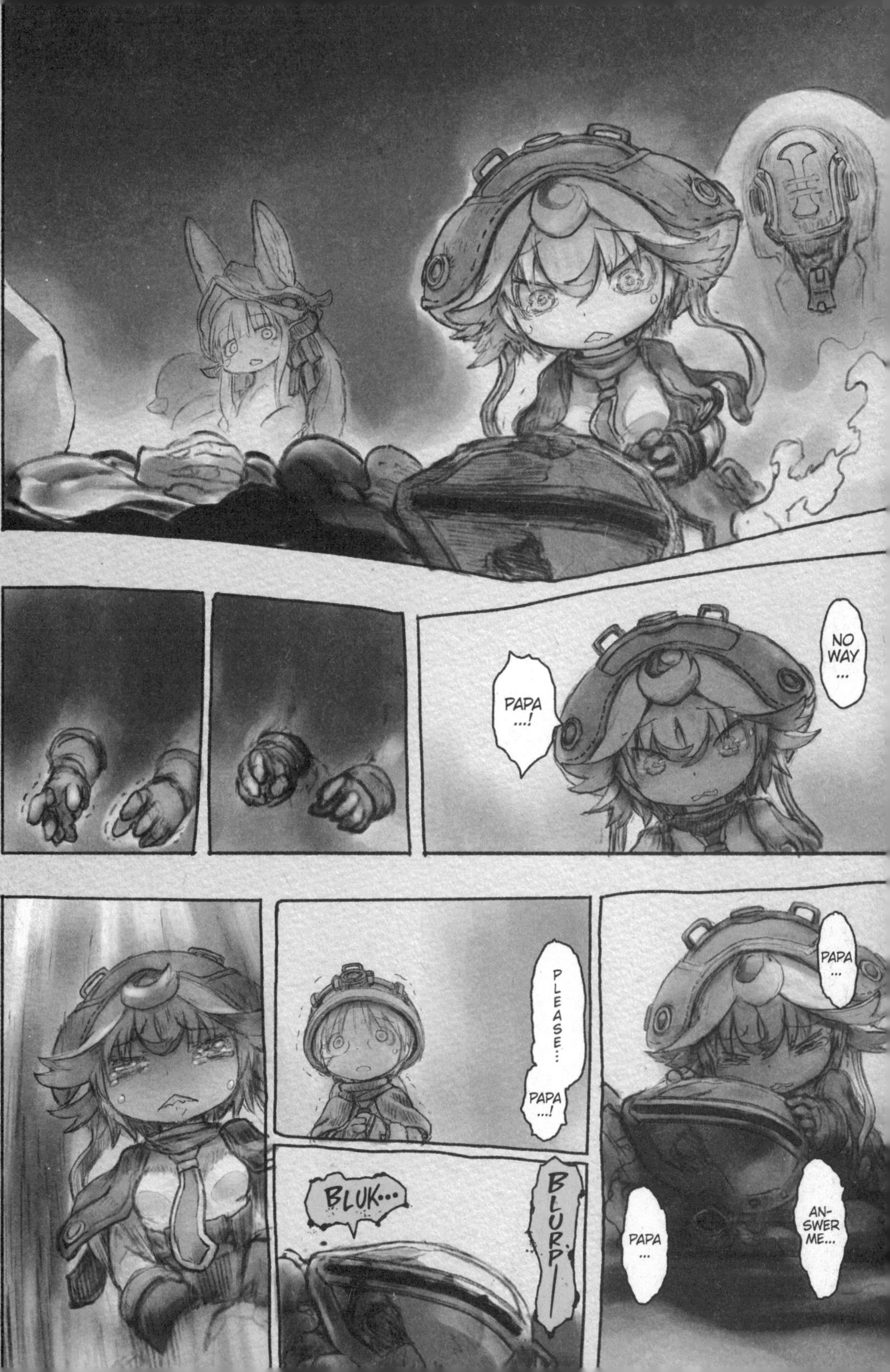
NO WAY ...
PAPA ...!
PAPA ...
ANSWER ME...
PAPA ...
PLEASE...
PAPA ...!
BLURP
BLUK...

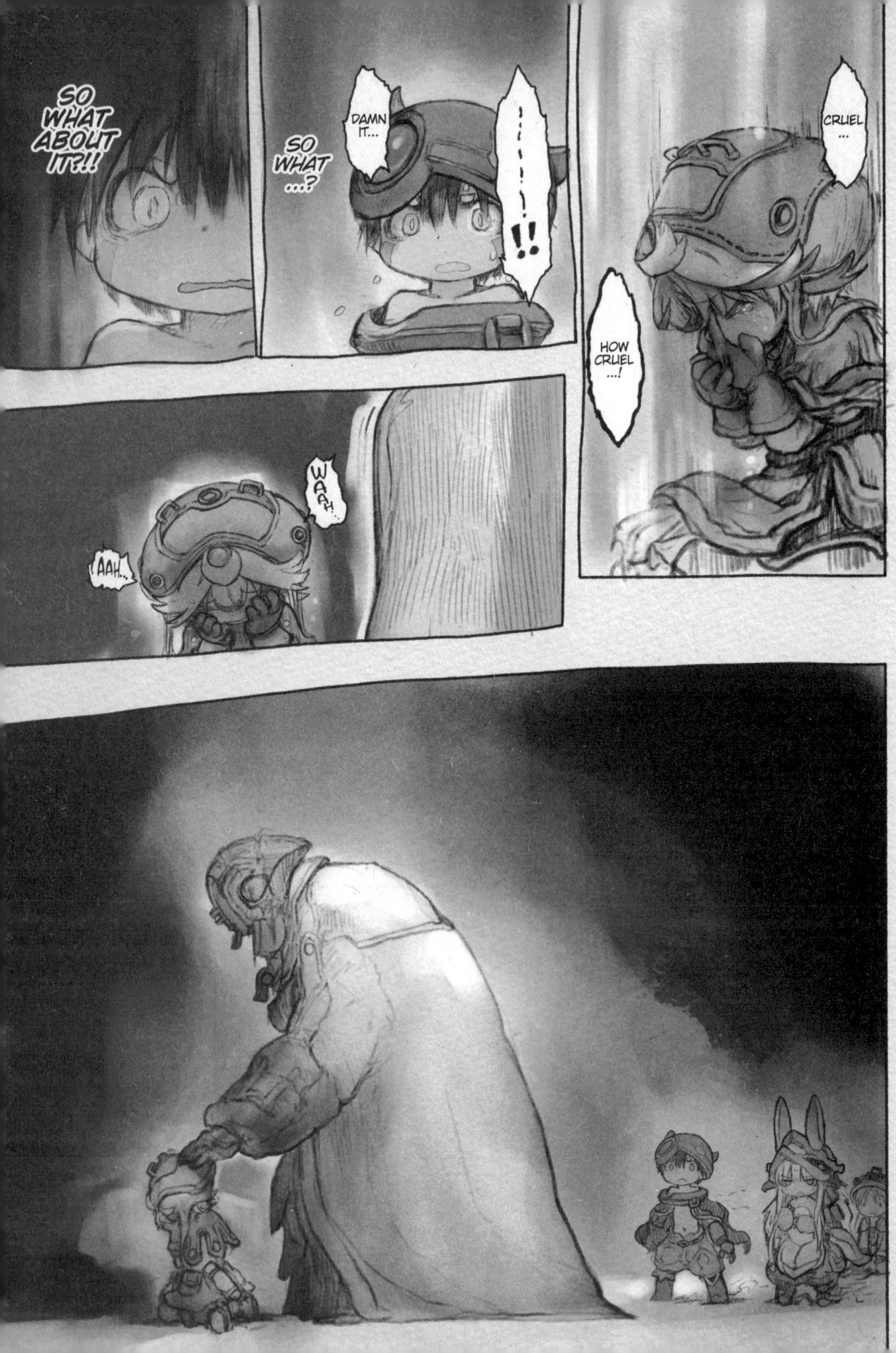
CRUEL...
HOW CRUEL...!
...!!
DAMN IT...
SO WHAT...?
SO WHAT ABOUT IT?!!
WAAH...
AAH...

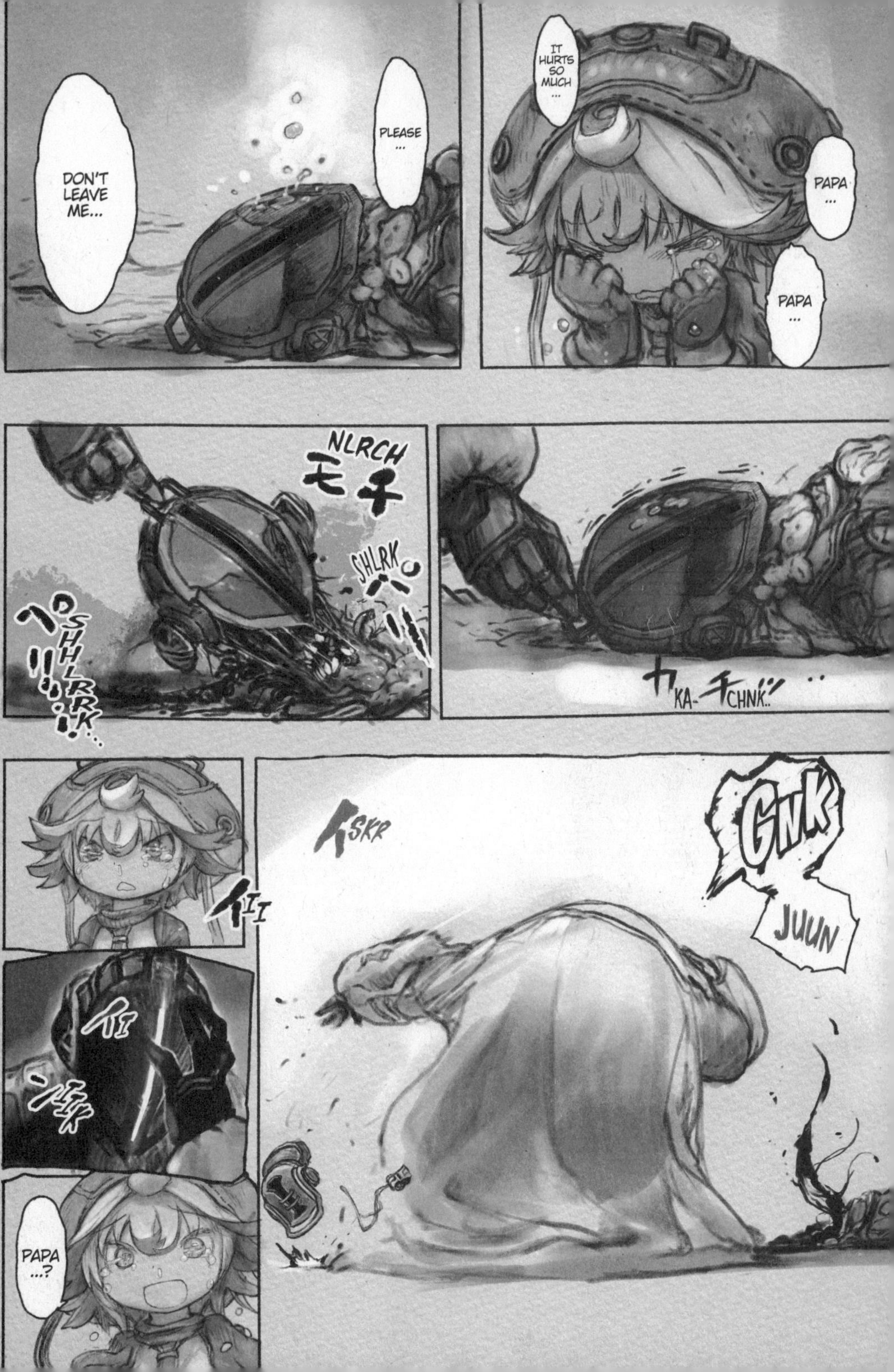
IT HURTS SO MUCH ...
PAPA ...
PAPA ...
PLEASE ...
DON'T LEAVE ME...
カ KA- チ CHNK..
NLRCH
モチ
SHLRK
パ
ペ SHHLRRK...
SKR
GNK
JUUN
III
II
PAPA ...?

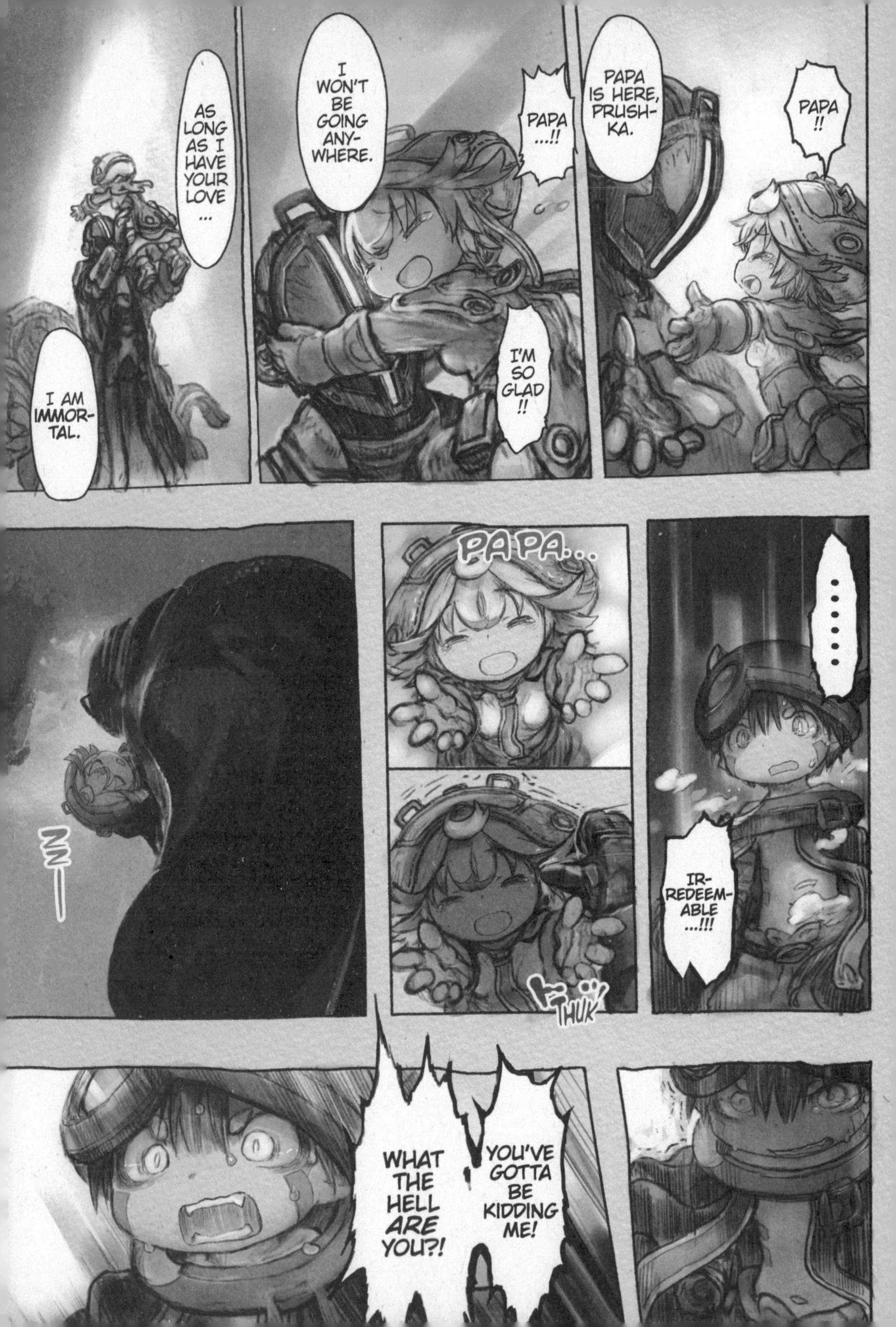
PAPA !!
PAPA IS HERE, PRUSH-KA.
PAPA ...!!
I WON'T BE GOING ANY-WHERE.
I'M SO GLAD !!
AS LONG AS I HAVE YOUR LOVE ...
I AM IMMOR-TAL.
......
IR-REDEEM-ABLE ...!!!
PAPA...
THUK
YOU'VE GOTTA BE KIDDING ME!
WHAT THE HELL ARE YOU?!

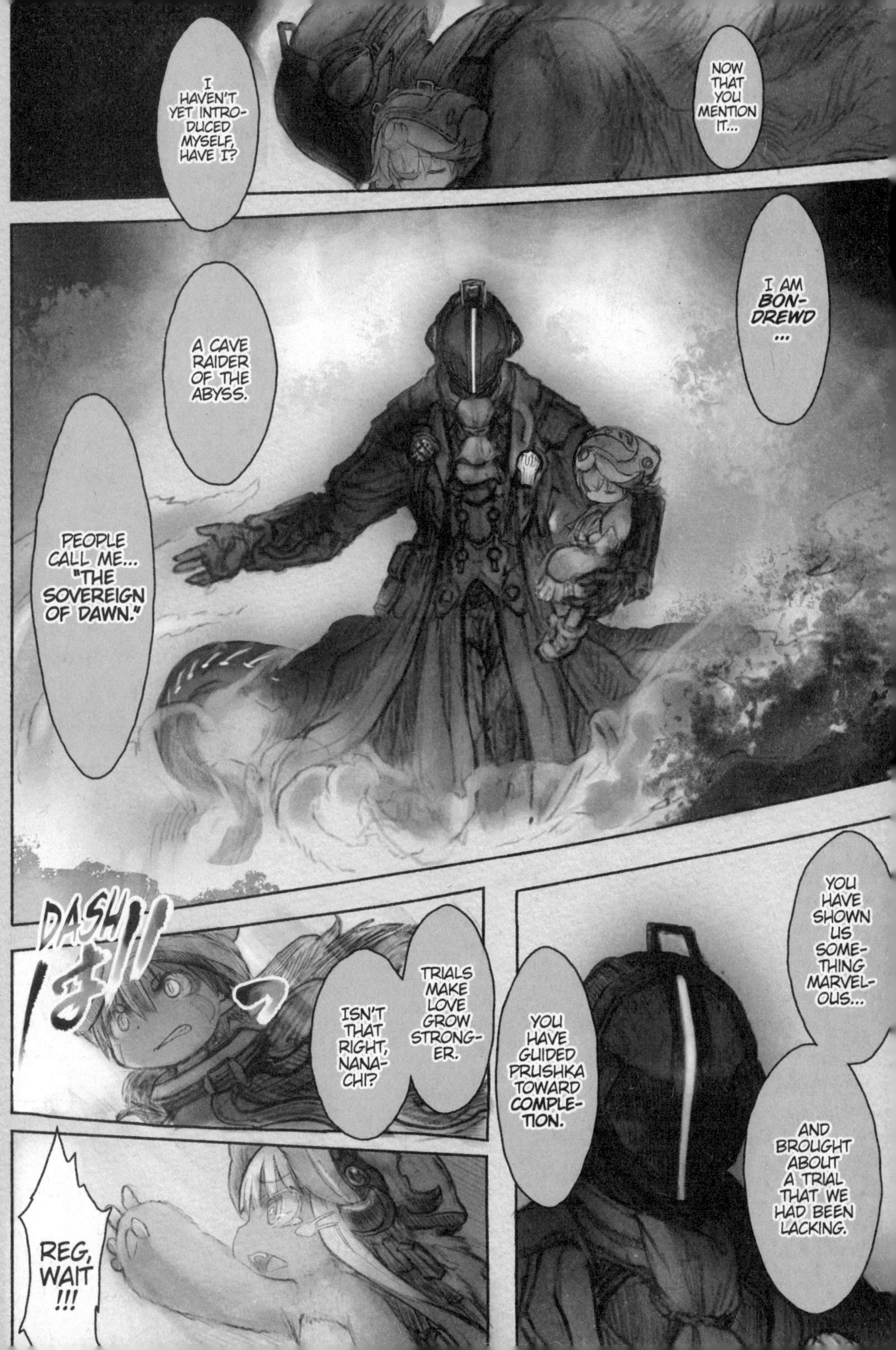
NOW THAT YOU MENTION IT...
I HAVEN'T YET INTRODUCED MYSELF, HAVE I?
I AM BONDREWD...
A CAVE RAIDER OF THE ABYSS.
PEOPLE CALL ME... "THE SOVEREIGN OF DAWN."
YOU HAVE SHOWN US SOMETHING MARVELOUS...
YOU HAVE GUIDED PRUSHKA TOWARD COMPLETION.
AND BROUGHT ABOUT A TRIAL THAT WE HAD BEEN LACKING.
TRIALS MAKE LOVE GROW STRONGER.
ISN'T THAT RIGHT, NANACHI?
DASH
REG, WAIT!!!

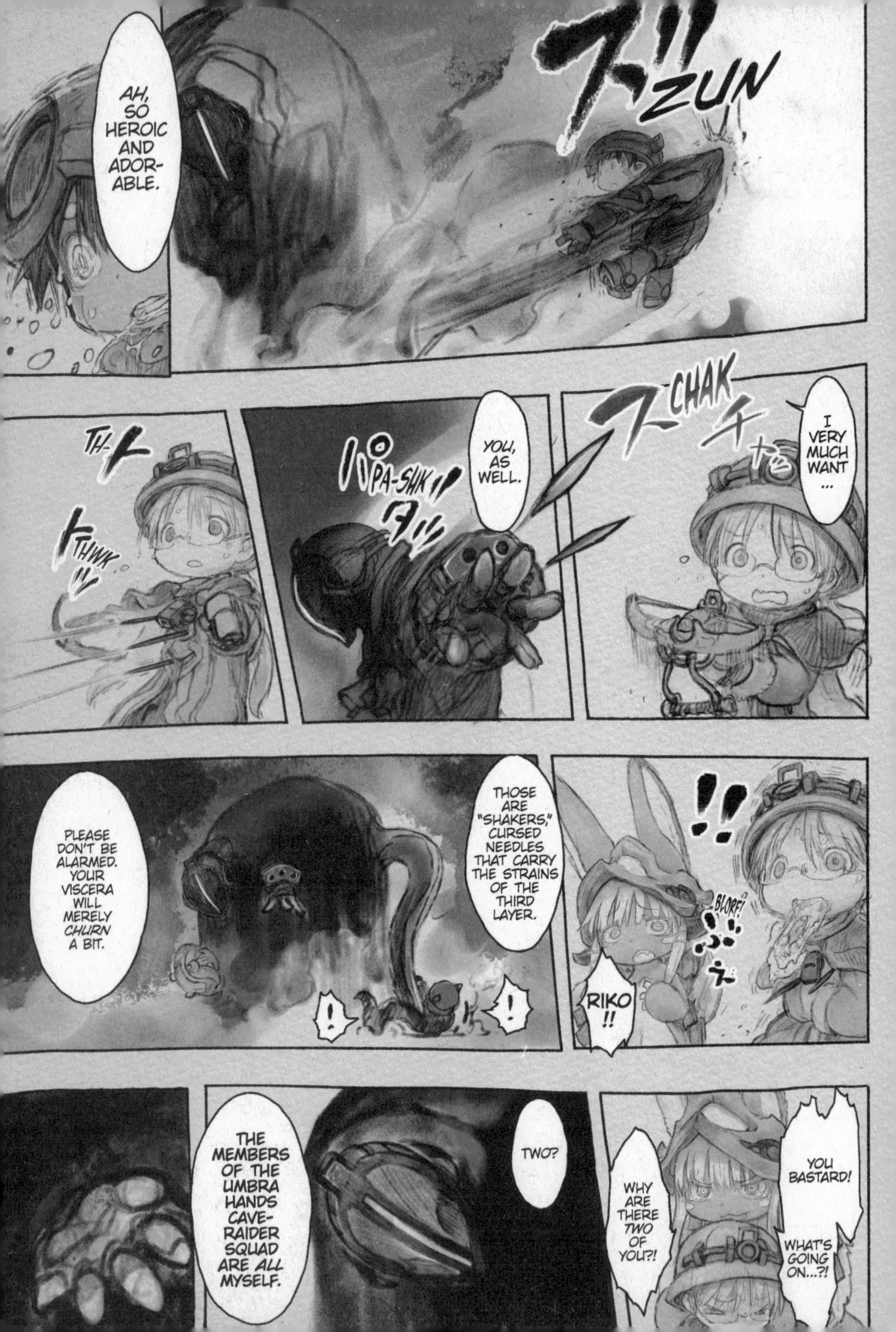
ZUN
AH, SO HEROIC AND ADORABLE.
CHAK
I VERY MUCH WANT...
YOU, AS WELL.
PA-SHK
TH-
THWK
!!
BLORF!
RIKO!!
THOSE ARE "SHAKERS," CURSED NEEDLES THAT CARRY THE STRAINS OF THE THIRD LAYER.
PLEASE DON'T BE ALARMED. YOUR VISCERA WILL MERELY *CHURN* A BIT.
!
!
YOU BASTARD!
WHAT'S GOING ON...?!
WHY ARE THERE *TWO* OF YOU?!
TWO?
THE MEMBERS OF THE UMBRA HANDS CAVE-RAIDER SQUAD ARE *ALL* MYSELF.

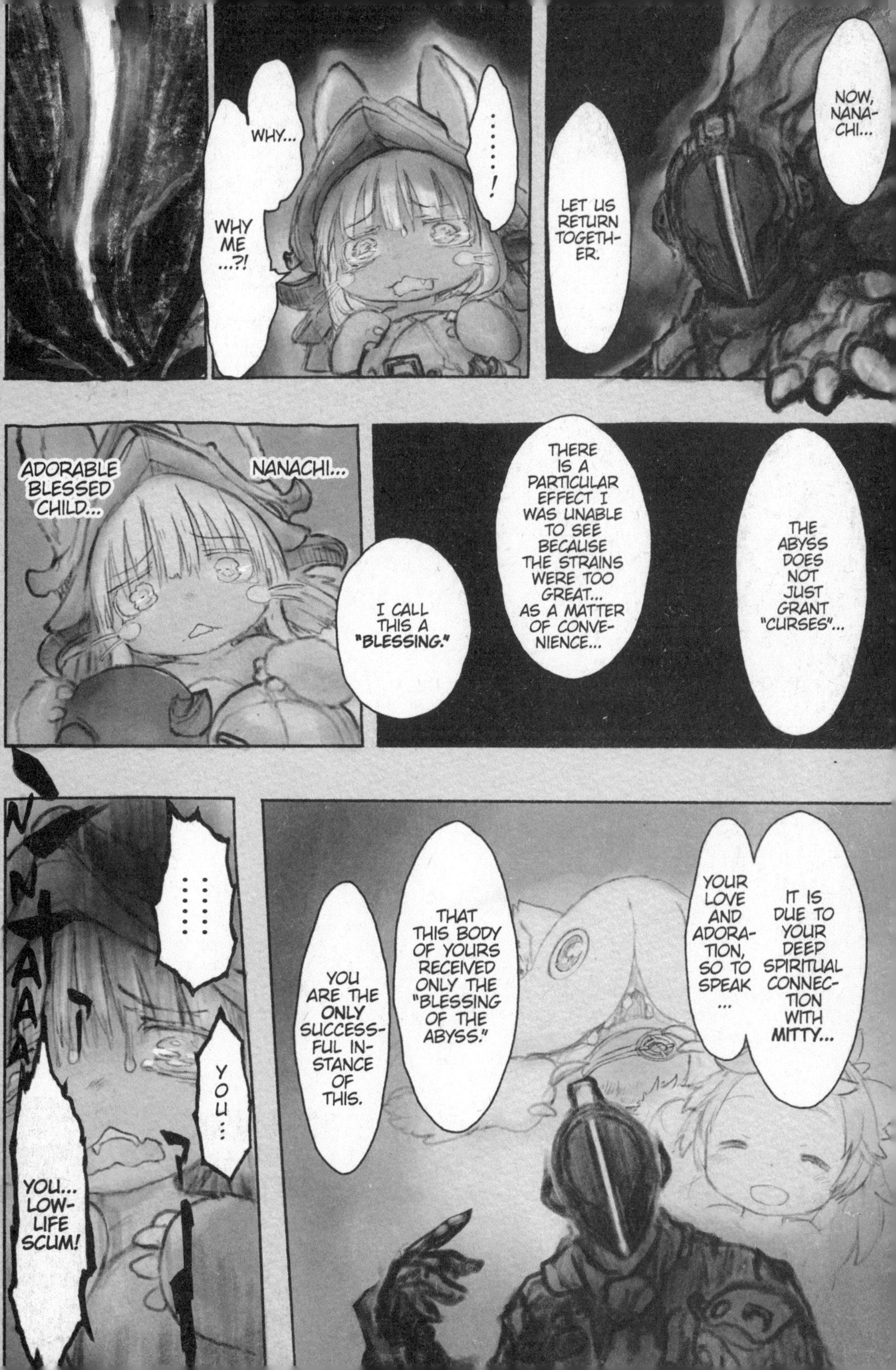
NOW, NANACHI...
LET US RETURN TOGETHER.
......!
WHY...
WHY ME ...?!
THE ABYSS DOES NOT JUST GRANT "CURSES"...
THERE IS A PARTICULAR EFFECT I WAS UNABLE TO SEE BECAUSE THE STRAINS WERE TOO GREAT... AS A MATTER OF CONVENIENCE...
I CALL THIS A "BLESSING."
NANACHI...
ADORABLE BLESSED CHILD...
IT IS DUE TO YOUR DEEP SPIRITUAL CONNECTION WITH MITTY...
YOUR LOVE AND ADORATION, SO TO SPEAK...
THAT THIS BODY OF YOURS RECEIVED ONLY THE "BLESSING OF THE ABYSS."
YOU ARE THE ONLY SUCCESSFUL INSTANCE OF THIS.
......
YOU...
YOU... LOW-LIFE SCUM!

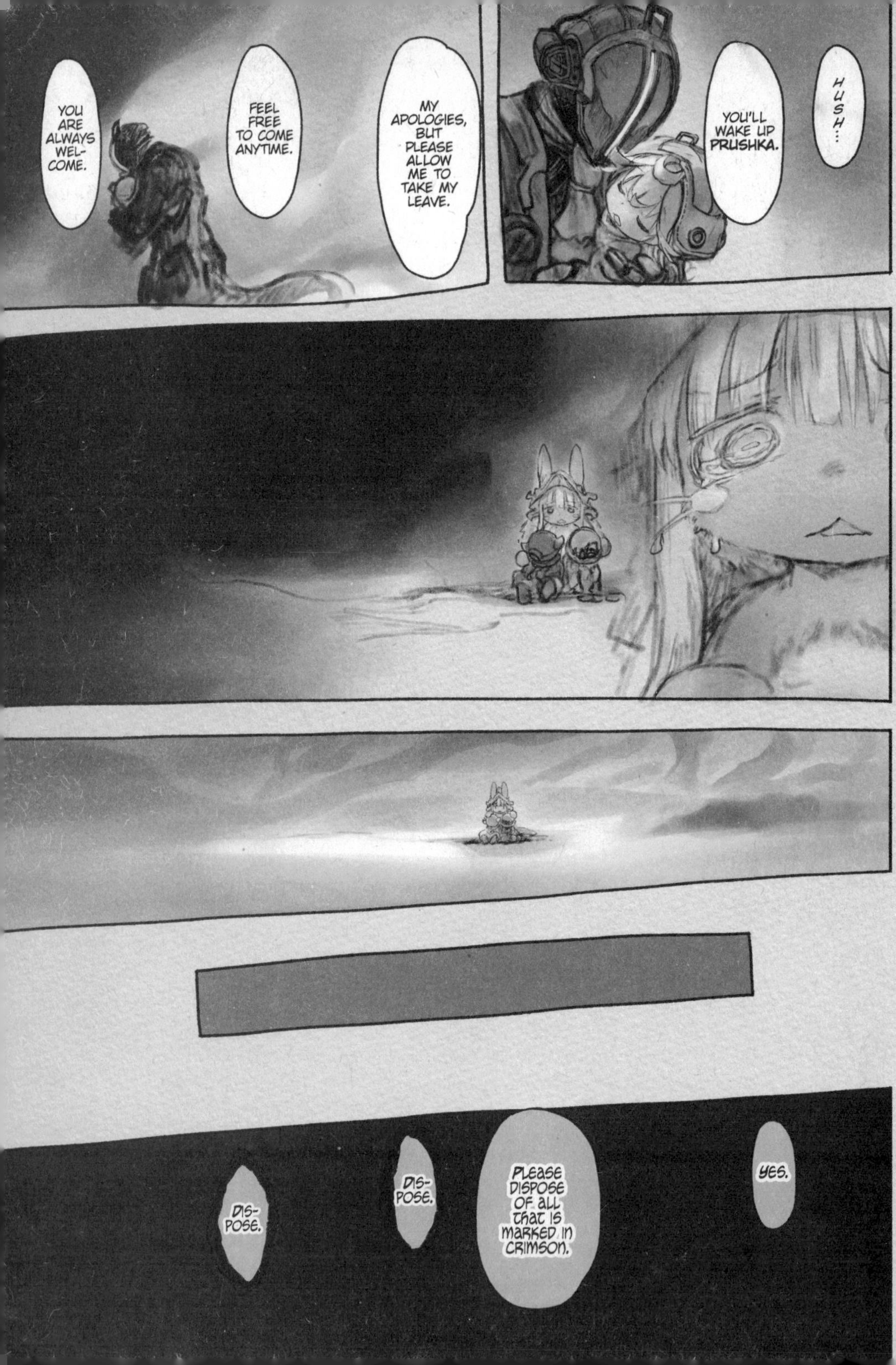
HUSH...
YOU'LL WAKE UP PRUSHKA.
MY APOLOGIES, BUT PLEASE ALLOW ME TO TAKE MY LEAVE.
FEEL FREE TO COME ANYTIME.
YOU ARE ALWAYS WEL-COME.
YES.
PLEASE DISPOSE OF ALL THAT IS MARKED IN CRIMSON.
DIS-POSE.
DIS-POSE.

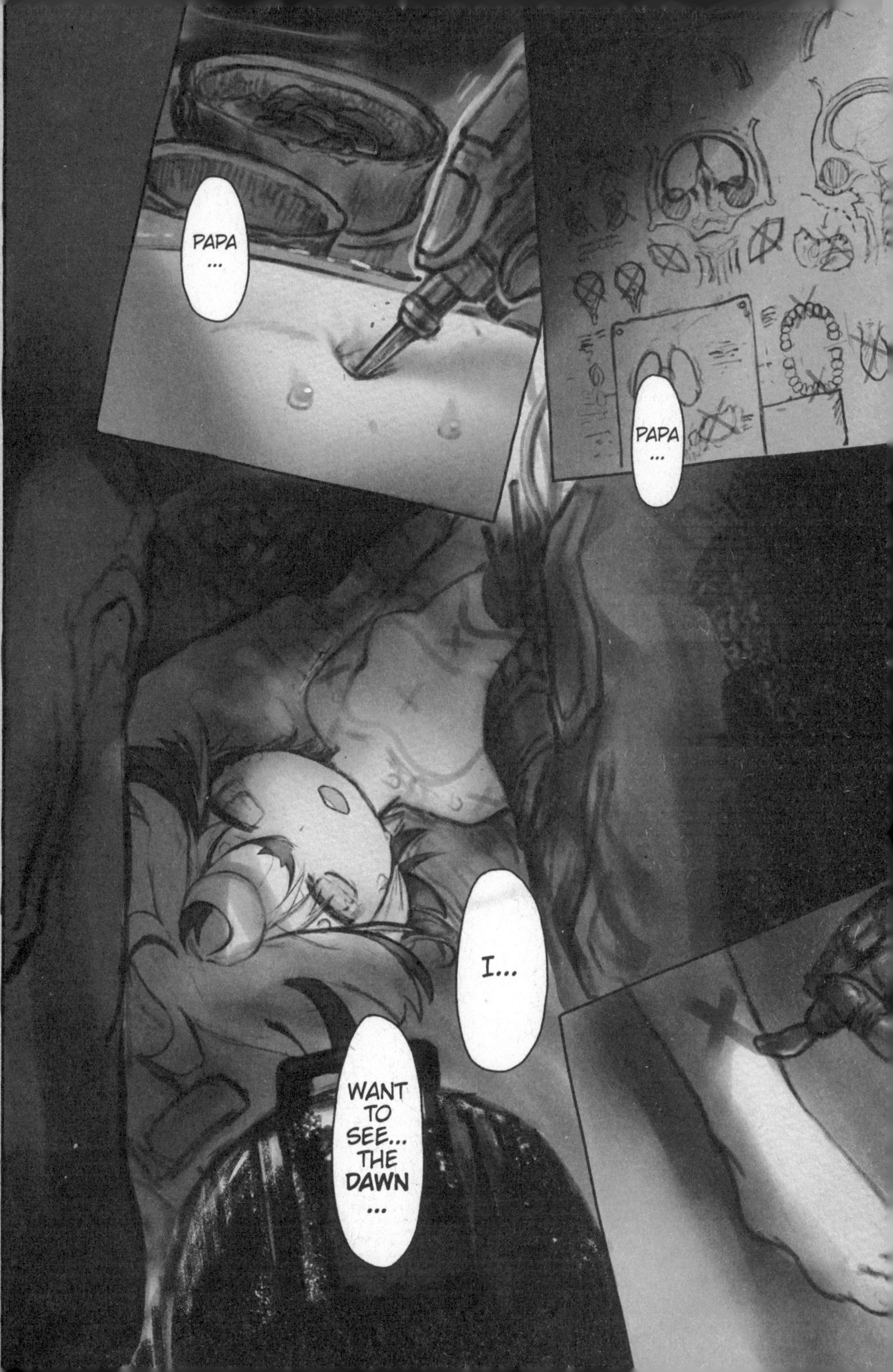
PAPA...
PAPA...
I...
WANT TO SEE... THE DAWN...

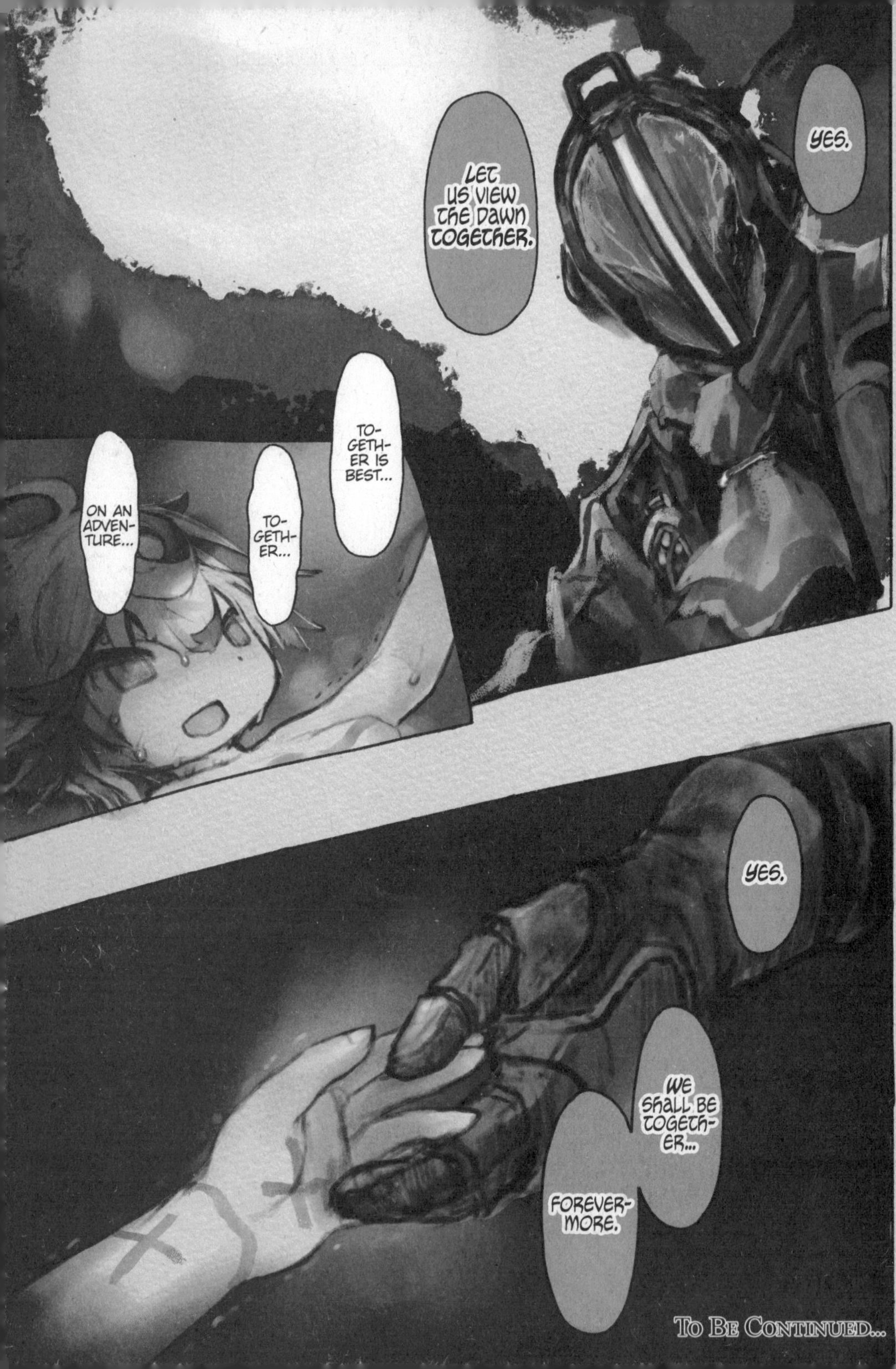
YES.
LET US VIEW THE DAWN TOGETHER.
TO-GETH-ER IS BEST...
TO-GETH-ER...
ON AN ADVEN-TURE...
YES.
WE SHALL BE TOGETH-ER...
FOREVER-MORE.
TO BE CONTINUED...

SEVEN SEAS ENTERTAINMENT PRESENTS

MADE IN ABYSS

story and art by AKIHITO TSUKUSHI

VOLUME 4

TRANSLATION
Beni Axia Conrad

ADAPTATION
Jake Jung

LETTERING AND RETOUCH
James Gaubatz

LOGO DESIGN
Andrea Rodriguez

COVER DESIGN
Nicky Lim

PROOFREADER
Shanti Whitesides
Danielle King

EDITOR
Jenn Grunigen

PRODUCTION ASSISTANT
CK Russell

PRODUCTION MANAGER
Lissa Pattillo

EDITOR-IN-CHIEF
Adam Arnold

PUBLISHER
Jason DeAngelis

MADE IN ABYSS VOLUME 4

Originally published in Japan in 2016 by Takeshobo Co. LTD., Tokyo.
English translation rights arranged with Takeshobo Co. LTD., Tokyo,
through TOHAN CORPORATION, Tokyo.

ISBN: 978-1-626929-19-7

Printed in Canada

First Printing: October 2018

10 9 8 7 6 5 4 3 2 1

FOLLOW US ONLINE: ***www.sevenseasentertainment.com***

READING DIRECTIONS

This book reads from ***right to left***, Japanese style. If this is your first time reading manga, you start reading from the top right panel on each page and take it from there. If you get lost, just follow the numbered diagram here. It may seem backwards at first, but you'll get the hang of it! Have fun!!

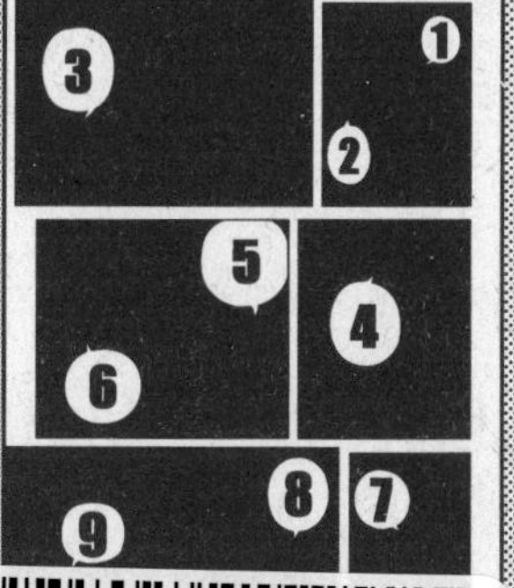
1
2
3
4
5
6
7
8
9

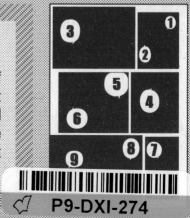